STILL LIFE

ELISABETH LUARD is an award-winning food writer whose work includes *European Peasant Cookery* (published in the US as *The Old World Kitchen*, a *New York Times* benchmark cookbook of the twentieth century), *The Food of Spain and Portugal, European Festival Food, Sacred Food* and *The Latin American Kitchen*. She has also written a couple of doorstopper novels including *Emerald* (WH Smith Thumping Good Read Award), and a trio of memoirs-with-recipes including *Family Life* (Guild of Food Writers' Book of the Year 1997), and was awarded the Glenfiddich Trophy for Food Writing in 2007. She contributes regularly to national newspapers and magazines including the *Telegraph, Daily Mail, Country Living* and the *Oldie* and is currently Director of *The Oxford Symposium on Food & Cookery*. Brought up in South America, Spain and France as a member of a diplomatic family, married for forty years to the late Nicholas Luard – novelist and founding father of the satire movement of the 1960s – she brought up their family of four children in a remote valley in Andalucia, where she developed her early career as artist and illustrator. She still travels widely, continues to use sketchbook and waterc[...]ges and recipes, and now happi[...]a remote farmhouse in the wil[...]*Welsh Farmhouse* is her most rece[...]

BY THE SAME AUTHOR

COOKBOOKS

EUROPEAN PEASANT COOKERY
THE PRINCESS AND THE PHEASANT AND OTHER RECIPES
THE BARRICADED LARDER
EUROPEAN FESTIVAL FOOD
THE FLAVOURS OF ANDALUCIA
COUNTRY COOKING
SAFFRON AND SUNSHINE
SACRED FOOD
THE LATIN AMERICAN KITCHEN
THE FOOD OF SPAIN AND PORTUGAL
CLASSIC FRENCH COOKING
FOOD ADVENTURES
TRUFFLES
CLASSIC SPANISH COOKING
SOUP GALORE
RECIPES AND RAMBLINGS
TAPAS: CLASSIC SMALL DISHES FROM SPAIN
A COOK'S YEAR IN A WELSH FARMHOUSE

MEMOIRS–WITH–RECIPES

FAMILY LIFE
MY LIFE AS A WIFE

NOVELS

EMERALD
MARGUERITE

STILL LIFE

Klipfisk, Cloudberries and
Life After Kids

ELISABETH LUARD

B L O O M S B U R Y

LONDON · NEW DELHI · NEW YORK · SYDNEY

First published by Bantam Press 1998
This paperback edition published 2013

Copyright © Elisabeth Luard 1998

The moral right of the author has been asserted

No part of this book may be used or reproduced in any manner
whatsoever without written permission from the Publisher except
in the case of brief quotations embodied in critical articles or reviews

Bloomsbury Publishing Plc
50 Bedford Square
London WC1B 3DP

Bloomsbury Publishing, London, New Delhi, New York and Sydney

www.bloomsbury.com

A CIP catalogue record for this book is available from the British Library

ISBN 978 1 4088 3142 7
10 9 8 7 6 5 4 3 2 1

Printed and Bound in Great Britain by CPI (UK) Ltd, Croydon CR0 4YY

Every reasonable effort has been made to trace copyright holders of
material reproduced in this book, but if any have been inadvertently
overlooked the Publisher would be glad to hear from them.

Contents

'With the loss of tradition we have lost the thread which safely guided us through the vast realms of the past, but this thread was also the chain fettering each successive generation to a predetermined aspect of the past. It could be that only now will the past open up to us with unexpected freshness and tell us things that no one has yet had ears to hear.'

HANNAH ARENDT (1906–75), *Nomos I: Authority*.

Carl J. Friedrich, ed. 1958

Acknowledgements

My thanks are most particularly due to my husband Nicholas, who accompanied me with fortitude and a firm finger on the map on forays into unknown territory in Eastern and Northern Europe; and to those kindly and generous souls who so patiently and tolerantly shared their hearths, skills and daily dinners with us along the way. On later journeys, while making *The Rich Tradition* for SBS Australia and BBC2, to Carmelo Musca, wizard of the camcorder, and the stoic Piercy Porter, our man with his finger on the recording button – camera-director and soundman respectively – both of whom left the tranquillity and sunshine of Perth to film, come rain or storm, in outlandish places and eat weird food; not least among their many virtues being that they only rarely complained about an excess of cabbage soup. And to all those who helped in the making of the series, both as participants and performers, and who contributed so much to my particular sum of human happiness.

Gratitude is also due, as always, to Broo Doherty, the best and most tolerant editor in the business, and to my beloved agent Abner Stein whose support is and has always been above and beyond the call of duty. Thanks are also due to Hazel Orme who took on the Herculean task of copy-editing the manuscript; to Julia Lloyd who designed the book and smacked all my little drawings into shape; and to Shauna Newman who heroically collated the proofs.

PROLOGUE

It is not a bad thing that children should occasionally, and politely, put parents in their place.

COLETTE (1873–1954), *Chéri* (Paris, 1920)

THIS BOOK IS HEREBY DECLARED A FAMILY-FREE ZONE.

There's nothing more liberating in the life of a mother than that moment when the offspring declares unilateral independence – the connection can never be severed, but independence is a heady feeling. There'll undoubtedly come a moment when I'm too old to spoon in the pap and I find myself in an old folk's home sitting against the walls while they vacuum in the middle, but now it's time to spread the wings and fly.

I make an exception for my companion of these past thirty-five years, Nicholas. Husbands don't count as family – after all, they're no relation. Absolutely not, I can reply with confidence when asked if I am related to the father of my children – well, as much confidence as family trees can deliver – I'm just his wife.

My children are up and running. We only come together at those feasts and festivals that remain central to our lives, spent, as always, round the kitchen table. This is the only time when I shall permit myself a mention of their presence; otherwise, it's every man for himself.

Fifty years on the planet is not much in the sum of human experience. Nevertheless, the fiftieth is a milestone. It marks the end of the breeding years for women, even if not for men – a time of change, mental no less than physical, a rite of passage from which some of us never recover. At such a time we need all the help we can get.

My fiftieth birthday present to myself was to ask questions of others rather than of myself. As a mother of four children, my experience of living had been largely through my children's eyes. It was time to move on, intellectually and physically, both directly, by asking questions of my contemporaries and friends, and indirectly, since in my chosen career as a food-writer I believed that it was in domestic habit that we knew who we were – that the lessons of the past could be more easily assimilated through the language of the senses rather than that of the intellect.

I would not be so foolish as to expect that through asking questions I might find answers, simply that throughout my life the experience of others has taught me how to understand myself.

The women I count as friends among my contemporaries were gathered at a time when we were still unformed – scarcely more than girls, not even women. At that time, none of us could be sure of what we might become. Now, thirty years later, some, like me, are still married to the men by whom they had children, others are divorced, some remarried, some resolutely single, some busy with careers, some even with grandchildren.

I started cautiously, skimming the surface, with a friend from my schooldays, not a natural beauty although a glamorous media career has ensured she must always present herself as such. 'You probably won't believe me, but I really don't bother at all. I'm not at all organized. I never worry about beauty routines, things like taking off my makeup before I go to bed. Of course I cover up the grey hairs and retouch the rust, but when I get myself together and go out to a party, I know I can knock spots off the thirty-somethings – the young marrieds with their babies, looking podgy and plain and exhausted. I keep the body in shape – swimming, yoga, properly supervised exercise. I always keep in trim but, then, I think it's easier for those of us who have never been through pregnancy. My doctor says that whatever happens to the woman, you can always tell if she's had children – the muscles change after childbirth, and after fifty they won't stretch.'

Friendships between women are no threat to the men in their lives. Two such among my friends have gone into business together, more for the stimulus than because they are obliged to earn a living. Both are married, both comfortably off, both have teenage children. Physically, they're as unlike as any two women could possibly be.

The younger of the two, initially a bouncy brunette, is easy-going and full of laughter. She is undeniably well rounded – and perfectly happy to remain so. 'I'm no good at dieting, I have the wrong metabolism. I love going to a health farm to tone up my body and just to get away from everyone. You forget your age until you look in the mirror, but there's no doubt that middle-aged women who are fatter look better.

'Just the same, when I was fifty, I decided to change the way I look. I was talking to my business partner about losing weight, and she suddenly said, "Why don't you go blonde?" So I did. It was terrific. Going blonde is the poor woman's face-lift. My husband was quite shocked at first. But I did it gradually and it took four goes to get it just right. Then he loved it, and if anyone criticized it, he'd go wild. Let me tell you, gentlemen really *do* prefer blondes. It's quite different in the street. Workmen wolf-whistle, and you turn heads all the time. It's a revelation – a whole new world.'

Both women love clothes, both are dedicated shoppers. 'Before Christmas, after I'd gone blonde, we went to Miss Selfridge to buy stuff for the children. We had all these packages and we were just leaving when my friend spotted something on the rail. "Look, you just *have* to try that on." It was a leopard-printed body stocking with a tulle tutu – quite crazy. I bought it, of course. I wore it a lot to all the Christmas parties, bosoms and everything, terrific. I had some of those black stick-on patches – hearts, clubs, diamonds – I wore one on my cheek, one on my chin, and one on the *décolleté*. One man, the handsomest man I know, greeted me with a kiss on the bosom. Imagine being greeted and kissed on the bosom! The hair and the outfit made men enormously cheerful. And even the women cheered up. Someone would say, "Look, it's Madonna!" and for a moment people believed it. It was a very *jolly* outfit. The only time it didn't work was when the kids gave a party and I wore it to that. They didn't approve at all.

'I don't want to grow old gracefully. I hate those newspaper articles which say so-and-so, *still* beautiful even though she's a hundred and one. There are women who weren't beautiful when they were young, but who grow beautiful as they get older. Look at Gladys Cooper – she looked wonderful as she aged. When my mother was fifty she was so much more elegant than when she was younger. You learn that. Your aesthetic perceptions change. My mother's face became more beautiful over ten years, between thirty and forty. Her face lost that raw look, and fined down. She never had high cheekbones or anything that obviously improves. Of course, some people look better when they are all young and juicy, and less good as they dry out. As for a face-lift, it's not for me. It looks good when you're looking in the mirror to put on the makeup, but it changes your expression – it's as if your smile has been moved back several inches. I know a man who's had his eyes done. Now he looks like a surprised Pekinese. My husband says I'm looking good even when I know I'm not. Sometimes I rather wish he wouldn't because if I notice *he's* looking older, I think maybe he notices I am too.

'My father used to say to my mother: "You look scrawny, put on some weight." He buys her clothes and she loves the things he buys. He went to India and bought her a wonderful coat. I was in the house on the day he came back. My mother was out and he was rushing round the house saying, "Look what I got for your mother! Where shall I hide them so she finds them?'' He put all the bits and pieces under her pillow, and the coat on top. It was green leather with fur. She adores it. She's always wearing it.'

Is it all in the look of the thing?

'No. Intimacy matters. Pillowtalk and cosiness is very important – being with someone you're used to. In a way, it's just as important as sex. A permanent, fixed man is vital to women, for their well-being. Although I *do* have a friend, a career girl, who's never lived with anyone. She has had lovers – usually other people's husbands – but the relationships are quite long-term. She's a sort of serial mistress. She's sixty, although you'd never know it. She cares for herself because she really wants to be attractive.'

The other member of the duo is a year or two older. Tall and slender, with brown curly hair streaked with grey, she wears little makeup. Her clothes are romantic, long skirts, silk-pleated evening dresses, caped coats. Married to a man a few years younger than herself, she has two children by a previous marriage. 'My husband is very absent-minded so I don't know how much he notices if I look older. But I did have my hair frizzed last year and he loved it. But he absolutely doesn't want me to get my face lifted. He always says he doesn't mind wrinkles, and I believe him. Anyway I really like faces that have aged.

'My mother's different. She's seventy-five and still very active, and she's had, oh, I don't know how many face-lifts. She says she had the first one when her face looked *sad* – so she just had it jacked-up. My father always wanted my mother to be a tootsie. He loves display, likes her to dye her hair, wear incredibly high-heeled shoes. I don't know how she manages them – I couldn't. I remember not long ago walking with her round Sloane Square and we passed an elderly Sloane Ranger, all coiffure and tailored clothes and good shoes. Ma looked at her and said: "Look at that. She looks so horribly *dignified*. I'd rather look like a clapped-out ballerina."

'My mother was very beautiful when she was young. I don't think she has changed her attitude to clothes at all. In the fifties she wore hand-woven things, lovely materials made up into full

15

skirts and tight waists and dolman sleeves and *décolletés* – very feminine and romantic, Bohemian chic. I remember she had a wonderful jacket with a lining of tiny patchwork. Beautiful linings are sexy – real silk and satin or even fur. I have a raincoat lined with my grandmother's old mink. And detail is sexy: perfect French seams and double-stitched pockets. Initials *inside* things, like on a man's shirt-tail instead of on the pocket – they were supposed to be a reminder for the laundry, so they were not for public display. Horn or mother-of-pearl buttons, hand-finished buttonholes, things you don't notice until you look closely. And underwear, of course, really beautiful, well-cut underwear. I always change my undies in the evening if I'm going out. I like little pure-silk bodice-tops and cami-knickers, black or flesh-coloured, with fine details. Underwear is something special. I have a friend whose husband has just left her, and the first thing she did was go out and buy some glorious silk underwear, all lace and pin-tucks. Then she ran into an old flame and celebrated by going to the movies with him. She *knew* that underneath her ordinary clothes, she had this wonderful silk underwear, and that's a very erotic feeling. And if you *feel* erotic, men seem to know.'

Then there's the visible evidence, the bits which can be rearranged by the plastic surgeon. To tuck or not to tuck? An American friend – one of the first feminist authors – finds English women neurotic about their face-lifts. 'I've reached the age when all my friends both here and in America are having the nip-and-tuck. The difference is the English tell such lies about it. They say they fell downstairs when they've had the eyes done. I have a friend who says she had cancer of the hairline to explain the old snip – who'd believe *that*? I have women friends who ring me up and say things like: "Well, I've *done* it. It's a really good one, no one can tell." Well, if you don't look so much better, why spend a fortune on having it done? If you had a new dress, you'd want everyone to notice. Why not if you have a new face?'

What of the long-term? Fifty, after all, is only a beginning. I sought enlightenment, as I do on all important matters, from an old friend – in both senses of the word. A woman of letters, the ninety years to which she admits have in no way dulled her intellect. She remains a working scientist in a field in which her talent for observation, allied with an anarchic aptitude for crossing the disciplines, has served her well. These talents she has applied to the consideration of her own species.

'I think I didn't notice the fiftieth myself – too busy. Seventy was different. That was when I decided to give up sex, not because I'd finished with it, just that it became impractical. I've always enjoyed it – biologists always do, they're a very sexy lot, no doubt because we deal with it all the time. We humans like to think we're different, above such things. Of course it's not true. We may not be aware of it, but we think about sex all the time. We travel through life on three intellectual levels, three pathways running parallel to each other. The first, the one we're most aware of, we can call shopping – the everyday running of life, worrying about housework, peering down a microscope, thinking about what to make the children for tea. The second is poetry – an awareness of beauty, a magnificent sunset, new leaves on trees after winter, a butterfly spreading its wings. The third level is sex. I don't mean the act itself – that takes up very little time – but just walking down the street or into a room and thinking, I like or I don't like the look of *that*. However old we are, that never stops. Sex, poetry, shopping – we can transfer from one path to the other, but the other two are still there, still operating. It's just that we don't happen to be walking down that particular one at that particular moment. Plenty of people will tell you they never think of sex, or you might imagine they can never be thinking about poetry, or they never do the shopping, but the truth is they don't happen to have chosen that particular pathway at that moment, not that it isn't there. The most troublesome path is sex. Believe me. I know.'

Sex seems to be the key to much of our concern about ageing. Among those of my mother's generation, I have a particular friend, an aristocratic Spaniard, who chose an alternative path. 'You'll find it not uncommon among women of my age and social position. Homosexuality is not something which everyone has in them, but in many ways it's the easiest choice. We turn to our own sex when we've had our children, fulfilled our obligations to the marriage. In Spain, that's very important for a woman. The men have always been promiscuous – it's part of the culture, almost an obligation. But the women are expected to remain faithful, even when their husbands don't sleep with them. So I fell in love with a woman, and had a wonderful relationship with her which continued for the rest of her life. We had both had our children, and they had already had their own families by the time we decided to live together. We never ever quarrelled, and if we were apart – she, like me, was extremely busy with her working life – we wrote to each other every day.

'I first came across the arrangement during the war, when I worked for the Red Cross. There were two nurses, sisters – one was twenty-two and the other a little older – and each of them had female lovers, nurses like themselves. They lived, they said, in great peace. There was none of the jealousy and scenes which seem inevitably to accompany heterosexual relationships. After the war, they both took male lovers and married. The weddings were from my family house. They didn't dislike men at all – they just found them rather troublesome except for the breeding. And then there was the usual problem in an enclosed hierarchy such as a hospital: if a junior doctor is living with the matron, it undermines authority. Nowadays it happens in the workplace. There are many more who make the arrangement than you would ever know. I think perhaps my own mother would have chosen the same path but she died when I was a child, so I never knew. Women are so much gentler. They know so much more about their own bodies. Even so, you can't make a conscious decision about your sexuality. Homosexuality is not a choice – it's there or it's not. And if it's there, it's always been there.'

For the intellectual effects of ageing, I talked to a former journalist, mother of three, who trained as a counsellor with a private practice. A few years older than myself, she had left her own fiftieth behind. 'Fifty to seventy – I'd call them the middle years. Middle age now starts between forty-eight and fifty-three – the dividing line has shifted a decade. At fifty, or even fifty-five, we now expect to be as our mothers were at forty, the direct result of better diet and exercise. You have only to look at the photographs of the models of the sixties – their bodies are completely different from the models of today. Nowadays the top models all work out, and they have the muscles and bodies which go with it.'

She herself works out once a week with a trainer. 'I need the discipline – I wouldn't do it otherwise. But I don't take hormones myself. Observation tells me the problems associated with menopause are likely to occur anyway, whether the chemistry is replaced or not. I'd never directly recommend a client to try it, but I might suggest they talk to their doctor. If someone comes in with a physiological pain, they're not talking psychosomatic. Even so, there's no doubt there's a psychological element. The change of life is a very important event. It is still vital to think that you *can* breed, even if you've had absolutely no intention of doing so for twenty years.'

How about the men? There's been much talk of the male menopause. 'I'd subscribe to the idea. I've no doubt it exists. I would certainly describe some of my male clients as menopausal, but it's more psychological than physical. As a man, until you're fifty, you feel you can do anything. But after fifty you begin to see the writing's on the wall. The physical changes are subtle. After fifty the sexes start to look more alike. Men somehow look healthier – they become nice and pink, and round-faced, like girls. Women go the other way, they get a grey tinge to the skin, and there are the obvious things, like an increase in visible facial hair. It's much worse for women who trade on their looks. But ageing is, above all, in the genes – ask your mother what happened to her. You'll follow the same pattern, but later.'

Wrinkles, she thinks, don't matter as much as the way you see them – and, consequently, yourself. 'You can't blame women for going for the cut if they really feel they have to. If your face is your future as well as your past, what can you do? Ultimately, you can't postpone age. A wrinkle is a wrinkle, and once it's there, that's it, however much you iron it out. But hormone replacement may well slow down the process of collecting more. It's hard to tell. Curiosity is crucial – that's one thing you should never lose. If you are naturally curious, you don't worry about ageing. Walking and talking are important, finding out about new things. Surface things matter. A new haircut, a facial, all these things are good. When you *look* better

19

there's no doubt you start to *feel* better. I've noticed a physiological correlation between the looks of women who have a girlish attitude to life – women who were girlish when they were young continue to be girlish as they get older. I believe middle age is the time plain women come into their own. Middle age is a time when you should have evolved spiritual strengths and balance, an introverted, less public attitude. The best tonic is loving another person. Ultimately, if you have a steady relationship, ageing isn't important.'

For the last word on what the benchmark birthday means to someone whose life is cluttered with neither husband nor children, I turned to a woman I count among my closest friends. She chose a very different path from mine, but over the years this disparity has strengthened rather than diminished the friendship. 'I never felt the need for a husband – a lover, of course, but never a husband. I felt the same when I was young as I do now. Marriage is only useful if you have children, and I never wanted to breed.

'I have no problems with turning fifty. It's a good time for a woman. As we grow older, men and women are no longer looking for the same things from a relationship. At fifty, paternal and maternal qualifications are not important any more. If you're a woman, you've earned your status, whatever it is, so that's not something you need from a man. You can actually have a relationship based on sex, but with a heightened sensuality because it doesn't demand society. There's no public display of possession. It can be an enclosed relationship, a private affair, a secret, if that's what suits you both. And it can go on feeding on itself, getting better and better as the shared experience stacks up.

'I would always choose an older man. I find the company of young people boring – I don't have much in common with them. That doesn't mean I wouldn't pick someone younger, but certainly I wouldn't contemplate anyone under forty.

'I appeal to young men because I have something the young women don't have: I know exactly what I want. Young women give out confusing signals. They might deliver the right image, but they're not really interested in sex. Underneath it all, they're interested in breeding and babies. But they're also trying for status. The dressing-up and the socializing – parties and so on – that's all jockeying for position, a necessary part. The man you get is the man who gives you your social standing. You're looking for the best man to bring home the bacon. And that's fundamentally true whether you have a career or not.

'Older women are capable of eroticism. I mean erotic enjoyment – conducting a seriously sexy relationship, creating an atmosphere where absolutely everything is erotic: touch, taste, scent, sight, sound. But it's not purely sensual, above all it's in the mind. Sex is a battleground. Eros is pure pleasure. There's one thing about procreation – it proves you can do the business. It's the *balls* that men mind about. They can all convince themselves they're good lovers – best, bigger, whatever. But the seed they sow – that's what separates the men from the boys. Once they've done that, the whole thing changes. Then they can enjoy eroticism for its own sake. And I don't want anyone too old either: sixty's my outer limit. After that it's all too complicated.'

Her reaction to the physical symptoms of ageing is characteristically practical. 'There's only one answer, zap in the hormones. Pick the one that suits you, and hang the consequences. When my long-time lover left, as one might expect, the whole business coincided with the onset of the menopause. I was very depressed, found it difficult to cope. My legs were getting thin – skinny calves just like my mother's. Fortunately, my local doctor's a woman. She took one look at me and gave me a blood test for hormone levels. For me, the build-up to the menopause was headaches, insomnia, a general feeling of misery it was hard to shake off. You have to remember that the cycle of reproduction is different today – without efficient contraception there would have been endless children, endless breastfeeding. You have to remember the price: thirty years of menstruation is unnatural and takes it out of you. But once I started on the hormones, you could see the change immediately – muscle-tone, hair, everything. The stuff's going to be as liberating to our generation of women as the contraceptive pill was in the sixties. We're simply not going to feel old.

'The important thing is to feel good when you walk into a room. First impressions count. It doesn't matter if your makeup makes you look older. I use plenty of glitz, dark red lipstick, the lot, and I reckon I can get the attention of any man I want. If I set my mind to it, I can beat the competition into a cocked hat, even if it's half my age.'

What about life on your own, without a permanent man in your life? 'It isn't easy – sometimes I think I'd like a man to share my house but not necessarily my bedroom. In fact, I really like my bedroom to myself, and my bathroom even more so. But you need a man to look after the nuts and bolts. I miss the shared life, a life that still goes on, whatever. The knowledge that there's another rhythm in the household. The day had a form and a shape when I lived with my lover, even if we quarrelled all the time. Things got done without me – someone else took half the decisions, but now I have to make them all. I'm used to living on a domestic level: now I have to remember to buy the washing-up liquid and get the logs split.'

Maybe she might like to go back to work to pay for some of the things I know she enjoyed but can no longer afford? 'Absolutely not. My lover left me with enough money to live perfectly comfortably. When I was with him and I chose to go out to work, it was to buy things for myself, my own clothes and the luxuries I like. Now I wouldn't dream of working just for the money. It would have to be more than just sitting in an office – it would have to be satisfying, and that's not an option I can choose. If you haven't made the money or the career you want by the time you're fifty, you're in competition with the nineteen-year-olds, and as we all know, that's another ball-game in more ways than one.

'I prefer to stay at home and deal from strength. I'm at my best in the environment I've chosen, and I've enough money to make it work. I like men, but I'm not sure if I want a permanent one. I know how and where to seduce. I would never entertain anywhere else than at home. It's the only place where I'm at an advantage. My house and my garden are mine, I invented them, this is where I can load the dice. That is why my house is so important to me and why I fill it with flowers and as many beautiful things as I can. I've just redone the drawing room – it looks like a tart's boudoir, and I *love* it.

'There's no doubt that to run your social life successfully as a single woman takes money. You must be able to pay for yourself. It goes without saying that single women are a social threat to the married. To counteract that, you must have a walker, a tame male who can be asked as your escort. Never neglect your homosexual friends in the good times – they make perfect walkers when times are lean. The first thing I learned when my lover left was, don't rush out and look for another. You have to normalize your life. Find a balance.

'Cooking is a powerful weapon in the erotic armoury. I really like to cook for the men in my life – but I'm well aware it can also be a major turn-off. The food must be delicious, but above all it must look easy. There's nothing sexy about a woman slaving over a hot stove, coming in all sweaty with the *poulet à la mode* and worrying it to death with little dabs of this and dollops of that. Perfect smoked salmon with impeccable scrambled eggs is sexy. Roast beef and all the trimmings simply isn't. And it must be sensual. My food is always very highly spiced: I love strong flavours, and I'm crazy about smell. I have a whole bed of scented salad leaves, rocket and tarragon and chervil, lovage and basil and coriander, all the things which smell good. I always take the food into the garden in the summer when the evenings are long – there's a sheltered corner and I light candles.

'I love my garden when everything is overblown and overscented, and the apples and plums are ripe. I never want to go anywhere else and I never want to live in the city again. All the things I do well, I do in the country – and I do them all within my own space. But when I *do* go out, go up to London for a party maybe, every now and again I dress purely to attract a man. I wear something that makes me look really good. Real jewellery, beautiful shoes, perfect nails. It's the overall effect that counts. I know I can go to a gathering where there are ten women of thirty, and I'll look infinitely better than any of them. Maybe it's because I have no children, so I have the time. And I always paint my toenails. It's very surprising to find immaculate toenails when the woman has not painted her fingernails. Such detail, not publicly visible, is the essence of eroticism. At our age, one is prepared to put oneself on the line. To say, "Here I am. And, as you can see, I'm pretty good. So what about it, lads?" '

23

So there it is. Make of it what you will. We all need the experience of others to help us make sense of our own. As for me, I do what I can with the talents I have at my disposal; my only obligation is to use them to the full. I would certainly agree with my counsellor friend that a steady relationship is important – but I would push the parameters further. Friendship is my own face-lift, my drug, my cure-all. Husband, good friends, my favourite (and only) sister – but above all, my children. And since I have promised I won't mention them ever again in print, the matter must stop there, except to say I have no doubt they take pride in what I do. But even so, their lives are very separate, and rightly so. There's no doubt that their choices are different from my own. The world has changed, so how could it be otherwise? Their horizons are far wider than mine could ever be. In my time and theirs, men have set foot on the moon. In half a day we can be half-way round the world. We travel faster than the speed of sound – perhaps soon, faster than light. We have constructed equations capable of calculating the length and breadth of the universe. Time – eternity itself – is no longer a mystery. We have at our disposal machines capable of exploring the composition of the planets. We may soon, the scientists tell us, unravel the secret of life, know where we will meet our end as well as our beginning.

As yet we have no notion what this knowledge may mean – or even if we were right to ask the questions. This, the world in which we live, is our reality, our responsibility. It is our children and our children's children who will reap the rewards of our stewardship, or pay for the consequences. Each generation must ask its own questions, find its own answers.

Mine was the generation that believed in the power of change. We had no choice: we were the children born on the battlefield, the sons and daughters of war. Many of us were fatherless, most of us came from broken families, few of us escaped unscathed.

When I was a very young woman, after a late and well-lubricated lunch at Wheeler's with my soon-to-be-husband – if I remember rightly, in the company of Francis Bacon and Lucian Freud – I walked down a Soho street with the poet Christopher Logue. I was on my way to a clerical job at the newly nascent *Private Eye*, while Christopher was delivering his anarchic lyrics for Annie Ross to sing to Stanley Myers's music at Nicholas's and Peter Cook's Establishment Club, where Lenny Bruce – that arch-subversive – was performing nightly.

When we parted company at the corner, Christopher asked me where I was going. 'Down the road to change the world,' is what he tells me I replied. I don't remember, but the words ring true – and, if so, the reply was not born of arrogance but of hope.

Arnold Wesker warned my generation: '*If we do not change, we die.*' I believed it then and, Heaven help me, I believe it still.

PART ONE

Into The East

CHAPTER ONE

The Open Road, September, 1985

> *If you are wise you will not look upon the long period of time occupied in actual movement as the mere gulf dividing you from the end of your journey, but rather as one of those rare and plastic seasons of your life from which, perhaps, in after times, you may love to date the moulding of your character – that is, your very identity. Once feel this, and you will soon grow happy and contented in your saddle home.*
> VITA SACKVILLE-WEST (1892–1962), *Passenger to Teheran* (1926)

FIVE YEARS BEFORE MY FIFTIETH BIRTHDAY, I HAD ALREADY reached a milestone in my life. *European Peasant Cookery* was the book I had always wanted to write, but when I embarked on the undertaking the prospect was truly daunting.

My area of knowledge, though acquired through direct experience and without expectation of any but the most practical application, was deep but not broad. I had lived with my young family in southern Spain, I knew France well, Italy since girlhood, Britain through work as a food journalist.

But there were many geographical gaps to be filled: all of Scandinavia, the Germanic and Slav traditions, the Balkans. But, above all, I had always been fascinated by the Ottoman Turks, not least because they were to the Balkans as the Moors were to Spain. By way of introduction, I should explain my chosen subject.

The peasantry, say the ethnologists, are those for whom agriculture is a livelihood and a way of life, not a business for profit. What I had learned was that self-sufficient smallholdings depend on access not only to arable land but to pasture and sufficient uncultivated land to provide wild-gatherings. The peasant crop is dictated by the nature of the land, the season and the weather. This is not to say that the diet is necessarily poor or monotonous, simply that it's limited by what can be grown, herded or gathered locally. The first requirement is that meals must be balanced and healthy. The peasant housewife needs to keep her family in good health or they will not be able to work and the group will suffer.

Abundance is strictly seasonal and must be preserved for those times when the fields and woods are bare. The store-cupboard is of the utmost importance: its stocking requires judgement, patience and skill. The peasant larder can contain such luxuries as *foie gras* and the finest hams, truffles and ceps, the best of olive oil and the most fragrant herbs. Variety is harder to come by: eighteenth-century farm labourers in Scandinavia as well as Scotland had agreements that they should have to eat salmon no more than three times a week.

Imported luxuries – sugar, tea, coffee – were always limited by trade-routes and vulnerable to shortages. Pepper and spices were used only when there was ready access through exchange and barter.

My neighbours in Andalucia could remember times when these things were not available. Salt, essential for the conservation of food in winter, was brought to the valley from the salt flats in Cadiz. Nevertheless, our climate being damp, we sent our Christmas hams to the mountain villages to be cured in the cold, dry air of the sierras.

If the factors that govern peasant cookery are seasonality, geography and access to trade-routes, those that govern the two other great culinary traditions also have their limitations. Bourgeois cookery, the culinary habit of those who live in towns, is limited by price and perishability. The rich might eat the prime cuts of beef and the choicest fish, taking their pick according to their pocket; the poor would make do with the tougher cuts, the innards and the fish that was too perishable to transport to the inland markets. Where anything and everything is available at a price, recipes have to be invented to accommodate them. The peasant tradition prefers accommodation to invention.

The third tradition of the European kitchen, *haute cuisine* – offspring of the medieval banquet and grandchild of the extravagant cooks of Rome – is the province of professional chefs, who must play to the gallery with sophisticated sauces, exotic ingredients and glamorous presentation. The home cook, bourgeois or peasant, has a captive audience, but restaurant chefs have to satisfy the paying customer. 'A nation's gastronomical level should be examined by tasting both the products of the best private kitchens and restaurants, and the dishes from the kitchens of the peasantry,' said Curnonsky, France's foremost post-war authority on culinary matters, best known as the first compiler of *Larousse Gastronomique*. 'Somewhere in between lies the true level of excellence.'

My neighbours in the Andalucian valley stocked their store-cupboard every autumn with home-grown beans and chick-peas, dried red peppers, garlic, onions and a good selection of salt-cured pork, sausages, bacon and hams. The lard was melted down, spiced with paprika and marjoram, to be spread on bread instead of butter.

This store-cupboard, supplemented by vegetables from the garden and fresh greens from the wild – most European country people still crop the wild for mushrooms, berries, leaves and herbs – provided the basis for what my children called beans-and-bones dishes. These one-pot stews, cooked over a top heat, which was all most country people had, remain my own family's favourite food. Variations on the theme are found all round the Mediterranean: cassoulet in France, Italy's minestrone, the

Balkan bean stews. Seasonal fruit – oranges, grapes, melons – cheese from the valley's herd of goats, rough red wine, olives and olive oil, eggs and the odd young cockerel or old boiling fowl completed the menu. Almonds, sunflower seeds, pine kernels and honey were the treats. The diet included practically no dairy products, no butter and very little sugar. My family thrived on it.

It is this balance in diet, this understanding of the composition of a healthy meal, established by trial and error over the centuries, which is more important than the nutritionist's facts and figures.

On a cold evening in late September 1985, when we landed at Munich airport, I carried a notebook and sketchpad, a handful of travellers' tales from the nineteenth century and nothing else in the way of a writer's equipment. Maps and guidebooks were Nicholas's department – I had dragooned him into accepting the position of chauffeur and carry-your-bags-miss when I committed us both to spending the autumn in Eastern Europe.

We had arrived four hours behind schedule, with no hotel reservation. Appropriately enough, soldiers with machine-guns patrolled the arrivals hall – a salutary reminder that this land has always been a battleground. Other passengers had been similarly delayed. Skirting the throng, we joined the queue for accommodation. 'You are part of the group?' enquired the brisk young man at the desk. I glanced round. Behind us, a noisy black-clad crowd, Homburg hats perched on inky ringlets, jostled for position – tourists from Israel.

'Absolutely,' I agreed, never one to reject the easy option.

'Hotel Imperial.' The brisk young man banged a stamp on a ticket and pushed it across the desk. 'Next.'

There were five of us in the communal cab: three of the ringleted ones and ourselves.

'You are members of the group?'

'Of course.'

'Jerusalem?'

'Certainly.'

Munich was in the grip of its annual beer-festival. The streets were thronged with revellers in sweat-stained *Lederhosen*, so woe betide anyone who was neither Bavarian nor full of beer.

Inside the hotel, the lobby's anaglypta–clad walls were plastered with posters of suspected terrorists wanted for questioning. Ulrike Meinhof and Andreas Baader were giving the Bavarian police a hard run for their money. A transit hotel was just the place you might be likely to bump into both.

The ringleted ones set about demanding kosher refreshments from a sullen young woman with blonde pigtails and steely blue eyes. Kosher refreshments? In Munich? With the beer-festival in full swing?

'Anyone care to rewrite *Kristallnacht*?' asked Nicholas cheerfully, never one to pour oil on troubled waters. We deposited our luggage in our spartan quarters – hard little beds welded to the wall, Good News Bible on the bedside table, crumb-dusted carpet, broken shower – and departed swiftly, before the victors of the Six Day War took offence at Reception's lack of co-operation.

Picking the back-streets rather than the main thoroughfare, the revellers being no respecters of person, we made our way cautiously towards a neon sign that held out the somewhat bleak promise of *Essen und Trinken*. *Essen* turned out to be tepid brown soup and cold pink sausage, but the beer was truly magnificent.

Spirits somewhat restored, we returned to base, threading our way down the alleyways like Montagus threatened by Capulets. The night passed, but only just. Nicholas, plagued by an overindulgence in beer and sausage, was up and down all night like a sailor in a brothel. Sleep descended at dawn. Not for long: the ringleted ones were up at cock-crow, performing their necessary ablutions with a mighty rattling of drains. We gave up the unequal struggle, rose, dressed and went in search of breakfast.

The morning repast, served in the hotel's grim cafeteria, turned out to be more of the non-kosher sausage whose acquaintance we had made at supper. The ringleted ones mounted further protests. We called a cab. We had our rented vehicle to collect, and Nicholas was anxious to satisfy his craving for English newspapers – a preoccupation that does not afflict his wife. I have always been more than happy to let the world turn without me.

The streets were deserted at this early hour – presumably none of the natives worked during the Oktoberfest – and only the *Gastarbeiter* are about. Fortunately it is they who provide the essential services. The Turks drive the cabs, the Argentinians control the newspaper pitches. The tourist services alone are staffed with admirable German thoroughness. I had done a deal with Hertz, hoping that a rented vehicle with German numberplates would make our travels behind the Iron Curtain less suspect. All was in order. We were allotted a splendid silver Mercedes. With some relief we paid, packed and got on our way.

Munich to Weiz is a full day's drive through the Bavarian Alps into Austria. We made stately progress through the orderly, well-tended countryside. On either side, hills were grazed smooth by flocks of fat sheep, parkland was dotted with little huts for winter feeding. In the meadows were placid, dun-coloured cows.

We stopped for lunch in Schladming, a little market town with a pretty sixteenth-century posting-hotel. On the menu was more *Wurst* in all its guises: with sauerkraut, with apples, with potatoes – even, most magnificently, *Wurst* with sauerkraut, apples and potatoes. The alternative was frankfurters. These came in pairs, each one at least a foot long, garnished with pungent piles of freshly grated horseradish, dark brown mild mustard, bread spiced with caraway.

In Weiz we were booked into the Hotel Romantik, which had allotted us rooms in the geriatric annex, with full provision for wheelchairs and doors that swung in both directions to accommodate zimmer frames. In the bathroom were curious fitments and handles designed for the convenience of those deprived of the use of their extremities.

The fierce *Frau* behind the desk explained, with some severity, that supper was sharp at six thirty, lights out at ten: Austrian trencherpersons allow plenty of time for digestion. The dinner was a dream. The stars of the show were the *Steinpilze* – boletus, known in Austria as stone mushrooms – sautéed in butter and served with little semolina soufflés; a robust tomato soup heavily spiked with chilli; a salad of fine strips of celeriac blended with tiny new potatoes drenched in a creamy, mustardy, honey dressing; thick slabs of salty pink bacon heaped on tiny buttery dumplings speckled with fronds of dill. To drink, a jug of iced wine, pink and fragrant as rose-petals.

Next morning, mindful of my responsibilities, I went in search of the kitchen. Here, amid stainless steel counters and all the soulless paraphernalia of modern catering, were two well-upholstered *Hausfrau* kneading dough. The hotel might have been romantic, but its kitchen was a model of practicality. I enquired after the little dumplings.

'*Die Nockerln? Kein problem, Fraülein.*'

A mound of flour, a handful of creamy curds, a knob of yeast and the dumpling dough took shape. It was quickly made – soft, yeasty, white as snow and smooth as silk. Small pieces were broken off, each nugget swiftly worked into a tiny ball and just as swiftly tossed into a gleaming copper pan of simmering water. Within moments the whole surface was covered with tiny pillows, soft and light as swansdown. A swift flick of the wrist and the swansdown pillows were dropped in a pool of melted butter in a deep dish. Another flick of the wrist, and the pillows were covered in crisp, buttery breadcrumbs.

A spoon was produced, a huge helping ladled on to a plate.

The two round pink faces, wreathed in smiles, watch me triumphantly as I taste. Good cooks are never in doubt of their worth.

'*Ist gut?*'

My smile matched theirs. 'Is better than good. Is perfect.'

The following day belonged to Nicholas.

In 1956, he was a young officer in the Brigade of Guards stationed in Germany, when the tanks rolled into Budapest. Although under orders to do no such thing, he took French leave and made his way to Heiligenkreuz, one of the few border posts between Austria and Hungary that had not yet been closed. Somewhere to the south lay one of the escape routes for the refugees.

The day was warm and wet. There would be a storm before nightfall. We took the road to Heiligenkreuz. No man's land

Austrian Steinpilze mit Himmelthausoufflé
PORCINI IN CREAM WITH SEMOLINA SOUFFLÉS

Steinpilze – *Boletus edulis*, otherwise known as *porcini*, ceps, *bolet*, penny bun – are the real treasure-trove of the autumn woods. Austria's favourite wild fungi is exquisite cooked in cream and served with delicate little semolina soufflés. *Himmelthau*, heavenly dew, is old Austrian for the Habsburg Empire's favourite grain-food.

――――――――――――― SERVES 4 – THE SOUFFLÉS ―――――――――――――

1 pint/600 ml milk	*a little flour*
3 oz/85 g semolina	*1 tablespoon grated Parmesan*
2 eggs, separated	*salt and pepper*
small knob butter	

―――――――――――――――― THE MUSHROOMS ――――――――――――――――

1 lb/500 g fresh porcini mushrooms	*1 tablespoon kümmel* or *eau-de-vie*
1 tablespoon butter	or *vodka*
2–3 tablespoons olive oil	*4 tablespoons double cream*
salt and pepper	
1 tablespoon marjoram, finely chopped	

1. Make the soufflé base first: bring the milk to the boil and stir in the semolina. Cook it steadily for 10 minutes, stirring all the time.

Remove and leave it to cool.

2. Preheat the oven to 425°F/220°C/mark 7.

3. Whisk the egg whites. Butter and sprinkle with flour 4 individual soufflé dishes. Stir the yolks, Parmesan, salt and pepper into the cooled polenta. Fold in the whisked whites. Drop the mixture into the little soufflé dishes – they should be no more than two thirds full. Bake for 40 minutes.

4. Meanwhile, prepare the *porcini*. Pick over and wipe the fungi and dust off any loose earth and leaf-mould – don't wash them, and discard any that are wormy or past their best. Slice thickly. In a frying-pan, melt the butter with the oil. As soon as it foams, throw in the mushrooms. Season with salt and pepper (the salt helps the juices run), and toss over a gentle heat until the mushrooms release their water. Turn up the heat, sprinkle in the marjoram, and let everything bubble fiercely until the water has all evaporated and the mushrooms begin to fry. Splash in the liquor and set it alight – this helps the caramelization and concentrates the flavours. Stir in the cream, taste and adjust the seasoning. When you're ready to serve, bubble it all up again.

5. Unmould the soufflés on to hot plates, and serve with the creamy mushrooms.

Austrian Rindsuppe mit Speck und Butternockerln

BEEF BROTH WITH BACON AND BUTTERED BREAD DUMPLINGS

The Austrians like their soups based on beef broth and enjoy combining different kinds of meat. You can add a boiling sausage for an even more substantial dish.

———————————— SERVES 6 – THE BROTH ————————————

2 lb / 1 kg shin of beef	½ celeriac root or 6–8 celery stalks
2 lb / 1 kg smoked bacon, pre-soaked	2 onions
2–3 mature carrots	2–3 garlic cloves
1 parsley-root or a small parsnip	1 teaspoon allspice
small bunch parsley	½ teaspoon peppercorns

———————————— THE DUMPLINGS ————————————

2 oz / 50 g unsalted butter	1 egg, lightly forked
1 small onion, finely chopped	2–3 tablespoons plain flour
7 oz / 200 g day-old bread, diced small	salt and white pepper

1. Make the broth first. Put all the ingredients in a large pot, pour in enough water to cover generously – about 5 pints/2.5 l – bring to the boil, skim off any grey foam that rises, turn down the heat,

lid loosely and leave to simmer gently for 2 hours or so, until the meat's perfectly tender. The water should tremble, with the odd belch. No salt required – there's plenty in the bacon. Add more boiling water if necessary. A pressure cooker will do the job in a fraction of the time.

2. Remove the meats when they're quite soft, and reserve. Strain out and discard the flavouring vegetables (for a good clear broth, strain through a clean cloth in a sieve). Boil down the remaining broth until you have about 3 pints, 1.5 litres.

3. Meanwhile, make the dumplings. Melt the butter in a frying-pan, and fry the onion until soft but not brown. Add the bread cubes and continue frying until nicely golden. Transfer the contents of the pan to a bowl and pour in the beaten egg. Mix well with a fork and work in the flour – you may need a little milk if the mixture seems too dry, or a little more flour if it looks too wet. Season lightly. With wet hands, form the mixture into dumplings the size of large golf balls.

4. Drop the dumplings into the boiling broth – not all at once, do them in three batches. Turn down the heat to a gentle simmer and poach them for 10 minutes, until firm and light – they'll rise to the top when they're ready.

5. Ladle the broth into hot plates. Finish with slices of meat and the dumplings.

was marked by two concrete pillars linked by an arch. Framed in the semicircle of steel, the plains of Hungary stretched towards the Urals. In the distance, a small family of fallow deer, three does and their fawns, crossed the road, dainty as dancers. Earlier in our married life, Nicholas had spoken of that time. Young men confronted by death have little choice but to be heroes, and I knew he had been heroic. But when he spoke of it, there was little of heroism. He talked instead of the noise bullets make when they rip through flesh, of women and children wounded, of babies stranded on barbed wire, of bodies rotting in wheatfields churned by the treads of tanks.

It was through this border that he had driven to Budapest – and he was anxious to set ghosts to rest. This is one of the reasons, I knew, that he had agreed to accompany me.

A young soldier came towards us, enquiring courteously if we needed assistance. Nicholas woke from his sombre reverie. 'Thank you, but I know the place well.'

'You were here in the war?' The young man's voice was sympathetic.

Nicholas shook his head and smiled. 'Too young for that. In 'fifty-six – the time of the troubles.'

This border was always no man's land, a sombre place, not somewhere to linger.

As soon as we turned south, the storm broke. We drove through sheeting rain into the hills. I, too, had memories to revisit, but of a rather different sort.

Bad Gleichenberg is one of those curious spa towns built to accommodate those who pin their faith on the miraculous restorative powers of sulphur waters. It had managed to survive modern medical scepticism. Pretty young nurses were shunting elderly gentlemen in wheelchairs between the baths, the drinking fountains and the consulting rooms.

In the evening, a soft blanket of silence descended. I remember the routine all too well. I spent many a school holiday in such places – my American-born grandmother was an addict of the fashionable watering-holes that flourished after the war: Marienbad, Eugenie-les-Bains, MonteCatini. Never, as far as I can remember, Bad Gleichenberg, but it would do well enough to satisfy my memories.

All I remembered of such places was that the people were old, the diversions few. Only the food was of any interest. The more fashionable, the better the chefs, the more exquisite the menus. My grandfather was a gambler with enough money to satisfy his craving – until even his considerable fortune could no longer cope with his habit and my grandmother's extravagance.

Curiosity, and my own hazy memories, led me to one of the luxurious hotels. My grandparents had been friends of the Duke and Duchess of Windsor. Like that spoiled pair they never travelled without a brace of their own personal servants, a cabin trunk full of monogrammed linen and enough clothes – breakfast-gowns, cocktail frocks, smoking jackets – to sink the *Titanic*. My grandmother required similarly high sartorial standards of her granddaughter, and would insist on cramming my plump teenage form into end-of-season bargains from the great Paris fashion houses, outfits designed to fit the twig-slender house-models. Wallis Windsor may have declared that a person could never be too rich or too thin, but I was neither. Nevertheless, I tried hard to please my grandmother, and it was many years before I realized that a weekend abroad did not always require a forty-pound suitcase with matching vanity-case, or that the achievement of a plank-flat body was not necessarily the ultimate good.

The hotel had no room for passing strangers. Watering-hole hotels are booked up for years in advance. Nevertheless, the concierge, a stern, grey-uniformed matron with a clutch of keys at her belt, took pity on us. She could offer us a small room in the attic. In all my years of travelling with my grandparents' retinue – one bit of baggage among many – I had never seen what were then the servants' quarters. They were forbidden territory, and the opportunity to inspect them was too good to miss.

The upper storeys, no longer required for servants and pressed into service for the more impecunious guests, were reached by a long corridor lined with gilt-framed sepia photographs of plump ladies in crinolines. Their tiny waists and pinched faces indicated that the commonest complaint was a surfeit of rich food and too-tight laces.

We inspected the bedroom. It was furnished with a washstand, a commode and a very narrow single bed designed to accommodate one very small, very tidy person.

'I don't think so, thank you very much,' said Nicholas politely.

'Perhaps you are right.' The concierge smiled. 'Ach. This was once where I was sleeping. It is many years. I think I have forgotten.'

Seeing our disappointment, she relented. 'Perhaps, *meine Herren*, I can find you somewhere where you might be not so comfortable but you can perhaps take rest. Is my uncle – he has a small *Gasthaus* in the hill, for the walkers. *Das Zimmer –*' she raises her eyes to the heavens '– is not of the best. But *das Essen* is good. I go there myself and I know.'

The guesthouse was full of boots and wet mackintoshes.

The rooms, pointed out through the rain, were small wooden chalets set among the trees. The beds turned out to be bunks, but at least they were large enough to house the sturdy Austrian hill-walkers who made up the clientele. There was no bath but the shower water was hot, and we were happy to have found shelter. Meals, advised our hostess, were taken communally. As it was past six o'clock, dinner was already in progress. We changed quickly out of our wet clothes and made our way back through the trees.

A scrubbed wooden table reached the full length of the dining room under the mournful gaze of a regiment of stuffed and mounted heads – stag, boar, moufflon. The diners were equally silent but far from mournful. A dozen spoons worked busily in reverent silence. The windows were frosted with steam and the air was filled with the scent of bacon broth.

Three families with two children apiece were already tucking into basins of semolina-thickened soup. By their dress – leather shorts for the men, green corduroy knickerbockers for the women, matching green loden jackets complete with braces, epaulettes and braiding – it would have been easy to mistake them for some kind of school outing.

Austrians, Nicholas pointed out cheerfully as we took our places, never could resist a uniform.

The green-clad ones inspected us briefly, then returned to the happy enjoyment of their dinner. Fulfilling all expectations, the meal was not only good but gargantuan. The broth was followed by a huge plate of veal cutlets bathed in cream. The accompaniments – sliced onions fried in goose fat, spiced cranberries, buttered pumpkin, potato pancakes – were piled liberally into bowls set at intervals along the boards. We could not hope to match such prodigious appetites. By the time the dessert appeared, we were flagging. Dumplings – four fat snowy globes to each serving, stuffed with plums and hatted up with hazelnut crumble – spelled defeat.

Our host inspected our plates severely. '*Das Essen ist nicht gut?*'

We smiled weakly. '*Sehr gut*. Fine, delicious. It's just that . . .'

Our host roared with laughter. It was clearly not the first time English appetites had fallen short of Austrian expectations.

'*Die Engländer*, they do not eat. *Die Engländer*, they drink. I say to English, first we eat. Then we drink.'

Nicholas brightened. Our host grinned and clapped him on the back. 'Ach! I see we have interest. I think perhaps for you I find something special.'

The something special turned out to be a fiery collection of illicitly brewed *Kirschwasser* trawled up from the dusty depths of the cellar. The junior hill-walkers were shooed off to their bunks, the table was cleared and a regiment of short, stubby glasses lined up on the board. This, announced our host, was to be a formal tasting, and a formal tasting demands no shirking.

The tasting was followed by drinking. The drinking was accompanied by singing. National priorities surfaced.

The Austrians delivered a rendition of '*Unter den Linden*' in close harmony, with descant. They were members of a glee-club. Nicholas countered with six robust but out-of-tune choruses of 'D'ye ken John Peel with his coat so gay?'.

The green-clad ones professed themselves mystified by the lyrics. Nicholas obliged with a learned discourse on the usage and abusage of the word 'gay' when applied to a coat which, although red, is none the less held to be pink.

Austrian Zwetschkenknödel
PLUM-STUFFED POTATO DUMPLINGS

The proper conclusion to an Austrian meal. The potato makes the dumplings lighter, and the finishing with butter-fried breadcrumbs and hazelnut gives a deliciously crisp coating.

—————————— MAKES ABOUT 12 DUMPLINGS ——————————

1 lb/500 g floury potatoes, unpeeled	about 6 oz/275g plain flour
1 oz/25 g butter	12 small blue plums
1 tablespoon cream	12 small sugar lumps
1 egg	¹/₂ teaspoon salt

—————————————— TO FINISH ——————————————

3 oz/75 g butter	powdered cinnamon
4–5 tablespoons fresh breadcrumbs	icing sugar
1 tablespoon hazelnuts, chopped	

1. Boil the potatoes in their jackets until soft. Skin them while still hot and mash them with butter and cream until you have a homogeneous mass. Leave to cool for 10 minutes, then work in the egg. Stir in some of the flour and tip everything out on to your

work surface. Knead in the rest of the flour until you have a soft, pliable dough – depending on the wateriness of the potatoes, you'll need more or less flour. Cover with cling-film and leave aside for 30 minutes.

2. Meanwhile ease the stones out of the plums with a skewer. Replace each stone with a sugar lump. Divide the dough into 12 pieces. Work each piece into a ball and flatten into a thin round. Brush the edges with water and use to wrap each plum – the dough should cover the fruit completely.

3. Bring a large saucepan of water to the boil and turn down the heat till the water's just at simmering point. Add the salt and lower the dumplings into the water – as many as you can, depending on the size of the pan. Simmer steadily for 10–12 minutes, until white and puffy and firm. Remove to a colander and rinse quickly with cold water from the tap.

4. To finish, fry the breadcrumbs in the butter in a frying-pan until crisp. Add the finely chopped hazelnuts right at the end, and let them toast a little. Leaving the pan on the heat, roll the dumplings in the hot crumbs. Keep frying and turning to give them a crisp coat. Serve sprinkled with cinnamon and sugar.

'*Bitte?*'

Two hours later, after an in-depth examination of Austrian versus British hunting philosophies – the needs of the trencherman versus the requirements of the sportsman – no one was any the wiser.

This, we finally agreed, was as it should be. All the best parties ended in confusion. Confusion is only to be expected when *vino* looks for *veritas*.

CHAPTER TWO

The Country Formerly Known
as Yugoslavia

*I am interested in growing food for its own sake and in
appetite. The health-giving and prophylactic virtues of a meal
depend on the zest with which it has been imagined, cooked
and eaten.*

PATIENCE GRAY, *Honey from a Weed* (Prospect Books, 1986)

THE NEXT MORNING, THE STORM HAD LIFTED. THE TOWN
sparkled in sunshine.

Rays of multicoloured light filtered through the chestnut
woods and the hard brown fruit crunched under our wheels as
we took the highway south towards the border.

The Austrian approach to what was still Yugoslavia ran
through open country. Golden plain met blue sky on a grey
horizon. The crops had long since been harvested, and the
brown plough was slicked with a green mist of winter wheat.
Those fields that had not yet received the attentions of the

ploughman were, like an unshaven chin, still prickly with autumn stubble. There were blackened patches where fires had been lit to clear the straw, but these had been extinguished by the previous day's storm.

This was to be our first Iron Curtain border. Anticipating interrogation, we had rehearsed our story carefully.

Smiling confidently, Nicholas wound down the window. '*Entschuldigen Sie bitte*. Excuse me.'

We needn't have worried. The Austrian border guards waved us through without a second glance. The Yugoslavs were equally indifferent. We were bewildered. Then we remember the licence plates. No need for explanations, we were German – to all appearances, wealthy burgers of Munich, tourists with wallets stuffed with Deutschmarks. Signs by the roadside offered directions in German to the coastal resorts – Sibenik, Split, Dubrovnik. Although the contours of the landscape had not changed, the difference in husbandry was startling. Long narrow fields rayed out from the road, the effect curiously medieval, like diagrams of feudal crop-rotation reproduced in history books. The last harvest of the year had not yet been gathered: a second crop had been planted among the stubble – there was still fertility to be sucked from the autumn sun. Tall stands of rattling maize and broad rows of dark-leaved brassicas streaked the fields.

Ignoring the signs to the coast, we chose the road for Belgrade. Soon the strip-cultivation was replaced by vast unfenced fields littered with gourd-bearing vines. In the fields, at well-spaced intervals, groups of women had set up circles of kitchen chairs beside piles of the gourds. Sprigged aprons and floral headscarves fluttered like bright butterflies in the breeze. It was apparent that this was a work party; what was less clear was the nature of the work.

Intrigued, we drew to a halt. A few moments' study revealed that the gourds were pumpkins. A brawny-armed matron was splitting them with a single deft blow of a large sharp knife. Another retrieved the halves and scooped out the seeds into a bucket. A third spread the contents of the bucket in a wide circular sieve, shaking it to separate the seeds. A fourth was operating an instrument that looked like a large coffee-grinder.

As we approached, the women halted in their work studying us with calm faces.

'*Was ist das?*' I gesture towards the pumpkins. 'What are you doing?'

A puzzled moment of silence was followed, in formal old-fashioned German, with the explanation: 'We're milling for oil, of course. What do *you* do with your pumpkins?'

Nicholas translated my explanations about pumpkin pie, pumpkin soup, pumpkin mash with butter and nutmeg. My recipes were greeted with astonished laughter.

'You mean you eat the flesh? We give it to the cattle. The seeds are what we harvest for ourselves. They give good oil. We put it on salads, eat it on our bread. Sometimes, even, we use it for frying, but it burns easily, so we use it only if we have no other.'

The oldest woman, who had resumed her work, smiled at me. 'Perhaps you would like to taste?'

'*Bitte.*' I glanced hesitantly at the thin stream spouting into a bucket from the little hand-cranked mill worked by one of the younger women. None of the women had paused for long.

'*Nein.* This one is for cooking and for softening the skin.' She reached out her hand to pat my cheek. 'I shall give you something special.'

From a basket by her side she pulled out a bolster-shaped loaf and a small ceramic bottle with a cork stopper. She wiped the knife on her apron, and used it to slice off a knuckle of dense-textured bread speckled with poppy-seeds. With a careful hand, she drizzled the crumb with oil from the bottle, and held out the slice. 'Eat. It's good.'

I accepted the offering. The bread was fresh and crisp-crusted. The oil was dark in colour – almost as black as molasses – and so liquid it had already vanished into the crumb. The flavour was delicate, nutty and sweet.

She prepared another slice, thicker this time, and handed it to Nicholas. 'Your wife might like to learn of the preparation. We do not roast the seeds until we are ready to mill them. This is because the oil must be fresh. *Verstehen Sie?*'

We understood. 'The bread's very good,' said Nicholas, chewing appreciatively. This brought more nods and smiles. 'It's

Pumpkin Pecan Pie

A favourite recipe of my American-born grandmother – it's the maple sugar that makes the difference.

4 oz / 100 g plain flour
pinch of salt
2 oz / 50 g cold butter

2 oz / 50 g caster sugar
2 egg yolks

THE FILLING

1 lb / 500 g piece pumpkin,
 peeled, seeded and chunked
4 tablespoons double cream
2 eggs
4 tablespoons maple syrup
4 tablespoons brown sugar

2 eggs, forked
1 teaspoon ground cinnamon
$^{1}/_{2}$ teaspoon ground nutmeg
2 oz / 50 g shelled pecans
 (walnuts could substitute),
 finely chopped

TO FINISH

maple sugar or soft brown sugar

extra pecans for sprinkling

1. Make the pastry first: this is easiest in the food processor. Start with the flour, salt, butter and sugar, then drop in the egg yolks,

allowing the mixture to come together in a crumbly dough (if the yolks are small, you'll need a few drops of water). Pack together in a ball, wrap in cling-film and set aside in the fridge for 30 minutes to firm. If you make it by hand, grate the *cold* butter into the dry ingredients and mix lightly before working in the egg.

2. Now for the filling: cook the pumpkin chunks in a closed pan in very little water until perfectly soft – about 20 minutes. Drain, mash and dry over the heat. Let the purée cool, then drop it with all the remaining ingredients, except the nuts, into the food processor. Process to a purée.

3. Preheat the oven to 400°F/200°C/mark 6.

4. Roll out the pastry to line a 9 in/23 cm pie tin – don't worry if it rips, just patch it firmly with a wet finger. Prick the base and bake it 'blind' (without filling) for 10 minutes to set the pastry – don't bother to line it with foil. Let it cool a little. Sprinkle with the finely chopped nuts, spread in the filling, decorate with the reserved nut halves and bake for about an hour, until the pastry is crisp, the filling set and the top nicely browned.

5. Grate the maple sugar over the top, or sprinkle with soft brown sugar, and serve with whipped cream.

my mother's recipe, I will tell her of your appreciation. She is ninety-two, she still bakes bread three times a week. Here.' She hacked off more slices, urging us to eat. Money seemed inadequate payment for such courtesy, so I settled down on a vacant stool and completed two small sketches of the ladies at their work – one for our generous hosts, and one for myself.

Both curiosity and honour satisfied, we drove on through the shimmering heat of the hills. After the long summer, the landscape was dry and parched, littered with tall stands of yellowing maize stalks and a few swathes of bright blue flax and purple lupins. As we approached the central plateau, villages rimmed the road, each house with its pumpkin patch, its little square of vines and rows of potatoes. Domestic animals were few – a tethered pig, hens scrabbling in the dust, rabbits in hutches. Goats and yellow-fleeced sheep grazed the stony ground, with here and there a dun-coloured cow. All along the road verges, a mist of pale blue flowers – escapees from the flax fields – contrasted with the darker violet of autumn crocus.

Although we had chosen the main arterial route to Istanbul and the east, there were few ordinary travellers on the road and no signs of any facilities that might cater to tourists. At midday, we turned off the highway and followed the signs to the town of Ljutomer. It seemed reasonable to assume that a wine-making centre must boast a restaurant.

Factory sheds and public-housing tower blocks ringed the town. Enquiries of the few passers-by in the main square revealed that the only public eating facility was to be found in the Hotel Jeruzalem, whose name held the promise of a picturesque coaching inn outside which a Victorian postilion might expect to be struck by lightning.

The Hotel Jeruzalem, however, revealed itself to be a large grey building with plate-glass windows through which could be seen the steel counters and Formica tables favoured by municipal caterers. Instead of pilgrims travelling the well-trodden path to the birthplace of Christianity, the only guests – judging from the samples in the vehicles lined up in the car-park – were travellers in fertilizer and bottled bull-semen, advisers on the use of pesticides and all the other man-made paraphernalia essential to modern industrial farming.

As it was well past midday, the canteen was almost empty. Four tables were still occupied by grey-uniformed municipal workers masticating in silence. In one corner, elbows on a table scattered with overflowing ashtrays, a small party of Russian lorry-drivers were working their way through thick slabs of black bread and pickled cucumbers, washed down with vodka. The food slumbered sourly in tin trays set into the counter: sulky slabs of boiled beef, boiled onions, boiled carrots, boiled macaroni. On the wall behind, a pictorial menu promised richer pickings.

'*Ja?*' The serving woman was as thin and grey as municipal gravy.

Ever the optimist, Nicholas pointed to a full-colour photograph of steak and chips. The answering burst of verbal gunfire caused the masticating workers to swing round and choke on their gristle.

Nicholas withdrew swiftly and settled for the boiled beef and carrots. I went for the whey-coloured macaroni, which came with equally grey meatballs floating on a watery scarlet sauce and slabs of the same black bread that the Russians were shovelling down in a somewhat more appetizing form. I had hoped for better commons. Serbians, my Yugoslav informant had told me, had a taste for Turkish food, spicy and fragrant. Clearly he had never experienced the Hotel Jeruzalem.

A tentative request for a bottle of Riesling, the area's most famous product, produced loud guffaws and reinforcements in the form of the canteen manager, a large woman with severely scraped-back hair and the air of a disapproving headmistress.

Oliver Twist could not have received a less encouraging response. Certainly the wine was made, and in considerable quantity; it was a peasant product, not state-controlled, but all of it went to the state collective. The peasantry were permitted to keep a proportion of production for their own use, but the rest was for export. Yugoslavia was a poor country, explained the headmistress severely. The state needed all the foreign currency it could earn. It was a patriotic duty not to drink it. The delicate dry wine was not to be had for love or money.

The choice was between Bulgarian bottled beer and a syrupy

cordial of a peculiarly virulent yellow. Clearly the vodka-swigging Russians knew the way things worked.

It was beginning to dawn on me that this particular research trip was likely to turn into a struggle for survival. The midday meal had been an experience neither of us would care to repeat, although it had certainly established what might be expected of Communist canteen catering. If I was to find what I needed, I must head for the markets and follow the housewives home.

Meanwhile, we needed somewhere to spend the night.

The highway led to Zagreb, which, explained the only tourist guidebook available, was a grim industrial city not recommended for casual tourists. I was learning to be a little nervous of casual tourism. Instead we headed through the gathering dusk for Plitvice, a summer resort in the heart of what the guide assured us was Yugoslavia's very own Snowdonia. Billed as a tourist destination popular with English holiday-makers – notably those from Bromley – Plitvice might confidently be expected to welcome the traveller, however casual.

Quite why Bromley and Plitvice should have chosen each other was to remain a mystery. There were no foreign tourists, English or otherwise, in the streets of what proved to be a pretty little resort town. Signs directed us to the holiday village. This being a weekend, it was full of prosperous shopkeepers and their wives enjoying an autumn break with their families. Presumably they, too, were escaping the grim industrial suburbs of Zagreb.

The charter season over, the individual chalets designed for tourists had all been bedded down for the winter. The only accommodation available, explained the young woman in the reception centre, was in communal wooden bunkhouses. These were strictly segregated and lights went out at midnight. Blankets were provided, but not pillows. Furthermore, she added, with the air of one conferring unusual privilege, occupancy of a bunk entitled us to eat in the National Restaurant.

'We'll take it,' announced Nicholas, with a decisiveness born of desperation. 'Just like being back at school.' With a cheery wave of the hand, he headed off for the ablutions with the casual confidence of a man returning to his roots. Curious how men seem to enjoy dormitory living, whereas women need their space.

Mercifully the women and children's bunkhouse was deserted, although there was plenty of evidence of occupation. I chose an empty bunk, decanted the minimum of overnight necessities, and made my way through the darkness towards the shadowy bulk of the communal eating facilities.

The National Restaurant, a log-built *Bierkeller* the size of a small cathedral, featured a bank of wood-fired brick barbecues (unlit), rustic tables with benches and a well-stocked bar. The place was already crowded, with most of the tables occupied by diners. The Croat table has never been noted for its daintiness. Waiters bustled back and forth bearing foaming tankards of beer and plates of pickled vegetables. The choice of solid refreshment was limited to sauerkraut with sausage or sausage with sauerkraut.

After the meal the barman took charge of our alcoholic education. 'You are English, no? Good. So I am mixing you a Partisan. When you are drinking it I am telling you how it got its name.'

Ice clinked into two tumblers, which were then filled with a triple measure of slivovic, the lethal white brandy of the Balkans, minimally diluted by a single measure of sour-cherry juice.

'Bottoms up,' said the barman in English, pushing the glasses across. He waited until we had both taken the first sip before launching into a vivid reconstruction of what the partisans did to the Germans during the Second World War, and what the Croats were likely to do to the Serbs when a similar opportunity arose in the future.

Mindful of his obligation to maintain the reputation of the absent inhabitants of Bromley – as he explained it later – Nicholas downed double rations.

By the time I returned the communal billet was full of sleeping bodies. I passed an uneasy night, aware of the small noises babies make when they sleep – as are all mothers, even if the infant is someone else's responsibility.

I met Nicholas in the ablutions at dawn. He reported that the hours of darkness had passed alternately in fitful sleep and attention to the demands of a digestion poleaxed by too much Partisan. We were on our way just as soon as the sun lifted over the mountains.

The lower slopes of the mountains were heavily wooded. Above them, the high tops gleamed with the first snows of winter. In the valleys, where the land might be cultivated, maize leaves and stalks were stacked to dry in baskets ten feet high – the leaves provide fibre for carpets, the stalks serve as firewood. The cobs were stacked neatly against the walls of the farmhouses, providing winter fodder for beast and barnyard, or, in hard years, the people themselves.

The houses were set back from the road, each fronted with its well-worked patch of garden in the centre of which was a vine arbour, an arched trellis of bent sticks and woven willow that seemed to serve as a makeshift dairy. At this time of the morning, with the air still cool from the night, aproned housewives were renneting the morning's milkings, lifting and turning the curds, sleeves rolled up above the elbows, their arms and hands pink from the cold.

Every few miles we passed a trestle table loaded with round cheeses of a size that can be held comfortably in the hand, some the colour of new parchment, some smoked to a rich nut-brown. Drawing to a halt, we accepted a taste proffered on the blade of a knife. The flavour was mild, the texture dense, the curd delicate and white. I had learned my lesson: I bought supplies for the midday meal.

At each curve in the road was a young girl or boy holding up a flat basket filled with wild-gathered mushrooms. These too I bought. I had no means of cooking them, but at least I could make a record with my brush. The children had gathered three varieties, all good for drying for the store-cupboard to make soups and flavour stews: winter fungus, pale-gilled and smelling faintly of honey; smooth brown porcini, thick-capped and firm-fleshed; horn-of-plenty, smooth and velvety, black as night, known in France as *trompettes de mort*. Occasionally we passed orchards of apple and plum trees laden with fruit, and these, too, had their roadside vendors.

On the outskirts of a village, we found bread for sale, cut

open to show the crumb, dense-textured and yellow with cornmeal.

At lunch-time we drew off the road and followed a path up into the hills to picnic on the edge of a meadow bright with butterflies and cropped by curious goats with long brown coats and expressionless golden eyes.

Our evening's destination was Belgrade. As we drew nearer the city, the offerings on the trestle tables became more sophisticated: there were wicker trays of doughnuts; round breads pyramids, each big enough for a fistful, split and filled with thick slices of smoke-cured bacon; triangular stacks of strudels – not the Ottoman-inspired filo fantasies of Austria, but the sturdy German *Beigli* made of yeast-raised pastry-dough filled with curd cheese, poppy-seeds, crushed walnuts. Here, too, were bottles of the elusive white wine we had been unable to find in Lutomer, and the slivovic all too familiar from the night before.

Belgrade turned out to be a grimy city with cracked pavements, gap-toothed rows of apartment buildings, piles of rubble trawled by flea-racked dogs. After a night in a tumbledown guesthouse on the outskirts of the city I made my way to the central market and settled down to sketch.

Lacking the language, I had it in my mind that this might be a way I could communicate more easily. Sure enough, I quickly acquired an audience, first the children and then the adults. Even I, wielding the brush, still find the process of painting extraordinary. I keep to a limited palette, the colours I have always used – never black or white, but cobalt and raw umber to make a delicate grey, or rose madder to blend with viridian to make a softer shadow. Each pigment has its own viscosity and scent. Madder smells of rose petals, the earth pigments – the terracotta colours – smell dusty, like the hot hillsides where the colours are mined. Each behaves in a different way when it encounters another: some pool in concentrated heaps, some break and spread like raindrops landing on the surface of a puddle. The mineral-based pigments, cobalt and umber, blend easily with each other, but maintain their separation on the paper. There's magic in the way the loaded brush makes its arbitrary mark, the instant likenesses that appear, however crude. Unlike the camera, the sketchbook is friendly, communicative, a shared experience.

Mindful of this, I used my skill to ask questions with the brush, drawing pictures of cloves, or almonds, or the shape of a cooking pot.

'What's the filling in that pastry? What spices?'

I searched out these stallholders who presented their wares as a visual recipe. If local custom was to cook broad beans with marjoram, the vegetable seller arranged the two ingredients in proximity. Peppers, onions and potatoes grouped together revealed a local recipe for a *djuvedj* – a vegetable stew found all over the Balkans. I already knew that in Bulgaria I could expect a dish of the same name to be thickened with rice and finished with yoghurt; in Hungary, with paprika and soured cream; in Croatia with caraway and garlic. In Serbia the preferred vegetable is aubergine, a Turkish favourite, and the dish is called *ajvar*. A Montenegran pilaff picks up everyone's habits.

At that time Belgrade was a cosmopolitan city in which each group retained its own culinary habit. By the scents that curled under the kitchen doors in winter, billowed through the open windows in summer, every inhabitant knew his own.

This culinary diversity, so fiercely defended, can identify foe as easily as friend. The Inquisition, I remembered from my years in Spain, relied heavily on culinary habit to single out those who might be suspected of non-Catholic recidivism. The diligent interrogators filled fat manuscript ledgers with questions and answers that were almost complete recipes. A direct refusal to eat pork or drink wine, or to combine certain foods with others, as in the Muslim or Jewish traditions, earned the backslider a place on the bonfire. But even if the obvious questions were answered satisfactorily, there were more subtle interrogations on the use and choice of spices, shapes of pans, rituals of preparation, even table manners.

At this time, in the autumn of 1985, the inhabitants of Belgrade were enjoying a rare period of peace. The old dictator – one-time leader of the partisans who proved a painful thorn in the side of the Third Reich – brooked no ethnic quarrelling. Belgrade had always been of considerable stategic importance. The city commanded the highway to the east, the pilgrim road

Montenegran Pilaff
RICE WITH LAMB AND MEDITERRANEAN VEGETABLES

This dish combines Turkish rice in a Serbian stew with an Italian garnish. Ecumenical as well as economical.

──────── SERVES 4 ────────

8 oz/250 g round rice (Arborio is
perfect, pudding rice is fine)
12 oz/350 g lean lamb
or pork, cubed
2 oz/50 g lard or 2 tablespoons
corn oil
2 onions, skinned and chopped
2 garlic cloves, skinned and chopped

1 green pepper, seeded and chopped
1 lb/500 g tomatoes, scalded,
skinned and chopped (or a can)
1 tablespoon paprika
about 2 pints/1 l vegetable or
chicken stock
salt and cayenne pepper

──────── TO FINISH ────────

slices of tomato and green pepper

1. Pick over the rice and remove any little stones. Trim the meat, removing any bits of extra fat or gristle.
2. Preheat the oven to 350°F/180°C/mark 4.
3. Heat the lard or oil in a heavy pan. Throw in the onions and garlic and cook them until they soften and take a little colour. Push them to one side and add the meat and the green pepper. Turn everything in the hot oil until it browns a little. Add the tomatoes, then turn up the heat to bubble it all up. Turn down the heat, put on a lid and leave to simmer for about 10 minutes.
4. Tip the contents of the pan into an ovenproof casserole and stir in the rice. Add the paprika, then season with salt and cayenne pepper. Pour in enough boiling stock to cover the rice completely. Bake it, covered for the first 30 minutes, for 40 minutes, until the rice is tender. Add more boiling liquid if it dries out too much. Taste and season.
5. Tip the pilaff out onto a pretty dish and decorate it round the edge with slices of pepper and tomato.

Serbian Ajvar

AUBERGINE AND PEPPER DIP

Serve as an appetizer with olives and bread. Keeps for a week at least in the fridge.

SERVES 4–6

2–3 sweet red peppers
2–3 fine fat aubergines
6–8 cloves garlic, skinned and
  chopped

1–2 tablespoons wine vinegar or
  lemon juice
1/2 pint / 300 ml olive oil
salt and pepper

1. Preheat the oven to 400°F/200°C/mark 6.
2. Arrange the peppers, aubergines and garlic in a baking tin, drizzle with a little of the oil and bake for 30–40 minutes, until the vegetables soften.
3. As soon as they're cool enough to handle, skin the peppers, then halve and seed them. Hull the aubergines and pop the garlic cloves out of their skins. Chop all thoroughly together and mash until you have a heavy purée, then add the vinegar or lemon juice. Beat in the rest of the oil – as much as the mixture will absorb. Add salt and pepper to taste. Or use a food processor: put all the ingredients into the chopping bowl except the oil, and blend thoroughly. Add the oil in a steady stream until the mixture will absorb no more (the point at which it starts pooling).
4. Serve at room temperature, with bread and Cos lettuce leaves to act as scoops.

Croatian Djuvedj

PORK AND POTATO HOT-POT

If there is no meat, the bacon will have to do on its own. If there's no bacon, wish for better times and use extra mushrooms. As reflects their politics, the Croats look north for their culinary inspiration while the Serbs look east.

4 oz/125 g streaky bacon, cubed
1 lb/500 g lean pork,
  cubed smallish
1–2 tablespoons oil or butter
1 large onion, skinned and sliced
2 garlic cloves, skinned and crushed
2 large carrots, scraped and diced
1 tablespoon wine vinegar

about 2 pints/1 l water or stock
2 lbs/1 kg potatoes, scrubbed and
  scraped (if old, peel them)
8 oz/250 g mushrooms, sliced
2 green peppers, seeded and sliced
1 tablespoon marjoram,
  finely chopped
salt and pepper

1. Render the bacon down in a heavy casserole until the fat runs. Add the pork and turn it in the hot fat. Push the meat aside, add the butter or oil, then the onion and garlic. Fry these a little, until they soften, and then add the carrots. Sprinkle with the vinegar and enough water or stock to submerge the meat. Bring all to the boil, season, turn down the heat, lid and simmer until the meat is tender, or cook in a medium oven (350°F/180°C/mark 4) for 50–60 minutes.

2. Chop the potatoes into bite-sized pieces and stir them into the stew along with the mushrooms, peppers and marjoram. Add more water or stock – enough to submerge everything. Reboil, then simmer for another 20 minutes or so, until the potatoes are tender. Check the seasoning. Serve with pickled vegetables.

to Jerusalem, the trade-route to Russia – a citadel irresistible to any conqueror. The old Stamboul Road, now converted to a motorway, ran outside its walls. Trouble in the Balkans had always started here. Forty-one times in its history it has been destroyed. The vigour of the market-place – the need to trade in food, the one commodity essential to the countryside as well as the town – ensures it has always risen from the ashes.

Belgrade's central market reflected the culinary habits of the inhabitants: here a kiosk selling Turkish coffee brewed in a *briki*, over there a stall selling Bulgarian yoghurt, another offering Greek honeys and syrupy jams, still another piled with German *Wurst* and sauerkraut, another with Italian rolled and shaped pastas. The Balkans have their pastas, but these are of the more primitive kind, finger-pinched dumplings and the tiny hand-rolled doughs that dry to look like rice. The street food was *kajmak*, a cheese and spinach pie, baked in huge metal trays and sold by the slice.

On the fishmonger's slab, for those of a Mediterranean cultural inheritance, were sardines, anchovies, octopus, tuna hanging by the tail alongside salt-caked dried cod, the Catholic fasting food. Most patronized by the Croatians, whose culinary habit is German, there were crates of mackerel, eel, and live carp in tanks.

The fruit and vegetable stalls told a similar tale. For those who cook in the Turkish tradition, there were sacks of Eastern spices displayed alongside huge bunches of mint and coriander. Another stall was piled with bunches of Mediterranean herbs: rosemary, sage, thyme, oregano. On a third could be found the pot-herbs of the German kitchen: chives, dill, horseradish, parsley root.

The vegetable sellers had bunches of fat white garlic, so young the cloves inside had not yet begun to suck the moisture from their coverings, plaits of purple onions and rosy shallots, cucumbers, leeks, aubergines, tomatoes, grapes, watermelons, apples, pears, figs, peaches and apricots.

Aproned and kerchiefed countrywomen, with live chickens tethered to a socked ankle, had set up their little trading posts in the gaps between the commercial stalls. Their wares mirrored those of the roadside stalls, but in greater profusion: barrels of fresh curd cheese sold by the ladleful; blocks of butter, unsalted, pale as cream, kept cool in muslin wrappings and damp sacking; fresh walnuts, in shell or shelled, with or without salt; bolsters of country bread, some round and rough, others of fine flour and just of a size for the pocket; Turkish pastries – *borek* and *kataifa* stuffed with chopped pistachios or almonds; yeasty strudels rolled around savoury stuffings made with greens and curds.

One corner of the market was occupied by Turkish traders: rug merchants, vendors of coffee, spices and sugar. Their wares, imported luxuries from across the Bosphorus, were carefully displayed in labelled jars screwed down to foil those disinclined to pay for what they couldn't afford. In another corner, spread out on sacking in gleaming pyramids, were home-grown substitutes for imported spices: paprika for colour, chillis to replace imported pepper, herbs for infusions, bundles of liquorice twigs for chewing and used by the country people as a toothbrush.

Piled in slate-coloured heaps were the seeds of *Papaver somnifera*, the opium poppy, a by-product of the opium trade that once flourished throughout the Balkans. Nineteenth-century travellers documented with some surprise the remarkable docility of those who lived under Ottoman rule. Their Turkish masters were well aware that, unlike the liquor forbidden by the Prophet, opiates kept a conquered people quiet. The seeds have no hallucinogenic properties and prodigious amounts are used in breads, stuffings for dumplings and fillings for strudels. No one enquired too closely what happened to the sap.

That evening, in spite of our spartan billet, I was content. Thanks to my brush, I had better material than I had dared hope – I had been shown how to make a *djuvedj*, how to roll pastry to make baklava, how to stuff and bake the poppy-seed strudels we had so far only been able to taste.

The next day we were on the road early, travelling southwards into Macedonia, or that part of Macedonia which the treaty of Bucharest had assigned to Serbia, since with the casual cruelty of the conqueror, the remainder had been divided between Albania, Bulgaria and Greece. As was abundantly clear from the culinary habit, nothing in the Balkans has ever been simple.

Serbian Kajmak
CHEESE AND SPINACH PIE

The Turkish influence comes through quite clearly in this filo-pastry pie with its cheesy, creamy filling. Really an Eastern quiche, the filling is fresh, clean, and a perfect match for the delicate pastry.

———————————————— SERVES 6–8 ————————————————

1 packet (about 14 sheets) filo pastry
12 oz/350 g spinach or mixed
  leaves (rocket, borage, beet tops)
about 4 oz/100 g flat-leaf parsley
4 eggs
8 oz/250 g cream cheese (the real
  stuff – not low-fat)

8 oz/250 g feta or any other
  strong cheese, grated
4 oz/100 g clarified butter, melted
salt and pepper

1. Allow the filo to defrost so that you can separate the sheets. Take care to keep the pastry covered while you work – it dries out and cracks very easily.
2. Wash your chosen leaves and shred them roughly. Put them in a pan with the water that clings to their leaves and shake over a high heat until well wilted – 3–4 minutes. Drain in a sieve, squeezing to

remove as much liquid as possible. Squeeze again with your hands as soon as the greens are cool enough to handle. Chop thoroughly with the parsley.

3. Beat the eggs and cream cheese together in a bowl, and stir in the greens and feta. Taste and add salt – how much you need depends on the saltiness of the cheese. Be generous with the pepper.

4. Preheat the oven to 350°F/180°C/mark 4.

5. Brush a 10 in/25 cm diameter round shallow cake tin (or a 12 in x 8 in/30 cm x 20 cm rectangular baking tin) with melted butter. Line with two sheets of filo pastry, leaving the edges flopping loose – they'll be tucked up and over the filling later. Brush the top sheet generously with butter, lay on another 2 sheets, brush with butter, and so on until you have 8 thicknesses of filo.

6. Spread on the filling lightly, so that you do not press the air out of the layers, then cover with 6 more sheets of filo and butter in layers as before. Fold the sheets delicately up and over, all rumpled and airy like an unmade bed. Drizzle with the remaining butter and sprinkle with a little water from your fingertips.

7. Bake for 40–50 minutes, until well-risen and golden. The pie will stay crisp even when cool. Cut into squares or wedges, as you please.

Lorries blocked the roads and the journey was slow. We ate on the move – delicious things from the Belgrade market pressed on us by the stallholders or recommended by their customers. It was sunset before we reached the little town of Titov Veles, the end of the railway line and the furthest outpost before the border. The Macedonians are a Mediterranean nation. Dark-skinned, bright-eyed, their doors remained open to admit the last of the summer's sunshine. Grannies and grandfathers had set their chairs by the edge of the road to watch the world go by. Children played in the streets, shopkeepers and their customers had time for a gossip.

The houses were half-timbered, balconied, no more than two storeys high, with the overhanging roofs that tell of rainy winters. As yet it was still the end of summer, and the *paseo* – the evening stroll that underpins all social life in Mediterranean lands – was in full swing, part social occasion, part opportunity for flirtation. Handsome well-dressed youths and pretty girls in flowered frocks circled the town square in single-sex gangs. Every now and then, a couple broke away, linked arms, vanished round a corner to hold hands or even steal a passionate embrace. Their elders kept a wary watch on the proceedings – one eye on the giggling gangs, the other on the babies and young children scampering underfoot.

As in all Latin lands, the evening meal is a moveable feast and a pause for refreshment was part of the evening's entertainment. One of the houses that fronted the square was doing a roaring trade in charcoal-grilled kebabs – *raznici* – handed out through the open window on a skewer with a hunk of bread. Another served paprika-spiced sausages – *pljeskavica* – grilled to a crisp and wrapped in a paper napkin. A third offered tiny hamburgers – *cevapcici* – stuffed into a pitta pocket with chopped cucumber and pickles.

We joined the strollers, spent a couple of happy hours sampling the street foods, and finally turned our attention to the night's accommodation. Driving into the town, we had noticed a pretty little inn overlooking the river. However, closer inspection revealed it to be closed for refurbishment. The guidebooks listed no commercial alternatives. 'Should the casual

Macedonian Raznici

SPICED MINCEMEAT KEBAB

The Yugoslavs pride themselves on their grilled meats. You will
need small skewers, and a hot grill or barbecue. These delicious
little kebabs are sold on street corners in the markets and from
little snack bars all over the towns and villages. Small paprika-
flavoured sausages are often grilled alongside them.

SERVES 4
---

1 lb / 500 g minced meat (pork and
  beef is the street mix)
1/2 teaspoon salt
plenty of freshly ground
  black pepper

8 oz / 250 g onions, grated or
  finely chopped
1–2 green chilli peppers,
  seeded and chopped

1. Pound the meat with the salt and pepper. Knead it thoroughly
until you have a soft paste. Form the paste into small sausage shapes
with wet hands and push a wooden skewer through the middle of
each. Best to soak the wooden skewers first so that they do not
burn over the coals.
2. Cook over a little charcoal brazier or under a hot grill. Serve
with a dish of grated onions, the chilli peppers, and a thick slab of
country bread. That's all. Simplicity itself – street food at its best.

For a main meal, serve with a salad of roughly chunked onions,
tomatoes and cucumber dressed with a sprinkling of crumbled
strong white cheese, and a sliced green chilli pepper. Quartered
lemons go alongside.

tourist require budget accommodation, it may be possible to negotiate with private householders.'

Negotiations with private householders seemed a little unlikely at this late hour. We returned to the main road, almost resigned to finding a parking spot and spending the night in the car.

Then Nicholas remembered that a few miles back on the highway there had been a filling station with a lorry park and a sign offering *Zimmer*. We retraced our path. Sure enough, the billboard offered beds. We parked the Mercedes alongside the juggernauts and made our way towards the lights of what appeared to be a cafeteria on the filling station's forecourt.

We peered in through the steam-misted window. The place was clearly well patronized. Encouraged, we went inside. Neon striplighting flickered through a thick pall of cigarette smoke, rock-and-roll music pounded from a juke-box. At the rear, a Formica-topped bar ran the full length of the room. The patrons appeared to be mostly truckers, many of whom were drinking at the bar. The café tables were occupied by small gaggles of brightly dressed young women in the mini-skirts and beehive hairdos that seemed the height of fashion in Macedonia. At the far end was a crowded dance floor on which, in spite of the energy of the music, couples were moving very slowly.

At one end of the bar was a frosted-glass screen. Through this we could see a corridor lined with doors. On the bar was a small brass bell and a framed notice in German and Cyrillic script, which listed room rates. Nicholas picked up the bell and tinkled it tentatively. It was nearly midnight, we were tired, and we had already satisfied our hunger at the little kiosks in the town. We waited. The Rolling Stones replaced Helen Shapiro on the juke-box. Nicholas rang the bell again.

'*Ja?*'

A little old lady popped out from behind the bar. Her hair had been dyed a brilliant shade of red, her lips and cheeks were painted shiny pink. A low-cut scarlet blouse displayed a wrinkled bosom. The message delivered by the upper body was contradicted by the lower, which was snugly encased in a pair of pyjama bottoms and well-worn trainers.

'What you want?'

'I – we – we're hoping for a room.'

The apparition examined us thoughtfully.

'American? I speak American. I speak with American sailors good.'

'English, actually.'

'Hah! Winston Churchill, Morecambe and Wise. Hah!' She grinned triumphantly, showing a mouthful of wobbly false teeth. 'You see? I know English very well.' She pushed the notice towards us. 'How much time you want? Ten, thirty minutes?'

Nicholas stared at her for an instant, then answered briskly, 'Eight hours.'

'Eight HOURS!' The bosom quivered like a pink blancmange. Its owner leaned towards me. 'Fine fellow – plenty fucking. Where you find him, lady?' She shook her heavily bangled wrist in an international gesture of appreciation, replaced the key on the hook and selected another. 'I give you number six. Good bed, plenty bouncy. I give discount.' She scribbled a figure on a scrap of paper. 'See? Very good price.'

Negotiations satisfactorily concluded, she clapped her hands to achieve a momentary lull among the audience of ladies and their truckers, and relayed the outcome of the negotiations in rapid-fire Russian with accompanying gestures. The roar of laughter was followed by a round of applause for the stamina of those who needed eight hours to accomplish what lesser mortals could manage in ten minutes.

Scarlet-faced, we made our escape.

Number six was half-way down the corridor, conveniently situated next to the communal lavatory. The night passed with incident – all of a thoroughly personal nature, none initiated within our own four walls. Had she been a fly on the ceiling, our landlady would certainly have revised her opinion of her star guests' capacities. It was not until dawn broke outside the uncurtained window – and with it a mighty revving of trucks – that we finally slept.

Breakfast was chick-pea soup and slivovic. We did it justice.

CHAPTER THREE

Among the Hellenes

*But in spite of all my troubles, give me leave to eat my supper.
For nothing in the world is so shamelessly demanding as a
man's stomach.*

  Odysseus in the palace of Alcinous, Homer's Odyssey,
Book 7, trans.

E. V. RIEU (Penguin Classics, revised 1991)

IF THERE'S ANYTHING THAT MAKES GREEK BLOOD BOIL — AND FIRE
in the belly is a characteristic of the Hellenes — it's the matter of
Macedonia. Macedonia, say the Greeks, is not in Yugoslavia but
Greece. Anyone coming from Yugoslav Macedonia is no friend
of the Greeks.

The border guards on both sides turned the contents of our
vehicle inside out. Dirty washing, guidebooks, intimate articles
of underwear — everything was spread out on the counter for
official inspection. Nicholas's travel diary, camera and my

sketchbooks were subjected to particularly thorough scrutiny. Our passports vanished for an anxious hour while mysterious telephone calls were made.

Nicholas becomes agitated at customs posts. Even if he hasn't done anything he shouldn't, he gives out the wrong signals. I have no such inhibitions. Accustomed in childhood to being ushered through all obstacles as just another bit of diplomatic baggage, I remain blithely confident that although there's something tucked into my luggage that contravenes someone's regulations somewhere, I shall not be required to pay the price. When the children were little and we were travelling from one end of Europe to another in a van, I used to carry a small automatic pistol in the map pocket. I had no clear idea of how to fire it, but it was my security blanket. When Nicholas discovered it, in spite of my protests, he turned it over to the authorities: his reward was an intimate body search and a thorough interrogation by Our Man with the sniffer-dog.

This time, my illicit luggage happened to be nothing more dangerous than a pair of Krugerrands tucked into the little pouches in my bra that were meant to hold breast-enhancement pads. Wonderbra never struck it so rich. As a mother of four, breasts have never been my problem, gold coins rather more so. I think I'm now on my sixth replacement pair of coins – never leave home without 'em.

In confident anticipation that his wife was likely to have something illegal about her person, Nicholas took a hike round the lorry park, looking for a social life among the drivers. I sat on the tailgate, watching the bustle. I had just taken out my sketchbook when the top brass arrived to inspect the vehicle.

'You make picture?'

I nod.

'*Iconostasi?*'

'Not icons. Nothing religious.' I gestured at the surrounding landscape. 'Just what I see.'

'Good. You are an artist. My son – he is only five years old – he will be an artist. I myself was an artist until I am becoming a policeman.'

'Would you like to see?'

'I like it very much.'

I handed over the sketchbook. The pumpkin ladies were much admired. The sketchbook was passed to his colleagues. 'In Greece you will make pictures of Greek people. Greek culture is very good. Greek temples very beautiful.'

'Greek everything very beautiful,' I agreed, pressing home my advantage. 'But first you have to let us through.'

Gold teeth flashed. His laughter was rich with the scent of black tobacco and roasted garlic. Then he shook his head, lowered his brows in what I hoped was mock disapproval. 'Your Lord Elgin, he steal our Marbles. You must tell him he give them back.'

'I'll have a word.'

'You do that, lady.' A broad grin, a shake of the hand, and the barrier swung open.

We drove onward towards the sunshine. I'm a creature of the sun – like a lizard I cannot function without warmth.

The first glimpse of the blue Aegean made our hearts leap. The earth was warm among the silver trunks of the olive trees. Our destination was Thessalonica, one of the great cities of Byzantium, guardian of the gateway to mainland Greece. No more than a spear's-throw from the Turkish border, proximity to the heirs to the Ottoman Empire induces a certain paranoia – a Greek word, if ever there was one – in the inhabitants. For some five hundred years, the city was an outpost of the Turkish Empire. The Turks invaded once; there's no reason to suppose they won't do it again.

Few of the city's buildings are ancient. The old Ottoman houses on the water-front that escaped fire in 1917 fell to the earthquake of 1978. Among the modern apartment blocks that line the orderly modern thoroughfares, a few Byzantine church façades and a handful of Roman ruins tell of more glamorous days.

The city's streets were deserted. Sunday is the one day of the week when the Greek male turns into a family man. Sunday is for wives and children, a day out by the seashore with maybe a meal of fresh-caught fish in one of the little shacks on the beach, or for packing a picnic and heading for the hills.

Commercially and philosophically, the capital of the north

has no reason to bestir itself on a Sunday, particularly not a Sunday in late September when most of the tourists have already flown home to their chilly northern eyries. No doubt those foreign visitors who still remained were making a final attempt to blister their pale skins on the beaches of the coastal resorts.

We had arrived in Greece's second city at what, under normal circumstances, would have been the perfect time for a leisurely lunch. Idly, I hoped for tripe. Ship-victualling ports are always skilful with offal for the obvious reason that there's always plenty of innards left over from the barrelling up of salted meat. Triperies are, equally obviously, mostly to be found in the vicinity of the market. Unfortunately Sunday isn't market day.

Despairing of anything the natives might patronize, we set off in search of the tourist cafés by the harbour. A line of small restaurants stacked like dominoes along the promenade were doing a steady trade in the usual tourist fare. Unusually, this also happens to be the way the Greeks themselves like to eat: the only real difference is that the restaurants used by the Greeks are cheaper, and raw materials of a higher quality.

In spite of the shuttered kiosks, Nicholas wandered off in search of a newspaper. Meanwhile I made my way down the line of restaurants, inspecting the counter displays with mounting gloom. On a trip like this, you can only eat so many meals and each must earn its space.

Restaurant food in Greece is exactly what you would expect: taramasalata, aubergine dip, black olives, feta-cheese salad. The main dishes are equally predictable: frittered fish with chips, stuffed vegetables, fish or meat stews all bathed in the same tomato sauce. Greeks go out for company rather than gastronomy: culinary skill is something you can expect to find at home.

As I was finishing my inspection, Nicholas reappeared, empty-handed but beaming.

'Something interesting?'

'See what you think.'

I followed him round the corner. The seductive scent of slow-simmered spices curled down the narrow alleyway. I sniffed appreciatively. 'What is it?'

'You'll see.'

Greek Taramasalata
SALTED FISH-ROE DIP

This dip is familiar from every cook-chill cabinet – but the commercial version is a pale shadow of the real thing. In Greece, the basis is *tarama*, the salted, pressed roe of the grey mullet that frequent Greek harbours and come up to the quayside to be fed, curious as cats. The potato that replaces the bread in the ancient recipe is considered more delicate. If you have no fish roe, use double quantities of garlic and make a *skordalia* – good for the *mezze* table or as a sauce for frittered aubergines or courgettes. It is also the traditional accompaniment for a beetroot salad (the Greeks like to use the leaves as well as the roots).

--------------------------------- SERVES 4 ---------------------------------

2 large potatoes   1 lemon, juice
$^{1}/_{2}$ pint/300 ml olive oil   salt
2 garlic cloves, skinned and crushed
6 oz/175 g tarama or *smoked cod's*
   roe, skinned

--------------------------------- TO SERVE ---------------------------------

1 black olive   pitta bread for dipping

1. Boil the potatoes in their jackets in salted water until tender. Drain – save a little of the cooking water. As soon as they're cool enough to handle, skin then mash them with a splash of their cooking water, 4 tablespoons of the olive oil and the crushed garlic.
2. Beat the roe into the warm potato together with enough olive oil to make a thickish purée. Add lemon juice to taste.
3. Serve swirled on to a shallow plate, topped with a single black olive and maybe an extra drizzle of oil, with pitta bread for scooping.

The little taverna was not much from the outside, but inside it was packed. The scent of spices combined with the fragrance of garlic and chicken, overlaid with the thick sweet aroma of Turkish tobacco. I don't mind tobacco smoke at meals: I have always associated the scent of the burning weed with good food. My gambling grandfather smoked cigars.

We slipped quickly into a just-vacated table.

No menu was produced. Instead, the proprietor – cheerfully pot-bellied, with a round pink face and glasses misted with exertion – produced a pottery dish of olives (mauve, juicy and scented with thyme), another of roasted garlic and a basket of sesame-sprinkled bread-rolls just hot from the oven. A carafe of yellow wine and a jug of water arrived unbidden. Unless the vintage is distinguished, the Greeks always water their wine – only barbarians and northerners drink their liquor undiluted.

A plate of chips, crisp and hot and sprinkled with salty grated cheese was soon followed by an earthenware dish of chicken stew spiced with cinnamon and nutmeg, the source of the perfume that had drawn Nicholas down the alleyway in the first place. This particular stew, the proprietor confirmed, was the speciality of the house. Both recipe and main ingredients, prunes and chicken, came from his wife's home village on the Halkidiki peninsula. His wife was in the kitchen, helped by his two unmarried daughters. They were Asia Minor Greeks, he explained gravely, as were the diners in his restaurant. The Asia Minor Greeks kept themselves to themselves, and their dishes were often spiced in the Turkish manner.

And the name of the dish? I enquired, opening my notebook diligently. Stupid tourist question. The proprietor shrugged and spread his hands. '*Kotopoulo yiahni*. Chicken stew.'

The triple-fingered Halkidiki has a large population of those whom the Greeks themselves still view as refugees. Fifty years ago the inhabitants of Turkish villages of Greek descent were 'repatriated' by agreement with Kemal Atatürk, the man credited with the creation of modern Turkey. On Halkidiki, every second village is new – Neo Marmola, Neo Salonika, Neo Neo.

We took the road into Halkidiki. The northern arm of the peninsula is home to the monks of Mount Athos, for five

Greek Kotopoulo Yiahni

SPICED CHICKEN CASSEROLE WITH RED WINE AND PRUNES

Here's a fine dish from the Halkidiki peninsula in northern Greece. *Kotopoulo* is the onomatopoeic Greek word for chicken, and *yiahni* is a casserole – the word pops up under various aliases all over the Balkans.

———————————— SERVES 4 ————————————

1 chicken, jointed – include the
  whole bird: back, neck and all
1 heaped tablespoon seasoned flour
6 tablespoons olive oil
1 large onion (red if you can find
  one), skinned and sliced
3 garlic cloves, skinned and chopped
1 lb/500 g plum tomatoes, skinned
  and chopped

6 cloves
1 short stick cinnamon
  or 1 teaspoon powdered
1/2 teaspoon grated nutmeg
1/2 pint/300 ml dry red wine
8 prunes
salt and pepper
1 teaspoon chopped mint (in Greece,
  dried is preferred for flavouring)

1. Toss the chicken joints in the seasoned flour – just a sprinkle. Heat the oil in a roomy casserole. As soon as it's hot enough to fry, put in the chicken pieces – not all at the same time. Fry until they take a little colour, and remove. Put in the onion and garlic, and let them fry until they soften and gild.

2. Return the chicken pieces to the casserole and add all the other ingredients except the mint. Pour in a glass of water. Let everything bubble up, turn down the heat, and let it simmer gently for about an hour, until the chicken pieces are tender and the sauce nicely reduced.

3. Stir in the mint and adjust the seasoning. Let the stew cool a little before serving. The Greeks don't approve of piping hot food. You'll need plenty of bread for mopping fingers and sauce.

centuries a beleaguered outpost of Christianity in a sea of Muslim Turks. The inhabitants of the other two arms earn their living mainly from the tourist trade. The coastal strip, warned the guidebook, has concentrations of high-rise hotels and yacht marinas. In the southernmost and least-developed of the three we hoped to find a fishing village where we could settle down for a few days to catch our breath and the last of the summer sunshine.

The guidebook recommended a National Hotel at the coastal village of Ounanopoulos. Before dropping down to the coast, the road wound its way through hummock-shaped hills clothed in chestnut groves. Instead of villages, there were beehives, miniature townscapes of wicker and mud.

The National Hotel was well signposted. We left the car in the empty car-park among olive trees, their branches laden with the purple fruits of autumn, and went in search of some form of authority who might be able to give us a room.

The hotel appeared deserted. We found its sole employee sleeping off his Sunday lunch in a deck-chair on the beach.

'*Haben Sie Zimmer?*'

There was, indeed, a room, but only for one night. Tomorrow, he explained, in international hotel-speak – mostly German, with a little Italian for good measure – was the last day of the season before the hotel closed for the winter.

'*Hotel ist chiuso. Restaurant ist kaputt. Nicht tourist mangiare. Essen und trinken in das Dorf, bitte.*' He waved his hands to punctuate his message. '*Verstehen Sie?*'

Absolutely we understood. We didn't mind a bit that we would have to go to the *Dorf* for our *Essen und Trinken*. Whatever the morrow might bring, for tonight we had found safe haven.

Later, as dusk fell over the Adriatic, we wandered slowly along the beach towards the village in search of supper. Small waves nibbled at the sand and the sun set in a wild extravagance of scarlet.

The village was considerably livelier than the hotel. The single street had three souvenir shops, a small supermarket, all closed. But the café and taverna were both open for business.

77

The tourists might have vanished, but these establishments were clearly popular with the locals.

In one corner of the café, the television rambled on to an enthralled audience of small children while their mothers gossiped among themselves, occasionally exchanging banter with the men who occupied the tables on the street. The women's fingers were busy with those strange little scraps of crocheted lace with which Greek babies are bedecked on the evening promenade. The husbands' diversions were chess and backgammon.

The taverna was empty but for one large party of Greeks. We ordered the only thing available, macaroni with mince. Nicholas added a bottle of retsina – just for old times' sake, he explained. Nicholas is a romantic at heart: we drank retsina many years ago on a stolen holiday before we were married. Those were the days when cohabitation was not what nice girls did and we were both fearful that our families might put two and two together and make three.

Even for old times' sake, retsina is always a mistake. We had both forgotten it tastes like horse embrocation and gives you a terrible hangover. Actually, even through the mists of first love, I remember I hated retsina even then – almost as much as I dislike macaroni and mince.

Meanwhile the occupants of the next table were celebrating the Sabbath with pre-ordered roast pork and copious quantities of Italian white wine, undiluted. By the time we were half-way through our dismal platefuls, we had been invited to join the gathering, treated to a passionate polemic on the Greekness of Macedonia (again), the iniquity of the Turks, the perfidy of Albion in partitioning Cyprus and, once more, the necessity for returning the Elgin Marbles so that the pollution in Athens could finish the demolition so effectively begun by his lordship.

The next day, somewhat the worse for wear, we made our way back up the road to the Palace Hotel, a luxuriously appointed establishment set among imported palm trees, which had caught our attention the previous evening. At the time, with the National Hotel within our sights, we had rejected the place as almost certainly beyond our modest means.

Emboldened by retsina hangovers – nothing like a hangover

for ridding one of inhibitions – we opened negotiations with the proprietor. Surely he could make us a special price. Indeed he could. A pretty little beachside bungalow might be ours for the winter rate.

'Restaurant is close,' he said, as soon as the deal was struck. 'You eat in village.'

We were more than happy to settle down for a few days. There was work to be done, I needed to empty my head of what I had learned, and I find it almost impossible to make sense of anything on the road. There were diaries to be filled, sketches to be completed, telephone calls to be made. Our experience in Yugoslavia had taught us that a little more planning was necessary. We couldn't just trust to luck.

I worked all through the day in the shade of the olive trees, while Nicholas explored the hinterland. In the evening we retraced our steps along the beach, passing the National Hotel which was indeed closed and shuttered.

The village, on the other hand, was about its daily business. The supermarket was open and a queue of housewives had formed behind the vegetable van. I have always loved shopping in unfamiliar supermarkets. As a child, I was never allowed souvenirs, but as an adult I have more than made up for early deprivation. This is not to say I shop aimlessly. Far from it. There's deliberation, consideration. My collection of kitchen instruments is legendary. Strange saucings and seasonings crowd my larder shelves, their use long since forgotten, their presence talismanic.

On this occasion, I had spotted an embroidery display at the back of the supermarket. What I had in mind was a round tablecloth with matching napkins, all in white. I love white linen on the table – an early training as a housemaid left me with an appetite for bluebag and flat irons so I never mind doing the laundry. Laundering comes easily to the Greeks. They *do* like a well-blanched table.

'Very beautiful, you like? All is made by hand.'

The Greeks, say those who have no reason to love them, will sell anything including their grandmothers. Failing Granny, the labours of the blind nuns of an enclosed order who have taken a vow of silence.

'Is from Mount Athos,' says the plump young salesgirl, flashing a set of imperfectly mended teeth. 'Is made by lady monks.'

'Really? I thought there were no ladies on Mount Athos.'

'This is true. It is my grandmother. She is working very hard, sewing, sewing, sewing all the time.'

'She must be a very busy lady.'

'Please?'

'Very busy. Your grandmother is a very busy person.' I flapped my hands to demonstrate. 'Working all the time to make all the tablecloths.'

'Is from Mount Athos, is what I tell the tourists, lady. You know what is happen on Mount Athos?'

'Tell me.'

I waited for the punchline. I had only been on Halkidiki for a day, but I was already aware that the locals regarded the celibate monks of Mount Athos with that peculiarly Greek mixture of ridicule and respect that has always characterized its dealings with the Church.

'No ladies on Mount Athos, not even lady sheeps.' Roars of laughter punctuated this possibly obscene but unarguable assessment. Shepherd–and–sheep jokes are universal.

The next day dawned dull and cloudy. With the beach unwelcoming, we set out to explore the peninsula.

The old villages, those that have survived the earthquake and the waves of emigration, are built high above the harbours for safety against the pirates: Turkish corsairs, Crusaders, Vikings. Produce vans with dropped tailgates displayed the autumn harvest: tomatoes, thin-skinned green peppers for frying, cabbage, okra, parsley, carrots, onions. Housewives bearing baskets, summoned by a blast of the horn, crowded round to argue and squeeze.

The balconies were draped with scarlet curtains of paprika peppers – some small and fiery, others mild and sweet – threaded on strings for drying. A chilli puts fire in the belly on a cold evening in the long winters, and you don't have to pay good money to the Turks for them. Along the roadsides, apples had been set out in great yellow piles, fragrant as spring blossom. Customers helped themselves and left the money in a jar. We exchanged a few coins for a bagful, and ate them as we drove. They were crisp, sweet and juicy, a reminder of the pleasures of autumn in northern lands.

The road wound back to the coast, narrow as ribbon etched into the cliffs. Beneath us the peacock sea was pearled with the spume of waves breaking on rocks. Greek men go to sea, leaving the women to work the land. By the shore the trees crouched low against the wind, their gnarled knees garlanded by heather and rosemary, sage and fennel. Grey branches, grey rock shimmered against the summer's late growth of green leaves on the scrub oaks.

Soon after midday we reached a little seaside village, a Hellenic St Tropez waiting for Bardot to rescue the rust-coloured dogs and tuft-eared cats that haunted the doorways. Here, too, the season was nearly over. Shutters were up and small knots of shopkeepers were discussing the summer's takings at the café tables. Beyond, as far away as a child might spit the husk of a sunflower seed, white yachts bobbed by the quay, sails furled, their naked masts towering like trees in winter.

One of the few tourist shops still open for business sold pottery of a singing cerulean blue, bowls and dishes washed with pure cobalt. In another corner, stacked one upon the other, were plates glazed with pink or violet, little dishes slicked with a sea-green sheen. I love pottery. I will always spend my money on a dish that is just the right size and colour for olives or almonds, or the perfect bowl for a salad, or a purpose-made cooking pot for a stew I have enjoyed that day.

At one end of the village was a sweet factory – or what might pass for a factory in a land where industrial production is likely to be a kitchenful of working women. It was seasonal, producing nut-based sweets for the Christmas market. Samples were already on sale to those who might be thinking of their festive store-cupboard: sugared almonds dyed red for luck, walnuts bottled in honey, sticky squares of caramel with sesame seeds, a curious almond nougat that fizzed and vanished on the tongue like marshmallow.

Knowing there's an autumn crop, I wanted to buy figs – Nicholas loves figs. I made a sketch, ripe figs with tiny seeds, all scarlet and juicy, to explain what I wanted. The fruit seller pointed to the clouds and made trickling gestures with her fingers. After the rain, no more figs. We could have melons or grapes, but no figs. Or perhaps we might like a slab of salty feta cheese made with the milk from her own goats?

We acquired a translator, a young man who had been a seaman in the Queen's Navy. He explained that the cheese was good, hand-made, the fruit seller was his aunt. The country people, he continued eagerly, like to eat the curds fresh, mashed up with chilli and vinegar – *tipspti* is the name of the dish. Very hot, very good, a peppery dip with a kick like a mule. But when it is very new and rich, they eat it with honey. If we were to buy some of his aunt's fresh cheese, he would take us to his brother's restaurant where we could eat it with honey from his uncle's bees. And before that we could enjoy his mother's fish soup, *psarosuppa avogolemono*, very good, thickened with egg and sharpened with lemon.

On the wall of the taverna were huge mussel shells, green and pearly. Our translator explained how deep his uncle had had to dive to harvest them, as deep as the Empire State Building – deeper.

The soup was fine, the cheese with honey exquisite. But I didn't believe his mussel stories. Mussels that size can only be gathered in the Pacific. The Greeks are tellers of tall tales. They like their gods and heroes nimble, two-faced, as capable of flight as fight. The Turks, spotting a talent for sweet-talking in uncomfortable situations, employed them as tax-collectors.

The restaurateurs all looked as though they might be brothers. In Greece everyone knows their relatives to the hundredth degree. You are either a cousin or you are no connection at all.

For the journey home we chose a different road, a bumpy track that curved through the interior. There were boulders every-where. The fields were stone-bound, walled with rocks. Among the rocks were stunted pine trees and hard grey cushions of the aromatic thyme whose volatile oils scent the air even without the pressure of foot or fist. Abandoned orchards of wild pears dropped their little woody fruits in circular carpets beneath the branches, but the olive groves looked husbanded:

the ancient trees were still yielding their crop. In these uplands, the olives for pressing are gathered when still unripe – green olives that have had plenty of sunshine in summer yield a peppery green oil, strong and rich.

An old man had set out a table in his olive grove to sell his produce. He smiled when he heard our voices. He was, he explained in English, always pleased when English people stopped to buy his oil. He hoped we would take it home to England, where it would speak to us of the sunshine of Greece. He himself learned English in Birmingham where he worked in a Greek grocery store whose imported produce he could not afford to enjoy. Sometimes the scent of the oil he sold was all he had to remind him of home. 'I drank it with my nose. It made me weep.'

He filled a wine bottle with the lush green oil and wrapped it carefully in newspaper. 'You will find it good. My olives are picked by hand so they are not bruised. I take them to the mill myself, I wait while the oil is pressed. I must be sure it is my own oil that comes back – I would never trust anyone else, not even my own wife Domenica, who works hard and never lies.'

The flavour, he continued, was good because of the company the olive trees kept on the hillside. There was rosemary, oregano, mint, sage-brush, but particularly the arbutus, the strawberry tree, which flowers one year and ripens another, so brings luck.

'There is, too, you will excuse me for saying so, the animal droppings. That is good for the trees. But it must be special – not goat droppings or pig droppings, but donkey.'

Sure enough, the old man's black donkey stood tethered in the shade beneath the spreading branches of an ancient tree, straining his rope to reach a bouquet of pink-flushed belladonna lilies. The lilies, I remember from my time in Spain, are hallucinogenic. A snap of the rope, and the olive trees would receive a dose of mood-altering donkey droppings.

This was a hard land to work, said the old man. At the first opportunity, the people bought their food in supermarkets. The housewives no longer went into the countryside to gather wild leaves, but bought them from the herb sellers in the market. They did not understand the wilderness or its denizens – the striped polecats, the fat grey slow-worms with yellow eyes, the snakes with crosses behind their heads, which go into the Virgin's sanctuary to mate on her name-day. In the winter, he added, there was snow on the hills, which sometimes settled in the valleys. The hard winter made fine olives, but that's all it was good for. His was the last generation that would work this land. After that, there would be no more oil from his trees.

We discussed the goodness of the oil, its virtues over what was sold in shops. Its properties were miraculous, health-giving, ensuring fertility in women and potency in men, the food of the gods, better than the oil pressed from the olives that grow on Mount Olympus. But the gods, too, had had their day, although even this might not be true. If a Greek tells you the truth, he is insulting your intelligence. It is not for nothing that Ulysses is a hero to all Greeks. He got what he wanted by tricks, by thieving, and lying to women, as all good Greeks do – including those who sell you the best olive oil from their own olive grove. As a stranger, you may ask questions for the joy of hearing the answers, but don't believe for a moment you'll be told the truth.

Nicholas laughed. 'We know.'

We drove on, deeper into the hills.

Greek roads meander like the trails left by goats. The blistered tar was patched and mended with gravel, littered with rocks from the hacked precipices, dry cliffs of ochre and rust and shimmering chips of marble. Pushing their way through the verges were stiff pincushions of shrub, tall as a man. The tips had sprouted tiny bunches of green leaves: the sap rises at the end of the summer to carry the plants through to the spring.

Greek sheep have ochre-tinted fleeces and brown faces. Greek goats have long silvery hair with slate markings, streaked like the trunks of the olive trees, blue-black and steel and pearl. The olive trees here were very ancient, their trunks as thick as oaks. Fat clusters of leaves flipped in the breeze, glittering like frost. Here, too, the olives had not yet ripened: they were bright green and hung in clusters like emerald earrings. Swallowtail butterflies, their wings the colour of old parchment traced with Chinese ink, hung like upside-down candles from the few fruits that had ripened, fastidiously sipping the juice.

We did not hurry our journey, reluctant to leave such beauty so little explored. We halted once to drink at a spring whose waters, guided by a spout and provided with a copper cup on a chain, were as cold as melted snow. We halted again to pick prickly pears from a hedge, sucked the soft flesh, careful to avoid the spines; and one last time to gather green almonds from a roadside tree so that we might nibble the translucent kernels sitting on a bank by a stream patrolled by kingfishers.

Every year, fires rage across the hillsides of Halkidiki. No one knows who sets them alight. The unspoken truth is that flame is man's most ancient agricultural tool and he will still use it when the authorities are looking the other way. Last year's scorched earth was still flecked with charcoal; the spring's regrowth would bring a fine crop of mushrooms and wild asparagus.

The next day was to be our last. The clouds had lifted, the sun was warm on our skin. We passed the day lazily on the beach, our pale faces turning pink in the reflection from the silk-smooth sea. The beach-front bar offered mackerel cooked over a brush-fire, and for a sauce, we had the old man's olive oil, unctuous and rich as melted butter.

In the evening we returned for the last time to the taverna. The place was packed, but not with diners. The whole village had turned out to watch *The Dirty Dozen* dubbed on to video in fast-talking Greek. The proprietor presided over his customers from a huge corporate desk in one corner, swinging round to inspect his clients like a Mafia godfather.

The previous evening, for our final meal, I had ordered a fish. As soon as we arrived, the cook, an ex-sailor, emerged from his kitchen to demonstrate his personal recipe. 'You take this fish . . .' In his hands was a handsome gilt-head bream – I would have guessed its weight at a couple of kilos . . . 'You clean him and scrape him and chop him in pieces. You take this of potato . . .' He held up two big handfuls of waxy yellow potatoes, peeled and quartered into fat yellow chips. 'These for flavour.' In his hands was a bundle of green celery, carrots, a jar of paprika. 'You cook for twenty minutes. And when you cook, you raise the heat and drop it, and raise it again and drop it.'

'Like the bouillabaisse of Marseilles?'

The cook looked puzzled, but his employer swung round in his chair. 'Of course is like the bouillabaisse. Where you think the French learn to cook? Everything, everything is learned from the Greeks.'

A chorus of agreement from the television watchers confirmed this to be no more than the truth.

The proprietor nodded in satisfaction. The pre-eminence of all things Greek was undeniable. We ate the fish, took a glass of a sticky orange liquor with the cook, and said our goodbyes.

The proprietor did not approve of our travel plans. 'Turks very bad people. Dirty, lazy, steal your wallet.'

Above us as we left Halkidiki, a pair of buzzards rode the thermals on broad brown wings. Over a field of saffron crocuses, kestrels hovered.

After lunch we passed a Roman bridge, a single curve of mortarless hand-chiselled stones, one of those magical feats of engineering that have survived merely because the roadmakers have decided to thread their tarmac across a different path.

On either side were terraces, cultivated since the days the bridge was first built, abandoned now as too labour-intensive, too costly to produce the ancient crops. Among the grey, lichen-encrusted stones could be seen the soft russet-coloured leaves of pomegranate bushes, densely fruited spikes of sloe, wild cherry, the fruiting branches of stunted walnut trees.

Across the valley, above a chestnut grove, a peregrine falcon dropped down to roost in a crag. Beneath it were more of the domed beehives, this time in preformed plastic, set out in long numbered rows like beach chalets. A bend in the road revealed two men with donkeys. On the animals' backs were balanced towering bundles of kindling: sticks and branches gleaned from the tangled scrub, the prunings and clippings from the vines, the husks and stalks of maize. Fuel is hard to come by: a few thousand years of shipbuilding have taken their toll of the timber trees. The olive trees alone are untouchable. Their rootstock, say those who tend them, never dies. Country people will point out the ancient twisted stumps of trees whose fruits victualled Caesar's armies, whose branches shaded Socrates.

Occasionally we drew to a halt to explore the cool interior of a church. Even when empty of people, Greek churches are full of presences – painted saints, wax flowers, votive offerings, the scent of incense and the flicker of oil-lamps. The names of the artists who painted the icons that cover the walls are not known. There is no master-painter, no Leonardo or Fra Angelico, to praise or follow. The paintings are God's gift to his people, anonymous and formal. There are rules to be obeyed and grace from God to guide the hand. The painters are always men. The embroidered hangings are the work of women – although, as secular artists, among these, the names are much more likely to be known.

The cemeteries have survived far longer than the villages they served. Cypress trees, high and tall and dark, stand sentinel over the stones. Even in abandoned places, you will always see people coming and going from the boneyards. Ancestors, if they are to speak for their descendants in the next world, must always be kept informed of events – betrothals, weddings, christenings, but never funerals. It can be assumed that death will need no heralding. So that the living may be reminded of the faces of the dead, small faded photographs are embedded in the marble memorials.

We halted for lunch at a roadside taverna. Salt herring was on the menu. Curiously, Mediterranean upland villages have a taste for salt cod and salt herring, a harvest from the Atlantic. In the days when sea voyages were long and hazardous, the fishermen's catch was salted for conservation, serving as trade goods as well as stores. Here, the herrings were dressed in the Greek way with a sauce of oil and lemon – delicious with the salty flesh. To complete the meal, a mound of fried eggs dewed with green oil, a dish of rice cooked with okra and flavoured with mint.

Hearing our voices, the proprietor came to join us while we drank our coffee. 'You know Pinner? I have my own restaurant in Pinner. Very nice place, but no good for Greeks. No olive trees. I cannot live in Pinner because no olive trees.'

We agreed that no olive trees was indeed a reason for a Greek not to live in Pinner.

'You know Melbourne, Australia?'

'I visited—'

'Visit is good. My brother is living long time in Melbourne. Is marry nice Greek girl – Australia many Greeks. Melbourne,' he held up his hand proudly, 'second biggest Greek city after Athens.'

What about Thessalonica?

'Thessalonica, chicken-shit. Thessalonica full of Turkish people.'

Right.

'You want *loukoumades*? Today we make loukoumades. We put honey. Autumn honey, thick and black.' He smacked his lips appreciatively, then frowned. 'Turkish cooking chicken-shit. Only Greeks cook good.'

Absolutely. Who were we to argue with a Greek bearing honey-soaked doughnuts? Particularly autumn honey of a dark velvety viscosity, thick with the richness of summer hillsides. Autumn honey has the scent of heather and pine. We already had some in our basket – sold by the roadside in big plastic buckets at six hundred drachmas for a two-kilo drum.

With the syrupy sweetmeat came more coffee – black, strong and bitter, just as the Ottomans liked it.

'This is not Turkish coffee. It is *Greek* coffee.'

Wisely, since we had to be on our way, I did not embark on a discussion of the similarities between Greek and Turkish cooking, although the truth is that it is only their beloved olive oil that distinguishes Greek cooking from that of their sometime overlord.

Some miles further on, our minds on other matters, we found the narrow road blocked by two plump brown donkeys, tails swinging, their long ears pushed through battered straw hats, slowly ambling down the centre of the highway.

We slowed down and hooted, not in the ear-splitting Greek fashion but a polite little parp. The donkeys halted, but did not yield.

'Hello?' A wrinkled brown face topped by a straw hat of the same vintage and design as those worn by the donkeys, popped up at our wound-down window. 'You want photo-opportunity?' Bright blue eyes examined us speculatively.

Nicholas shook his head. 'Thank you very much, but no.'

A leathery hand reached through the window, searching for something to shake. 'My name is Aristotle. Pleased to meet you English.'

Greek Loukoumades
HONEYED DOUGHNUTS

The Greeks are justifiably proud of their beautiful honey. On the three-pronged Halkidiki peninsula, where the tall peak of Mount Athos shelters an autonomous republic of black-robed monks, the summer air is filled with the hum of millions of honey-bees. Their nectar comes from the wild herbs – rosemary, lavender and thyme.

―――――――― MAKES ABOUT 20 DOUGHNUTS – THE DOUGH ――――――――

1 lb/500 g strong bread flour   *about ¹/₂ pint/300 ml warm water*
1 teaspoon salt
1 oz/25 g fresh yeast or ¹/₂ the quantity of dried yeast

―――――――――――――― TO FINISH ――――――――――――――

light olive oil for frying   *1 lb/500 g Greek mountain honey*

1. Sieve the flour with the salt into a warm bowl. Rub in the yeast (if using dried, follow the instructions on the packet). Work in enough warm water to make a soft dough and knead well, working with the heel of your hand. Form into a ball, cover with a clean damp cloth and set in a warm place to rise for an hour or so, until doubled in bulk.

2. Pummel the dough-ball with your fists to distribute the air bubbles. When you have a soft smooth ball, cover it again and set it to rise for another half-hour, until it has regained its bulk.

3. Put the honey jar in a bowl of hot water to liquefy its contents. Heat up a panful of oil. As soon as the surface is faintly hazed with blue, wet your hand and pick up a handful of dough. Squeeze the dough gradually through the top of your fist into short lengths. Drop the pieces of dough into the hot oil, slicing them off your fist with a knife. Allow them to puff up and fry golden. Turn them once. When well risen, take them out and drain them on kitchen paper. Pour the warm honey over the hot doughnuts. Accompany with a tall glass of iced water, a small glass of *raki* and a tiny cup of Greek coffee.

Nicholas was suddenly curious. 'How do you know we're English?'

The hat came off in a sweeping gesture towards the heavens. 'Minerva and Athena tell me.'

'Minerva and Athena?' Nicholas's voice had risen an octave, his hand hovered on the gear-lever.

'Don't go, English.' The groping hand landed firmly on the steering wheel. 'Donkeys. Donkeys tell me you English. This Minerva. This Athena.'

'Scottish, actually,' says Nicholas, absent-mindedly, in his best Jeeves-and-Wooster voice.

'Good. Scottish is good.' An encouraging pause. 'What part Scotland? Long time ago, I visit Aberdeen.'

'The islands – the West Coast,' said Nicholas, uncertain of this sudden intimacy.

'Like I say, donkey tell me you English – Scottish.' Aristotle waved his hand at the patient brown rumps. He had the tact of the true philosopher – the kind who lies in wait for tourists and offers them photo-opportunities.

'*Really*? How?'

Aristotle's face set into an expression of cunning. 'Donkey, she walk slow, very slow. Make car slow. You tootle horn. Not impatient like Greek peoples, not loud like German peoples, not scream and wave hands like Italian peoples. You tootle nice and quiet, like English peoples.'

A moment passed while we all considered this thumbnail sketch of national characteristics.

'English peoples like animals. Very much like animals,' added Aristotle helpfully. 'You like photo-opportunity?'

'I don't think so. Really.'

'Your lady-wife Scottish too?'

I received the full beam of Aristotle's Greek charm.

'Scottish ladies *very* nice. Minerva and Athena very happy with English – Scottish – ladies. See?'

Right on cue, the leading animal curled back one hairy brown lip from a set of yellow teeth and gave voice to one of those heartrending, ear-shattering guffaws with which donkeys everywhere announce their requirements.

Aristotle patted Minerva's nose – or it might have been Athena's. 'Donkeys very nice to nice ladies.'

By this time both animals had turned full circle. Huge brown eyes fringed by impossibly long lashes were watching us with what might have been curiosity, but was more likely to be hope that nice lady might produce something to eat.

'Athena like you very much. She want to have her picture taken with nice English – Scottish – lady.'

'Only half Scottish,' Nicholas offered unnecessarily.

'Good. Aristotle only half Greek.' Aristotle patted his heart. 'This part Greek. Other part,' he glanced downwards mischievously, 'Turkish. My mother is Turkish. My father is Greek. Greek father, Turkish mother meet in Tottenham. Many Turkish peoples in Tottenham. This is why I speak such very good English. Not leave England till I leave school. Then come back to Greece.'

'Tottenham?'

'That what I say.' Aristotle had tired of these topographical exchanges. 'Now we have photo-opportunity. Aristotle make very cheap price.'

'No,' said Nicholas.

'How much?' said I.

'Whatever you want, lady.'

'*No.*' Nicholas's voice held a note of desperation.

'Oooh, go on,' said I.

Naturally, I had my way. English ladies, particularly those of Scottish extraction on the one side and straight American-Jewish on the other, usually do.

'Lady stand here. Smile nicely for Aristotle.'

Aristotle and his twin donkeys Minerva and Athena posed obligingly by the blue Aegean. Three hats, two with holes for ears, glittered in the sunshine. Unfortunately, as we discovered later, Nicholas forgot to wind on the film.

'Now we take coffee,' said Aristotle firmly. 'Greek custom is always take coffee. Turkish custom is always take coffee.'

Before we knew it, we had parked the vehicle in the shade of the olive tree which had previously hidden the philosopher-muleteer, and were making our way up the hill in the wake of the two swaying brown rumps.

By now, Aristotle had the bit between his teeth. 'I got watermelons. You like watermelons? I give you watermelons. I give you whatever you want. I got shirts – good Greek cotton for Scottish gentleman. Whatever you want, Aristotle got.'

The door to a small shack swung open to reveal a rough table, a bench, a fireplace with a gas-ring balanced on the empty grate, and a large double bed.

'Nice bed,' offered Aristotle, bouncing on it to demonstrate its niceness, then added, glancing suggestively in my direction, 'many ladies.'

'Really?' I said.

Aristotle changed intellectual direction. 'You like *ouzo*? I got *ouzo*. Very fine *ouzo*. My family make since—'

'Since they left Tottenham?' prompted Nicholas slyly.

'Yes, yes, English joke,' Aristotle agreed enthusiastically. 'You can drink. Is good Greek *ouzo*, is very good with Turkish coffee.' He grins. 'I make Greek joke. I make Turkish coffee. And then you see all my pictures of my ladies.'

Aristotle's gallery of conquests turned out to be as exhibitionist as his coffee-making. There could be no doubt at all of our host's powers of seduction. Aristotle's ladies appeared to have thrown their inhibitions to the wind along with most of their clothing.

'This Lisa, very nice German lady. This Anneke, beautiful Swede.' Pale billows of female flesh posed coyly in the olive groves, smiled suggestively over slabs of watermelon.

'Goodness me, what we have here?' What we had here was two large breasts, nipples a-twinkle, topped by a sulky face squashed into a Brigitte Bardot pout. Sure enough, 'This Françoise. Very nice French lady.'

Aristotle unearthed another bundle of photographs. This time any doubts over the authenticity of the material were dispelled by the unmistakable presence of Minerva and Athena, partners in pornography.

Aristotle selected one particularly well-fondled item. 'Don't I tell you Minerva and Athena like nice English ladies? This Doris. Doris very good woman.'

We nodded gravely. Goodness seemed a surprising virtue in a lady of such ample attributes with so little to disguise them.

Aristotle has a sudden attack of generosity. 'Here, lady. I give you. You take. Show your husband when he say, "Not tonight, Josephine." ' Aristotle paused for effect. 'English joke! English lady tell it me. "Not tonight, Josephine" – you get it?'

We got it. 'We really must go now. We'll be late.'

Late for what?

'Mount Athos,' I offered, too late to take it back.

Aristotle slapped Athena's rump, his belly rippling with laughter. 'You no go to Mount Athos. No ladies, not even Scottish ladies, on Mount Athos. Not even Minerva and Athena allowed on Mount Athos.'

We made our escape before the sheep-jokes cracked in.

Barbed wire barred the way to Mount Athos. Beyond, glimpsed through a no man's land of thornbush and black scrub, stretched a wilderness of red earth and dry rock. It was impossible to imagine a life lived in such a desert. There was nothing to eat for man or beast. Perhaps the monks threw lines for fish, or limed the branches for birds – it seemed that no other husbandry could be possible.

Nicholas settled himself on a rock to contemplate the narrow path to sainthood. 'No wine, no women, no song.' He shook his head. 'It's not for me.'

There was a village by the frontier. We walked down to the harbour to watch the fishing fleet return. The mystery of the monks of Mount Athos was solved at a stroke. Even the holy go shopping. As soon as the first boat docked, a tall young monk in a black robe appeared as if from the ether, loaded the catch into twin baskets slung on the back of a mule, and vanished as silently as he had appeared.

We saw no more of Mount Athos than the black-clad monk. Permission to enter might have been granted to Nicholas, but it would have taken weeks to process. We had to be on our way.

What I had in mind was a little bird-watching. Porto Largo, said the manual, is best for birdwatchers. Permission to view might be obtained from the guardian, who lived in a hut just by the salt-pans, a broad expanse of shimmering grey crystals that crunched beneath our wheels.

Miraculously, since bird-wardens are not usually to be found in obvious places, we found him dozing peacefully in an old car-seat installed on his salt-streaked verandah overlooking the sea. The shoreline was innocent of birds. Our pocket dictionary did not run to sophisticated enquiries about the non-availability of the lesser black-backed shrike, so we pulled out the identification manual.

All gone to Africa, said the guardian, rising sleepily from his couch as soon as he saw our binoculars, the badge of the serious birdwatcher. This information was conveyed by means of wildly flapping arms and a spread-handed shrug.

Nicholas flicked over the pages, picking out the little pictures of pelican, flamingo, heron – the trophy birds, the kind that twitchers tick off on their life-lists and all wardens can recognize immediately. Twitchers are the head-collectors, their life-list a running tally of all the birds they have managed to identify. Certain birds are rarer than others; some, like a Penny Black to a stamp-collector, appear once in a lifetime.

The guardian pointed to the purple heron and waved his hand. Within the species, some birds are more valuable than others. The grey heron is an everyday bird but its purple cousin is a trophy. Inky-crested, polka-dot bibbed, chestnut-breasted, with plumes of a singing purple, this is a rare bird that rates a detour.

The flats yielded a whole family of the imperial birds, dainty as dancers. As we watched them pick their way round the reedbeds like ballerinas negotiating a piece of fallen scenery, a flotilla of pelicans crash-landed into a wall of bulrushes, scattering a gaggle of rose-pink flamingos which had been peacefully trawling the shallows.

Unable to resist, I settled down with brush and sketchbook. By the time I had finished, the sun was setting in a soft haze of violet and gold, and it was already too late to cross the frontier.

We would have to eat and sleep in Alexandropolis, appropriately named for the warrior-king of Macedonia since it is the last Greek town before the Turkish border. The guidebook did not have much to say of the city, apart from registering its lack of interest. We followed its advice on the selection of a modest hotel with a car-park by the railway station. After the day's exertions, we wanted only to eat quickly and sleep soundly.

Our host explained his wife was visiting her sister, so there were no facilities for supper.

I enquired where we might go to eat.

He shrugged and spread his hands. 'You go to Ilya's, of course. Everyone go to Ilya's.'

And what might we expect to be served?

'Everything is good. You eat what you want.' This, the standard Greek reply to such enquiries, is not a recommendation to be taken literally. Nevertheless, we had no choice but to take his advice, not least because Ilya's was just round the corner, the lighted window glowing invitingly through the darkness.

A glance through the open door revealed a busy, noisy throng, and all but one of the scrubbed-wood tables occupied by family groups cheerfully eating out of communal dishes. The air was thick with the mingled scents of garlic, eau-de-Cologne and perspiration.

What we ate was not so much what we wanted, but what everyone else was eating. As soon as we sat down at our table, a sizzling copper dish of *saganaki* – roasted cheese – appeared. With it came the now-familiar appetizers: a dish of smoky-flavoured aubergine purée – *melitzanosalata* – deliciously sprinkled with toasted sesame and cumin; a bowl of *tsadziki*, the yoghurt thick and creamy, the cucumber finely chopped, the garlic mild and sweet. Greek garlic is strongly perfumed and hot to the palate. As a flavouring, it is not well seen by the bourgeoisie. Greek recipe books, designed for the upwardly mobile urban housewife, often include dire warnings about the undesirability of over-indulging in garlic. The country people have no such inhibitions.

The salad was, by Greek standards, unusually elegant, the onion mild and thinly sliced, the feta cut into neat little cubes, the tomatoes seeded, the lettuce patted dry, the olives neatly pitted. The guidebook might not rate the town, but clearly the citizenry appreciated refinement. Contrary to expectations – the guidebook advised fish – the house speciality was *souvlaki*. Fat pink cubes of lamb were weighed to each customer's

Greek Horiatiki Salata

GREEK SALAD

This is a peasant salad, so make it rough and ready.

———————————— SERVES 4 ————————————

1 Cos lettuce, chopped	4–6 tablespoons olive oil
2 large ripe beef tomatoes, chunked	juice of 1 lemon
1 cucumber, chunked	salt
1 mild onion, sliced into fine rings	4 slices feta cheese
1 tablespoon black olives	

1. Toss the lettuce, tomato, cucumber, onion and olives together. Dress with olive oil, lemon juice and a very little salt – the olives and feta provide plenty of salt. Top with the slices of feta cheese. That's all.

Greek Souvlakia

KEBABS WITH LEMON AND MARJORAM

'Kebab' is an ancient Indian word meaning 'cooked meat', a modest beginning for a dish that has inspired so many cooks. The secret of good kebabs lies in the marination. Lamb, or kid, is the usual (and the best) meat: it is delicate enough to take the flavourings, and tender enough not to harden under the fierce heat of the grill.

———————————— SERVES 4 ————————————

1 lb/500 g lamb off the bone, shoulder or *fillet,* or *pork*

———————————— THE MARINADE ————————————

4 tablespoons olive oil
2 tablespoons lemon juice
2 bayleaves, crumbled
2 teaspoons marjoram or *oregano, chopped*

1 teaspoon thyme, chopped
1 teaspoon black pepper

1. Trim the lamb and cut it into bite-sized cubes. Mix all the marinade ingredients together and toss the cubed meat very thoroughly in it. Leave to absorb the flavours overnight, or for several hours at least. Thread the meat on fine skewers (if using wooden ones, soak them first so that they do not burn).
2. Grill the kebabs. The best cooking medium is a charcoal fire, but a grill will do well enough. All but pork kebabs should be cooked quite close to the heat so that the outside chars but the meat remains juicy. Turn the kebabs once or twice. They will be ready in 10–12 minutes over or under not too fierce a heat. Pork kebabs will need 15–18 minutes further away from the heat. Serve with rough chunks of bread, or rice. Accompany with lemon quarters.

requirement, threaded on fine skewers with little squares of scarlet pepper, and cooked to order on a charcoal brazier, whose smoke curled out from the patio behind. The lamb was exquisitely pink and juicy inside, deliciously charred on the outside, and arrived with a risotto whose curious consistency and complex flavour led me to investigate its composition. Customers are always welcome to wander in and out of Greek restaurant kitchens, so this was nothing unusual. An inspection of the cooking pots and a few questions with my sketchbook revealed that the risotto included pine kernels and tiny rice-shaped scraps of pasta dough, a surprisingly sophisticated combination.

As was to be expected after so magnificent a supper, we slept soundly. We didn't expect to be so fortunate the following night. Our host, enquiring after our next port of call, told us that the state of the border was dire. There were reports of delays of two or three days. We would be advised to be well prepared. We might not find food. We might even have to sleep in our fine vehicle while the Turks decided if we rated admittance.

'Turkish people do not like tourists coming from Greece.'

CHAPTER FOUR

Oriental Habits

*This question of horizon, however; how important it is; how it
alters the shape of the mind; how it expresses, essentially,
one's ultimate sense of country! That is what can never be told
in words: the exact size, proportion, contour; the new standard
to which the mind must adjust itself.*

VITA SACKVILLE-WEST, *Passenger to Teheran* (1926)

'MR HERTZ? WHO THIS MR HERTZ?'

It's a widely acknowledged truth that the quantity and
brilliance of the gold braid worn by the official representatives
of any nation is in inverse proportion to that nation's ability to
influence world events. It is also well known that the thicker the
braid, the thicker the brain. Nowhere is this more evident than
at a frontier post.

'Hertz is a hire-car company, very big, very famous,' I
answered, with mounting panic. I had already offered this

explanation to several minor officials, but clearly this was a big cheese. From the size and splendour of the moustache, a *very* big cheese. 'It's like going to a hotel – you borrow a room, and then you give it back.'

'You are perhaps Mrs Hertz?'

The officer's face was impassive. He stared down at my passport. I always smile for my passport photo in the belief that this will make immigration officers more kindly disposed. However hard I smiled, it was clear that I was not Mrs Hertz.

'Not exactly,' I answered, fearful that a complete denial might lead to instant incarceration in some rat-infested Turkish jail.

'Your husband is friend of Mr Hertz?' My interrogator pushed his heavily gilded cap back on his tight black curls and raised his eyebrows.

'In a manner of speaking . . .' I agreed, with desperation. 'My husband will explain.'

'Where your husband?'

I glanced round. Where, indeed, was Nicholas, now that I needed him? He has an extraordinary knack of simply absenting himself at such moments. I'm sure it's not deliberate – just a bit feline, as if he can scent trouble in the air.

'Lady, this not your car. This not your husband car. This car belong to Mr Hertz. You say he is not friend of Mr Hertz. You have letter giving permission to borrow?'

'We don't need a letter. We have a *contract*.'

'Hah.' An expression of cunning passed across the official face. 'I think perhaps you steal.'

'We don't steal. We *borrow*.' I told myself to remain calm. Customs officers are like terriers: they can smell fear. 'We hired the car. In Munich. You know – like a taxi,' I added.

My own face stared back at me in double miniature in sunglasses glazed like small mirrors. 'Taxi? Where the taxi-driver?'

'Taxi-driver – my husband.'

'Ah. Your husband is taxi-driver.' For one incapable of grasping the notion of a hire-car, the official had a surprising command of the language.

'No, no. He's a writer. My husband writes books.'

Silence. Then, 'Books? What kinda books?'

'Good books.' I waved my hands. 'Stories. Travel. Adventure. Love.'

'Love?' The teeth flashed. Ringed hands sketched out a pair of ample breasts. '*Playboy* magazine.'

'That kind of thing,' I said, with alacrity.

'OK, lady. He write books. What he wanna write about Turkey?'

'He doesn't. It's me. I'm a cookery writer. I write about food.'

'What kinda food? Mr McDonald hamburger?'

'Good food. Turkish food.'

The sunglasses and the teeth flashed. The atmosphere was distinctly lighter. 'Turkish cooking good. Not like Greek cooking. Greek cooking . . .' An expressive glob of spittle hit the dust.

'Absolutely. That's why I have come,' I expanded hastily. 'To find out about good Turkish cooking and how much better it is than Greek.'

'My wife Turkish woman. Turkish women cook good. Make many children, eating all the time. You have children, lady?'

'Four children,' I answered, making a mental note that next time I made a trip like this, I must carry family photographs.

'You leave children at home, all alone?'

'My children are all grown-up. They don't need me to cook for them any more. All grown – tall, big.' I made growing gestures, not wishing to be thought an inferior mother.

'Ah. Many sons.'

'One son. Three daughters.'

A sharp glance. 'Daughters? They have husband?'

'Not yet.'

'Whatsa matter? They ugly?' A roar of laughter. 'Poor, maybe? No money for marrying?' He looked at the car. 'Not poor. If poor, you sell car.'

We stared at each other. Clearly this conversation was heading in a direction I did not understand. He removed and polished the dark glasses thoughtfully, replacing them carefully on the bridge of his nose.

'I have many daughters. Daughters very expensive.' He

rummaged in a pocket of his uniform and pulled out a well-thumbed photograph. Five small girls in identical lace-collared velvet dresses, as alike as peas in a pod, posed solemnly in front of a photographer's backdrop of some highly ornate mosque.

'Very pretty – very beautiful daughters,' I said. 'You are very fortunate.'

'Not fortunate. Daughters very expensive,' he repeated, with exaggerated gloom. Then added, wearily, as if talking to an imbecile, 'You have picture?'

'Picture?' I repeated stupidly.

'Picture? You have picture of daughters?'

'No – I mean, I'm sorry—'

'Lady, you *find* picture.' The voice contained a note of exasperation. At this moment a movement caught the corner of my eye: the unmistakable rubbing of the officer's index finger against the thumb. Finally, the penny dropped.

'Of course I have picture.' Fumbling in my pockets, I found what I imagined to be a postcard, behind which I tucked a twenty-dollar bill. The note vanished smoothly, but the card remained for examination.

'Very nice picture, lady.' A broad grin spread across the swarthy features. 'My congratulations to your husband.'

At this opportune moment Nicholas chose to reappear on the horizon. 'All well, sweetheart?'

'I think we've reached some kind of agreement,' I answered cautiously.

The beringed hand of my interrogator came up in a laconic salute. 'Lady, here is your papers. I wish you and your husband many years of happiness.'

The barrier swung up.

'Welcome to Republic of Turkey, Mr and Mrs Hertz.'

A mile down the road from the border post, we joined the tail end of our particular batch of vehicles, all anxious to put as much distance as possible, as fast as possible, between themselves and the frontier.

Ten minutes later, with a scream of sirens, the motorcycle police pulled us all in. From the moment we had left the barrier to the moment we were pulled over confirmed that we had all broken the speed limit.

The cops moved down the line imposing fines, like over-eager vergers collecting for the new church roof. Tourists pay double. The Greeks pay twice as much as the tourists.

A plump Mimi Papandreou lookalike in an open-topped Mercedes was both Greek and angry. The cops listened impassively and charged her triple. A fine is a fine. A Greek is a Greek.

A swarthy face in the regulation mirror-glasses appeared at the window. 'Hundred thousand lira. Fifty dollars.'

Resignedly, I pulled a fifty off the rapidly diminishing wad. The policeman handed over the receipt with a somewhat over-familiar salute. 'Very nice picture, lady.'

My cheeks flamed. It had only just occurred to me that what I had thought was a postcard of fishermen picturesquely mending their nets with Mount Athos in the background, had been nothing of the kind. As we drove on, I flicked through the passports and car papers, although I really needed no confirmation that Aristotle's photograph was missing.

'The Turkish police have a reputation for – how shall I put it? – *thoroughness*,' a diplomat friend had warned me. Thoroughness, in the elliptical language of diplomacy, is not something one wishes to encounter in policemen. Particularly those who are under the impression that the lady they have just admitted to their country, whose vital statistics they have no doubt filed in triplicate, spends her evenings stark naked under an olive tree keeping company with an ass.

'What was all that about?' enquired Nicholas.

I told him.

Nicholas thought it very funny. I had somehow managed to mislay my sense of humour. Furthermore, I pointed out, negotiations with policemen, whatever the outcome, left a person hungry.

While my husband never seems afflicted by the need to fill the belly, I need regular meals. My faith in humanity in general and Nicholas in particular can always be restored by a decent lunch.

With this in mind, we turned off the highway towards

Rodosto, the first stop on the road to Istanbul. A single main street led to a harbour-front whose half-finished buildings gave the place an air of dilapidation. This, as with so many things in Turkey, was not entirely true. In reality, the inhabitants make an adequate living – by Turkish standards – from restoring the frayed nerves of tourists such as ourselves. Since taxes are not payable on new buildings until they have been completed, new edifices are left unfinished. Television aerials, washing lines, dustbins brimming with all the evidence of habitation tell a different story: that it is financial acumen rather than necessity that leaves the iron stakes protruding from naked ceilings like unmade beds.

Restaurants – well patronized by large family groups taking advantage of the tables set out in the golden autumn sunshine – lined the harbour-front. Young men, in what looked like short Victorian nightgowns that flapped merrily over their jeans, bustled up and down carrying the makings of mint-tea: trays of steaming tea-kettles, bowls of brown sugar lumps and tiny glasses full of green leaves. The trays swung from the hand on three chains, like old-fashioned scales. Others had wooden yokes slung over their shoulders from which dangled rush-baskets filled with sesame-sprinkled bread rings, round and shiny, like golden amulets. Still others presided over hand-carts filled with stalks of bright yellow bananas, prized for their rarity since all other fruit is free for the gathering, the scent cheerfully tropical.

The restaurant owners did not appear to discourage these itinerant food-pedlars from approaching their clients. On the contrary, the street-sellers provided a service the restaurants themselves had no interest in supplying. Their business, the main attraction, the reason for the presence of Turkish tourists, was fish – perfectly fresh fish of every colour and shape, very expensive by anyone's standards. The catch of the day was on display at the front of each restaurant in a refrigerated cabinet, with the skills of the cook advertised alongside. The fish was weighed, scaled and cooked to order. It might be grilled, kebabed, fried, stuffed, or baked, depending on the speciality of that particular establishment's cook.

But the breads, sherbets, fruit, coffee and various delicacies to

104

be added to the *mezze* selection were provided directly to the customer by the pedlars. This arrangement required the employment of a great many people – a kind of ambulatory chef's brigade.

We chose tuna-fish steaks to be cooked on the grill. When they came, they were deliciously crusted with paprika. As a *mezze* we ordered *imam bayildi*, aubergines simmered with oil and onion. From one pedlar we bought bread, from another mussels stuffed with rice, the two shells of the mollusc sandwiched together with a dab of saffron-coloured pilaff. Ripe bananas from the cart served us well enough for dessert.

The coastal road to Istanbul is a pitted highway that links the sprawl of half-completed tourist hotels set in concrete dustbowls fringed by ramshackle shanty-towns, like grey lace on the edge of a grubby petticoat. Muezzin towers and industrial installations pierced the pink drift of baked earth. Beyond the shingled beach, the sea was gun-metal grey. To the casual traveller hurrying on his way, there is nothing much to draw him into the towns, unless to visit one of the numerous mosques the guidebooks recommend.

It was already late afternoon by the time we reached the outskirts of Istanbul. Signs to the centre threw us into confusion. We drove round and round the commercial area like gerbils on a wheel, attempting to rejoin the main coastal highway, which would take us to the fishing village of Terabaya, ten miles north of the city. There was no particular reason for the choice except that I had an idea we might catch a glimpse of the autumn bird migration. Terabaya, according to our adviser on all things Ottoman – an ex-diplomat of impeccable taste, a collector of rare Islamic artefacts – is the St Tropez of the Bosphorus. On his advice, we had booked ourselves into the Pera Palace, a hotel he assured us overlooked the Golden Horn and would give us the best possible view of the avian passage, should we be so fortunate as to coincide with it.

After an anxious half-hour diving in and out of a mass of tiny streets interspersed with high-rise office blocks, I hailed a taxi, leaving Nicholas to follow behind. Usually this technique worked well in unfamiliar cities. Istanbul turned out to be the

Turkish Imam Bayildi

AUBERGINES WITH ONION AND TOMATO

The most seductive of aubergine dishes, aubergine being the Turkish national vegetable. The name is most nearly translated as 'the Imam swooned with pleasure' – propaganda on a plate. The secret is to keep all the ingredients distinct: they must be delicately intertwined rather than a mush.

———————————— SERVES 4 AS A STARTER ————————————

2 large firm aubergines, halved
lengthways
salt
1 large onion, finely sliced vertically
3 large tomatoes, skinned and
chopped
6 garlic cloves, finely chopped

bunch fresh parsley, dill and basil,
finely chopped
¼ pint / 150 ml olive oil
4 tablespoons water
1 teaspoon sugar
1 lemon, quartered

1. Sprinkle the cut flesh of the aubergines with salt and leave to weep for 15 minutes. Rinse and place the halves side by side, cut side up, in a wide pan in a single layer.

2. Mix the onion, tomatoes, garlic and herbs in a bowl with a teaspoon of salt and a little of the oil. Carefully pile the mixture on top of each aubergine half until all the flesh is covered. Mix the rest of the oil with the water and sugar and pour it over and around.

3. Set the pan over a gentle heat, cover and leave to braise for about 1½ hours – if you prefer, you can bake it in the oven at 325°F/160°C/mark 3. Baste occasionally with the oil, pushing the onion and tomato mixture down into the aubergine halves as they cook. The aubergines should end up soft and flat, sitting in a golden, slightly caramelized, pool of oil, with a topping of aromatic vegetables, which still retain a little bite. Leave to cool. Spoon over the oil before serving with quartered lemons.

exception. To the Turkish male, driving is fiercely competitive, a matter of honour, a replacement for the exploits of the battlefield. In vain I explained that the Mercedes behind us did not contain a representative of the secret police whose attentions must be shaken off at all costs. In spite of my pleas in every language at my disposal, it was only by the skin of his teeth that Nicholas managed to hang on to our tail-lights. While gesturing frantically through the rear window, I could see his face pink and his knuckles white on the steering wheel.

As might be expected, German engineering turned out to be more than a match for the pride of Turkey. Round and round we screeched in a cloud of burning rubber. Louder and louder became the cursings of the taxi-driver. Half an hour later we came to a clattering halt with a simultaneous howl of brakes beneath a beflagged canopy. The hotel was disconcertingly huge and modern. Like some monstrous one-eyed Cyclops clad in steel and glass, it glowered over the Golden Horn.

Our room was on the nineteenth floor – just as I had requested, as near the top as possible. Being small, it was relatively cheap. The very topmost, explained the lady behind the desk, were huge and expensive and reserved for the penthouse guests. Signed photographs of the fortunate luminaries – movie stars, politicians escaping the boredom of Ankara whose features were no doubt equally familiar to those who followed Turkey's labyrinthine politics – adorned the reception area.

Our room was like an eagle's eyrie. A large bed occupied most of the floor space, but the outer wall was made entirely of glass. An uninterrupted view of the Asian shore and the white-capped stretch of water between made it the perfect bird hide. It was a clear evening, the sun had not yet dropped behind the hills. We were just in time. Big birds and little birds, broad-winged buzzards and slender-bodied hawks, storks – both black and white – too numerous to count, eagles, bee-eaters, swallows, finches, it seemed as if the entire avian population of the Western world was on the move.

'Wonderful,' said I, settling down contentedly on the edge of the bed with my binoculars and sketchbook.

Unfortunately, I had forgotten that Nicholas suffers from

vertigo – a common enough affliction, but which had come upon him only lately. He refused to train his binoculars on the avian travellers and declared his intention of spending the night with a pillow and a blanket in the bath.

The first day in any new city demands orientation. We booked a day-trip on the tourist bus, lunch included.

The twin trading posts of the Bosphorus were once the capital of the Ottoman Empire. Culturally, socially, gastronomically, the great city serves as a link between Europe and Asia. Two magnificent bridges now span the divide, but for thousands of years the ferries ploughed back and forth, exchanging Eastern spices for Western wheat, wool for silk, New World gold for coffee, tea and Indian rubies.

Built to the glory of a pagan goddess of fertility, a harlot of a city, not even her name is truly her own. Even the archaeologists cannot be certain when the beaten earth of the market-place turned into a city. All we do know is that there have been traders here since our ancestors first discovered how much tastier their food could be when they sprinkled it with pepper. Those were the glory days of the Orient: at the same time as the Chinese were exploring the possibilities of pasta-making, pastry-rolling, dumpling-stuffing and all the other little culinary tricks that so delight both heart and stomach, our ancestors in Europe were still boiling bison in its skin.

The pagan city of Byzantium became the Holy Roman city of the Emperor Constantine at the moment of change, when the fusion of Eastern philosophy with Western romanticism gave life to modern Christianity. The city fell to Muslim rule when Suleiman, architect of the military empire of the Ottoman Turks, made her the centre of his dominions. From here his turbaned armies marched into the heart of Europe, their advance contained in the East only by the natural wall of the Urals, and halted in the West, almost by accident, by the walls of Vienna. It was seven centuries before the Turkish conquerors went home.

The Ottoman garrisons marched on their bellies. This may be true of all armies, but the Turks set rather more store than most by the daily dinner. The rank-and-file were accustomed to show their disapproval of their officers by kicking over the supper cauldrons: no food, no fight. The officers, possibly hoping that such mutinous gestures might be avoided if the scent from the stewpot was irresistible, recruited the best of the local talent and taught them how to cook the kind of dishes the sybaritic Turks enjoyed at home.

The Slavs and Germans co-opted to work in the garrison kitchens quickly acquired a whole new culinary vocabulary. When the Ottoman filo pastry wrapped the German dumpling, the result was the Austrian strudel. The brewing of coffee – the Viennese will tell you that the first coffee-house was established with the sacks of beans the Ottomans left behind – was learned from the Ottomans, as was the trick of frying the meat before making a stew. The art of fine pastry-making – even the creation of what are now known as Danish pastries but which the Danes call Viennese. All these skills were Ottoman-taught. Yoghurt, imported by Turcoman nomads from Central Asia, is another Ottoman gift.

For all these reasons and more – although politicians may deny it and historians excise it – their legacy cannot be ignored. The kitchen never lies. The true history of a nation is to be read not in libraries, but in the domestic habit of the people.

In Istanbul, the steps of the market lead directly to the quays on which, before bridges spanned the channel that divides the continents, the wooden barges unloaded their treasures. Sacks and trunks of the precious spices were haggled and priced before being loaded on donkeys and mules for the journeys to the great medieval fairs of France and Germany, Holland and Hungary. Maybe it was in this same market that Alexander's soldiers first acquired a taste for soporific saffron, blamed by the warrior king for his late arrival to do battle with the Persians. From here, too, Richard the Lionheart's Crusaders took home sugar and oranges to please their abandoned wives. Here, Vikings traded with Phoenicians, exchanging wind-dried cod for the spices that enliven a dull Northern diet.

By the sixteenth-century, through her trading partners, the Renaissance merchants of Venice, Constantinople controlled a new market: the incoming New World trade. Shipments included not only gold and silver but a variety of mysterious vegetables previously unknown in Europe.

The Turks transported the seeds of these new plants to their colonies, which by then stretched from Egypt to the forests of Transylvania. Courtesy of the Ottoman conquerors, Hungarians received their first supplies of paprika, and maize flour replaced dried chestnuts in the stewpots of Romania. The green-fingered Bulgarians, master-gardeners of central Europe, cultivated everything they were given: potatoes and marrows, sweetcorn, tomatoes, capsicums, beans, pumpkins. To a traveller through the vast territories that were, until after the First World War, the European provinces of the Ottoman Empire, this legacy of the Turks has survived long after the mosques and minarets have tumbled.

We took our places on the bus. By the time we had reached the golden walls of the city, the group had established its individual identities. Right at the back four Dutch tourists, two male, two female, in tracksuits and running-shoes, bickered quietly over the accuracy of the guidebook. The remaining passengers were a French family with three impeccably dressed teenage children, and two Americans, both female, in well-tailored linens and sensible shoes.

The first stop on the tourist tour was Topkapi Palace, once the sultan's domestic dwelling but now a vast museum, its treasures seamed into alarm-linked glass cases. The opulence startles: necklaces studded with rubies the size of birds' eggs, suits of armour so heavily inlaid with gold they look like ceremonial robes, porcelain dishes from China of such exquisite fragility it's impossible to imagine anyone actually using them for the purpose for which they were made. The carpets, the only truly Ottoman art form, are astonishing, the patterns so intricate, the silk so soft, the pile so dense, the knots so tiny that they can only have been made by fingers as light as butterflies.

The eye first takes pleasure in symmetry, the curves and geometric tracings that are mirror images of the shapes to be found in nature. There are no human images to divert the eye, to instruct the warrior or tempt comparison with the beauties of the past. The deeds of heroes are not recorded in paint or stone, they live on only in story and song. But if you let your imagination wander through the shimmering halls, the ghosts of the perfumed ladies of the seraglio laze on the silk-embroidered cushions, the shades of long-dead warriors slip through the shadows.

The halls were cool. The patchwork colours danced in the slanting sunshine from the high windows, the light filtered through the filigree screens. Water trickles from carved spouts into clear pools lined with exquisite mosaics into which the optimistic had thrown coins for luck. The pennies and francs, Japanese yen and American dimes seemed oddly disruptive, anachronisms, as in a movie when the Roman legionary has forgotten to remove his watch.

For me, at least, a visit to a habitation preserved for posterity is always an unsatisfactory experience. Neither guest nor participant, the visitor for whom all this magnificence is displayed has no part in the reality. We can change nothing, contribute nothing – all the more so here, where there were no human images to stir the imagination, to people the empty rooms with those for whom these things were made.

We behaved as all tourists behave, furtively, shuffling slowly round the caged treasures like a herd of antelope inspecting tigers in a zoo, or grave-robbers plotting the desecration of a tomb.

In the cavernous kitchens, I felt more at home. Here, locks and bars were not considered necessary – domestic pots and pans are not obvious fodder for thieves. Lining the walls were floor-standing cauldrons as high as a man, pyramid-lidded baking dishes as wide as a car wheel, huge frying-pans, stewpots, ladles as big as birds' nests. The palace food was plentiful and rich – visitors described rolls of buffalo cream atop honey-soaked pastries – but not over-elaborate. The Seraglios employed a thousand kitchen workers and fed up to ten thousand daily, but few of the dishes were complicated, none beyond the capacities of the domestic cook.

We re-embarked. The bus hooted and rattled through streets crowded with people on their way to market. Turkish countryfolk transport their produce as they have since medieval times: on flat-bedded mule-carts. The only innovation is that, these days, the wooden wheels are protected by tattered tyres.

At my special request, we halted at the fish market for a quick trawl round marble slabs piled with crates of sardines, emerald-flanked mackerel, prawns with turquoise-streaked heads and whiskers as long as Atatürk's moustache.

Market-places serve a double purpose. The daily visit to buy fresh food for the family provides social contact for women who might otherwise be isolated, a gathering-point for political argument, exchange of news both political and personal, a confirmation of national identity, an opportunity for new-comers to integrate into the community. In commercial terms, it ensures direct contact between producers and consumers, a chance for the country to come to the town and assess the needs of its customers – an exchange essential to the health of a food-producing nation. The market-place provides a forum for innovation, common ground available to all where even the most gastronomically conservative can learn new tricks and try new flavours.

Market food requires an element of theatre. Presentation must be persuasive. The food has to look good, taste good, and whoever prepares it has to demonstrate a high level of expertise. It's a skilled chef who can persuade the shrewd housewife to pay a premium for something they could very well take home and cook for themselves. Standard fare in every market-place that has not lost its soul and turned into a second-hand supermarket are restorative soups made with market-leavings. Ingredients must be cheap – tripe, trotters or oxtail require time in the preparation, but they are plentiful where the butchers are busy. There is a ready market, too, for wrapped foods that can be carried in the hand – flatbreads stuffed with a slice of meat or cheese, a little dab of a savoury stew enclosed in pastry. These ideas are universal – no single culture has the monopoly: the Turkish *gozleme*, the chapattis of India, China's delicate pancakes, all are sisters under the wrapper.

The market traders are full of tall stories. A taste for bending reality is their stock-in-trade. The spice-traders of the Egyptian souk can sell you the very perfumes with which Helen scented her marriage bed at Troy, the incense burned by Cleopatra when she set her mind to conquer Caesar. Ginger-root and

Turkish Gozleme

FLATBREADS WITH PARSLEY, ONION AND CHEESE

This is not a bread you're likely to find in a bakery, although you might find a lady preparing it to order in the corner of the market square. Although it looks like a large pancake, the method brings it closer to an Indian *chapatti*. Easy to make, even if few of us can achieve the sleight of hand with the broom handle that seems to be the birthright of every Turkish cook.

―――――――――― MAKES ABOUT 8 ――――――――――

4 oz/100 g strong bread flour   *1 tablespoon olive oil or melted butter*
½ teaspoon salt   *about 5 tablespoons warm water*

―――――――――― THE TOPPING ――――――――――

4–5 spring onions, trimmed and   ½ teaspoon Turkish mild chilli flakes
 finely chopped   *(kirmizi biber), or paprika with a*
1–2 garlic cloves, skinned and   pinch of cayenne pepper
 finely chopped   about 4 oz/100 g fresh white
a big handful (about 200 g) fresh   cheese, crumbled (could be
 spinach, shredded   cottage cheese)

―――――――――― OPTIONAL EXTRAS FOR SPRINKLING ――――――――――

hard cheese (Cheddar or Parmesan), grated
parsley, chopped

1. Sieve the flour and salt into a bowl. Work in the oil and water and knead thoroughly. Divide into 4 and work each piece into a ball. Cover with a cloth and leave for 20 minutes.
2. On a floured board with a thin, well-floured rolling-pin, roll out each ball into a very thin disc 5–6 in/12–15 cm in diameter.
3. Next mix all the topping ingredients together in a large bowl, and set on one side.
4. Heat and lightly grease a heavy frying-pan and slap on one of the discs. Use your fingers to move it about so it blisters and browns. Brush the top with more oil and flip it over.
5. Sprinkle the cooked side with a quarter of the topping mixture while the underside is cooking. When done, lift the *gozleme* on to a piece of greaseproof paper and roll it up into a cone. Continue with the other three, and eat hot, straight from the griddle.

Turkish Boreki

FILO PASTRY ENVELOPES WITH SPICED LAMB AND SPINACH

A little bit of glamour for the *mezze* table – triangles of filo pastry filled with a delicately spiced stuffing. The main difference between Turkish and Greek cooking is that Turks use spices while Greeks use herbs. You can stuff the envelopes with any spicy little stew, whether meat or vegetable, so ring the changes with whatever comes to hand.

--------------------- SERVES ABOUT 8 AS AN APPETIZER ---------------------

1 packet filo pastry (1 packet yields
  about 24 sheets)
8 oz/250 g spinach, rinsed
  and shredded
1 tablespoon oil
1 onion, grated

1 garlic clove, finely chopped
8 oz/250 g minced lamb
1 teaspoon ground cinnamon
1 teaspoon ground cumin
¹/2 teaspoon ground nutmeg
salt and pepper

--------------------------- TO FINISH ---------------------------

oil for shallow frying

1. Defrost the pastry, if necessary, and keep it covered while you work so that it doesn't dry out.

2. Cook the spinach in a lidded pan in the water that clings to the leaves. Drain and squeeze out all the water. Chop finely.

3. Heat the tablespoon of oil in a frying-pan. Fry the onion and garlic until they soften and gild. Add the lamb and stir over the heat until it begins to brown a little. Stir in the spices and fry for a moment more. Add the spinach and allow it to cook gently for about 5 minutes, loosely lidded, to blend the flavours. Let it cool.

4. To assemble the *boreki*: lay out the filo pastry and cut it into strips 2½ in/5 cm wide by the full length of the pastry. As you work through the layers brush each strip with oil or melted butter. Put a teaspoon of the filling on the near corner of the strip. Fold it over to make a triangle, fold again to make another triangle, and so on up the strip, always rolling away from you, until you have a well-wrapped little *borek* covered in half a dozen thicknesses of pastry. Seal the last fold with a wet finger. Continue until all are done; keep them separate or they will stick to each other.

5. In a frying-pan, heat enough oil to submerge the *boreki*. When the oil is lightly hazed with blue, fry them a few at a time, turning once, until the pastry is well puffed and golden. Drain on kitchen paper.

6. Serve warm. Nice with a mint and yoghurt dip.

grain-of-paradise, fenugreek and mastic, rosewater and sandal-wood, nutmeg, pepper, allspice: name your potion, the spice merchants of Istanbul will tell you they've been supplying all these things to their customers since Scheherazade first filled the sultan's nights with her thousand tales.

The interior of the souk was arched and dim as a Gothic cathedral. In early September, the honeycomb of spice-merchants' kiosks was lit by shafts of autumn sunshine. Bright beams danced along the graceful alleyways, picking up spirals of dust. Everywhere was the scent of spices, drifting from the warren of shadowy tunnels that accommodate the merchants' wares, spiralling upwards to lose itself in the white domes that tented the vaulted aisles.

It was the end of the morning by the time we were free to wander and the heat had gone out of the salesmen. Perched on upturned baskets, oblivious to customers, a pair of chess players huddled over a board, the game as ancient as their trade. At a neighbouring stall, loose-robed black-clad peasants and veiled housewives waited patiently for slivers of paprika-crusted dried beef, sandwiched between slabs of yellow dense-crumbed bread – a pleasure to be completed by a tiny cup of bitter coffee, the beans milled to order and sweetened to the customer's preference, brewed in a brass *briki*.

Kiosks that sold honey and sweetmeats had the longest queues – the Turks love sweet things. Piled on the counter were hunks of dark honeycomb robbed from wild bees' nests; sandy blocks of sesame halva studded with pistachios or swirls of chocolate, walnuts, coconut; in wooden drawers behind the serving counter, *loukum* – Turkish delight – transparent as amber, flavoured with rosewater and half buried in drifts of icing-sugar, nut-stuffed baklava, and least familiar – reminding me of the sweetmeats on sale in Chinese pastry-shops – discs of crisp-fried noodles drenched with syrup.

Spices are the real business of the Egyptian souk – known as such for its principal customers in the days when Egypt was an outpost of the Ottoman Empire. All the flavours of the Orient are displayed in open-mouthed sacks which crowd the alley-ways. The aroma and the brilliance of the colours so seduce the senses that it's almost impossible to resist the urge to plunge headlong into the shop's interior. The dust that rises from such disturbances fills the air like fragrant smoke. Ridiculous to resist the merchant as he weighs out on tiny brass scales the grains-of-paradise, the galingale, the fat rolls of cinnamon bundled up with string. Impossible, in passing, not to thrust a hand into the mouth of a sack and let the seeds, the grains of rice, the cloves and cumin and cardamom, trickle through the fingers like perfumed sand. Each sack or box or jar is marked with its place of origin: sandalwood from Lebanon, jasmine tea from China, Bulgarian rose petals, figs from Smyrna, almonds from the Jordan valley – when each provenance is declared, its value is understood.

Salt has been stored in crocks large enough to hide a man. The crystals, not yet purified or processed, were multi-coloured: some pure white, others a soft slate-grey or rose-pink. Unrefined salt contains the minerals valuable in the preservation process. Even today, when there are many easier ways of conserving glut, the taste for salted foods remains. When preparing recipes, housewives will adjust the seasoning to take account of the salt in the ingredients. No need to salt a stew that has been prepared with salted fish or meat. The brine from vegetable pickles can be used to salt a soup, and you will often find unsalted bread in places where there's a tradition of preserving butter or lard with salt.

The salt trade was once as vital for preservation as refrigeration is today. The salt-roads – the tracks down which the barrels of salt were brought to the market-place – are still known to country people, even though the highway may now follow a different route. The year's supply of salt was bought at Easter, the time of the spring planting, so that when the crops matured the excess could be barrelled up for winter. Salt and sugar, knives and needles – these were things that self-sufficient communities valued, the only things they were prepared to pay money for were those they couldn't make.

The traveller can only be an observer at such a feast – without a kitchen, there's no chance to buy or try – so I settled down at a café table, prepared my paints and ordered a salep ice. Salep is the powdered root of the European ground-orchid – almost any orchid will do – and is used to thicken and perfume the ices of which Turkish ladies are inordinately fond. Frozen but not thickened, the fruit juice is a sherbet, but the powdered root gives a creamy consistency and a fortifying dose of protein. Chemists have confirmed that the twin tubers of *Orchis mascula* pack a higher protein punch than fillet steak.

Even at this late hour, trade was still brisk at the spice-merchants. The precious powders were blended and weighed to each customer's order, tiny quantities twisted into scraps of brittle sugar-paper. Most of the preparations were familiar to me: a mixture to serve as a marinade for meat or fish, another to be used as pickling spice. Most interesting to watch, since most complex, the swift blending of pungent powders called *ras-al-hanout* – top-of-the-shop – which serves the Middle Eastern cooks as *garam masala* the cooks of India. A few of the ingredients, stored in stoppered glass jars and carefully guarded from thieving fingers, seemed so odd they could only be medicinal – curious roots and twisted twigs, scraps of skin with fur, unidentifiable bits of bone, the iridescent wings of beetles and the dried bodies of insects. These were requested by veiled women or furtive menfolk, ground into potions no doubt guaranteed to promote passion, cure impotence, induce pregnancy.

As it was a Thursday, the day before the Muslim holiday, business in the everyday necessities was brisk. Turkish house-wives buy their spices weekly, sometimes daily, to match the contents of the shopping basket. Cumin for kebabs; coriander for stuffings; cardamom to perfume the endless procession of tiny cups of coffee that punctuate the day. Cassia-bark for the stew; cinnamon and nutmeg to scent the delicate pastries and creams with which Turks celebrate feast-days, holidays, or simply the joy of finding yourself among friends on a warm evening by the Bosphorus.

The souk was built to the order of the beautiful wife of a seventeenth-century Ottoman emperor. We must assume her beauty – no sultan's lady could ever be ugly – since, naturally enough, no portrait remains. The taxes imposed on the merchants who took advantage of the magnificent shelter – not only protection against winter rains, but also against thieves and cheats and those reluctant to pay their debts – endowed

Turkish Ras-al-Hanout
SECRET SPICE MIX

Otherwise known as top-of-the-shop, a spice mix with a thousand uses – and no doubt as many tales as Scheherazade. Start with a pinch in your favourite marinade and take it from there. To make powdered lavender, whizz up a few dried heads in the spice or coffee-grinder until well pulverized.

———————— MAKES ABOUT 8 OZ/250 G ————————

1¹/₂ oz/40 g ground coriander	*1 oz/25 g ground cloves*
1 oz/25 g ground white pepper	*¹/₂ oz/12 g cayenne pepper*
¹/₂ oz/12 g ground cumin	*¹/₂ oz/12 g ground ginger*
¹/₂ oz/12 g ground cardamom	*2 teaspoons powdered thyme*
1 teaspoon powdered rosemary	*1 teaspoon powdered lavender*

Mix all the ingredients together and lock up the treasure in a tight-stoppered glass jar. Store in a dark corner and use within 6 months. Keep the recipe to yourself – it's the stuff of which star chefs are made.

the sultana's mosque, the Yeni Valide Camii, with a royal revenue.

Appropriately, the steps of the souk lead directly past the mosque to the quay. Finishing my sketch and shaking off the crowd of urchins who had gathered to monitor its progress, I transferred my artistic attention to the comings and goings, the loadings and unloadings of the small boats, which are all that remain of what must have once been a whole flotilla of water-borne traffic.

Here, before the bridge-builders spanned the channel with iron and tarmac, the wooden caïques unloaded their aromatic treasure, to be haggled over and priced before they were offered for sale in the souk. Trade-routes run in both directions. In the domed kitchens of Topkapi I had noticed pyramids of Chinese steamers – perhaps the sultans employed Chinese cooks. Certainly it was through the merchants of the Egyptian souk that the New World's chillies made their way to the kitchens of the Orient.

From here, too, came the first maize-cobs that provided Africa with a new staple, a means of survival when all other crops failed. The merchants had a vested interest in the well-being of their customers and the reliability of the crops. Until recent times, well into the first quarter of this century, the merchants of the souk were as willing to trade in slaves as in any other commodity. A high infant mortality rate among the tribes of Africa was not good for business – and, furthermore, a well-fed slave fetched more in the market-place.

It was already late afternoon when we returned to the bus. The others had all made the tour of the sights, while I had satisfied my own interests. The tour was to make its way round the coastal road to Terabaya, conveniently depositing us back at our hotel.

Meanwhile, Nicholas had noticed that the younger and prettier of the two American women was sobbing quietly into a handful of shredded Kleenex. He is a man who can never resist a challenge, particularly if it's female and sobbing, so he made it his business to uncover the reason for her distress. Noticing that the tearful one's companion had her nose buried in a well-thumbed copy of Karen Blixen's *Out of Africa*, he enquired if they had both visited the continent. And if so, perhaps they loved it as much as he?

Indeed they did, confirmed the younger woman, blowing her nose with some ferocity. But she for one would be perfectly happy if she never saw it again in her life.

Why so?

At the suggestion of her fiancé, she explained, she had just completed a trip to Victoria Falls in the hope that it might cure her of hydrophobia. Her fear of water had revealed itself on a pre-nuptial weekend at Niagara when, confronted by a hundred and sixty feet of freefall, she had felt an almost overwhelming urge to throw herself over the rail. Following this unfortunate revelation, at her fiancé's prompting she had discussed her phobia with a therapist, who had suggested the visit to an alternative waterfall as aversion therapy. Since this particular fall was of an unthreatening kind, surrounded by virgin forest full of wallabies and parrots (natural history was not the therapist's strong suit), she might find it friendlier. This turned out to be the worst advice she had ever taken. A million gallons a minute of aquatic freefall, she sobbed, served only to confirm three things: water scared her witless, therapists were crazier than the people they treat, and she had made the wrong choice of fiancé.

Nicholas grinned. 'A lucky escape, no doubt about it. Far better to know exactly where you stand.'

She considered this seriously, stuffed the Kleenex back in her pocket, and agreed that he might be right. All men were bastards, but some were more so than others. So, with a sideways glance at she who might be assumed to be his companion, what was he doing for dinner that evening?

At this moment – fortunately for my faith in the sisterhood of women – the bus drew to a halt outside our hotel and our erstwhile companions vanished into the distance.

Terabaya had not yet lost its identity as a fishing port, it had simply added on the tourists. Behind the lines of working boats, rows of restaurants advertised belly-dancers and small birds. I enquired after fish, and was told to select my own from the fishermen's catch.

Alongside the quay, the evening's haul was displayed in rush baskets – octopus and squid, mackerel and sardines, mullet both red and grey. I picked out what I took to be a fine fresh bream, but forbore to ask the price. It had been scaled and gutted before I discovered it was sea-bass, much sought after and the most expensive fish in the market.

Back in the restaurant, the chef laid my offering reverently in a copper dish and admired it extravagantly. Nicholas, meanwhile, had gone in search of newsprint; he returned with a week-old edition of the *News of the World* and a copy of *L'Équipe*, his favourite sports newspaper.

Half an hour later the fish reappeared, head and tail still in place, the remainder neatly filleted but swathed in a thick grey blanket of Campbells mushroom soup, garnished with blobs of tomato purée, like a poorly infant with measles. With the fish came, unasked, a dish of exuberant yellow rice in which, just visible, were the roasted carcasses of small birds.

Nicholas poked at them doubtfully. 'I hope they're not what I think they might be.'

'Farmed quail,' I lied shamelessly, willing him to return to the results of the Tour de France in the hope that he wouldn't notice the collection of little bright-winged birds in full feather, bee-eaters among them, bunched in pretty little posies, hanging on a hook by the bar.

At this moment, the chef arrived. 'You like?' he enquired, beaming down at the tiny carcasses. 'I make for you express. Is special for this time of year. When birds come over the Bosphorus, we catch with nets like fish.'

The ex-diplomat who was my adviser on all things Ottoman had provided us with an introduction to the granddaughter of Atatürk's last prime minister. 'Her name is Ruya. You'll find her delightful, the last of the Ottoman princesses. Charming and very cultured. Speaks French, of course, and perfect English. She shops in Paris. She's married to a successful young banker – a golden couple.'

Between them, my sponsor continued, they were restoring the family's summer house, a beautiful old wooden *yali*, one of the trellised and balconied pavilions that line the water-front beyond the crowded wharfs of the city's harbour, on the Asian side of the water.

'Fortunately he has the money, and she certainly has the taste.'

I had made the telephone call as soon as we arrived at the Pera Palace.

The voice at the other end was young and confident. Her English had no trace of an accent. 'Of course you must visit. You will enjoy the *yali*. We will have dinner together. It will be a pleasure.'

We followed Ruya's directions across the bridge, threading our way past modern villas with high walls and wrought-iron gates through which could be seen tall trees and manicured flower-beds.

Halfway down the street, Ruya – as promised, a Turkish beauty in the kind of well-tailored patterned silks which are only found in one of the most expensive shops in Florence – was waiting for us. The entrance to the *yali* was marked by a pair of intricately carved wooden doors set into a high wall. 'Welcome. I see you found your way quite easily.' She swung the doors wide. 'You can leave the car in the drive.'

Chattering happily, she led us across a little formal garden towards a graceful wooden pavilion, double-storeyed, generously verandahed, canopied with lacy fretwork painted in pastel colours. Tumbling down the slender pillars that supported both the verandah and the roof were the dark, almond-shaped leaves and starry white blossoms of a climbing jasmine.

'Are you enjoying Istanbul? Of course you are. How could anyone not adore it? We have a saying—'

At this moment her husband, a tall blond young man in a tweed jacket and corduroy trousers which could only have been tailored in Savile Row, appeared, laughing and holding out his hand. 'You must forgive Ruya's enthusiasm. It's wonderful when friends from England come to visit – or friends of friends. I know Ruya is longing for a gossip. Please come in – forgive me if I lead the way.'

We followed our host up a wide wooden staircase, ornately carved and gilded, and through what, from the almost total absence of any furnishings, seemed to be a huge anteroom that led directly on to a wide balcony beneath which sparkled the waters of the Bosphorus.

On the balcony was a garden table with chairs, and a trolley with bottles and glasses. 'We have no live-in servants, and we have not yet finished the restoration. But I make a fine Martini – and I'm hoping you'll join me.'

We could think of nothing more delicious.

'Perfect. Then I shall mix the drinks and Ruya shall show you around. This is *her* family home, not mine; I just make it easier for us to live here.'

'Of course. If you're sure you really want to?' Indeed we did. More than anything in the world. 'I shall show you the rooms we have finished, although to Western eyes, you might not think so.'

In stark contrast to the outside appearance of rustic flamboyance – like a Russian *dacha* of the old Imperial days, or a showgirl who married a lord and retired to country – the simplicity of the interior seemed strangely modern. The ceilings were high, the windows uncurtained, the floors of pale, polished wood. Over the white walls, reflections from the water danced like dragonflies. The rooms led from one to another, each subtly different from the last.

Her face bright with pleasure, Ruya led us through each in turn, explaining the stories in the patterns of the carpets, the images stitched on the cushions – this one was made by a nomadic tribe who had fought a great battle, by another whose favourite daughter was the sultan's most beloved mistress. Everything seemed to have a tale to tell, as if the impersonality of the designs, the lack of human or animal images, made the stories they evoked an essential part of the pleasure. 'You must tell me if I'm boring you. I'm afraid I can be very passionate about my home. There used to be hundreds of these places, now there are so few. After the war – the First World War – there was no longer a need for them, and they reminded people of the old days. It's a terrible shame that most of them have already fallen down. If not, they soon will.' She sighed. 'But what can we do? This one we can save because it belongs to my family. But the others – who knows? Wooden walls need constant attention. We have water, we have wind, we have wars – what can you expect? It is only because my husband makes money that we can afford to restore it at all.'

The almost total absence of furniture or pictures on the walls made the rooms seem vast, like an abandoned film set, or an empty ballroom waiting for the dancers.

'I can tell you the restoration is absolutely accurate,' said Ruya. 'This is how we lived – with few possessions, like nomads. We valued only what we could carry. These carpets and cushions were all the furnishings we required.'

She flung open the final door. 'Except her. This was my grandmother's drawing room. She insisted on one room with proper chairs and tables, and this is the one we always use when we're alone.'

The contrast was startling. While the other rooms had a tranquillity entirely in keeping with the place, the drawing room seemed vulgar and overcrowded. On one wall, heavily framed in gilt, was a hand-tinted photograph of a moustachioed patriarch leaning towards the camera, cigarette dangling from the lower lip, fedora tipped rakishly over one eye.

Ruya smiled up at the portrait. 'That's my father. As you can see, he was a great admirer of Humphrey Bogart. We used to watch all his films over and over again. We knew them by heart – *Casablanca*, *The Maltese Falcon*, *The African Queen*. When the celluloid wore out he just ordered a new one.'

Two ornate sideboards stood on either side of the double doors which led to the verandah. The windows were draped in dark Victorian cut velvet. Back to back, in the centre of the room were a pair of button-backed upright sofas, four stiff little chairs and a mahogany table with incongruously fat legs like a seaside landlady. Smiling, Ruya laid her hand on the polished wood. 'Imported, of course. The whole lot arrived packed up in a box, like chocolates. They were a present to my grandfather from Queen Victoria. Her Imperial Majesty paid a state visit to Turkey when my grandfather was the king's first minister. She expressed a desire to take tea with my grandmother at the *yali*. I'm told she enjoyed her tea, but I think she found our Turkish habits a little primitive, so Her Imperial Majesty decided to take pity on us poor savages and send us some proper furniture.'

Ruya walked over to the double doors, which led to the verandah, and flung them wide open. The platform ran the full length of the *yali*. At the far end, Ilyun was putting the finishing touches to the Martinis. 'I hope by now my husband will have something a little more modern for us to enjoy. We must make the most of it. As you know, we are a Muslim country and women do not drink in public – at least, not in places where we are known.'

'And that, I'm afraid, is almost everywhere,' Ilyun added, smiling. 'My wife is very well known in the city – not only because of the family but because of what she has done for the *yalis*, bringing them to the attention of the government. We are raising money for the restoration of others.'

We sipped our drinks and watched the sun stain the water scarlet. Beneath us, steep terraces descended directly to the water. These, Ruya told us, could be viewed from the overhanging balcony, but were inaccessible from within. 'Because of the servants,' was her somewhat mysterious explanation.

The terraces were marble-edged, the beds planted with white-blossomed oleander, a drift of daisies, madonna lilies in clumps, orange trees in pots. A few slender trumpets of datura bent towards their own reflection in a mosaic-encrusted fountain – stylized shapes of fishes, butterflies and flowers.

'We are taking you out. I would like to have entertained you here, but the kitchen is not yet finished and I have nowhere to cook. But Ilyun has made a plan. He is a man, so what can you expect? We shall visit all my favourite places because that is how we Turks like to eat – something here, something there. You will see. It will be an adventure.'

We finished our Martinis and piled into Ilyun's gleaming Volvo.

'Much easier if we all travel together, like a caravan into the desert. First we are going to a little fishing village called Sariyer. Very small, very simple, but everyone goes there for the mussel fritters.'

The big car swung back across the bridge. 'Most of the eating places are on the European shore. There are twice as many people on the European side as on the Asian. It has always been so.'

Each little settlement, Ruya said, specialized in one thing.

126

This might be fresh figs in the proper season, or perhaps candied fruit. Or it might be something savoury – mackerel stuffed with pine kernels, or the promised mussel fritters. 'People will drive out from Istanbul just for one thing. And then they will move on to another.'

In Sariyer, alongside the line of moored fishing-boats, a queue had already formed by a line of frying vats. The mussels of the Bosphorus are fat, orange-fleshed, juicy as melons. Here they were dipped in batter to order, fried crisp, sold by weight, to be eaten wandering down the quay, or sitting on the sea wall. With them was offered a bowl of *tarator* – a pungent walnut and garlic sauce.

'You know how the mussel fishermen came by the recipe for the *tarator*?' asked Ruya as we chose a place on the wall, swinging our legs over the water and eating the mussels straight from the paper cone. 'You must listen while I tell you. The Turks have a tall tale for everything, but particularly for our favourite dishes. The story goes that it was a princess of Georgia who taught the palace cooks the secret. She was the sultan's favourite wife and the mother of many sons. She had golden hair, skin like a peach and eyes the colour of sapphires – but that's only to be expected of the sultan's favourite. There are many songs about her beauty, but even more about her cooking. She taught the secret of the sauce to her favourite serving-girl, a young woman from this village, and the people have followed her recipe to this day.'

Ruya pushed herself off the sea wall, and leaned over to exchange greetings with an old man shucking mussels on the deck of a fishing-boat bobbing at anchor below.

'You must come back tomorrow. The old man says tomorrow the fish will run.'

Nicholas woke up. 'What fish?'

'The tuna, of course – the famous migration. Have you not heard of it? It's the most exciting thing you have ever seen – like a big black thundercloud, the water dark and churning and all the people wading in up to their armpits. When they know the fish are running, the people go crazy. They bring baskets, buckets, anything that comes to hand. The fish is for everyone, the excitement is the same for everyone – the rich and the poor,

Turkish Midye Tarator
MUSSEL FRITTERS WITH WALNUT SAUCE

The mussels dredged from the Bosphorus are the size and colour of baby tangerines – succulent and delicious. I have included a spoonful of roughage in the batter: our fine-sifted modern flours are far too smooth. The walnut sauce is the traditional accompaniment – very pungent, but delicious.

─────────── SERVES 4 AS A STARTER ───────────

24 mussels (more if they're small), shucked	$^{1}/_{2}$ pint / 300 ml beer
4 oz / 100 g strong bread flour	1 tablespoon olive oil
1 teaspoon salt	oil for deep frying
1 tablespoon semolina or finely ground polenta	

─────────── SAUCE ───────────

6 garlic cloves, skinned	$^{1}/_{2}$ pint / 300 ml olive oil
1 teaspoon salt	2 tablespoons hot water
4 oz / 100 g walnuts	juice of 2 lemons
1 slice bread, torn into small pieces	

1. Pick over the mussels and remove any grit. Sieve the flour into a bowl with the salt and semolina or polenta. Beat in enough beer to give you a smooth batter about the consistency of pouring cream and add the oil – or drop everything in the liquidizer and give it a good whizz. Let it rest for half an hour.

2. Meanwhile make the tarator sauce. Pound the garlic cloves with the salt with a pestle and mortar. When you've achieved a smooth paste, add the walnuts and pound some more. Soak the bread in the water and squeeze dry, then stir it into the garlic mixture. Gradually trickle in the oil, adding the lemon juice to taste, as if making a mayonnaise, beating vigorously. Dilute with hot water. The result should be a thick paste which can be used as a dip as well as a sauce. The whole job can be done most effectively in a blender.

3. Heat the oil till you can see a faint blue haze rising. Dip each mussel in the batter and deep-fry – not too many at a time. Drain on kitchen paper. Serve piping hot, accompanied by the sauce.

the shopkeepers, the housewives. Even Ilyun, he too will be there.'

Ilyun laughed. 'Beggars, bankers – even Ottoman princesses!'

Ruya's eyes gleamed. 'Yes, of course. Every year since I was a child, unless I am abroad, I never miss it. My grandfather once told me that when *he* was a child there were so many fish so tightly packed together you could walk on their backs right across the straits and not once would your toes dip in the water.' She shook her head, her face thoughtful. 'My grandfather used to tell me many such stories, some of them true, some of them – how shall I put it? – fanciful. But not *not* true. True or false, it was the listener's business to choose. Typically Turkish – and why not? Scheherazade was one of ours. We're story-tellers, it's in our blood.' She laid her hand on my arm. 'That, too, you must learn since you wish to write about these things. People will always tell tales. This is not because they wish to lie. Good manners require you to be told what they think you want to hear. It's a courtesy, a way of acknowledging that your truth is as true as theirs. You want to learn how Turkish peasants eat? In Turkey all our peasants are poor. The answers that poor people give will show not what is the truth, but the truth of what the people want you to believe.'

There was no need for me to question this. In Spain, living among peasant farmers who depended on their own labours to fill the store-cupboard, I realized that my neighbours had one set of answers for the look of the thing, another for the reality. I soon learned to phrase my questions to take account of the sensitivities of others. Among peasant communities money is a crop like any other, useful but not indispensable. An excess of crops that can be exchanged for cash provides proof of good husbandry. Shop-bought goods are valued for this reason. Ready-sliced white bread, tinned milk, imported coffee are luxuries to be offered to a guest: the purpose is to display wealth, to deliver a message that the household is well fed and therefore well able to defend its own. Famine is always a disgrace: no one wants to admit to empty store-cupboards. Answers to questions about everyday diet are always embellished.

I smiled. 'I understand exactly what you mean. Myths are made that way.'

Meanwhile, Nicholas, a fisherman himself, wanted to know more about the tuna migration. Perhaps that, too, he enquired, was one of Ruya's myths?

Ruya laughed. 'The migration is real enough. I have seen it many times, though I cannot speak for the truth of my grandfather's tales. But when? When will they come? The old fisherman says tomorrow, but only because he understands I am anxious for you to see it. Next day, next week, next month the fish will come. They go up to breed in the Sea of Marmora, but they always return. The Golden Horn is a cornucopia, and that's why it has its name. People will tell you romantic stories of sunlight falling on golden stones, of sunken treasure ships. They will fill your ears with tales of Byzantine gold – they know that foreigners tip well for fantasies, poorly for the truth. But the truth is that people need to eat. Only a fool would value a piece of gold more highly than a fish.' She teased her banker husband. 'Is it not so, Ilyun?'

'Anything you say, Princess.'

Ruya touched his cheek. 'You see what an amiable husband I have found myself? Well, if it is indeed to be anything I say, we've a busy night ahead.'

As the sun dipped over the Galata bridge, we paused by the roadside for sweetcorn roasted over an oil-drum, and drew to a halt in the shade of a tree where a young woman with kohl-rimmed eyes presided over baskets of figs arranged in perfect cartwheels on their own dark leaves, the purple skin slashed with scarlet. As we moved from one little café table to another, Ruya entertained us – a responsibility, she explained, that was part of her duties as a hostess.

'I learned to tell stories from my grandfather. It is a tradition among our people, so you really have no choice. But you must eat while I tell my tale. The food is good, so you mustn't waste it. I shall tell you the story of the sultan's mule. Ilyun will forgive me since he has heard it many times, but you have not. And if you listen with your heart as well as your head, my tale will tell you more about my people than you will ever learn from books.'

Each time we halted, she loaded our plates, picking out the tenderest cubes of meat, the most succulent morsel of fish. And every time she returned to her storytelling.

'A mule, as you may know, is a eunuch, the product of the union of a horse and a donkey. He is a useful beast, but can bear no issue. At the beginning of my tale, the sultan had a muleteer who had an understanding with a particularly fine mule, the strongest beast in the stable. The muleteer had a beautiful wife, too, but he was often away on the sultan's business. And, like all beautiful wives who are left alone, his wife was unfaithful.'

The tale-telling stopped − delivered in spoonfuls, like sugar.

'The muleteer came back from the sultan's business, and found his wife in bed with her lover. He was very angry. He was so angry he used his strong right hand to strangle his wife and her lover to death. The murders had been seen by many people. The muleteer could not deny what he had done. He was brought in front of the sultan for judgement. The punishment for murder is the forfeit of whatever is used to do the deed. In this case, the muleteer's right hand.'

We moved on, but when we halted again, Ruya returned to her story.

'The muleteer refused to accept the sultan's judgement. He was a good muleteer, he had served his master well. The sultan had no desire to lose him. Knowing this, the muleteer proposed a pact: "Master," he said. "If I lose my right hand I could no longer serve the sultan as I would wish. The mule would not obey my orders and the sultan would lose not only his most faithful servant but his strongest beast of burden. Let a year pass before you deliver judgement. In that year, if the mule has had a foal, you must let me go free. If the mule remains without issue, you may cut off my head."

'Intrigued by what he thought must be a riddle, the sultan agreed. Later, in private, he sought out the muleteer: "What is the meaning of the riddle? How can a mule have a foal? Why should you want me to cut off your head?" But the muleteer just bowed his head and would not speak.

'The year passed. On the last day, the sultan called the muleteer to his presence. "Foolish man. If you cannot tell me the meaning of the riddle, I must cut off your head." The muleteer bowed his head once more but still he would not speak. The crowd began to laugh. "Off with his head!" cried the sultan, who was not a man who liked to be made to look foolish. All was made ready, the executioner summoned, the people called to witness the sultan's justice. As the sultan's executioner raised his scimitar over the muleteer's bowed head, the sultan himself appeared on the palace balcony. "Tell me the meaning of the riddle, muleteer!" the sultan called out over the heads of the crowd. "And I will pardon you!"

'This time the muleteer raised his head and looked his master in the eye. "The meaning is this, my master. When the year began, I had only one choice. At the end of the year, I had three."

' "And what are those three choices?"

' "The choices are these. At the end of the year, the sultan might be dead, I might be dead – or the mule might have had a foal." On hearing this, the sultan laughed so much he fell right down and died.'

'And the muleteer?' asked Nicholas.

Ruya smiled at him. 'What do you expect? The muleteer went free. Next time he took to himself a faithful wife who gave him a beautiful daughter and the beautiful daughter – but that's another story. You must understand there's no morality to our tales, no beginning and no end. They fit one inside another, like Russian dolls.'

Midnight found us serenaded by gypsies and nibbling *dolmades* – vine leaves stuffed with rice and raisins, exquisitely spiced.

Later, much later, Ruya led us to the pastry shop for pistachio *kataifa*, tiny rolls of shredded pastry soaked in honey. Last of all, as the soft light of dawn flooded the east, our hostess chose a table by the quayside for ices, a sip of black coffee scented with cardamom, rose-perfumed liquor, lemon-scented sherbet, sugar-dusted *loukum*.

And all the while, like Scheherazade she told of the splendours of the Topkapi while it was still a sultan's palace, the magnificence of the processions, the silks, the damasks, the jewels, the beauty of the women of the seraglio, the deviousness of eunuchs, the power wielded by mothers over sons.

And then, as our host and hostess had always intended, we took our ease on the balcony of the palace by the Bosphorus and watched the sun rise over the Golden Horn.

Next day, we were on the road again. We never had a chance to see the tuna migrate – perhaps we never would. Or perhaps one day we might return to watch the waters churn and hear the fishermen rejoice as the nets are filled with fish. Who knows?

And that, as the last of the Ottoman princesses would have it, is just as it should be. Another story for another day.

CHAPTER FIVE

Of Cabbages and Kings

> They are a fine people with a PASSION for freedom: so great
> that it made them able to remain 500 years under the Turk
> and come out pure Bulgar at the end.
>
> FREYA STARK, *The Coasts of Incense* (1953)

THE BULGARIANS HAVE A PARTICULAR REASON TO DISLIKE THE
Turks. Like parents whose child reminds them of their own
shortcomings, they come from the same stock. Whereas the
Turks' relationship with the Greeks was an uneasy truce, in
Bulgaria five hundred years of Turkish suppression has left scars
too deep to heal.

The border guards on the Turkish side waved us through
without comment. Those on the Bulgarian side expressed their
dislike in not only the time but the displacement imposed on
those attempting to pass the barriers. In two shakes of a Turk's
fez, the entire contents of our boot was spread on the inspection

counters, a line of rickety tables presided over by a ramshackle army of semi-uniformed officers.

Had my sketchbooks not been removed for examination along with the passports, into which I had remembered to tuck the necessary note, the scene would have provided good material for my brush. There were crates of live poultry, sacks of cabbages, packets of spices and coffee, carpets and copper pans and household goods – the detritus of that temporary migration that occurs across all those borders where goods and services are more available on one side than the other.

The highway that led to the border from Istanbul was like an extended market-place. At regular intervals there were corrugated-iron shacks advertising the sale of snacks and soft drinks, fronted by tables set out with backgammon boards. Alongside were kiosks selling vegetables, meat, lead-glazed cooking pots with reversible domed lids for cooking over coals, brass trays, copper kettles and the highly decorated glasses used for *chai*. Veiled women squatted beside bundles of green leaves – mint, parsley, dill.

The route was hazardous not only because of the mule-carts, donkeys, goats, women with bundles on their heads, but also because of the gaggles of ragged children who rushed towards speeding vehicles, holding up strings of chilli, plaits of onions, white discs of home-made cheese. One small girl had positioned herself in the middle of the road with a wicker cage as large as herself in which were red-and-yellow fig-peckers – the only small birds likely to survive the hunters' snares since, like Scheherazade, their song protects their lives.

Absorbing all of this, I settled down to wait, frontiers being my business, while Nicholas strode off as usual to join the action in the lorry-park, returning at intervals to report on his discoveries.

'There's a bunch of Turks just back from Kiev. They say there's nothing to eat in the Communist countries. They have to take all their own food and cook it themselves. They told me if you wander through the lorry-park with a spoon in your pocket, you'll get something to eat.'

He rummaged in the glove compartment, emerged with an olive-draining spoon I'd bought in Thessalonica. This he tucked into his breast pocket. 'I'm going to see if it works.'

I pointed out that the spoon – wooden and perforated – was unsuitable for any other purpose but that for which it was designed.

'It's the thought that counts.'

I watched him vanish among the juggernauts.

A few minutes later, a man in a shiny blue suit appeared from the concrete bunker that housed the customs officers. In mounting panic, I watched him striding purposefully in my direction. In such a situation, there was only one thing a man in a shiny blue suit could be: a secret policeman. At best I might expect a spell in jail. At worst – well, Bulgaria's security services had just disposed of one of their own defectors on the streets of London in broad daylight with a poisoned umbrella.

The secret policeman was carrying my sketchbooks. These he laid on the table with the utmost delicacy, as though the pages might suddenly detonate, spraying bits of body all over his blue suit and requiring the filling in of endless forms.

He flicked slowly through the pages, studying each in turn. A stubby finger jabbed downwards. The moving finger had stopped at the little watercolour of the Roman bridge we had passed before we encountered Aristotle and the donkeys. 'Military installation. Why you make picture of military installation?'

'It's not installation. It's Roman. A bridge built by the Romans.'

'Romania? Why you make picture of Romania military installation?'

'*Roman*, not Romanian. The Romans built bridges. Very old, built very long time ago . . .' I windmilled my hands in what I hoped was the international gesture for way-back-when, but could just as easily be something insulting involving other people's ancestors.

'Julius Caesar. Alexander the Great—'

'Ah!' The dark face brightened. 'Alessandro. I know Alessandro very well. Alessandro hero of Bulgar people.'

I nodded eagerly. 'Good man, Alessandro. This,' I pointed helpfully to the sketch, 'is Alessandro's bridge.'

136

The suited one frowned. 'Alessandro make *military* bridge. Alessandro *military* man. Kill many, many Turks. I salute Alessandro. I kiss his feet.' His face lit up. 'Battle of the Shipka Pass, eighteen seventy-seven, very great Bulgarian victory. Kill many, many Turks.' He drew a finger across his throat. 'Turks *kaputt*.'

He paused. The sketch came under fresh inspection, this time the stubby finger almost caressed the page.

I had an idea. I tore the sketch out of the book and held it up. 'Take it. I make you a present.'

Alexander's fan-club raised his eyebrows enquiringly. Seemingly, 'present' was not a word which featured in his vocabulary.

'*Baksheesh*,' I offered suddenly, surprised at myself. The word had popped into my head, but I had no idea if it might be insulting.

'*Baksheesh?*'

'Yes – for you.' I smiled ingratiatingly and pushed the sketch towards him. With the closest thing a Bulgarian plain-clothes policeman can manage to a smile, the little sketch vanished among the bulges in the blue suit.

The Iron Curtain had lifted. Bulgaria beckoned.

The Bulgarians have no time for trade, still less for the social interaction that accompanies the selling. Although the Turks occupy every inch of roadside with commercial activity, here were neither stalls nor pedlars nor players of board games.

In their place, every inch of terrain had been turned to productivity. The roundabouts had been planted with maize. It being the last crop of the year, the plants were ten feet tall and ready for harvesting. Down the verges were lines of cauliflowers, fattened on the exhaust fumes of the juggernauts trundling down the road to Russia. Just by the frontier post we stopped at a trucker's pull-in for a meal. All the dishes were vegetarian – spinach cakes, salads of green peppers, potatoes and tomatoes stewed with onion.

As evening drew down, the cultivation vanished into the darkness. Bulgaria generates her own hydro-electricity, but Mother Russia had sucked her dry. Domestic power was only

Bulgarian Kyufteta ot Spanak
SPINACH CAKES

A useful little recipe that can be adapted for chard, greens, cabbage or cauliflower. The breadcrumbs can be replaced with mashed potato.

————————————— SERVES 4 —————————————

1 lb/500 g spinach, or *any other*
  leafy greens, shredded
1 teaspoon salt
1 large or *2 small eggs, beaten*
2 tablespoons toasted breadcrumbs

1 oz/25 g hard cheese (mature
  Cheddar or *Gruyère), diced small*
1/2 teaspoon chilli pepper
oil for frying

————————————— TO SERVE —————————————

yoghurt

garlic, crushed

1. Cook the shredded greens in a lidded pan in the water that clings to the leaves after rinsing. Drain well, squeezing out the excess water – use your hands. Chop finely.

2. In a bowl, mix the spinach with the salt, eggs, breadcrumbs, diced cheese and chilli. Divide the mixture into 8 mounds, roll each into a ball (wet hands make the task easier) and flatten into little patties.

3. Fry over a moderate heat in oil (maybe a little butter for the flavour) until browned on both sides. Drain on kitchen paper and serve with a dipping sauce of yoghurt into which you have stirred a little crushed garlic.

Bulgarian Salata ot Piperki

GREEN PEPPER SALAD

This simple salad makes a fine first course. For an ethnically mixed plateful, team it with *Serbian ajvar* (see page 60) and a salad of grated carrots dressed with pumpkin oil and lightly toasted pumpkin seeds.

———————————————— SERVES 4 ————————————————

1 lb/500 g green peppers
2 tablespoons finely chopped parsley
2 garlic cloves, peeled and finely chopped

2 tablespoons wine vinegar
4 tablespoons olive or walnut oil
sugar, salt and pepper

1. Preheat the oven to 350°F/180°C/mark 4. Roast the peppers whole until soft – 30–40 minutes will do the trick (most economical to do while you have something else in the oven).
2. Hull, halve, seed and remove any easily detachable skin from the peppers. Cut them lengthwise into ribbons and dress with parsley.
3. Mix the remaining ingredients together thoroughly and pour over the peppers. Toss before serving.

available for certain hours of the day, and these did not include those of darkness. At night in rural areas, the authorities simply turned off all the lights.

The night was dense and dark, and we were obliged to navigate by a map printed before the Second World War. We headed for Plovdiv, capital of eastern Bulgaria, where we might find somewhere to spend the night. An hour passed, and then another. An increase in crossroads and the presence of a few parked vehicles indicated we were in a built-up area. Nicholas climbed out with a torch to inspect the signs. All the street names were in Cyrillic script. We crawled round in the silence, looking for lights, action, people – anything that might indicate this was the land of the living.

The moon appeared in a gap in the cloud-cover. The outline of a large building became visible against the sky. As we drew nearer, lights glimmered behind drawn blinds.

Plovdiv, it seemed, was blessed with a people's palace, a conference centre where the Soviet masters gathered to do what business there was to be done, and took their leisure in whatever way they could. Bulgaria had two things to recommend it to the Russians: fruit brandy and slender young girls with dark eyes and an urge to better themselves with fur coats and Russian roubles.

We parked in the forecourt and made our way up a grand flight of steps. In the dimly lit foyer, a female figure, who may once have been a slender young girl but was now a beetle-browed matron, her ample frame improbably embedded in a steel-and-plastic chair of surprising modernity, was crocheting an absurdly dainty scrap of lace.

'Do you have a room? *Haben Sie Zimmer?*' enquired the bilingual Nicholas, enunciating carefully in the manner of all educated Englishmen everywhere.

The guardian of what was probably the only accommodation available in Plovdiv at this late hour wound the white thread back on to its reel, tucked the lace into the pocket of her apron, and finally raised her eyes to inspect us, but without interest. This chore accomplished, she produced a key from a chain round her neck, waddled slowly across the foyer towards the reception desk, also in modern steel and plastic, and unlocked a drawer. From it she took out a printed notice encased in yellowing plastic and held it up, turning it from side to side for our inspection.

One side was in Cyrillic script, the other in various European languages, including English. The notice read, 'People's Socialist Republic of Bulgaria Welcomes Foreign Guests to International Trade Fair. All Prices Doubled. Room with Bath $100 per Night. Breakfast Not Included.'

Nicholas nodded. 'We'll take it.'

She pushed a form towards us, following it, after a moment's thought, with a stub of pencil. She pointed at two words. Passport. Signature.

We signed. We handed over the precious passports. A crooked finger indicated we should follow. Finding a torch in the same murky depths that had delivered the pencil, our guide led us up several flights of unlit stairs and down a labyrinth of corridors. The hotel was vast and impersonal, like an ocean liner. The room was tiny, with two prim little beds, clean sheets, plastic-coated chairs, and a bathroom with a shower.

Up to the moment when she received a five-dollar tip, our guide had not spoken a single word – in fact, I had begun to think her silence was because she could not speak.

The money had an astonishing effect, producing a sudden flood of information in strongly accented German. The hotel dining room was closed, but there was a party in the town, and we – undoubtedly distinguished foreign visitors – would most certainly be welcome. A taxi might be summoned. She would see to it immediately.

When we found our way back to the foyer, our transport, an elderly Lada, awaited us.

The centre of Plovdiv, the Kapana district – the part of the old town that successive waves of invaders had left standing – was visible in short bursts in the vehicle's headlights. We bumped slowly down cobbled streets under overhanging balconies. On either side, tall thin houses with flaking plaster leaned one against the other like sailors after shore leave. The buildings were half timbered in the Macedonian style, the ironwork painted ox-blood red. Through the small windowpanes candlelit interiors could be seen, like the set from some expensive production of a costume drama, *Tamburlaine*, perhaps, or a dramatization of one of Balzac's novels.

The taxi-driver deposited us beside an alleyway. Through the tunnel of the entrance we could see a wide, well-lit courtyard. One side was formed by a three-tiered restaurant of which only the upper tier, magnificently roofed with tiles, was enclosed.

We walked through. Long, damask-covered tables were crowded with diners – no doubt delegates to the conference, portly bellies bulging from beneath badly tailored grey suits. Dinner was already half-way through. Young men and girls in smart black and white uniforms raced around with bowls of meat set in flaming saucers. On a wooden stage, raised above the tables, a small group of brightly costumed musicians were tuning their instruments: violin, accordion, and an assembly of oddly shaped wind instruments. They began to play gypsy tunes – the kind best heard by firelight, in places where owls call at twilight and wolves howl under the moon.

We found a table just beneath the stage. There was no need to order from a menu, no need to explain our presence. It was as if we were guests at the wedding of strangers, passers-by for whom good manners, or fear of the wrath of the gods, dictated we must be made welcome. Dishes of stuffed marrow came, followed by the bowls of stewed meat, *kapama*, dark and rich, scented with garlic and wine, which closer inspection revealed to have been set in saucers filled with flaming alcohol. The purpose of these rings of fire remained a mystery. Perhaps they were purely decorative, or a practical device to keep the food hot, or simply to suggest the flavour of the fire. Whatever the reason, the evening air being chill, the flames were comforting.

The music started up. Down the stairway came a troupe of young women, blonde and pigtailed with pretty, painted faces like Russian dolls. All were dressed in velvet boleros laced tightly over white blouses, with brightly coloured voluminous skirts tied with flower-embroidered black satin aprons. They linked arms and formed a circle. Young men with soft blue-black hair and thick moustaches, all in a uniform of black breeches and full-sleeved white shirts, took up positions as if interested observers. The girls linked arms, the dance began.

Bulgarian Kapama
LAMB AND ONION STEW

A gently stewed dish of lamb perfumed with onions and mushrooms. For a touch of drama, serve in small earthenware bowls set in saucers of flaming brandy. Rye bread and boiled potatoes accompany.

———————————— SERVES 4–5 ————————————

2 lb/1 kg boneless lamb, diced
8 oz/250 g mushrooms, sliced
2 tablespoons oil
1 lb/500 g mature onions,
  sliced vertically

6 spring onions, sliced with their
  green tops
3 garlic cloves, finely chopped
$^1/_2$ pint/300 ml boiling water
salt and pepper

———————————— TO FINISH ————————————

2 tablespoons mint or dill, finely chopped

1. Trim the meat. Fry the mushrooms in a little of the trimmed fat in a casserole. Add the oil, sliced onion and meat, and fry until lightly browned. Add water and season. Bring to the boil, turn down the heat and lid tightly.

2. Stew gently on top of the stove or in a moderate oven, 325° F/ 170° C/mark 3 for a couple of hours, until the onions have melted into a shiny little sauce and the meat is soft. Taste and add more salt if you need it, then stir in the spring onions, chopped garlic and plenty of fresh black pepper. Add the mint or dill right at the end of the cooking.

Bulgarian Tikvichi Pecheni
STUFFED MARROW WITH YOGHURT AND HERBS

The marrow is the perfect background for the flavour of the herbs, and the yoghurt-and-egg baked custard provides a delicate sauce.

———————————— SERVES 4 ————————————

1 whole young marrow	2 egg yolks
1 tablespoon wine vinegar	1/2 pint/300 ml thick yoghurt
1 oz/25 g butter	1 teaspoon flour
1 tablespoon marjoram, chopped	1/2 teaspoon ground nutmeg
1 tablespoon dill, chopped	salt and pepper
1 tablespoon chives, chopped	2 tablespoons cheese, grated
1 tablespoon mint, chopped	

1. Preheat the oven to 450°F/230°C/mark 8.
2. Peel the marrow, quarter it lengthways, remove the cotton woolly centre with the seeds, and cut the flesh into bite-sized chunks. Put them in a saucepan with 3–4 tablespoons of water, the vinegar and the butter. Lid tightly and cook on a high heat, shaking so that the pieces don't stick, for 4–5 minutes, until the marrow is tender. Remove the lid and boil fiercely for a moment or two to evaporate any extra liquid, sprinkle with the herbs and turn to coat.
3. Whisk the egg yolks with the yoghurt and flour, seasoning with nutmeg and plenty of salt and pepper. Arrange the marrow pieces in a gratin dish then pour over the yoghurt custard. Sprinkle with grated cheese and bake for 15–20 minutes, until brown and bubbling.

Feet flashed while bodies were held rigid. The ribbon-plaited pigtails bounced like tiny semaphores.

The Russians moved on to the fruit brandy, cheered loudly, yelled raucously and began to thump the tables with their shoes.

It was time to leave. We did so as anonymously as we had arrived, before the young men by the stage felt the need to defend their women's honour.

The following morning, we headed north.

The eastern provinces of Bulgaria, being most distant from the capital, were of most interest to me.

Along the way, I had work to do. Much could be learned from the landscape, still more from peering into backyards, looking for bakeries and inspecting the shelves of grocery stores.

The state-owned supermarkets were dismal. Half-empty shelves were stacked with unwanted goods: herring in jars with German labels, faded blue packets of macaroni made in a factory in Sofiya, rusting tins of tomatoes, pickled cucumbers in smeared jars, cracked plastic tubs of marrow jam. The refrigerated cabinets had been unplugged and served as display counters for slabs of bright orange processed cheese, tubes of pink luncheon meat encased in plastic, tubs of yellow maize-margarine and white lard.

At first light – the days were shortening rapidly – a fleet of ancient buses cruised slowly down the highway, collecting workers from the verges. During the remainder of the day, the countryside appeared empty of all life, whether furred, feathered or human.

All able-bodied persons, men and women, went to work in the factories that ringed the towns, leaving only the old people and young children in the villages. Occasionally, in the distance, an elderly tractor could be seen dragging across the furrow, gulls screaming in its wake. All land in common ownership had been given over to the cultivation of commercial crops that required processing: sugar beet, sorghum, clover for cattle-fodder.

We went hungry at midday. As the Turkish lorry-drivers had warned us, there were no roadside restaurants to cater to passing travellers, presumably because these were so few. At the border we had exchanged dollars for meal vouchers and petrol coupons. These proved impossible to negotiate. Hard cash delivered fuel, but there were no cafés or lorry-drivers' pull-ins where the vouchers could be used.

The markets delivered no better fortune. Although it was autumn, a time when people might hope to fill their winter store-cupboards, nothing could be purchased without a ration book. Even bread was unobtainable without coupons. We took to scavenging rolls from the breakfast provided by our evening's lodgings, and ate them with slivers of dried beef I had bought in the souk in Istanbul – a purchase made out of curiosity, not with any thought of providence. By the third day, the meat was running low and we were longing for a fresh tomato, an onion, a cucumber – anything to relieve the monotony.

The journals of my intrepid Victorian lady travellers spoke of lush pastures in which milk-sheep grazed, of orchards with laden branches busy with the hum of honey-bees, of chestnut forests trampled by great herds of fat swine, of fields golden with corn. Driving through this abandoned countryside, it was as if these stories were fantasies, the meanderings of a romantic mind. What the sybaritic Ottomans would never have wished on their colonials for fear they themselves might suffer, the state had achieved at a stroke. Bulgaria, celebrated under the Turks for the fecundity of its soil, the diversity of its crops, the excellence of its market-gardens, had sunk into the apathy induced by state monopoly.

As we had noticed on the motorway from the border, only those small patches of ground which, for one reason or another, might be considered unsuitable for cultivation were well worked. The produce from these little plots did not appear to be available to any but the growers. There were no roadside salesmen, no sign of any gatherings of rural housewives round the back of the produce van. In the central squares of the towns, there would sometimes be a few stalls selling turnips, potatoes, parsnips, the overage from the state farms, but most were given over to dismal piles of factory seconds and cheap household implements. One or two had a few handfuls of tomatoes and other salad vegetables, but all attempts at purchase – even dollar bills – were met with blank stares and shakes of the head. Unless, suggested a smooth young man with slicked-back hair and dark glasses – who had somehow managed to evade the factory floor – we had music cassettes for barter. The Beatles, the Rolling Stones, the Monkees – he wasn't particular. We offered him a choice of Carly Simon or Nicholas's African birdsong tapes. He chose the former, offering in return a jar of pickled vegetables. We accepted gratefully.

Late on the fourth afternoon, before sunset, we had no desire for any more nocturnal wanderings, we reached Veliko Turnovo, Bulgaria's ancient capital.

The suburbs were a thick tangle of prefabricated factory buildings and goods-yards interspersed with blank-eyed blocks of state housing. Signs to the centre led us into a vast open space, entirely featureless, as if someone had dropped a huge concrete pocket handkerchief on a hillside and then forgotten to collect it. Set on a terrace overlooking this dismal architectural feature, a line of neo-brutalist buildings. The lack of advertising made it hard to identify which might be shops, which a town hall, or which might offer shelter to the weary traveller.

We parked on the edge of the concrete hankie and inspected the buildings discreetly on foot. One was indeed a hotel. We booked in. I shall skip lightly over the accommodation – at least there was a washstand, the double bed was large enough for two adults, and the communal lavatory facility was only two doors down the corridor.

As every evening, we were famished. We were encouraged to find that the concierge was not the usual crocheting dragon but a smartly dressed young woman with excellent French.

We explained we were in search of a neighbourhood restaurant, nothing grand, just somewhere we might be able to appreciate what had so far been unavailable to travellers: the dishes Bulgarians liked to cook for themselves.

The young woman looked doubtful. There was a pizza parlour in the hotel. What did we have in mind?

Something more . . . *Bulgarian.*

She considered this thoughtfully. Then her face lightened. '*Mais oui.*' There was indeed such a restaurant in Veliko Turnovo. It was newly opened and offered a *menu touristique.* She herself hadn't eaten there, nor had any of her friends. When they had any money to spare, which was not very often since the state paid poorly, they liked to eat pizza and pasta – anything but the food they got at home. The day-shift concierge had told her that the restaurant was popular with Russian visitors who had plenty of roubles. It was not far. We could reach it on foot. She drew us a map and accompanied us to the door to set us on our way.

Meanwhile the central square was no longer deserted but packed with people. They did not seem to be involved in any business, but were standing around in groups, forming and re-forming.

What were they doing? Nicholas enquired of our young informant.

Waiting for transport, she explained, with a shrug. Waiting for transport was the national pastime. She herself worked in a shoe factory by day. Since her own village was twenty miles away, it could take her until midnight to make her way home. For this reason she did the night shift at the hotel – at least she could be sure of a few hours' sleep.

'*Vous comprenez?* It's not the money but the convenience. I have a chance to practise my French and learn a little of the outside world.' She smiled. 'And, then, sometimes the guests are generous, and I am saving up to be married.'

The restaurant was housed in a building of similar elegance to the one in Plovdiv – almost its twin – but there the resemblance ended. On the ground floor a single long table was occupied by a party of grey-suited businessmen – they might well have been the Russian delegates from Plovdiv. A waiter fielded our attempts to occupy one of several empty tables, pointing upwards to the first-floor balcony.

One table was free. We settled down unopposed, and waited for service. The table offered a grandstand view of the gastronomic activity below. A flock of waiters and waitresses fluttered back and forth carrying loaded trays and generously piled plates. Half an hour later, we had still received no attention from the single elderly waiter on our floor.

At the tables all around us, our neighbours received little dishes of pickled vegetables, plastic baskets of thick-cut yellow bread, plates of rice, pork chops, bowls of some kind of red sauce.

In the well below, the privileged ones were tucking into chicken. Herb-scented steam rose into the sterile air of our unproductive corner, arousing my professional interest.

'Marjoram and garlic,' I announced.

'Don't count on it,' said Nicholas bleakly. He succeeded in buttonholing the waiter. We acquired a menu. The list of possible dishes was very long and almost totally mysterious.

'Let's ask.'

We looked around for the waiter. He was nowhere to be seen. Meanwhile, the party below was just beginning to relax. Bottles of wine that had arrived full had been removed empty. Jackets had been slung over chairs, shirts rolled up to the elbows. The noise level had increased in direct proportion to the bottles.

'Please?'

The voice was that of a solitary diner, a corpulent gentleman, with a gold chain looped across his waistcoat and a hearty appetite, whose progress through the menu we had already observed. Now he folded his napkin carefully, placed it on his table and rose to join us.

'May I perhaps join you for a moment? I speak a little English – perhaps I can assist. These people,' he waved his hand at the diners below, 'these people are Russian.'

We admitted we thought that might be the case.

'Russians eat all the food. The waiter, he is ashamed to tell you there is nothing to eat.'

'*Nothing?*'

Our new companion shrugged. 'There is pork chops. There is always pork chops. If you wish to eat pork chops, I will tell the waiter.'

'Pork chops would be fine – really they would.' At that moment, almost anything would have been fine.

As if by magic the food appeared. Plates, cutlery, bread and an unexplained dish of tomato paste mixed with chilli were set on the table. We ate the bread dipped in the tomato. This gastronomic treat was swiftly followed by two plates of pork chops with matching dollops of reconstituted dried mashed potato. However terrible, at least it was edible.

Our new friend nodded approval as we wiped the plates clean.

'Good. These people will be pleased. You see how it is. These people are proud. They have ancient tradition of hospitality. They are ashamed because they have not enough food for foreign guests.'

I digested this information with some gloom. 'You are Bulgarian yourself?'

He shook his head indignantly. He was, he explained, from East Germany, a tractor salesman from Lübeck.

'You know what is Lübeck? Is Hansa. Is Hanseatic League. You know what is? Is very important merchants, is controlling the fur trade, the gold trade, many many trades. Not now. Now is tractors and machinery. But long ago, very long time ago, is very rich people. Eat caviare all the time.'

We were silent while we contemplated the possibility of eating caviare. Below, the Russians were eating pancakes stuffed with jam.

'You do not mind I sit with you a little time? Good. Now we must drink. To friendship. To caviare. To Helga, my wife. To you, my English friends.' The tractor salesman snapped his fingers. A bottle appeared. He poured out three measures of a clear liquid and raised his glance. 'We drink, my friends, to friendship between German and English people.'

We raised our glasses and drank. From below came the sounds of breaking glass. The Russians had moved on to the slivovic.

The tractor salesman leaned over the balcony, withdrawing his head with a scowl. 'Fucking no-good Russians,' he announced with the passionate conviction of a man who knows a fucking no-good Russian. He warmed to his theme. 'Fucking Russians no good. No good fucking Russians.'

He paused for breath. 'You want to know something, English friends?' He reached under the table and lifted up his bulging attaché case. 'What you think I got in here, my English friends?' he enquired in an aggrieved voice. 'I know what you are thinking. You are thinking I got tractor business in here.' He shook his head vigorously. '*Nein. Nicht* tractor business.

150

Cabbages. I got cabbages.' A theatrical pause. '*Beautiful* cabbages. I guard them with my life.'

'Cabbages? With your life?'

'*Ja.*' He nodded vigorously. 'You are thinking the man is mad.'

'Not at all,' I said soothingly. 'I'm sure you have very good reason.'

Nevertheless, since there were cabbages growing in profusion all down the motorway, they hardly seemed so valuable a crop as to require such extreme measures of protection.

'Still you do not understand. I must explain what I mean. *Meine Frau* Helga is from Stuttgart. Helga, she says, "Hansi" – this is my name – "when you come to Bulgaria, bring me cabbages. Do not bring me gold, but bring me back beautiful cabbages to make the sauerkraut." ' He stared at us. 'Ha! Now you understand?' He shook his head. 'My wife say, "Hansi, we have two sons, Otto and Klaus. I ask you, Hansi, how can they grow into men without the sauerkraut?" ' His arms waved expansively. ' "Helga, my dumpling," I say, "in Democratic Republic of Germany we have already many cabbages to make the sauerkraut, why do you need cabbages?" But Helga tell me lorries come in the night,' he dropped his voice to a whisper, '*take all cabbages*. In Romania, I find same thing. Russians come in the night, no cabbages. In Bulgaria, same thing. Everywhere I go, no cabbages.' He paused again. 'You want to know where goes cabbage?' He glanced round and put his finger to his lips. '*Moscow.*'

He paused dramatically. 'Russian five-year-plan say farmers not plant cabbage. Next year, maybe. In Russian markets, no cabbage. Russian people want cabbages to make the sauerkraut. People say to Kremlin, "Give us cabbage." Kremlin telephones German government, tell them send all good German cabbage – buy now, pay later. Telephone Romanians, same thing.' He leaned back in his chair, his face twisted with emotion. 'You tell me, English lady, what kind pig-country steal other people's cabbage?'

This was unanswerable. The future seemed bleak indeed for a nation that wasn't even capable of growing its own greens.

'How can we be *German* without the cabbage? You have

Bulgarian Svinsko s Kiselo Zele
PORK CHOPS WITH SAUERKRAUT

A winter dish, simple but good. If you can't get sauerkraut, use shredded fresh cabbage.

――――――――――――――――――― SERVES 4 ―――――――――――――――――――

4 pork chops
2 oz/50 g butter
2 large potatoes, cooked, skinned
  and sliced
2 crisp green apples, peeled, cored
  and sliced

1 lb/500 g sauerkraut
4 tablespoons seed oil, pumpkin, for
  preference
1 teaspoon cumin seeds, lightly
  toasted in a dry pan
salt and pepper

1. Season the pork chops, dot with a little of the butter and slip them under the grill or fry until the meat feels firm when you prod it – about 5 minutes a side. When deliciously browned and sizzling, remove to a warm dish.

2. Add the rest of the butter to the fatty juices in the pan, and fry the potatoes until nicely browned. Remove and reserve. Fry the apples lightly and briefly – you may need a little more butter – until the edges caramelize, no more.

3. Meanwhile, put the sauerkraut in a bowl of cold water and work it with your fingers. (If using fresh cabbage, cook briefly in a lidded pan in the water that clings to it after rinsing, with a little oil and a good seasoning of salt – dress as for the sauerkraut.) Drain off the water, and wash it again, dump it in a colander to drip, and when you are confident that it can lose no more water, put it into a salad bowl and dress it with the oil, cumin and a little pepper.

4. Serve with the pork chops, fried apples and potatoes, blending the salad with the hot pork fat as you eat.

rosbif, we have sauerkraut. You have your Queen Elizabeth, we have . . .' His voice trailed away. Failing to find an equivalent for royalty, he ordered another bottle of slivovic.

Later, much later, arm in arm, liquor having made the heart grow fonder, we returned to the hotel. It was well past midnight and the crowd in the market square had thinned, but not yet vanished.

Our pretty young informant was slumbering in her chair. Mindful of her marriage plans, we slipped five dollars under the ashtray. We might not have eaten well, but the experience had been illuminating.

Dawn was already thrusting dirty fingers through the thin curtaining when the Russian contingent returned, pausing beneath our window to deliver a soulful rendition of some gloomy Russian ballad. Somewhere in the distance the tractor salesman's voice rose in protest. The crash of breaking china brought the singing to an abrupt conclusion.

When I woke once more it was well past nine o'clock, the usual hour when the townsfolk were about their business. Sure enough, I could hear sounds of activity in the square below. I dressed quickly and made my way outside. A line of market stalls had been set up in one corner of the concrete dustbowl. A brief inspection revealed neither meat nor fowl nor fish on sale, but a few stalls with potatoes, various store-cupboard beans, a few lemons artfully arranged in a pyramid, mint and parsley in parsimonious handfuls. There was no cabbage.

Sauerkraut is more than a food, it's a declaration of national identity. Very ancient, talismanic, no one who is not of Slavic origin can understand its appeal. Barrels of salted cabbage travelled with the Mongolian herdsmen who surged across the plains of central Europe when Rome pulled back to her boundaries. Salt-fermented cabbage – sauerkraut – is eaten by all Northern peoples who have come under the influence of the nomadic people of the steppes. It is an Eastern taste, the flavour of the Orient. The people of the Mediterranean do not eat sauerkraut – in fact, they find it inexplicable, as odd and unpalatable a foodstuff as boiled baby.

A taste for salt cabbage explains more about the turbulent

history of the Balkans than any transient political allegiance. Ask any native of the Mediterranean what he or she feels about salt cabbage and you'll understand exactly what I mean. A passion for sauerkraut makes one group as different from another as chalk from cheese. The Bulgarians belong to a cabbage-salting culture. They salt a great many other things for winter, but sauerkraut is the staple.

All this I learned late one evening in a cavernous kitchen lit only by candlelight in a monastery in the hills of northern Bulgaria. My instructor was Brother Boris, whose enquiring mind, sharpened by an Oxford education and his duties as the monastic librarian, had led him in search of a soul, that of his country rather than his own.

The Bulgarian soul is not easily found. In Bulgaria, he explained, it was the life of the monasteries that had provided a blueprint for the modern secular state. The monastic life is highly disciplined, communal, deliberately choosing to suppress individuality for the good of all. Each monastery operated independently and had its own rules.

During the Ottoman ascendancy the monasteries were isolated, fortified and self-sufficient. The monks were scholars, educated and politically sophisticated. Loyalty to the order kept the communities closed, allowing sanctuary to be granted and dissidents moved to safety among brother orders in more tolerant lands. Among these dissident scholar-monks was Paissi de Hilendar, the Venerable Bede of Bulgaria, who chronicled his nation's past and mapped out its future from the safety of his cell on Mount Athos. His manuscript, *The History of the Slav-Bulgarians* – the title itself more than enough to warrant the attentions of the sultan's executioner – was copied and passed from hand to hand through the generations.

Although the written word was powerful, it depended on a literate population. Well aware of the limitations of libraries, the fortress monasteries ensured the survival of the old ways through the domestic habit – not only through the crops they grew in their fields, the herbs that flourished in the physic garden, the utensils employed in the kitchen, but through the methods and recipes employed to prepare them. The Church needed no reminding that it is through domestic habit that people know who they are.

Having no historical record to establish what might or might not be considered Bulgarian, the politicians found it necessary to invent. Invention delivered the Proto-Bulgars, a group of mythical early Bulgarians who were perhaps of Mongolian-Turkish origin, but who were most definitely not Ottoman. Since no one knew who these primitive Bulgarians were or what they might have done, they could be endowed with whatever characteristics anyone wanted.

By the time we encountered Brother Boris, we had already met the Proto-Bulgars. We had spent the day in what had once been a rural industrial centre, which would certainly have earned the approval of William Morris, had that vigorous Victorian advocate of social reform ever taken it upon himself to visit such a remote valley. The centre had been abandoned during the turbulences of modern times. In the aftermath of the Second World War, with Bulgaria delivered to the Communist sphere of influence, a new wave of somewhat more politically successful social reformers had decided to restore the model village and its semi-automated industries for educational purposes.

The Bulgarians are proud of their history. The trouble is, the record is somewhat hard to read when the trampling feet of successive hordes of occupying powers have flattened what little there was. History is hard to come by when the infrastructure has gone.

The slopes of the valley that sheltered the little settlement had been planted with Proto-Bulgarian crops. The crops that might be considered Proto-Bulgarian are those which predated the discovery of the Americas. Conveniently, the Ottoman tax-inspectors, mainly meticulous Greeks, had listed these for the purpose of imposing levies. Cabbage is particularly Proto-Bulgar, and the elusive greens lined the valley in serried ranks. The tractor salesman would have been overjoyed.

When the Ottomans encouraged their colonials to plant the New World crops, with seeds supplied by the merchants of Venice, the diet changed. To this day, maize is still known as Turkish wheat. The introduction of these botanical benefactors served a double purpose: the masters could enjoy exotic flavours without having to do the gardening, while the astonishingly high yield of the new staples ensured the survival and multiplication of a captive population whose function was to serve as field-workers to the occupying power.

This was the legacy – a rural service industry, based on producing goods for which the export market had vanished – that confronted post-war Bulgaria. The socialist solution to what was a national identity crisis was to present an idealized view of the past in a way that was easily understandable to a rural population which had had little access to the written word. Like their sybaritic predecessors, the bureaucrats of Sofiya decreed exactly what crops might be planted and what industrial endeavours should be undertaken. These tasks accomplished, they returned to their desks, leaving the community – craftspeople who had been encouraged to settle and provide their labour in exchange for a state wage – to its own devices.

Since the original village had fallen into disrepair, the buildings had had to be imported from elsewhere. Wooden dwellings of the appropriate date had been commandeered, along with their surrounding palisades and outhouses, dismantled and reassembled along the banks of a tumbling stream, whose waters had been harnessed to turn the cogs that provided the craftspeople with a primitive source of power. A mill-wheel turned to grind the wheat for a working bakery; a series of cogs operated the spit for the butcher to roast his meat; water-powered wheels spun the spools for a wool-weaver; another arrangement wound the thread for a producer of fancy ribbons and braids.

The enterprises were operated by gaily costumed state-funded peasantry – a neat reversal of Marie-Antoinette playing at milkmaid. The cloth they wove was handsome, the braid charming but, with true Communist logic, it was not for sale. The food looked good and smelt even better, but there was no possibility of tasting it. As with the medieval miracle plays, the medium was the message: these were actors charged with delivering a set of complicated philosophical ideas through a simple visual presentation. There was no need for the trappings of the tourist trade, the provision of refreshments or the sale of souvenirs, since the designated audience was the Bulgarians themselves.

The kiosk at the entrance sold tickets. The ticket-seller was an employee rather than a craftsman, and something of an entrepreneur. As is the way with entrepreneurs, he had decided to augment his income with a little private enterprise. Just as stuffed seals made in Taiwan are the most popular souvenirs in Eskimo trading posts, the only product for sale was rosewater. The rose of Damascus – used in the manufacture of attar of roses – is still cropped in vast quantities in the hills of Sredna Gorar, just to the east of us. Rose essences were distilled to perfume the ladies of the seraglio; the by-product of the industry is rosewater – the washings of the petals – used for various culinary purposes, but mainly to perfume Turkish pastries and *loukum*. The guidebook will tell you that attar of roses is the most expensive and luxurious perfume in the world, that some five thousand kilos of petals are required to make a litre of rose essence, and it will also tell you that the essences are distilled in huge copper vats. Until the Ottomans arrived, the Bulgarians used earthenware pots for cooking – they certainly had nothing capable of boiling five thousand kilos of rose petals.

Rosewater is undeniably Ottoman; the ticket-seller's enterprise, a popular sideline among the visitors, had destroyed at a stroke the whole philosophical purpose of his employ. No doubt next time the bureaucrats visit their fiefdom, he will be out of a job.

'Please, eat. You must be tired and hungry.' Brother Boris's words were as welcome as rain in summer.

After our visit to the Proto-Bulgarian village, we had not been looking for accommodation when we arrived at what we thought might well be an abandoned monastery, but we were certainly tired and hungry.

We had knocked at the massive iron-studded wooden door hoping for a caretaker who might allow us to view the frescoes recommended in our pre-war Baedeker. The guidebook mentioned that the monastery accommodated pilgrims, but we had no reason to suppose, fifty years on, that this would still be the case.

In fact, knowing that religious orders were banned in all Communist countries, we had expected the community long since to have vanished; still less had we hoped there might be the chance of a night's lodging.

Brother Boris's offer had seemed nothing short of a miracle – as miraculous as our benefactor's command of our own language, the first English speaker we had encountered since we had left the Ottoman princess in her palace by the Bosphorus.

Brother Boris smiled, shy when Nicholas complimented him on his English. 'I'm a little out of practice, but thank you. I read theology at Oxford.'

'Did you indeed?'

'Brasenose, actually. You know it?'

'Indeed I do.'

'You were there yourself?'

'Cambridge. Magdalene, actually. A bit before your time, no doubt.'

'Still, I don't imagine it has changed much. I well remember we trounced you at cricket. You weren't by any chance a cricketer?'

Brother Boris's cassock flapped wildly as he flailed his arms in an imaginary hit for six.

Nicholas laughed. 'Occasionally, but nothing to speak of. I was a boxer myself.'

'Were you, by Jove?' Brother Boris's English was becoming more Wooster-like by the minute. 'Cricket was more my game. Kept wicket myself – didn't have much choice. Nobody else wanted to take the risk. Girls, you know. But the chaps knew I was going to be a monk, so they persuaded me it didn't matter if I lost my front teeth.'

'And did you?' I enquired, examining his dentistry with circumspection.

'No chance.' He smiled again, revealing a perfect set of very white teeth. 'Actually, I was rather good. They asked me to play for the county. Couldn't, of course. Would have looked as if I wasn't taking my studies seriously enough.' His eyes took on a faraway look. 'As a matter of fact, I rather miss it. Kept the pads and the bat and stuff for old times' sake. Sometimes I get them out and make one of the brothers chuck a ball.'

For a brief moment, the ancient courtyard rocked with shared male laughter. Then the hands were folded neatly back under the robe, the laughter faded, decorum was restored.

'You are pilgrims, perhaps?'

Nicholas shook his head. 'I must tell you, in all honesty, we are not members of your faith.' At the mention of pilgrimage, my husband's Huguenot ancestry surfaced – much to my horror, for fear it might jeopardize our night's lodging.

Brother Boris considered his reply. 'It is not Christian to deny the traveller shelter, whatever his denomination. Our hospitality is free to those who cannot pay. But in the case of such as yourselves . . .' he glanced at our vehicle, somewhat travel-worn but undeniably expensive '. . . twenty dollars would be accept-able – in Deutschmarks, if you prefer. I'm afraid our own currency is a little unreliable – you know how these things are.'

Twenty dollars? It would have been cheap at triple the price. The money vanished swiftly into the depths of the monkly robe.

'And now, if you will kindly follow me, I shall show you to your room. There is ten minutes to vespers, when I must see to the Lord's business until supper-time.'

At the mention of supper, we both brightened.

'You will have to forgive my lack of culinary skill. We take it in turns in the kitchen. This evening it is my duty to prepare the meal. We no longer have lay brothers to see to our earthly needs. Actually, I rather enjoy it – and at least you will not go hungry.'

Brother Boris set off across the courtyard. We had to hurry to keep up. He had a long stride and was clearly anxious not to miss any part of his devotions.

The accommodation for pilgrims was set apart from the main buildings in a modern cloister whose whitewashed walls were pierced by wooden doors, each of which was neatly numbered in plain black lettering.

Our guide halted, fumbled within the folds of his robe and produced a bunch of keys. The door swung open to reveal a whitewashed cell with simple furnishings: two single beds decorously separated by a table, two chairs, a washstand. The only distraction, apart from a narrow window, unglazed and set

159

high enough to limit the view to a short stretch of limestone cliff, was a large crucifix.

'Not quite the Ritz, I'm afraid. But I'm told the tranquillity makes up for the simplicity.'

We expressed ourselves more than content, as indeed we were. Straw-stuffed mattresses and eiderdowns plump with goose-feathers looked like heaven.

'It's clean,' said Brother Boris – somewhat unnecessarily. There is nothing so demonstrably clean as a monk's cell, unless it might be, as Nicholas observed dumping his rucksack on the nearest bed, an Army dormitory with a sergeant major who makes his soldiers polish the floor with a toothbrush.

Brother Boris nodded gravely. 'I'll take your word for it, sir. I have had no experience of the military life. But perhaps ours is not so very different. We, too, must be disciplined.'

The loud clanging of a bell provided proof of the truth of his words.

'If you'll excuse me, please make yourselves at home. It is six o'clock. Your supper will be ready at nine in the building through which you entered. You will excuse the brethren if we do not invite you to join us at table. We observe silence at meal-times, and at all other times unless there is good reason. It will be my privilege to serve you, but not until the brethren are at prayer. I have special dispensation to care for our visitors. It is very fortunate for me. I shall be able to practise my poor English.'

With a swish of his long brown skirt, he vanished.

Nicholas occupied the intervening hours exploring the monastery's precincts, while I took my paintbox into the cloisters to take advantage of the last of the light.

If friend as well as foe can be identified by the steam rising from the cooking pot, there was no doubt we were among friends.

At the appointed hour for supper, the fragrance of a savoury soup, the scent of garlic and herbs, drew us through an open door into a cavernous kitchen. At one end of the echoing room was a huge iron range on which bubbled an earthenware pot, the source of the delectable scent and the object of the attentions of Brother Boris.

Seeing us arrive, he filled a couple of soup bowls to the brim.

I was curious. I had noticed mention of the recipe in several cookery books, but the ingredients and method varied widely. Nevertheless, it seemed to have the status of a national dish, but until now I had no idea of the rules that governed its preparation.

'What's it called, your beautiful soup?'

'Monastery Soup.'

What else?

We dipped in our spoons. The broth was exquisite. It tasted of vegetables just lifted from the earth, of pure water and fresh herbs. To accompany, a bowl of creamy yoghurt and thick slabs of home-baked bread.

Brother Boris smiled. 'It's only soup, but I think you will find it nourishing. We eat it every day, winter and summer, but it is always a little different and it is always good. We use what is proper to the season. The vegetables come from our own garden. The yoghurt we make ourselves. I have prepared some *nakip* apples with walnuts for you. It's something we make at this time of year.'

Brother Boris waited until our hunger was satisfied, removed the bowls and returned to the table with two glasses and a bottle of wine. He filled the glasses carefully, each to the brim, and waited – anxiously as any vintner – until we had taken the first sip. The wine was dark, almost black, the scent soft and rich as ripe blackberries.

'The wine is good?'

We nodded and sipped again. 'Delicious.'

He smiled happily. 'Father Dominic will be pleased to hear of your approval. We make all our wine ourselves from our own vines. The vintage is 1963, the year I was born. I am told it is a particularly good year, although I myself have never tasted it. We don't drink wine except when we come to the Lord's table. The special vintages we keep to honour guests.'

The candlelight flickered. The flame had burned too low. Brother Boris rose, rummaged in a drawer and replaced the candle, lighting the wick with a taper from the stove. The scent of fresh beeswax filled the air, fresh and fragrant.

'While you enjoy your wine, perhaps you can tell me a little

161

Bulgarian Monastirska Ciorba
MONASTERY SOUP

What goes into the soup pot depends on the season and availability, although all the vegetables in the recipe are authentically pre-Ottoman. The woods around the monastery were cropped for wild fungi; particularly suitable for drying are *porcini*, winter fungus, fairy ring, morels. Vary the recipe to suit the season and your own preferences.

─────────── SERVES 4 AS A MAIN DISH ───────────

2 oz/50 g dried mushrooms (porcini, for preference)
2–3 sticks celery, washed and sliced
2 large leeks or onions, finely sliced
2 mature carrots, scraped and diced
1 bayleaf
2–3 sprigs thyme
1 tablespoon marjoram, chopped

2 pints/1 l water
2 tablespoons rice
4 oz/100 g shredded spinach or spring greens
4 oz/100 g shelled peas or sliced okra
salt and pepper

─────────── TO FINISH ───────────

¹/₄ pint/250 ml thick yoghurt
1 egg

2 tablespoons parsley, chopped
2 tablespoons dill, chopped

1. Put the dried mushrooms, celery, leeks or onions and carrot in a roomy pan with the water. Bring to the boil. Add the rice and herbs and season with salt and pepper. Bring back to the boil, turn the heat down, lid loosely and let everything simmer very, very gently for about 45 minutes, until the rice is perfectly tender. Add more water if necessary. Five minutes before the end of cooking, add the green vegetables – if using okra, remember that when lightly cooked it doesn't become gluey.

2. To finish, whisk the egg with the yoghurt, and 1 tablespoon each of the chopped parsley and dill. Stir into the soup and let it sit on the side of the stove for 5 minutes to allow the egg to set.

3. Serve in deep soup-bowls, sprinkled with the remaining chopped herb. Accompany with pickled cucumbers and dark bread – black rye bread with caraway seeds for authenticity.

Bulgarian Nakip
MONASTERY APPLES WITH WALNUTS AND HONEY

Brother Boris served these honeyed apples after the soup – a lovely recipe, simple but delicious, made with apples from the orchard, honey from the monastery's bee hives and walnuts from the tree in the cloister.

———————————————— SERVES 4 ————————————————

8 crisp eating apples
½ pint/300 ml white wine
4 tablespoons honey

2 oz/50 g walnut pieces
1 teaspoon rosemary, finely chopped

———————————————— TO FINISH ————————————————

2 tablespoons honey
2 tablespoons white wine

2 oz/50 g butter

1. Preheat the oven to 350°F/180°C/mark 4.

2. Core the apples without going right through at the non-stalk end, and arrange them in an ovenproof dish into which they just fit. Stuff with the honey mixed with walnuts and finely chopped rosemary. Pour in the wine. Bake for 20–30 minutes until the apples are perfectly soft.

3. To finish, melt the honey with the wine in a small pan, and bubble up to evaporate the alcohol. Whisk in the butter in small nuggets until you have a smooth shiny sauce. Pour this over the apples and serve with thick yoghurt or clotted cream.

of what you seek. We are all seekers, one way or another, but more so when we travel to foreign lands.'

Briefly, I explained the purpose of our journey. As I talked, I felt the warmth of his interest.

'Thank you for confiding in me. In exchange, I shall tell you a story. It is a parable.'

He paused and composed himself.

'You may have heard of a certain village in the mountains of Bulgaria which has many centenarians. The village became famous when it became known that everyone in it ate yoghurt every day, and that none of them had ever been sick in their lives. Doctors came from all over the world to examine these remarkable people. Perhaps the answer lay in the diet of the sheep, whose milk was used to make the yoghurt? Or in the bacteria which turns the curd? They brought in chemists to analyse the grass the animals grazed, took scrapings from the wooden troughs in which the curd was set. They found certain things they thought might explain the miracle. They went home and told everyone what they'd discovered. They announced that the secret was indeed to be found in the diet of the villagers. They told the people they should eat yoghurt every day so they could all be as healthy as their days were long, save the state much money in hospital care and the wages of the doctors, and they would live until they were a hundred. Of course, this is what everyone wanted to hear. The sales of yoghurt soared. Soon someone had the fine idea of setting up a state factory and selling bottled yoghurt in the state supermarkets to all the people who lived in the cities.'

He shook his head, smiling. 'But the yoghurt in the bottles didn't make anyone live longer, nor did it make them any healthier and less dependent on the state. The doctors did not understand. This is because the scientists know everything and understand nothing. They did not know that this was not a medicine that could be trapped in a bottle, but a living thing that must be kept alive every day with love. The preparation of the yoghurt teaches us that life sustains life, and if it dies can be made to live again.'

He paused, absent-mindedly trimming the candle. 'You will please forgive me if I tell you what you already know. I have had to explain this many times to friends when I was at college. You think we are all the same. You think we belong to the West. You probably imagine – forgive me if I am wrong – that we, Bulgaria, Romania, Hungary and all the peoples of the Balkans, are just little bits of Europe, which happen to be in the East. This may be true of Romania, where they speak French and their culture comes from Italy. It may also be true of Hungary, which looks to Germany and formed an empire with the Austrians. But it has never been true of Bulgaria. To understand us at all, you must know that we are not really Europeans but Slavs. We came from the steppes. Genghis Khan was one of us. Our ancestors rode with Tamburlaine. Listen to our music, hear our poetry, read our language – although you will first have to learn our alphabet – and you will understand that what I say is true. If you understand that, you will understand a little of what we are.

'This is why it was easy for us to welcome the Russians as saviours rather than oppressors. We had two reasons to love the Russians. The first is because they, like us, are Slavs. They are neither Turks nor Germans nor a member of any group we had reason to fear. We can even understand each other's language.

'The second is what you might call historical gratitude. We have never forgotten it was the Imperial army who defeated the Turks – something we could never have done by ourselves. We learned about it in school. My grandparents took me there when I was a boy, I have seen the monuments for myself. After the battle, two hundred thousand corpses lay rotting in the rosefields the Turks had planted. Even to this day, roses smell to me of death. Even now, I cannot look at a rose, however beautiful, without anger in my heart.

'So when it was the Russians' tanks that rolled through our streets, we had good reason to remember and be grateful. Afterwards, we had new leaders, a socialist government. Georgi Dimitrov was the first. Although he had no love for monks, I personally admired him greatly. He was a hero of the people. He had fought in the revolution they called the Peasant Uprising. That was in 1923 – I remember the date from my childhood. Two of my father's brothers were killed, not bravely like men but crawling on their knees like dogs.

'Because he had seen such things and understood their meaning, Dimitrov knew that if there was to be a future, there must also be a past. Rebuilding cities is a matter of money and mortar. Restoring a nation's faith in its future requires different skills – philosophy, poetry, but above all an understanding of those things which binds us to places and people we no longer recognize with our conscious minds. Ancestral memory is not words. It is a sight, a sound, a scent.'

He looked at me, smiling. 'For you, because I understand your interest, we shall talk of that soup, our Monastery Soup. The whole history of Bulgaria is in that soup. I know because I have made a study of it.

'In the monasteries, our lives are communal. We have made a conscious choice to suppress individuality for the good of all. Like bees in a beehive, each member depends on the others. Because of this, we are in many ways the Communist ideal.

'When the socialists were making their new world, they came to us to see how they might live. They wanted us to tell them what crops we grew in our gardens. They asked to see our cooking pots. This is because they understood that we alone knew the old ways, even though they could not admit it. To admit this would be to admit that religion has a function in people's lives, and in a socialist state, nothing can function but the state.

'You will have noticed that the soup was very simple. You are a cook, so you will know that vegetables were put in the pot and cooked in water. We do not fry the vegetables or the flavouring ingredients in oil before adding the liquid. This is a Turkish habit, to fry the ingredients first before making a soup or a stew. Any dish in which the food is so treated is of Ottoman origin – a declaration of political allegiance, since it was the Turks who introduced the copper pans which made frying possible. The traditional cooking pot of the Bulgar people – remembering we were a settled community of peasant farmers with no direct access to mined metals, was made of clay. If too much heat was applied, the container cracked. Monastery Soup was the perfect recipe for such a pot.

'If you ask them, people will explain to you how to make our Monastery Soup. They will give you lists of what you should or should not put in. None of this has any meaning. For us of the monasteries, the preparation of food is more than a matter of satisfying hunger. From the time the seed is planted to the day of harvest to the moment the food is set upon the table, we know exactly what we do. Through our labours in the fields we learn our value to others, accept our place in the order of things, honour the achievements of our ancestors – these things need no education, cannot be learned from books. Because we monks are bookish, these are the tasks which teach us to be humble.

'In the first months of the year, when the fields lie fallow, our soup bowls contain not only those things we have saved from the previous year but also the first young leaves, the buds of birch and hazel, the top leaves of young nettles. By this we know that winter will soon be replaced by spring.

'In summer we have the young vegetables, and through this we learn to value our children, respect the generations yet to come. In autumn we reap the fruits of maturity, just as we ourselves come into full flowering when we have ceased the preoccupations of youth. But in winter, that's when we know the Lord has truly been good to us. When the snow blocks the valley, the water freezes in the wells, we give thanks that we have been wise enough to stock our own store cupboards.

'The food on our table is a daily reminder of who we are and where we come from. And that is the story of our Monastery Soup.'

By now the candle had burned down to its last scrap, and it was time for bed. We slept soundly, rose early to the sound of bells, and went in search of breakfast. Although the kitchen was deserted, there were bowls of the beautiful yoghurt set out for us. Of our companion of the night before, there was no sign.

We ate quickly, somehow uneasy, as if we were weekend guests who had overstayed our welcome. Nicholas busied himself leaving our rooms in military order, while I took time to finish a sketch of the monastery buildings. I did not carry it away with me, but left it on the table in lieu of thanks.

CHAPTER SIX

Beautiful Bucharest

The Romanians impressed me very forcibly by their skill in repartee. At table with these companions I heard again and again epigrams that would not have disgraced the Byzantine Greeks of the best period.

WALTER STARKIE, *Raggle-Taggle* (1933)

'ROMANIANS ARE CRAZY — TAKE MY WORD FOR IT, *GNÄDIGE Frau.* Crazy mad like dogs.'

Since the speaker happened to be a dog-food salesman, his opinion on canine craziness carried conviction. He reconsidered. 'Not crazy like dogs. Crazy like Cubanos.'

The Cubans were not a nation for whom he had any affection. He considered them thieves and murderers. He held them responsible for the death of his hero, President Kennedy.

The dog-food salesman and I had fallen into each other's company during the inevitable wait at the border between

Romania and Bulgaria. We had had two hours in which to tell each other our life stories. My new friend was somewhat more voluble than I. A West German by birth, his parents had emigrated after the end of the war. He had passed an unsatisfactory childhood in the Bronx, where he picked up a colourful accent and a deep loathing of foreigners. In his neighbourhood, this was anyone who spoke Spanish. He had also acquired a passionate dislike of cats, particularly unneutered toms of the rooftop kind. It was this passion that had led him into the dog-food trade, dogs being the only creatures who shared his dislike of felines.

He was now resident in Frankfurt, a place where the streets were clean and there were no fucking cats or shitting Spics – if I would excuse his language, since he was prepared to stand by both these epithets as the literal truth. He had just been on an incentive holiday on the Black Sea, a reward for selling more cans of dog-food than any other West German salesman. He was glad he hadn't come second, since the prize was a visit to Berlin to see a production of Andrew Lloyd Webber's *Cats*.

With his passport stamped and warnings delivered, he headed through the barrier in a cloud of dust. All the way to Hungary, no doubt.

Meanwhile, Nicholas had interviewed a few more lorry drivers, returning with news of gas shortages. 'Bit of a problem with the petrol.'

'I thought Romania had its own – bumping it up by the bucketful.'

Nicholas shook his head gloomily. 'Same as the cabbages. It all goes to Russia.' Furthermore, he continued, there were stories of hi-jackings at military road barriers.

'Don't tell me. Get the hell out to Hungary.' I laughed, and explained about the dog-food salesman.

Nicholas brightened at the mention of Germany. 'We can buy petrol coupons with German marks.'

'We've got dollars.'

He smiled at me and I smiled back, until I noticed the direction of his gaze. 'Absolutely not. Not the krugerrands. Absolute emergencies only.'

'This *is* an emergency.'

'Not yet it isn't.'

Another smile, this time ingratiating. Then, speculatively, 'I suppose we could crash the road-blocks and drive straight through to Hungary.'

I climbed into the driver's seat and put the car into gear. 'Let's go.'

I had no intention of driving straight through Romania. My heart warmed to it, not least because my negotiations with the customs officers had revealed that I could at least get a grip on a few words of the language. I badly needed an Eastern European nation with whom I had a chance of communicating directly.

The Romans left their stamp permanently on the country's name, the basic structure of her language, the lifestyle of her people, and the extraordinary wealth of gold and sculpted artefacts they left buried in her soil. For the next two thousand years, Greeks, Goths, Tartars, Bulgars, Turks and finally Russians washed over them. The tides of invaders flowed and finally ebbed, leaving the volatile Romanians still masters of their Latin island in a sea of Slavs. With the exception of Brother Boris, the Slavs had struck me as a gloomy bunch. It's probably a sauerkraut problem, but I have always been of a Mediterranean turn of mind.

In what had once been the Roman province of Dacia, I was looking forward to a little Latin volatility. Romania is a young country in its modern form, scarcely more than a century old. To the west, Transylvania, a former province of the Austro-Hungarian Empire, romantic and beautiful; to the east, Moldavia, a mountainous region on the borders of Russia. To the south, where we had crossed, the frontier marked by the mighty Danube, the land of Wallachia, a vast plain once covered with forest and marsh, but now the farming and industrial heartland of the country.

As we drove towards Bucharest, grain silos reared up like grey dinosaurs among the grainfields. Over the landscape hung streams of black smoke billowing from blazing chimneys, like half-extinguished candles. The flames marked the oil refineries which plumbed the subterranean petrol seams.

Our progress was slow, but not because of any military barriers. The broad highway – built, no doubt, on Roman foundations – was blocked at intervals by brightly painted wagons pulled by teams of heavy-shouldered cart-horses or by ancient tractors, behind which swayed high-sided carts, ambulatory silos piled with grain on which perched gangs of field-workers.

While the horse-drawn vehicles slowed the traffic but did not halt it, the tractors broke down in the middle of the road, their human cargo adding to the confusion by wandering along the verges, flagging down alternative transport with peremptory gestures, as if asserting a right rather than making a request.

Obediently we slowed, only to be rejected as soon as our foreign numberplates were identified.

At last the city of Bucharest rose from the plain, dimly at first, like a mirage, multi-spired, romantic. This impression of beauty vanished abruptly as soon as we approached the outskirts, resolving itself into the grey reality of factory warehouses and sprawling industrial suburbs.

The road from the south became the city's main artery, the Calea Victoriei, and spilled us into what must once have been the central market-place, but now served as a vast junction for the city's traffic.

'What now?'

Nicholas's voice was justifiably wary, the tone appropriate to a man who had just settled down with a beer and a week-old copy of the *International Herald Tribune*, and suspects his wife has made other plans.

He was right. Strange cities go to my head, and long before we arrived, I had already fallen in love with Bucharest.

We had established a convenient bridgehead at the very heart of the city. Our hotel, a faded rose of a place where once the belles of Bucharest had gathered to take tea, overlooked the central square. Immediately below our window was a courtyard with little groups of café tables balanced somewhat forlornly on a patch of cobblestones. The square was busy day and night, what with the comings and goings, the trolley-buses and trams disgorging passengers onto the pedestrian walkways which threaded their way gingerly between what appeared to be bomb-craters.

The hotel manageress, a young woman with impeccable French, chic as only Parisians can be, explained the phenomenon. Nicolae Ceauşescu had just ordered the digging of a Metro system. The enterprise required the demolition of all those buildings of architectural merit that had escaped the bulldozers in earlier rounds of municipal folly. The noise and dust continued until night-time, when the city's lights clicked off at random, leaving the unwary citizenry to stumble into the holes. Most of the restaurants had closed for the duration. Only the theatres were exempt.

'Naturally,' I explained cheerfully, 'I bought tickets for the theatre.'

'The *theatre?*'

'Well, not really the theatre. It's a kind of political cabaret. It's supposed to be killingly funny.'

'How the devil will we know if it's killingly funny if we can't understand the language?' Nicholas enquired, in one of his reasonable voices.

'We can get quite a bit of it from Spanish. The poster looked good. And the tickets weren't very expensive,' I added lamely.

Well, I admit I hadn't really thought it out, it had just seemed like a good idea at the time.

Our seats were high up in the third tier of the gallery. There were none available in the stalls – which, as I attempted to convince my companion, wouldn't have been half so much fun anyway.

Nicholas spent most of the first act with his bird-watching binoculars clamped to his eye-sockets. His explanation was that he had learned to lip-read as a child, which made it easier to understand a foreign language, but I suspect it was because the leading lady had terrific legs.

In the cheap seats, we were among a raggle-taggle audience of students, who behaved much as in a Victorian music-hall, their cat-calls and cheers spurring the actors on. The interior was as pretty as a Dresden shepherdess, painted with pastoral scenes set in peeling *trompe l'oeil* frames. Swags of tattered velvet were looped back by battered cherubs tinted an improbable pink.

The performance was a series of satirical sketches enacted by a cast of easily identifiable characters: the currency spiv, the black-marketeer, the lawyer with his briefcase.

But the most popular visual gag featured a young actress whose sole contribution was to walk from one side of the stage to the other carrying a typewriter. After this had brought the house down for the third time, I asked my neighbour, a young woman who had appointed herself our translator, to explain.

'*Pas compliqué*,' she replied. 'The very correct young lady is carrying what everyone knows is an illegal weapon. The government has ordered everyone to bring their typewriters to their local police station for registration and examination. The secret police think that if they have a record of all the typewriters they'll be able to tell who's writing anti-government propaganda. In Romania, even typewriters can be arrested if they have not the right papers. We find that very amusing. That is why everyone is laughing.'

'And the secret police? Are none of them in the audience? Aren't the actors scared they might be arrested?'

The young woman smiled. 'Yes and no. How to explain? Except that we are Romanian. Some of us are policemen, some of us are satirists. We make our choices. We follow our destiny.'

I was beginning to like Romania even more. There was anarchy about. I have a taste for anarchy myself, an instinctive urge to question all authority. It's been with me as long as I can remember – and it's got me into plenty of hot water in my time. I have never felt the urge to plant bombs, but I cannot help believing that human nature is fundamentally good and that, given a whisker of a chance, will conduct its affairs in a proper and godly fashion without the need for men with guns. History shows otherwise – but, then, history is written to justify the decisions of those who rule.

After the experience at the theatre, I fear I might have rather overindulged myself on Romanian pink champagne, because I woke up with a roaring hangover and absolutely no memory of what we had had for dinner. Or even if we managed to have dinner at all.

Next morning we needed to change money. The official rate of exchange, said the hotel's manageress, was three to the dollar.

She shrugged and spread her hands. Unofficially, of course, the rate was fifteen. This raised practical rather than moral considerations. In matters of currency, the free market is always right.

Caution won over cupidity. I had no desire to land up in a Romanian jail – the penalty, announced warning notices in public places, of changing money with the touts. We made our way along the main thoroughfare to the Bank of Romania, the only place where foreign currency might be legally exchanged.

The bank was shuttered and barred. Nicholas's interest in the padlock attracted the attention of a uniformed guard who reversed his sub-machine-gun and prodded him in the ribs.

'*Demain. Vous revenez demain.*'

We beat a hasty retreat. Round the next corner, a man in a Homburg hat who might well have been the uniformed guard's brother was loitering in a doorway. I loitered alongside.

'You wanna change, lady?'

'What's the rate?'

'You got dollar or mark?'

'Dollar.'

'I give you ten lei, one dollar.'

'Twenty.'

'Lady – I give you fifteen.'

I nodded. 'Done.'

'OK. How much you wanna change? Hundred? Two hundred?'

'Hundred.'

'OK.'

We had been warned by the hotel's manageress that we should make sure the bundle wasn't simply newspaper trimmed to look like banknotes, with real notes on top and bottom. A brief flurry of masculine misunderstanding followed while Nicholas checked the lei and the dealer checked our dollars.

'OK now?'

'OK.'

We did the deal. The dealer warned me against undercover policemen masquerading as currency spivs. I warned him against undercover policewomen masquerading as tourists.

Fortified with a fat bundle of lei apiece, Nicholas and I went

174

our separate ways, he to negotiate in one of the bookshops that specialized in rare editions of French poetry books, I to find myself a little refreshment.

I propped up my Baedeker while I sipped my herbal tea. There seemed to be no coffee.

'Psst, lady.'

I kept my head down. 'I have already changed my money, thank you very much.' I had lost my appetite for shady deals with men in Homburg hats.

'I got caviare, lady,' persisted the sibilant one, earning my immediate attention. It had already crossed my mind that there must be some other form of acceptable currency than money. In a closed economy with fixed exchange rates, such as Romania's, commodities quickly take the place of currency.

'What else have you got?'

'Cuban cigars. French condoms. Russian caviare. What you want, lady?'

I considered the offer. The caviare, of course – but the cigars were tempting. I had already fallen into conversation with a couple of members of a Cuban trade delegation staying in our hotel, and had been surprised to learn – since it would be hard to imagine two men whose ideologies were further apart – that two old dictators, Castro and Ceauşescu, were friends. It was entirely plausible that Havana cigars would have found their way on to the market so there was no reason to doubt their authenticity. And being beyond the breeding years, condoms were not exactly top of my shopping list.

It's the angler's particular skill to know which fly to choose to bait the hook. 'Wait here, lady. I fetch caviare.'

'Maybe,' I said.

Contraband transactions require special understandings. In contraband-dealer's language 'Maybe' means 'You bet your cotton socks I do.'

'Fresh caviare. Never been open. Come from Madame Ceauşescu.'

Really? Madame Ceauşescu's personal stock of caviare?

'Guarantee, lady. Big.'

'How big?'

'How big you want? Kilo? Half kilo?'

'Half kilo. How much?'

'You got cigarettes?'

I nodded. I had squirrelled six cartons of Marlboro under the spare wheel in the car. Miraculously these had survived unscathed. I had tucked one of the cartons in my shopping-basket before venturing out that morning – a precaution against not being able to change money.

'You got Kent?'

I admitted I hadn't.

A scowl. Then, encouragingly, 'One packet Kent, one half-kilo caviare.'

I shook my head. 'I haven't got Kent. I've got Marlboro.'

'You kidding?'

'What's wrong with Marlboro?'

'You kidding?'

'That's the way it is.'

'Wait here, lady. I ask my friend.'

With a flick of the raincoat, the negotiator vanished. For one wild moment, I imagined the friend might be Madame Ceauşescu herself – anything was possible in Romania. I was beginning to regret that I had embarked on the transaction at all. There was no guarantee that the mackintoshed one was not an *agent provocateur*. What would I get? Ten years? Twenty?

I slipped one of my newly acquired banknotes under the saucer to pay for the tea, and withdrew in the opposite direction to that chosen by my illicit tradesman.

One block further on, I changed my mind. Tonight was our wedding anniversary. Caviare would be just the thing, entirely appropriate to the place and the occasion.

I hesitated, but only for a moment. The tables in the café were well patronized, offering protective cover, so I could always change my mind again. I returned to my table and opened my book ostentatiously – the adventurous Tereza Stratilesco's *From Carpathian to Pindus: Pictures of Roumanian Country Life* (1906). 'Roumanian cookery is very elaborate. Dishes of herbs and vegetables, and of fowl and fish, are very numerous . . .'

'Psst.'

My personal pusher had returned to the fray. 'Half-kilo caviare cost you six packets Marlboro. Fresh.'

'Three packets. Better be fresh.'

'Kent, you pay one packet. Marlboro, you pay six. You want condoms?'

'Very kind, but no.'

'Good condoms – very big, very strong.'

'Just the same, I think I'll stick to the caviare.'

'Come along, lady. What you give?' This in a wheedling tone.

I held up three fingers. 'And I'll need a lemon.'

'What for you want lemon?'

I made a cutting and squeezing gesture. 'Caviare. Lemon.'

'You gotta get onion. Russian caviare good with onion.' He smacked his lips. 'You gotta get black bread, sour cream *smetana*, nice bottle Russian vodka.'

After a moment, 'Lady, you got husband?'

'I got husband.' You bet I got a husband. 'Very nice husband. Fresh.'

My dealer abruptly tired of this personal exchange. 'OK, lady. Last question. How much husband give for caviare?'

'Still three. Plus a bread coupon. I can't get bread without a coupon.'

'Five. My friend say last word, *five*.'

'My husband say *three*.'

'OK. Deal.' My dealer was keeping an eye on a man at the next table who was reading a copy of the *Bucharest Bugle* or the *Ceaușescu Clarion* or whatever the Party newspaper might be.

'Lady. You put basket on ground.'

I removed my purse and passport and did as requested. There was the rustle of paper as a bag was slipped into my basket, the scarlet flash as three packets of Marlboro were deftly extracted.

'There you are, lady. You take coupon to bread shop, they sell you bread.'

Inside the basket was the tin and a bread coupon. I joined the queue at the state bakery. There was only one choice: rye bread – black and sour and absolutely perfect as a vehicle for fish eggs. My coupon was accepted without comment. The state pays poorly. Its employees receive the same wage whatever the quality of their work, with the inevitable result that all customers are treated with exactly the same mixture of indifference and suspicion, an attitude entirely reciprocated by their customers.

On my return to the hotel I found Nicholas settling a somewhat rustic-looking bottle into a bucket of ice. He had also remembered it was our wedding anniversary, and he, too, had encountered a gentleman in a Homburg with something to sell, in this case, a bottle of plum brandy, *tsuica*, whose label recommended it as the favourite tipple of Vlad the Impaler. Since Vlad had provided a model for Bram Stoker's Dracula, I wasn't entirely sure this was the best possible recommendation.

What I had in mind was a table for two on the balcony, a romantic encounter of the kind enjoyed by one of Noël Coward's heroines, say, in *Separate Tables* or, possibly, *Private Lives*. I was a little hazy on the details, but one or the other would fit the bill. I explain my plans to the manageress. 'Of course you shall have a table on the balcony. You must leave all the arrangements to me. We are Latins, we understand romance. There must be violins.' She held up her hand to forestall any objections. 'It will be my pleasure. There will be no charge.'

'I don't know . . .' I answered doubtfully. 'My husband's never been much of a one for a violin.' This was something of an understatement. Serenading violins are just the kind of thing to send Nicholas howling for the woods.

'I absolutely insist, *chère Madame*.' She bustled off into the depths. There was no help for it but to accept her offer – and if I lost my husband to the night, so be it. An hour later, a table was laid on the balcony that would not have disgraced the Ritz.

We toasted, we drank, we broached the caviare – in that order – which might have induced the blunting of the palate that led to neither of us noticing anything amiss. We ate the whole tin. All of it – down to the last lick.

The violinists played softly under the balcony and not even Nicholas could find fault. We woke at dawn, stomachs churning. Delicacy dictates I draw a veil over the details of our ordeal, although there were moments that stick in the mind when death seemed a preferable option. Caviare past its sell-by date has much the same effect on the human digestive system as the wrong kind of Japanese blow-fish liver. Or, then again, it might have been Vlad the Impaler's revenge. Certainly the *tsuica* was lethal but it was hard to tell if it had tasted odd since it had tasted of nothing at all.

The manageress arrived with two coffee cups filled with well-brewed coffee grounds. In each saucer was a half lemon – the very thing I had been so anxious to find to accompany the caviare.

'You must squeeze in the lemon juice and eat it up with a spoon.'

We did as bid. It tasted disgusting, but seemed to calm the turbulence. Later, very delicately, our saviour enquired after the cause of our malaise.

'You are telling me you *ate* Madame Ceauşescu's caviare? *Mes pauvres amis*, has no one told you? Madame Ceauşescu's caviare is not for *eating*. It is for *trading*. You know, like Kent cigarettes, is like money. Kent is not for smoking, caviare is not for eating, unless you very rich or very foolish, like Russian.'

'And what,' enquired Nicholas, taking advantage of a brief lull in his digestive tract, 'do the Russians do with the condoms?'

She shook her head scornfully. 'We do not know, we do not care. In Romania we do not like the Russians.'

Next morning a market had taken over the central square, causing a complete blockage and the rerouting of the tram system.

The manageress, on learning of my interests, had volunteered to take me shopping in the market. This would be no hardship, she said, since the market was better than it had been for months. 'In the summer, the soldiers came and arrested everyone. The people who bought and the people who sold, they took them away and asked them many questions and wrote down their names and told them they will be put in prison. So the people of the villages stayed home and there was nothing to buy except what was in the official market. Soon there was no food in the official market and the people were hungry. When the people are hungry, first they are angry, and then they cannot work. So the government went out into the villages and asked them to come back. They are told they will not be arrested but will be given a paper saying they are *officially* permitted to sell in the *unofficial* market.'

'It sounds a little subtle.'

'I think perhaps you mean it sounds not quite honest. This may be so, but it is necessary to keep face. Many things in Romania are like this – we are Latins, we do not admit we're wrong. We prefer to make the *bella figura* – so that everyone knows and no one argues.'

The market was bustling – as busy, my mentor confirmed, as it had always been. We made a quick tour before she settled down to the real business of the morning: the restocking of the hotel's larder.

The official state-controlled market was no more than a single line of stalls selling officially priced vegetables and fruit alongside a prefabricated shed, whose shelves had been stocked with an arbitrary assortment of the same dreary goods we had seen in Bulgaria. The only item attracting public interest was several crates of beer of unknown provenance, and a box of what later investigation – using the corkscrew on Nicholas's Swiss Army penknife – revealed to be a truly terrible red wine.

Alongside this state-promoted gastronomic gloom, the black market thrived. The goods differed not so much in price but in quality and diversity: creamy heads of cauliflowers bibbed in their leaves, potatoes the size of baby melons, lettuces, pumpkins, tomatoes streaked with scars of golden juice, posies of scarlet radishes and purple artichokes as artfully arranged as a bridal bouquet.

Each stall had its own orderly queue. Among the customers were uniformed Army officers with leather briefcases into whose bulging depths vanished aubergines and peppers. The plot thickened. This was the *official* unofficial market. The *unofficial* unofficial market – the real black market – was a wholesale market, conducted with even more circumspection from the boots of elderly vehicles. The possession of private transport was itself a sign of the affluence that comes from illicit trading. The official black market provided a retail outlet in which shoppers negotiated for tiny quantities: a single leek, a carrot, a pound of potatoes. The vegetables looked dusty and in need of a good scrub, presumably because the gardens of those with access to city markets are inevitably close to the road. The high quality – explained my guide, cheerfully shouldering a sack of green peppers – could be attributed to the fertilizing fumes from the ancient trucks.

I wandered off through the unofficial market in search of picnic supplies when I spotted a gypsy-woman with a basket of wild fungi moving through the crowd. My attentions unleashed a torrent of high-pitched Romany, an identity card and what seemed to be an official permit. A small crowd gathered, eager to vouch for her integrity.

Bewildered, I attempted to explain in Spanish – with as much of a Romanian twist as I could muster – that all I wanted was a handful of fungi, for which I was willing and able to pay.

My attempts at communication simply roused the crowd to louder and more vehement protestations.

'Better go home, missy. They think you undercover police-man.' I swung round to identify the speaker, catching a flash of broad shoulders and a dark blue raincoat just before it vanished into the crowd. Retreating with as much grace as I could muster, I made my escape.

It was not until I regained the sanctuary of the hotel that it occurred to me there had been something odd about the warning. Who was my rescuer? It would have been worrying enough to be mistaken for an undercover policewoman in my own country but to be mistaken for one in Romania sent a shudder down my spine. Who *was* the man in the raincoat?

I went in search of Nicholas, who made absolutely no attempt to reassure me. On the contrary, he seemed to find the whole business highly entertaining. 'It'd have been a bit of a let-down if they hadn't been following us, presumably all the way from the border. How else would he have known?'

I considered the implications. 'Perhaps I'd better sign the book.'

'Signing the book' was a precaution left over from the days of the independent traveller whose presence might otherwise not have been known to the consulate. It was done partly for social reasons since, if the visitor was distinguished, the ambassador might wish to issue an invitation to one of the embassy's social gatherings; but partly as a precaution to ensure that the consulate could identify its own nationals in case of trouble.

'Margaret Maclean,' said the woman in the smart suit. 'So pleased that you dropped in.'

My informant had been a little vague about Ms Maclean: *Not quite sure what she does, but Maggie knows everything and everyone.*

Uncertainty about function, when applied to someone who knows everything and everyone, is usually an oblique way of describing a member of the embassy's intelligence unit. Usually, but not always.

I had attempted to telephone in advance. The result was a great many whirrings and clickings and no connection. The simplest thing seemed to be to take a taxi to the embassy and to have myself dropped at the gates. In the sentry box, two heavily armed policemen, both wearing dark blue raincoats, removed my passport before allowing me admittance.

Once inside the embassy, I signed the book – the phrase is no euphemism – and handed over my letter of introduction.

After a short wait in an anteroom, I found myself in a book-lined study overlooking a well-tended garden in the presence of a brisk, neatly dressed, bespectacled woman in her mid-thirties to early forties – just the right age for a spy-master. I very much hoped that this was what she was. Spies are useful in tight corners.

I apologized for interrupting her busy schedule.

'No interruption. We don't get many outsiders. Always glad of a little fresh blood.'

The phrase gave me pause for thought. I've worked in a consulate myself and am perfectly aware of the well-developed bush telegraph that identifies those who are being followed by men in mackintoshes, and might therefore be expected to give the consulates trouble. Trouble-giver was not a category into which I had any desire to be put.

'Now, my dear, what can I do for you?'

Taking care to leave out any whiff of politics, I explained the direction of my research. 'What I really need is someone who's a good cook, who can tell me about life in the rural areas. I was told you often went out into the villages and that you had many friends among the Romanians.'

She nodded. 'It goes with the job. But it's true that I'm particularly interested in the women. Some of their lives are quite remarkable.' She paused thoughtfully. 'But you must remember that Romania is . . . let's say, highly politicized. Contact with outsiders is not encouraged. You may think your questions perfectly innocent. But in a climate like this, where everyone's looking over their shoulders, they have all sorts of meanings – you need a reason to visit that doesn't put ordinary people at risk.'

She took off her spectacles, gave them a polish, and peered at me speculatively. 'Wasn't your stepfather in the FO?' I nodded. She smiled. 'Thought so. Someone said something. Better come to dinner tomorrow and we'll talk some more.' She waved her hand vaguely around the walls. 'Can't be too careful.'

She rose to indicate that the meeting was over, and handed me a visiting card. 'Take a taxi. Hopeless otherwise. They turn the street-lights off on a rota, a different district each night. They don't tell you which one because of the thieves. But everyone says the only people who've got a copy of the rota are the thieves themselves. Hand in glove, like everything else. Eight o'clock. Don't bother to dress – we'll be among friends. I'll see who's around.'

The taxi drew up outside what must once have been an elegant townhouse in the French provincial style, built round a courtyard large enough for a carriage-and-four to turn full circle. The apartment, a rambling suite of rooms, tall and well proportioned, occupied the whole fourth floor.

Two other guests had already arrived. One, introduced as Margaret's opposite number at the American embassy, was a woman with long blonde hair scraped back in a bun, and the handshake of a Texan cowpoke. The other, a young man with the dark gypsy good looks with which the young Romanian male is blessed before he slides into the corpulence of middle-age, was introduced by first name.

'Stefan's a curator at the National Museum. He's in charge of

Roman antiquities. They have some stunning jewellery. The gold's the best in the world, although it's been a good few years since anyone's seen it. The department's always closed for restoration and poor Stefan's stuck with empty shelves. Or that's the official story. The truth is, the powers-that-be have pinched most of it. Probably stuck it in some Swiss vault, just in case the natives get restless.'

Nicholas pricked up his ears. 'And *are* they restless?'

Our hostess looked at him severely. 'Politics before dinner is just not on. Not even among your lot, is it, Mimi?'

The Texan woman laughed and shook her head. 'Whatever you say, Maggie.'

'Good. Let's eat.'

In one corner of the room was a round table where small glasses and a bottle of well-frosted vodka had been set ready.

Beside the vodka, nestling in a bowlful of ice and garnished with quartered lemons and a napkin full of blinis, was an open tin whose contents were all too familiar. 'I hope you like caviare?'

Nicholas examined the arrangement cautiously. 'Not by any chance Madame Ceauşescu's caviare?'

Everyone laughed.

'No! Don't tell me you actually *ate* the stuff?' More laughter. 'No need to answer. I can see for myself. Oh dear. I usually manage to warn people. The Romanians have a rather odd sense of humour. It's a kind of code – means the stuff's not for public consumption. Trade goods. And when there's no fridge . . .' She spread her hands. 'Just be grateful it wasn't Madame Ceauşescu's condoms – they're probably responsible for half the inmates of the State orphanages.'

The conversation moved on to the state of Romanian roads – excellent where servicing the Russians, dire everywhere else. The caviare was replaced by what looked like a yellow loaf, round and moist, set on a circular wooden board with a handle round which had been wound a linen thread. This our hostess used to divide the loaf into portions, much as if cutting cheese. 'I thought you should try this. Here they call it *mamaliga* – but you'll recognize it as polenta. In Romania it takes the place of bread – there's always cornmeal in the shops even when there's

Caviare with Buckwheat Blinis

The best way to eat caviare – if you should be fortunate enough to get your hands on the necessary. Half a pound of fish eggs serves four people satisfactorily. Less is not enough.

─────────── SERVES 4 ───────────

12 oz/300 g strong white flour
4 oz/100 g buckwheat flour
1 level teaspoon salt
either *1 level teaspoon baking*
  powder or *1 oz/25 g fresh yeast*
  or *½ teaspoon dried or*
  instant yeast – follow the
  instructions on the packet

2 large eggs, beaten
1 pint/600 ml milk
oil or *butter, for greasing the pan*

─────────── TO SERVE ───────────

soured cream
spring onion, chopped

8 oz/250 g caviare or *pickled* or
  smoked herring or
  smoked salmon, chopped

1. *Either* sieve the flours with the baking powder and salt and then whisk in the rest of the ingredients, except the oil for greasing. The mixture is now ready to cook. *Or* sieve the flours with the salt into a warm bowl. Liquidize the fresh or dried yeast in a little warm water and stir into the milk (it should be at room temperature) in a jug. Whisk in the eggs, and stir into the flours in the bowl, whisking until all the lumps have vanished and you have a smooth, thick cream. Cover with a cloth and leave to rise for an hour or so in a warm place. You'll see the bubbles, which tell you the yeast has worked.
2. To cook, heat a griddle or heavy frying-pan, grease lightly, and test the heat with a drop of the mixture – it should sizzle and set immediately.
3. Pour on enough of the mixture to cover the base of the pan. Or you can make smaller pancakes – *blinchiki* – by dropping on little dollops. Cook over a medium heat until the top looks dry. Flip over and cook the other side. Continue until all the mixture is used up. Keep the pancakes warm in a clean cloth while you work. Serve with caviare, soured cream, chopped onion or whatever fishy thing takes your fancy.

Romanian Mamaliga
CORNMEAL PORRIDGE

A cornmeal porridge that has been cooked dry enough to be tipped out and sliced like a loaf, *mamaliga* replaces bread on the tables of Romania's peasantry. Serve it on its own or with soured cream, either between courses, or – like Yorkshire pudding – to satisfy hunger before the meat course. Served authentically, it's always a dish on its own.

———————————— SERVES 6 ————————————

8 oz / 250 g coarse-ground	*1 tablespoon salt*
yellow cornmeal	*2 oz / 50 g butter (optional)*
1½ pints / 1 l water	

1. The easiest way to make *mamaliga* is as if it was porridge: stir the cornmeal into the water in a heavy-bottomed pan, then bring to the boil and add salt. But if you wish to be authentically Romanian, start with boiling salted water and sprinkle in the cornmeal a handful at a time, beating constantly to avoid lumps. Either way, stir over the heat for about 40 minutes until the mush thickens.

2. Beat in the butter, if using, and tip out on to a wooden board to make a neat round pudding – it'll come out of the pan with a satisfying plop. Cut with a thread, like soft cheese.

3. To make feast-day *mamaliga*, pour a shallow layer of the cooked cornmeal porridge into a buttered gratin dish, dot with more butter and bake in a hot oven (425°F/190°C/mark 7), for 10 minutes. As soon as it's brown and bubbling, spoon on soured cream and cut it into squares for serving. Or fry breadcrumbs in butter and drop in spoonfuls, shaking them around to give them a crisp, buttery coating. Or layer into a buttered casserole with grated cheese. Dot the final layer of *mamaliga* with butter and bake (350° F/180° C/mark 4) for 20–25 minutes, until topped with a golden crust.

bread-rationing, which there almost always is. There's something to be said for eating differently from the Russians. In Russia cornmeal is famine food and people won't touch it unless they have to. *Mamaliga* is always served plain. You can sprinkle it with cheese, but otherwise it's eaten on its own. Nadia, my cleaning woman, makes it for me twice a week. She tips it out like this on its special board, makes the sign of the cross over it and makes sure I cut it with the thread and not a knife. She's very firm about how it should be handled. Says none of us foreigners know how to do anything properly. She'd probably hand in her notice if she knew I served it with a mushroom ragoût.'

The ragoût was an aromatic stew of wild mushrooms gathered by Nadia in the woods near her village. The varieties were the same as those the gypsy-woman had been selling in the market, and the combination of the earthy fungi with the sweetness of the *mamaliga* was delicious.

The main course was followed by pancakes stuffed with plum jam, and a little dish of what looked like miniature swiss rolls.

Margaret popped one of the rolls on my plate. 'Taste. Tell me what you think it is.'

I rolled it round my tongue. The substance was rich and soft, velvety, a little grainy. I considered my answer. 'Clotted cream?'

'Close.' She nodded approvingly. 'It's buffalo cream – much better than cream from cows. In the old days, cow's milk was thought very poor stuff, fit only for pigs. Good, isn't it? We've Stefan to thank for it. It's difficult to get hold of, these days, and he brought it from his village. Stefan's mum thought you simply had to try it with the pancakes – it's practically the national dish.' She patted the curator's hand. 'Dear Stefan, where would we be without you?'

With the arrival of liqueurs and coffee – Mimi's contribution, sent out in the diplomatic bag – tongues loosened and the talk turned to politics in general and the state of the Romanian exchequer in particular.

'It's far more than mismanagement, it's downright dishonesty. Romania should be the most prosperous country in Eastern Europe, not the lame duck. There's plenty of oil, the farmland's

Romanian Dragimiroff
MUSHROOM GOULASH

A simple way with any wild fungi – the more varieties the better, since each one has its own distinctive flavour and texture.

———————————————— SERVES 4 ————————————————

1 lb/500 g mixed wild mushrooms	1 scant tablespoon plain flour
2 oz/50 g butter	1/2 pint/250 ml soured cream
1 small onion, finely chopped	salt and pepper
1 tablespoon paprika	

———————————————— TO FINISH ————————————————

2 tablespoons breadcrumbs	2 tablespoons grated cheese
1 oz/25 g butter	

1. Pick over and slice the mushrooms. Melt the butter in a saucepan and gently fry the chopped onion. Add the mushrooms, stir and season. Lid and simmer gently until the mushrooms are cooked – about 15 minutes.

2. Sprinkle with the paprika and flour, stir to blend, and add the soured cream. Bubble up to thicken and transfer to a warm serving dish.

3. To finish, fry the breadcrumbs crisp in the butter, mix with the grated cheese, and sprinkle over the mushrooms. Serve before or after the *mamaliga*.

Romanian Clătite

JAM PANCAKES

Make double quantities for keeping – they freeze beautifully. Sweet pancakes are a favourite treat throughout the Balkans, a sophisticated little dessert, gorgeous with home-made jam.

MAKES 15-20 SMALL PANCAKES

4 oz/100 g plain flour
pinch of salt
1 tablespoon sugar
2 eggs

¹/₂ pint/300 ml milk-and-water
small glass fruit brandy (Tsuica) or
any white brandy

TO FINISH

butter for frying
1 lb/500 g jam, to stuff the pancakes

¹/₂ pint/300 ml thick cream

1. Sift the flour and salt into a bowl with the sugar. Stir in the eggs and then beat in the milk-and-water gradually until you have a thin cream – a job most easily done in a liquidizer. Leave the batter to rest for 20 minutes. When you are ready to make the pancakes, whisk or whizz it up again with the brandy and transfer to a jug.

2. Heat a small frying-pan – whatever you use to make an omelette. When it's good and hot, drop in a small knob of butter (clarified if you have any – it will not splutter and burn) and wipe round with kitchen paper (reserve the buttery paper to wipe the pan each time, and melt more butter as necessary).

3. Pour in a couple of tablespoonfuls of the batter and roll it round the pan so a thin layer sticks to it. Cook over a medium flame till the edges are lacy and curl away from the sides of the pan. Flip it over and cook the other side. Repeat until all the batter is used up. As each pancake is done, tuck them inside a clean napkin, one on top of the other.

4. Spread a spoonful of jam down the middle of each pancake and roll up into a little bolster. Tuck into a baking dish in rows. When you're ready to serve, preheat the oven (350° F/180° C/mark 4), bathe the pancakes in cream, cover the dish with foil, shiny side down, and bake for 20 minutes.

as fertile as West Germany, the roads are good, the workforce is willing. If it wasn't for the corruption. Bribery is like a disease. Everyone catches it. No one dares say anything about anything. The newspapers print nothing but what the palace wants them to print. There's no such thing as an independent media – the radio and TV are the same, a bunch of parrots. Palace propaganda, that's all the ordinary people hear. All the rest is rumour – and we all know what happens then.'

'What?'

'It's like laboratory rats. Something occurs. No one knows anything except that there are signs that something's wrong. So everybody panics.'

Mimi cut in. 'Let me give you an example. You've noticed the trolley-buses?'

We had. It would have been impossible to overlook the omnipresent grey buses, articulated like lorries, which lurched round every corner and were never less than packed.

'Then you'll also have noticed the gas cylinders on the roofs. Last year the buses suddenly vanished. A week later they reappeared, but without the cylinders, with the engines converted to petrol. No one knew why. Everyone thought it meant there'd be a shortage of butane. Most people use it to cook with so the black market price of bottled gas went through the roof. Everyone stockpiled.' She paused. 'Six months later the real reason emerged. Not even that was direct – nothing in Romania ever is. A story appeared in one of the underground newspapers about overcrowding in a certain cemetery in the northern suburbs. Stories like that are a way of telling people there's been an industrial disaster – even the underground papers have to be careful. And if there has been a disaster, there must be a reason. Well, right next to the report about the cemetery, there was an article on gas cylinders being fitted to a new kind of bus.'

She took a sip of her whisky, and then continued. 'After that, the real story came out. A cylinder on one of the trolley-buses had exploded. It was rush-hour. It's always rush-hour in Bucharest, but this was a particularly busy time of the morning when people come in from the country. There were bits of body everywhere and chunks of burning metal hurled right over the rooftops. It was dreadful. Everyone was killed, including the driver. The bodies were too mangled to be identified. Of course there were eye-witnesses and plenty of people looking for missing relatives, but they were only peasants, country people. No one pays any attention to what happens outside the capital. The incident was never reported in the bulletins from the palace. Even when it came out, the story took months to travel the grapevine. By the time the real reason surfaced, the cylinders were back on the buses, reinforced or not, no one knew. Meanwhile, the black-marketeers had made a killing – no doubt with a few backhanders to the officials.'

It was time to go. Before we left, our hostess called me into her study. 'I have someone for you to visit. His name is Vilmos. He's one of Romania's best known folk-artists, a glass-painter, though he'd probably say the painting just gives him something to do in the winter. He's a shepherd, like everyone else in the Carpathians. Last time I was up there he was complaining he was lonely. The young people were leaving the village to find work in the towns, the usual. But the other day I heard he'd found himself a woman, a local girl.' She smiled. 'They say she's a good cook – and he's certainly very knowledgeable. For two pins, I'd come with you.'

'Why don't you?'

She smiled. 'I think not. They follow the dips everywhere. You'll be much better on your own. You'll have no trouble finding the house. Just look out for the double doors – they're painted a rather chic shade of green. If you're in any doubt, just ask. Everyone knows Vilmos.'

She rummaged around in a drawer, pulled out a photocopied sheet and outlined a route in red biro. 'Here. You'll need a map so you don't miss it. The turning from the main road's not always marked. The shepherds take the signposts down. The Carpathian communities keep themselves to themselves, close as fleas in a fleece. You'll find they're the only Romanians with well-stocked larders. It's not widely known, but the state doesn't collectivize farming above five hundred metres, which means the villages actually control their own food stocks. And five hundred metres can mean anything – depends on who's doing the counting.'

She walked over to the window, lifted the edge of the curtain a crack, then let it drop with a sigh.

'I thought so. They usually follow the foreigners, particularly the ones who sign the book. You'll be on the record now, even if they didn't pick you up at the border. Gives the secret police something to do.'

'Too late, they're already on our trail.'

I explained about the incident in the market and the encounter with the man in the dark blue raincoat. I laughed, but Margaret frowned. 'Don't make the mistake of finding it amusing. Romania's not Ruritania, even if it can sometimes seem so. This government's a horror. We don't know the half of it. We probably never will. The provincial towns have the worst of it. Particularly the minorities – the Hungarians in Cluj, the Sibiu Saxons, the Germans in Brazov.' She paused thoughtfully. 'I made a telephone call to a friend of mine, the wife of Bishop Klein. He's the head of the Lutheran community in Sibiu. She's a wonderful old girl and a very good friend. She says the Bishop's away travelling, but she'll have her two teenage granddaughters with her, and you'll be welcome to join them. Be careful, though, what you write. Change the names, that kind of thing.'

'Of course. But if it'll get anyone into trouble . . .'

'Just a warning. It's all arranged. The Sibiu Saxons are proud of their community. It's hard for the old people – they've watched so many things being destroyed. She says it's important for others to know how things are.'

'I'll be careful.'

'Just be discreet, as they say in the Service. Send me a postcard when you get back to London – better through the FO, so it can come out in the bag. Let me know what you find in the market in Sibiu – I've been thinking it might be worth a trip. That's where the shepherds take their produce for sale – cheese and good fresh meat, the sort of thing we haven't seen in the capital all winter.'

Her voice floated down the stairwell behind us as we left.

'One last thing. That other stuff. Don't let it worry you. By signing the book and coming here tonight, you've told them you have friends. They're bound to follow you. They're just curious, like cats. Harmless if they think you're bigger than them. Nasty if they think you're a mouse.'

CHAPTER SEVEN

Carpathian Adventures

Romanian cookery is very elaborate, and there is a number of dishes a Romanian peasant woman can cook if she only can afford it, but as a matter of fact, want will come to the rescue and make things ever so much easier.

TEREZA STRATILESCO, *From Carpathian to Pindus* (1906)

'CARRY YOUR BAGS, MISS?' I SWEAR I WAS NEVER SO PLEASED TO see anyone in my life than I was to see Nicholas. Well – almost never. Actually, it ran a close second to my wedding-day, when my soon-to-be husband arrived five minutes late at the altar because he had been reading the inscriptions on the gravestones.

I had returned from a final foray round the market to gather supplies for the road to find both husband and vehicle vanished. The manageress spread her hands and shrugged. No, my husband had left no message. She had no idea where he had gone.

I knew exactly what had happened. My mind churned, sweat beaded my brow. My husband had been arrested. It was all my fault for persuading him to come with me on this lunatic adventure. It was my fault we had attracted the attentions of the secret police. It was because of me he had been thrown into the deepest and darkest of dungeons, to resurface in twenty years, haggard and brainwashed. Worse, he had been claimed by the frozen wastes of Siberia, never to be seen again.

It wasn't his fault, your honour, it was mine. I was the one who bought the caviare, who made the deal with the man in the Homburg hat. It was me. I was foolhardy – reckless, even. I was just rehearsing my speech to the public prosecutor, when Nicholas drew up with a screech of Balkan-battered brakes, cracking jokes about bag-carrying.

'Where the devil have you been?' Anxiety makes a person nervous.

'What kind of welcome is that for a man with a full tank?'

'You haven't? Really?'

The fuel-gauge had already dipped well below the half-way mark, and we both knew that unless the petrol coupons could be cashed or our dollars came good, any detours – even those suggested by Margaret Maclean – were out of the question.

'Where? How?'

He grinned happily. 'Took a leaf out of your book. Out of your bra, actually.'

I clapped my hands to my bosom. Until that moment, I hadn't even noticed that one of the krugerrands had gone.

'You didn't?'

'I did. Actually, it was that first edition I was after – you remember, in the antiquarian bookshop? The bookseller sent me down to a coin-dealer who was willing to trade in German marks. The usual – dollars no good, it had to be marks. And then I thought maybe it would work with the petrol, like the truckies said. And it did. Like magic.'

What could I do but pack my luggage into the car? We had introductions, we had a full tank of gas, we had a pocketful of marks, the mountains beckoned. How could I complain?

'Where to now, miss?'

I spread out the map. The taxi-driver was off to Transylvania.

The road to the north stretched straight as an arrow through the flatlands of Wallachia. A soft grey drizzle clouded the fields and dampened the blazing towers of the refineries, swirling round the factory chimneys, softening the outlines of the distant hills.

I had chosen a route recommended by the hotel manageress, which, as the scenic route, meandered through the hills rather than following the motorway.

'It will be longer, but you will not regret it.'

Soon after we left the highway, the route narrowed and we found ourselves among wooded valleys glinting with the red and gold of turning leaves. Hazel, walnut and chestnut copses edged the fields surrounding the little villages. Every now and then we saw pairs of yoked water-buffalo waiting patiently for the hay crop to be loaded on their brightly painted carts.

A signpost by the road told us we were passing Bran Castle, home of Vlad the Impaler – the title earned through a nasty habit of impaling his enemies on stakes on the castle walls. He whose mythical doings provided the nineteenth-century horror-writer Bram Stoker with much of his material, and Romanian plum brandy with its brand name. White-washed battlements topped by russet roofs, domed and turreted, beckoned amiably over the treetops. A handwritten notice announced it closed for renovation.

A few miles further on, just when I was beginning to consider the midday meal, Nicholas braked and drew into the side of the road.

'What is it?' I asked nervously, the secret police never entirely absent from my mind.

'Can't you smell it?'

I wound down the window. Floating down the street was the unmistakable perfume of hot butter. I wrinkled my nose reflectively. I could smell yeast too, and raisins and crystallized fruit. 'It's a wedding party. They've been baking *cozonac*.' I warmed to my theme. 'An enriched bread like the Austrian *kugelhupf* or the Russian *babka*—'

'For heaven's sake, woman, this is an emergency, not a menu. Just concentrate on the source.'

By now the scent was overwhelming.

Silently I pointed up the hill. In the distance, a beribboned cart was rattling up the cobbled street in the wake of a cheerful group who, from the colourfully embroidered skirts of the women and the Sunday-best of the men, must indeed be a wedding party. The cart, it could only be assumed, contained the wedding butter bread.

'*Bitte! S'il vous plaît! Excuse me!*'

Nicholas was off up the street like a hound on the scent of the hare. I followed at a more leisurely pace – loitering might be a more accurate description. Something told me that there would be tears before bedtime, as Nanny used to say.

Nicholas caught up with the cart just before it vanished into a courtyard.

'Excuse me!'

Unable to proceed without spreadeagling a stranger in the dust, the cart rattled to a halt. The exchange that followed was emotionally draining for both parties. The natural desire of the Transylvanian peasant to offer a stranger refreshment, particularly one so obviously willing to part with ready money, was as nothing to the desire of the Transylvanian peasant not to be parted from his wedding cakes, his babies. In the event neither Nicholas's pleadings, nor Romanian lei, nor American dollars, nor German marks, nor Mammon himself could have altered his resolve. The battle of the bread was lost before it had begun. Not since Napoleon retreated from Moscow had so much energy been expended for so little result.

'Never mind,' I offered soothingly. 'I'm sure I can get the recipe.'

'Shut up,' said Nicholas climbing back in the car.

I smiled brightly. 'There's a church a few miles back. We can have a picnic. It's a nice church, very well recommended. It's bound to have a churchyard, and I know you like reading the gravestones.'

This was probably a little near the knuckle, so I added soothingly, 'I've some of that black bread you like, and some pickled herrings.'

'I've got black bread coming out of my ears and I don't want herrings. I want butter bread – and I want to eat it at a nice comfortable table on a nice comfortable chair in a nice comfortable house. And I've had enough of picnics in the rain. And if you tell me that black bread and herrings is the traditional diet of the Romanian peasantry, I'm leaving. Right now.'

A rattle at the window interrupted this unproductive train of thought. A young woman in a flower-embroidered waistcoat and ribbon-patterned skirt, pink-cheeked, bright-eyed, wearing on her dark curls the bridal coronet of golden wheat, was smiling and gesturing that Nicholas should open the door.

'*Prenez. Pour vous. Un cadeau. Porte-bonheur.* It will bring you happiness.'

Into Nicholas's hands she thrust a package. Knotted into a bright kerchief was one of the beautiful wedding breads. What all the money in the world could not buy was hers for the giving. The bride on her wedding day, crowned with the garland of fertility, could never have allowed a stranger to go hungry.

'Goodness,' said Nicholas.

'*C'est beau, n'est pas*? They say it's a copy of the Sistine chapel. But I have never seen the Sistine chapel, so I cannot know if this is true. Perhaps you could tell me.'

The disembodied voice floated through the darkness, almost startling us out of our wits.

Finding the church mercifully unlocked and free of the usual renovations – probably only because the interior was pitch black and no one could see what there was to be renovated – we had carried our picnic inside.

We leaped guiltily to our feet. We had just finished the last of the wedding bread – that it might bring us happiness was an understatement since it had probably prevented instant divorce – when we were caught red-handed, like naughty schoolchildren at a midnight feast.

'*Excusez-nous*, Mademoiselle. We meant no disrespect,' said Nicholas, attempting to stuff the evidence back into the bag.

'There is no need to apologize,' the voice continued in excellent French. 'The Lord's house is open to all, and I am only the guardian. Sometimes I do the same as you, when it is raining, or there are no visitors, which I am afraid is most of the time. Please. Continue with your meal.'

'We've quite finished, thank you.'

Carpathian Cozonac
WEDDING BUTTER BREAD

Yeast-raised doughs enriched with eggs, rich milk and butter are the Balkan celebration cakes; tall and round-topped, the shape is supposed to be like a church bell. The plait symbolizes the long braid the bride cuts off on her wedding day.

———————————————— MAKES 1 LOAF ————————————————

1¼ lb/750 g strong white flour
1 teaspoon salt
1 oz/25 g yeast
½ pint/300 ml warm full-cream
  milk

1 egg
2 oz/50 g melted butter

1. Sieve the flour and salt into a warm bowl. Cream the yeast with the milk and fork it up with the egg and melted butter (reserve a little of the egg-and-milk to brush the top later). Pour the yeast mixture into a well in the flour and work it all together. Knead thoroughly until you have a soft smooth dough – you may need a little more milk.
2. Set the dough to rise for a couple of hours in its bowl in a warm place under a damp cloth, until doubled in size. Knuckle it down and cut it into three equal pieces. Roll each piece into a rope. Pinch the ends together with a damp finger and plait neatly. Coil into a tall round, buttered cake tin. Brush with the reserved milk mixture and set to rise for another hour, until doubled in size again.
3. Meanwhile preheat the oven to 400°F/200°C/mark 6. Bake for 35–40 minutes, until well risen and golden. Transfer to a cake-rack to cool.

'Then perhaps if you have the coins for the machine, I might suggest a little light?'

We had been unable to find a switch. Coins clicked into a meter, bringing life to a single bulb of such wattage as a penny-pinching Eastbourne landlady might provide for her benighted guests. Yet even this minimal illumination was enough to reveal that the interior was, indeed, of astonishing beauty. Its loveliness had little to do with architecture and everything to do with artifice. Like a plain woman transformed by powder and paint, the building was of no particular distinction, serving simply as a background for the frescoes that covered every inch of every surface of every wall, sprawling across the ceiling, creeping up the pillars. No corner, however dim, had escaped the attentions of the artist's brush.

It was not so much the skill of the painting as the sheer exuberance of the work, the astonishing fecundity of the images, the cumulative effect of paint layered on paint. Some of these layers had cracked or peeled to reveal the soft shadows of their predecessors beneath. Here marched a line of saints, here a line of sinners, over there a chorus of seraphim danced over a cloudful of cherubim. Heaven and hell stacked one above the other, God and the Devil face to face, fallen angels dancing among the blessed.

'*Que pensez-vous?*'

'It's – magnificent.' The light had also revealed the speaker to be a middle-aged woman with a trim figure, hair smoothed back in a neat chignon, perfect makeup. The whole package – high-heeled shoes, well-tailored skirt and blouse, silk scarf, a sparkle of gold at ears and wrists – had been put together with the attention to detail a chic Parisienne might devote to a morning's shopping in the Faubourg St Honoré.

'As magnificent, would you say, as the Sistine chapel?' Her voice was eager.

I could not imagine what I might answer. Nicholas, too, was silent. How to explain that the question was irrelevant? To compare the two would be like comparing the beauty of a butterfly's wings with the considered perfection of a Ming vase. How to explain that Michelangelo was an artist of extraordinary powers working within a sophisticated tradition of which he was the undisputed master. An individual, with an individual genius, satisfying a particular patron in a civilization where individuality was prized above all other virtues.

The appeal of this place was far more primitive, did not rely on a single hand or even a single vision, but on the work of many, as of voices singing in harmony; discord would have come from a need to express a single voice.

'I hope some day you will be able to judge for yourself,' Nicholas said, gently breaking the silence.

The light-bulb clicked off on its automatic switch.

Through the darkness came the reply, 'I do not think so. I have long ceased to imagine such a thing might be possible. The time for miracles is past.'

There was no more to be said.

As we walked back down the path in the gathering dusk, the voice called out behind us, 'Wait!'

We halted and turned.

The guardian came towards us, in her outstretched hand a red rose in bloom.

'It is the last of the year. Take it with you on your journey. It will travel with you for a time, as I may not.'

Such images are untidy, have no conclusion. I would like to be able to remember that I took the flower to the chapel in the Vatican, that there it miraculously bloomed anew. But that would be a lie. The rose lived for a time, and withered, and died and, being of no further use, was discarded.

We arrived late and tired at our destination, a ski-resort in the mountains. The mist had drawn down after we left the church, and we had driven through the darkness far longer than we intended.

Poiana Brasov, billed in the guidebook as offering modern comfort at reasonable prices, was a massive new development designed to attract package tourists, offering winter sports with all the facilities that might be expected of a fashionable resort in the West.

The complex was not yet fully operational, the season had

not begun in earnest, and only one of the several huge hotels was open to receive guests. We booked in, left our luggage, and made our way through the lightly falling snow to the building that provided such guests as there were with dining facilities. Lights blazed, the scent of roast chicken wafted encouragingly from the air-conditioning ducts, and even though it was already late, there was clearly no shortage of action.

The choice was between a cafeteria with steel counters and Formica-topped tables crowded with Romanian resort-workers drinking beer and eating the food they had brought for themselves; and a large dining room decorated with brightly painted folk-art and crammed with Eastern European tourists – family parties as well as the usual sober-suited apparatchiks whose massed Mercedes we had already noted in the car-park.

Having finished our stores at lunch and with no prospect of self-catering, we had no choice. There was no table immmediately available, but the dining room was provided with a separate bar for late-comers such as ourselves.

In one corner of the waiting area was a grotto protected by an iron cage. Within, much as a barman in Scotland might display his range of malt whiskies, was an astonishing array of foodstuffs: enormous jars of preserved fruit and pickled vegetables, huge bunches of onions, garlands of peppers, all displayed in glittering rows on wooden shelves. From the ceiling were suspended ranks of glistening hams and strings of plump sausages. In one corner were barrels of sauerkraut, in another sacks of yellow cornmeal, in another a display of wine bottles whose labels proclaimed provenance and vintage. All were spotlit to show everything to its best advantage.

Intrigued, I went looking for the manager. A gloomy young man in a shiny suit was eventually summoned from an office somewhere in the depths of the building. Was it possible, I enquired, that this bounty might be for sale? Absolutely not. The display was for the tourists to admire, visible evidence of the success of Romania's agricultural industry. 'We are a very modern country, as you can see.'

And were the tourists impressed?

'Of course.'

Was there some other commercial outlet in the complex where these splendid goods might be purchased?

A bewildered shake of the head. 'The tourists always eat in the restaurants. We have no self-catering facilities.'

What about the cafeteria? A shrug. That was for the workers.

Ah. Did he think there might be a moment when we might discuss the restaurant menu?

Gladly. That, too, was very modern.

In that case, I would very much like to meet the chef – I would like to discuss traditional recipes, the ones his mother used to make. The manager looked doubtful. Clearly no one had ever put this request to him before. I explained my particular interest. This did not seem to soothe him in the least: the very reverse, he began to look more and more like a rabbit cornered by a stoat.

At this moment, happily for the manager's tranquillity of mind, a waiter arrived with the news that our table was ready. The stoat, however, had no intention of letting its rabbit escape so easily, and we agreed to finish our discussion the following morning over breakfast.

By now, the crowd in the dining room had thinned considerably and service was swift. The menu was an ambitious list of international dishes of the kind found on airlines in superior class. Unfortunately absolutely everything was off except pork chops and chips. We had eaten a lot of pork chops and chips on our travels. Somewhere in Eastern Europe there had to be a chop-and-chip factory with our name on it. We asked for the wine list: this, too, promised all the pleasures of an international cellar. No wine. How about beer? The possibility of beer was grudgingly acknowledged.

A glance at the rest of the tables revealed that everyone else had had no better luck than we. Everyone, that is, but a lone Russian, pasty-faced and bald-pated, whose ostentatiously displayed briefcase marked him out as a member of the ruling class. On the table in front of him was not one packet but a whole carton of Kent. A virgin carton, still in its cellophane wrapper. This staggering display of wealth – rather as if some medieval prince had tipped a purseful of gold coins in front of a crowd of beggars – earned him the attention of every waiter in the room. Very slowly and deliberately, the owner of the objects of desire removed the cellophane, extracted two packets and placed them unopened on the table.

Then he asked for the menu.

The waiters fluttered back and forth in a flurry of anticipation. Two whole packets of Kent. Unopened. One brought fresh rolls, another a plate of butter, a third a bottle of red wine and a glass. One by one the dishes were placed on the table. Roast chicken with sauté potatoes, beetroot dressed with dill and cream, a dish of pumpkin purée from which rose the scent of cinnamon, even, finally and most triumphantly, a bowl of fresh peaches.

In short, the kind of food a traveller confronted by yet another portion-controlled pork chop with limp chips and thin beer would willingly kill for.

The rest of us masticated thoughtfully and watched the millionaire. At the end of the meal, when the waiters had received their reward, the bounder actually broached a new packet and *smoked* one – an action of such staggering profligacy that several of the waiters appeared close to tears.

The following morning I rose early to keep my breakfast appointment with the hotel manager.

I had given up all thoughts of discussing the menu, but hoped he might at least be able to cast some light on the curious lack of local dishes in public eating-places. Professionally, that was. Nothing personal.

Take pork chops and chips, for instance. Pork chops and chips did not seem to reflect what was for sale in the market-place. Where were the vegetables? What was happening to the aubergines, courgettes, peppers? Where was the much-touted *mamaliga* – so far only encountered at Maggie's table? I had read of the delights of *mititei*, grilled-meat patties flavoured with basil and thyme; of slow-simmered stews, *ghiveeiu*, made with veal and red wine and all manner of herbs; of *ciorba*, the famous soups.

Seeing his alarm, I added, 'You must forgive my curiosity. I have a deep admiration for your great nation. There are many

good things in Romania – the beauty of your cities and the
kindness of your people. Your traditional way of life.'

'We are very modern.'

'It's important to be modern?'

'Certainly.'

I waited for illumination.

'We are a modern nation. It is political.'

'Political?'

'Certainly. In Romania, everything is political.'

He glanced over his shoulder at a solitary breakfaster reading a
newspaper. It was impossible to see the man's face. Perhaps, I
thought, he was last night's Russian. The shoes were visible.
They were not the well-polished shoes of an apparatchik, but
well-worn brogues, scuffed and muddy.

Remember, you will be followed everywhere.

As if reading my mind, the young man rose to his feet.
'Perhaps you would allow me to give you a tour of the facilities?
We are very proud of our facilities.'

I followed him out into the pale sunshine. Poiana Brasov was
above the clouds. The first snow had fallen on the upper slopes,
bringing a sparkle to the air and a chill wind to whip the leaves
off the chestnut trees. A web of ski-lifts led up to the ridges of
the mountains, cutting through the forest in broad swathes of
white.

I said, 'The facilities do indeed look very fine. Very
splendidly modern.'

'The skiing is very modern. You should be here for the
skiing. We have many tourists. I'm sure the people who read
what you write would want to know about the skiing.'

'Of course. But I am a food-writer. I would like to be able to
tell them about other things as well. About the old ways, how
people like to cook when they're at home. The traditional
dishes of the countryside.'

'That will not be possible.'

'Why?'

'There are no dishes.'

'Really?'

'No. Romania is modern. Our food is modern. You have
seen in the restaurant, our menu is modern.'

We walked on slowly. I said, 'There don't seem to be many tourists at this time of year. The man reading the newspaper in the breakfast room, would you say he was a tourist?'

The young man shrugged. 'How can I know? You are foreign tourists. You are travelling in a car with German numberplates. Perhaps they are curious.'

'They?'

There was a silence. Then, 'Perhaps you do not understand my country. There are such people everywhere. Sometimes we know who they are, sometimes not. Him I do not recognize. He has written on his document that he is a salesman from Bucharest. He might be a salesman. He might also be a secret policeman. You have written in your document that you are tourists from England. You might also be spies.'

'I'm a cookery-writer,' I said. 'Cookery is not a subject for spies.'

He nodded. 'That is what you tell me. He might be a salesman. You might be a tourist. I might be a hotel manager. How can anyone know who anyone is?'

We walked on. After a moment, I said, 'And you, how do you come to be a hotel manager?'

'It is a position of trust. I am considered trustworthy.'

'And how did you become trustworthy?'

'I was brought up in the state orphanage.'

'I'm so sorry. Were you very young when you lost your parents?'

'I have no mother and father. The state was my mother and father. That is why I am trustworthy. It is political, like the cooking.'

'I still don't understand. If you can tell me why these things are political, I could stop asking stupid questions. Then I could go home and tell everyone how modern Romania is. The state would be pleased. You would be pleased. Everyone would be happy.'

A long silence greeted this subversive suggestion. Then, suddenly, a tumble of information: 'Perhaps you are right. I shall tell you a little of how it is. We in Romania do not cook in the old ways because it is unpatriotic. It would make us remember all the ways we are different from each other. That is not good.

We must be a modern nation – in our work, in our play, in the food we eat.'

'But surely people eat what they like when they're at home?'

'They do not eat at home. Our workers take their meal at midday in their place of work, and for this we have a manual which tells us how much and in what ways we must eat. The government gives us all the food we need and tells us exactly how it must be prepared for maximum nourishment. So much salt, so much oil, everything must be as it is written. In the hotels and restaurants it is the same. So much of that, in such a way as this, and we must not do anything which is not in the book.'

'Can I see the book?'

'No. It is a secret.'

'A secret?'

'Of course.'

'It is political?'

'Of course.'

'And what about the peasants?' I explained about the wedding party and the gift of the *cozonac*.

He shrugged. 'I cannot speak of others. I can only tell you what I know myself. I have received the proper training. I know what I must do. What others do – that is their business.'

As the Mercedes bumped up the unpaved street of the little shepherding village, Margaret Maclean's words came back to me.

You'll have no trouble finding the house. Just look out for the double doors. They're painted a rather chic shade of green. If you're in any doubt, just ask.

In the little mountain village of Rasinari, all the doors were double. All were painted green.

The high walls gave the street a curiously blank look, as if each household was a citadel, barricaded against not only the outside world but its neighbours as well. The wooden doors, though wide enough to drive two carts through abreast, gave no hint of any presence within.

It was mid-afternoon by the time we had arrived in the mountain fastness, and not because we had lingered long at the ski-resort. Something about the interview with the hotel manager had made me anxious to be on our way. As we took the road that led back down to the plain, I kept a careful eye on the rear-view mirror.

'What's up?' asked Nicholas.

'Wolves,' I said. 'Possibly bears.'

It's unwise to interfere with a driver's concentration with talk of secret police, particularly if there's a swirling mist cutting visibility to a few yards, and there's a fifty-foot drop on either side of the road.

As we emerged from the forest, the mist turned to rain. We had planned to spend the remainder of the morning wandering round the town of Brazov, recommended by the guidebook as 'charmingly medieval'. In the West, 'charmingly medieval' means heavily restored buildings, coach-loads of tourists, theme restaurants, souvenir shops and nowhere to park. In Eastern Europe at that time it meant exactly the same thing but without the tourists, the shops or the restaurants.

As soon as we reached the industrial outskirts what had started as gentle rain – dampening down the dust, bouncing prettily off the prefabricated roofs of the factories – turned into a steady downpour. By the time we reached the centre, the rain had already filled the gutters and was coursing down the cobbled streets in glistening streams.

Sightseeing was out of the question – even in a town as well equipped with charming buildings as this. We took shelter in the Black Church, the town's main attraction. The Black Church could never have been charming. Imposing, certainly; architecturally distinguished, without doubt; but charming – never.

Fortified churches have a peculiar poignancy, and none more so than those that bear the scars of battle. The interior of the Black Church had been burned out during one of the many wars with Austria, when the Catholic Austro-Hungarian Empire had decided to teach the refugee German Reformed congregations a lesson. Its subsequent restoration to its Gothic glory had not obliterated the scorch-marks on the walls. These remained, serving the citizenry as a permanent reminder that, in Transylvania at least, trouble comes from the West. The legacy of the Muslim Ottoman Empire seemed of an altogether more amiable nature. Turkish carpets glowed against the walls like sombre jewels. The prosperous burghers of Brazov were accustomed to commemorate their prominent citizens with prayer-mats bought from the merchants of Smyrna and Ladak.

When we finally emerged from the church, the rain was still bucketing down, the streets were still deserted and such public eating facilities as might be glimpsed through misted windows appeared to have given up the idea of attracting business.

We decided to cut our losses and head for the hills. There was a good chance the weather would improve in the highlands, and the mountain villages might be above the clouds. The shepherding communities of the Carpathians would surely pay no attention to a little rain.

The drive should have taken no more than an hour. The road to Rasinari, as marked on Margaret Maclean's map, turned off the main highway, a four-lane monster that carried traffic through from Russia to Hungary and served as the main trade route with the West.

An endless mass of thick yellow fleece and golden eyes flowed slowly down both sides of the four-lane highway: the pride of Romania brought to a halt by a sea of sheep.

We had no choice but to stop on the hard shoulder. We were not alone: a couple of overloaded elderly transport trucks, the shiny black limo of an irate apparatchik on his way home to the capital, a pre-war butane-fuelled bus full of women farm labourers, all were obliged to bow to the ancient right of transhumance, the biannual pilgrimage that brings the flocks from summer to winter pastures.

While we were waiting for the mobile road-block to clear, Nicholas found a new best friend among the truckies. He was a driver from Düsseldorf, his girlfriend lived in Brazov and kept him abreast of the latest shepherd jokes – among other things Nicholas was too delicate to relay.

Mercifully most of these were not the same as Greek shepherd jokes, having more to do with brass than bottoms.

'Have you heard the one about the shepherd who couldn't afford a helicopter because he only had a million dollars in his mattress?'

I conceded that this pleasure had so far escaped me.

'Don't worry. He borrowed the rest from his brother.'

Nicholas rocked gleefully. 'Here's one the shepherds make about the townies. Did you hear about the man who couldn't tell the difference between a wolf and sheep?'

I admitted I hadn't. Nicholas communicated something mystifying about the state-employed quota-fixer who tried to count a pack of wolves, and which might have had something in common with Greek shepherd jokes in that it certainly featured woolly yellow bottoms. Apparently it brought the house down in the bars of Brazov.

There were more in similar vein.

Forty minutes later, the rearguard appeared – two shepherds, a pack-donkey and half a dozen rangy pale-eyed dogs. The shepherds were lean, Mongolian-cheekboned, wrapped, like their charges, in heavy yellow fleeces. Black felt chimney-pot hats were pulled down over the ears to protect them against the rain. By this time Nicholas's new best friend had run out of jokes about mutton millionaires and had headed off into the distance in a cloud of black exhaust.

The road that led up into the mountains was no more than a cart-track and showed evidence of the passing of many sheep, but absolutely no sign of any vehicles. We began to worry that the entire population was off on transhumance and we had had a wasted journey.

The village street was formed not of houses or even cottages but of high walls pierced at intervals by the double doors. Each of the green-painted doors had a smaller person-sized door set into its centre. There appeared to be no alternative but to knock on every one until someone answered. I climbed out of the car. At this moment a small girl, followed by a large, mud-spattered pig, came running down the street. A torrent of Romanian appeared to invite us to follow.

The little girl and the pig bounced off up the street, checking our progress at intervals. Ten minutes later our guide halted, beaming, outside a pair of double doors – admittedly of a far more tasteful shade of green.

Beside the small central door, his hands extended in welcome, stood a figure who might have been the twin of the shepherds we had passed on the road. Broad-shouldered and stockily built, with a shock of grey hair and the high cheekbones, slanting dark eyes and bronzed skin of the mountain men, Vilmos was not only at home, he had already had notice of our impending visit.

In fact, he explained in fluent German as he made us welcome at a table set ready under the grape arbour, he had delayed his own departure to await our arrival.

How on earth, Nicholas enquired, had he known we were coming? There had been no sign of telephone wires along the road.

'We have ways.' Vilmos placed his finger against his nose, then, relenting, added, 'We are shepherds. We have short-wave radios. I had news of you from Bucharesti. The men you passed on the road are my two brothers – they warned me you were on your way.' A roar of laughter punctuated this admission. 'But we shall talk of these things later. First we must greet you in the proper manner.'

At this moment a young woman with pink cheeks and a heart-shaped face framed by a flowered kerchief came through from the interior of the house with a painted wooden tray. On it was set a little dish of sticky scarlet jam, a pair of silver spoons, very highly polished, and two tumblers of water.

'Eat, drink. It is the custom. It is in this way we say we sweeten the arrival of a guest. Also, you will find it good. My wife makes it herself with cherries from our own tree.'

We did as we were bidden. The preserve was of an intense syrupy sweetness, dark fruit suspended in a thick juice, like liquid toffee. The water was indeed necessary, if only to clear the palate.

'*Ist gut*. Now we may be friends. I already know your names, and you know mine – and this my wife Karina. I also know that you, *gnädige Frau*, are very fond of questions.'

I nodded gravely. 'Then you will also know I am discreet.'

'That too.' The dark eyes examined me shrewdly. 'But in these mountains we fear no man. Nor should you, while you remain with us. You may ask such questions as you wish, and I shall answer as I see fit.'

211

How was it, I enquired, that the villagers of Carpathians had escaped collectivization?

A shrug. It had always been so, back to the Romans. The shepherds paid no dues to the Tartars, even the Turks failed to tax them. What chance had the men from Bucharest, with their soft hands and their thin shoes? Naturally, the tax-collectors came to the village and asked questions and filled in forms. Unfortunately, they were very accident-prone. Most unfortunately accident-prone. Many times they slipped into the ravines on the way home, and if not, there were wild animals in the woods. I would understand how it could be. The mountains were full of hazards – bears and wolves and slippery ravines, and then in winter there were blizzards and avalanches.

But did they not send in soldiers? Of course. But the soldiers did not want what the tax-collectors wanted. The soldiers were only too happy to buy the shepherds' goods and take them home to their families. The bureaucrats too. The cities were starved for supplies. And the shepherds would take the produce down for sale only when the black market was operating. If the men from Bucharest closed down the black market, the people in the cities, even in Bucharest itself, were left hungry and angry, so the officials had no choice.

Strong white teeth gleamed against the dark skin. 'Bears – now, there's a creature worthy of respect. You notice the old man on the way into the village? No? He comes to rob our honey – but he is old and toothless and his claws are worn. Like the tax-collectors from Bucharest, all he can do is sniff the scent.'

A bellow of laughter punctuated this assessment. 'And wolves, they too command respect. We have reason to fear the wolves who steal our sheep. But when they come in the autumn to feed on the fermented plums in our orchards, they are like the apparatchiks on the vodka – harmless to everyone but themselves. It is the same in your country?'

More laughter, this time shared by all.

'*Ist gut*. We understand each other.'

Our host rose to his feet. 'And now, *die Herren* may leave *die Damen* to their own affairs. There is plum brandy, our famous *tsuica*, ready for distilling.'

The two men vanished down the street, leaving me to explore the little citadel with my young hostess. We communicated as the best we could, my Romanian being rather less fluent than what Karina described as a little English learned at school.

On the side facing the double doors, elevated on a wooden platform and shaded by a vine-covered verandah, were the living quarters and kitchen with its wood-fired stove and adjoining larder. The other three sides offered shelter for a water-powered generator, a store for firewood and sheds for domestic animals, chickens, a pig, a milk-cow and her calf. The cow, explained Karina, with much laughter and many gestures, provided the household with milk and butter, and there was cheese from the sheep-milking.

Flanking the living quarters was Vilmos's glass-painting studio. His work, primitive but confidently executed scenes from the life of the village, was neatly stacked on the workbench, ready for customers such as ourselves. On the other side was a sewing room piled with embroidered leatherwork; the sale of such goods, explained my hostess with apron-tying gestures, provided the corner-of-the-apron money every housewife needs for the purchase of small luxuries and those household items that cannot be home-made.

In fact, she had just sold an embroidered lambskin waistcoat, which meant she could afford to buy a chicken-brick she had long had her eye on in the market in the town. 'Many times I look. Many times I not have money. When I have money I buy. Wait. I show.'

Out came a basket. Within, still wrapped in newspaper, was a large oval pot of unglazed earthenware. This, demonstrated with much clucking and gestures designed to indicate neck-wringing, would be particularly useful when one of the hens was fit for nothing but the pot.

'First time, I cook chicken in water to make a *zupa*. Not eat chicken. I put here. I take—' She hesitated, frowning. 'Wait. I show you.'

A string of garlic and a pat of beautiful white butter were fetched from the larder. 'I do it like so, and so.'

The imaginary chicken was popped triumphantly in the pot

with what appeared to be at least a whole head of the rosy cloves and most of the butter. This, she explained, was an excellent recipe she had from her neighbour, also the proud owner of a chicken-brick, which would provide two dishes for the price of one.

'Is . . .' she hesitated again ' . . . *economical*. Is right word?'

'Quite the right word.'

'Good. Economical is good. I get this word from American lady who buy waistcoat.' She looked at me expectantly.

This was too strong a hint to ignore. I smiled. 'I, too, would like to buy waistcoat. And my husband, I know, would like to buy one of your husband's paintings.'

'Is good. Later we choose.'

Economy was what mattered most to the household. Nothing must go to waste. Everything in the compound had to earn its keep. The grape arbour, which shaded the verandah, provided not only fruit for the table and for the winter preserves but vine leaves, which could be rolled round a stuffing to make her husband's favourite dish.

'You mean *sarmale*?'

'*Da, da.* You know it?'

Indeed I did. Variations on the theme of stuffed leaves are to be found in all lands which come under Ottoman influence. The wrapper is as variable as the stuffing, but the principle remains the same. Of course, she continued, pleased to satisfy my interest, the vine leaves were for the summer-time. For the rest of the year, the wrapper might be spinach, or cabbage, or whatever was suitable for the season.

'Often I make, maybe two times a week. You like to try?'

Indeed I like to try.

Karina fetched what I recognized as a dutch oven, oval in shape and of heavy enamel, inside which were neatly packed many little dark, green rolls, much like the Turkish *dolmades*. The pot had a reversible lid on which, Karina demonstrated, might be placed hot coals, permitting the rolls on top to cook at the same time as those beneath.

'Here, take fork. You taste.' She watched me eagerly. 'Is good?'

'*Buna, buna – va multu mesc.*' This, my few words of

214

appreciation and thanks in Romanian, brought much giggling and correction of the pronunciation.

The wrapper of fresh vine leaf had a slightly acid flavour, like sorrel. The filling was of very finely minced meat and some kind of grain I did not recognize, flavoured with mint and the chilli that all self-sufficient households plant as a substitute for pepper.

'*Sarmale* good with meat. When no meat I make with . . .' A worried frown. 'Wait. I show.'

Down from the shelf came raisins, accompanied by gestures at the vine on the verandah, pine kernels, with wavings at the forest, a handful of tiny dried fungi, with a sweep of the hand towards the pastures.

'Also, I like to make a little sauce with . . .' From the larder came a jug of thick soured cream.

'For special days, we make with . . .' Out came a jar of rice, displayed with particular pride. 'Must buy in market. Cost money. For every day—' She frowned. 'You know what is *pasatul*?'

I admitted I didn't.

'Come, I show.'

I followed her out to the grain store, where she took a handful of dried maize kernels and tipped them into a little mill. She turned the handle a few times, producing roughly crushed grain. 'You see? Like this, no more. Is not same for *mamaliga*. For *mamaliga* we must turn many times. For *pasatul*, only little times. You see?'

I saw.

'We have meat. Last day we kill a man sheep, very old, very—' She chewed ferociously.

'Tough?'

'*Da*. First must be—' She made chopping gestures. 'Very many times. Very old sheeps, very, very many times. Then is good for *sarmale*.'

'Very good, very economical,' I said.

She nodded thoughtfully. 'Tell me, in your country, what you do when you have very old sheeps?'

I explained about shepherd's pie, Irish stew, Scotch broth.

'So. Which your husband like to eat?'

Carpathian Sarmale
STUFFED CABBAGE ROLLS

It was the Ottoman Turks who taught their subject nations how to stuff and roll a leaf. Among the shepherding communities of the Carpathians, these are made in winter with salt cabbage – *varza acra* – vine leaves in spring and fresh cabbage leaves at other times. A variable recipe: if you don't have any meat, use dried or fresh mushrooms.

─────────────── SERVES 4 ───────────────

1 green cabbage
4 thick rashers smoked bacon
8 oz/250 g long-grain rice
2 oz/50 g lard
1 medium onion, skinned and chopped
2 garlic cloves, finely chopped
salt and pepper

6 oz/175 g minced lamb, pork or beef
1 egg
1 tablespoon parsley, finely chopped
1 tablespoon marjoram, finely chopped
1 tablespoon dill, finely chopped

─────────────── TO FINISH ───────────────

1 glass white wine
1 tablespoon paprika

1 tablespoon flour, lightly toasted in a dry pan

216

1. Take off about twenty leaves of the cabbage and blanch them for 5 minutes in boiling water. Drain and set them aside. Shred the rest of the cabbage and put it in a casserole with the thick smoked-bacon rashers. Cover with enough water to submerge everything (only just), bring it to the boil, turn down the heat, lid loosely and leave it to simmer gently for 20 minutes while you attend to the rest.

2. Pick over the rice. Put half the lard to heat in a frying-pan and fry the chopped onion and garlic until soft but not browned. Add the rice and stir it over the heat until it's transparent. Season with salt and pepper and add enough water just to submerge the rice. Bring to the boil, turn down the heat and simmer for 10 minutes, when the rice will still be chewy. Tip the contents of the pan into a bowl with the minced meat, egg and herbs, and mix thoroughly with your hand, squeezing to make a firm mixture.

3. Lay out the blanched leaves, nicking out any particularly thick stalks. Place a small ball of stuffing (about a tablespoon) on each leaf, and roll it up neatly, tucking the sides over first to enclose the mixture. Lay the little parcels on top of the cabbage and bacon. Pour in the wine, cover and cook either gently on top of the stove, or in a medium oven, 350°F/180°C/mark 4, for an hour, until the cabbage is perfectly tender.

4. Mash up the remaining lard with the paprika and toasted flour, and stir it into the juices at the end of the cooking. Taste, and correct seasoning if necessary.

Carpathian Galuska
BUCKWHEAT PORRIDGE

Buckwheat is an upland grain, a quick-growing crop from Central Asia that enjoys poor soil and a cool climate. The grain has an unusual sweetish scent and gritty texture which is rather addictive. The porridge-stirrer is a small fir-tree branch, trimmed down to a joint from which protrude four twigs; the instrument can be held between the palms and whirled round, rather like a primitive food processor.

———————————— SERVES 2 ————————————

½ pint/300 ml milk   *2 oz/50 g buckwheat flour*
a large pinch salt

———————————— TO SERVE ————————————
fresh berries and cream or *sour cream and honey*
poppy seeds mixed with sugar

1. Pour the milk and salt into a wide, shallow, heavy saucepan. Bring it to the boil and sprinkle in the buckwheat flour a little at a time, stirring to mix it all in. Cook it over a low heat for 6–7 minutes, still stirring to prevent the mixture from sticking, until the porridge is smooth, and a spoon drawn across the pan reveals the bottom clearly. Pour into 2 little bowls and leave to cool.
2. Serve for breakfast or a light supper with fresh berries and cream – clotted is perfect – or sour cream and honey. Sprinkle generously with poppy seeds mixed with sugar.

I explained about the milk-simmered mutton of the Western Isles and oat porridge for breakfast.

Karina listened gravely. 'Here we make it with buckwheat. Next time I make it for Vilmos, I'll do it with oats. He will like to eat what Scottish people eat.'

At this moment the courtyard doors banged open.

An emotional rendering in close harmony of 'Return to Mingalay', one of those lugubrious ballads into which Scots are prone to tumble when in their cups, made it clear that the two men had already found much to share.

Thus fortified and equipped with our remaining stock of Deutschmarks, Nicholas negotiated the purchase of two paintings, one of a pig-killing, the other a sheep-shearing; plus three waistcoats, one for each of our daughters.

To this respectable haul he added a black felt flower-pot hat which had been treated with mutton fat to make it waterproof.

A man must do what a man must do. Nevertheless, I rather wished our host had not been impelled to add – by way of discount and to keep his new-found friend warm on the long journey home to the windy Hebrides – his second-best sheepskin overcoat, a gigantic garment whose rich aroma and lively secondary population of fauna were ample proof of authenticity.

In my view – and Nicholas being somewhat the worse for wear was in no position to argue the toss – transhumancing shepherds is one thing, transhumancing fleas is quite another. By the time we had reached our night's destination, I had quietly disposed of both hat and overcoat, leaving their owner none the wiser. Man proposes, woman disposes – and that's the way of the world.

CHAPTER EIGHT

Sibiu Saxons

> *The Saxons say it is such a town because they founded it, the Magyars because they once ruled it, and the Romanians because the air is so fine . . . The Saxon peasant women were easily distinguishable by their flat straw hats with immense brims, and their rather sombre clothes. They were not free and easy in their bargaining; they joked little and prospered exceedingly . . .*

D. J. HALL, *Travels in Romania* (1936)

'GOTT SEI DANK! I WAS WORRIED YOU MIGHT HAVE LOST YOUR way.' The Bishop's wife herself came to the door to answer my knock, hastily removing a flowered apron. 'I had word from dear Margaret two days, and I have been expecting you ever since. But now you are here, *alles ist gut.*'

The hand that grasped mine was bony and freckled with age, but surprisingly strong. The face was lined and weathered, the hair white and severely pulled back in a bun – but the eyes, of an extraordinary cornflower blue, were as bright and alert as a girl's.

The Bishop's Palace, a handsome baroque building at one corner of Sibiu's imposing central square, had the comfortable air of a family home. A cat was sunning itself on a window-sill, and net curtains of a dazzling whiteness shaded the narrow windows.

'Come in, come in, *bitte, gnädige Frau* – we cannot be seen like two old gossips on the doorstep.' Fran Klein's eyes examined me shrewdly as soon as I crossed the threshold.

Apparently satisfied, she nodded and added, 'We – my granddaughters and I – hope you and your husband will be able to join us for the evening meal. I'm sure we will have much to discuss. *Bitte* – come inside while I fetch my coat. I would like you to see our church before it gets too dark.'

The suggestion was no surprise. Margaret Maclean had already told me that religion remained a powerful unifying force among the German communities. 'The bishops no longer have the temporal power, but the spiritual remains,' she had said thoughtfully. 'The Sibiu communities have managed to keep their independence in spite of everything the regime could do. This is true of many minorities. Long after the blueprint has vanished, the isolated communities keep to the old ways. The Saxons are the most cohesive of all. You'll find them very remarkable people.'

The hallway was cavernous and shadowy, scented with lavender and beeswax. My hostess indicated an ottoman covered in buttoned velvet. 'Sit, please sit. You must be tired after your journey. I shall only be a moment to make myself respectable. You must forgive me – I have been in the kitchen, as you can see from my apron. It is time for us to make our jams for the winter and today, for the first time for many months, there was some sugar in the market.'

She reappeared almost immediately in a smart black coat, buttoned high under the chin. A dark felt hat had been securely anchored over her white hair.

'We must hurry. The children will soon be out from school, and then we shall have no time to talk until the evening.'

Frau Klein pushed her arm through mine, and set off purposefully across the square towards a large building with a green tiled roof and a square tower surmounted by a cupola. 'Our church is not ostentatious – I hope that is the word? – but we think it is appropriate. We say it is built for the glory of God, not the glorification of man. We are five churches round the *piata*. We are Calvinist, Orthodox, Catholic, Unitarian and ourselves. We are the oldest; we have been here for eight hundred years. You will be pleased to hear we do not quarrel among ourselves, even though our ways are very different. There is room in God's house for all.'

The church, she pointed out with pride, had recently been reroofed with handsome ceramic tiles of a glorious frog-green – the only frivolity. As for the rest, it had more the air of a fortress than a church. 'We are a minority,' Frau Klein explained. 'We needed our walls and our arrow-slits. We have had to defend ourselves many times in our history. It is the price of our religion.'

Beside the church was the Saxon school. 'This is very important. Without our children we are nothing. We serve not only the Saxon community in Sibiu, but the seven Saxon villages all around. We speak Saxon and this is the language in which the children learn their lessons. It is similar to German, but not the same.' A pause. 'You speak German, Frau Lisbet?'

'Very little, Frau Klein. My husband has enough to get by. I have only kitchen-German, because that's my interest.'

My guide nodded. 'Margaret has already told me this. It is a great pity my husband is not here. The Bishop is always glad to meet visitors and he knows many things which I do not. We live very much within our own community. And I am afraid your husband will be bored by all the talk of domestic matters. But my granddaughters will be happy to practise their English. We shall manage well enough.'

A bell clanged. The sound of children's voices rose, bringing a smile to Frau Klein's face. 'I think perhaps we shall go in before the children find us and we have no peace.'

The interior of the church, vast and austere, was made of pale stone. The glass in the windows was clear, letting in shafts of bright sunlight. The only concession to decoration was a line of military escutcheons supported by ample, somewhat Wagnerian, nymphs. These, explained Frau Klein, her voice low in deference to the Lord's presence, commemorated the lives of prominent and wealthy citizens. 'I cannot say that I approve. I cannot think it is proper that such eminence should be given to so few when so many go unrecorded.'

Candle sconces provided a soft illumination, but the air was chilly and we did not linger. Outside in the square, Frau Klein took temporary leave. 'You will forgive me. I must be with my granddaughters. But I shall expect you in an hour, if that is convenient. My granddaughters must attend school tomorrow, so you will forgive us if we eat at our usual time.'

That evening – although it was scarcely evening, since the family took its meal as soon as the sun set – all three were at the door to greet us.

Frau Klein beamed with pride as she introduced the two girls. 'This is Katrina – she is the eldest. And this is Silvya, we say she is the baby of the family, even though she is no longer a baby.'

With their bright blue eyes, round pink cheeks and long blonde hair worn in plaits tied round their neat little heads like crowns, the two girls looked like Saxon princesses painted by some medieval monk to illustrate a German princeling's Book of Hours.

Formal introductions completed, Frau Klein led the way to the upstairs living room, full of dark oak furniture, heavily carved, polished until the wood gleamed like silk. Against the wall a carved linen-press was piled with papers, and several mahogany bookcases held hand-tooled volumes bound in leather. There were no comfortable armchairs, but rather, formal groupings of upright chairs arranged as if for conversation.

Katrina had just returned from a visit to West Germany. It had been her first experience of Western culture. When Nicholas asked if she had enjoyed her visit, she considered the question seriously before answering in her careful schoolgirl English. 'It is a strange place. Very noisy, very crowded. You will forgive me if I say I found it ugly. So many advertisements for so many things that people do not need unless they are told they do. The people are not friendly. They do not talk in the street, but hurry past without looking at each other. I think they do not care for one another. I do not think I should ever want to live there.'

Even so, prompted Frau Klein gently, there are many good things in the West. And there was no doubt that ideas had changed in Transylvania from the days when she herself was a young girl. Even in Sibiu there had been many changes. She walked over to a small dining table the two girls had just moved into the centre of the room. On it was a white linen cloth inset with panels of hand-made lace.

'For instance, take this tablecloth. I am ashamed to tell you this beautiful work is not my own. I might say I have not the time – but it is also true I have not the patience. Instead, I must go to the villages and pay for the work of others.'

She ran her hand over the delicate embroidery. 'But I am glad to pay, when I have the money. If we do not value such work, the people will not make it any more. Many things are like that. When I was a child, the young girls all came to church in embroidered pinafores, very becoming, and you could tell which village they came from by the pattern and colours. Everyone knew who they were and where they belonged.'

She glanced at her granddaughters, smiling. 'Now the young people wear what *you* like to wear, my Katya, in spite of what you say about the West. Who was it who was asking for jeans the other day, so she could help with the harvest? And who was it who told me they could only be of one particular American make?' The teasing was affectionate, but it was enough to cause her granddaughter to blush. 'We must all change with the times, *Schatzi*. Not everything of the past is to be regretted.'

Katrina's eyes were sparkling. 'Of course, Grandmother. But, still, I am happy to be home.'

'If that is so, *Liebling*, you and your sister shall bring in the supper. Our guests have travelled far. They will surely be hungry.'

One by one the dishes were set on the table. A plate with slices of home-made smoked sausage came with cucumber dressed with sweetened vinegar and dill. Slices of pâté – pork liver with juniper, also of her own making, said Frau Klein –

arrived with a little dish of red peppers. There was bread of her own baking, milk-bread, said Frau Klein, very Saxon, the crumb pale and soft, the crust thick and golden. This was accompanied by a crystal dish of apricot jam and another of honeycomb, glistening chunks of translucent wax brimming with thick dark honey.

'This is our typical Saxon meal for the evening, a little bit special because we have guests. It is not our main meal of the day, you understand. That we take at midday, the *Mittagessen*. In the evening, we eat like this, using only what we can find in the larder.'

Katya came in with a rush basket lined with an embroidered napkin in which were tucked six freckled brown eggs. 'Thank you, Katya. My granddaughter thought you must taste our eggs. We are lucky to have our own hens.' She smiled. 'Enough talk for now. We have a saying, hunger is the best sauce, and I can see that you are hungry. Katrina will say grace.'

Heads were bowed and hands folded. Katrina delivered the Saxon grace in her high clear voice. 'Bless the Lord for his bounty. May the Lord make us thankful for meat.'

Frau Klein nodded approvingly. 'Silvya, pass round the eggs, *bitte, meine Liebling.*'

She noticed Nicholas struggling with a soft-boiled egg for which there was no sign of an egg-cup, and reached out her hand. 'Here let me show you how we do it.' Holding the egg delicately in her cupped hand, she tapped it sharply on the round end, then set it back on the plate. The egg balanced perfectly.

'There.' The blue eyes twinkled. 'Perhaps, after all, there are still some things we in the East can teach you of the West.' She watched Nicholas eat, then frowned. 'What am I thinking? There must be soup. Men are always hungry. I'm sure there's some left over from the *Mittagessen*. I shall fetch it at once. It will still be warm on the back of the stove.'

In spite of Nicholas's assurances that the table was already well laden, Frau Klein bustled out, to return moments later with a steaming bowl.

'Eat while it's hot. Tomorrow I shall give your wife the recipe. It is thickened with egg and we put in a little sour wine

Sibiu Salatsuppe
CREAMY LETTUCE SOUP WITH POTATOES

This Sibiu-Saxon soup, as with so many German soups, is sharpened with vinegar. Pretty as a picture and quick to prepare, it's also something useful to do with a glut of lettuces.

———— SERVES 4 ————

1 lb/500 g potatoes, peeled and chopped into walnut-sized pieces	2 large lettuces, shredded
4 oz/100 g smoked bacon, diced	4 eggs
generous bunch spring onions, trimmed and sliced with their green	$^1/_2$ pint/300 ml single cream
	$^1/_2$ pint/300 ml milk
	salt and pepper

———— TO FINISH ————

4 tablespoons wine vinegar
chives or *spring onion, green only, chopped*

1. Put the potato chunks to cook in 1 pint/600 ml lightly salted water until tender – about 20 minutes. Meanwhile, gently fry the bacon in a small frying-pan until the fat runs. Add the spring onions and let them soften a little. As soon as the potatoes are done, remove them and reserve. Add the bacon, onion and shredded lettuce to the potato water and reheat.
2. Whisk together the eggs, cream and milk with a ladleful of the hot broth. Add this creamy mixture to the pan and stir over a low flame until the soup thickens nicely – don't let it boil or it'll curdle. Stir in the chives or spring onions and the vinegar. Serve poured over the potatoes in individual plates, sprinkled with chives or spring onions.

– very typical of the Saxon villages. We eat bread with our soups, never *mamaliga* because we are Saxon. You have tried the *mamaliga*? You like it? My granddaughters too. But, in my grandmother's time, the Saxons never ate it – it was food only for the poorest villagers when there was no bread. But the children like it, so I think perhaps that, too, will change.'

Frau Klein surveyed the table. 'I hope it will be sufficient. Only on Sunday do we have meat, and then only at the *Mittagessen*.' She shook her head sadly. 'In my grandmother's time, there was always roasted meat on the Lord's Day. Now we cannot afford such luxuries even if we can find them. These days we must make do with the bacon or the sausage. We make our own after the pig-killing in December, after the first snows.' She smiled at me. 'When it snows the country people say St Elisabeth shakes her petticoat, so you would find yourself at home, *gnädige Frau*. We must not complain. Sometimes, if there has been a wedding or a christening, we might perhaps have a chicken brought in by one of our parishioners. The people pay the Church in any way they can. Often when there is very little in the collecting plate on Sunday there are eggs or a piece of cheese or a pat of butter left in a basket by the door. I always know whose gift it is because of the pattern on the butter.'

Her face crinkled with laughter. 'Once, at a time when I had been visiting in the villages and my husband too had been absent, in the basket was not butter or cheese but a fat little mouse. The mouse had made a nest of paper for her babies and they had eaten all the food. Do you remember, Silvya? You were the one who found her – and you cried so because she had eaten your butter.'

Silvya giggled and whispered in her grandmother's ear.

'My granddaughter says you will not think well of us if we have a mouse in our church. I tell her the Lord looks after mouse babies, just as He looks after her.' She put her hand gently to her granddaughter's cheek. 'What do you say, *Schatzi*? Now you are so old and wise, would you still mind if a mouse baby ate your butter?'

Her granddaughter ducked her head to hide her blushes, and set about clearing away the few empty dishes.

'Not so quickly, *Schatzi*. Our guests have not yet finished, and nor have I. They have not yet tried the *Leberwurst* with the peppers. Please, try.' She helped us to the food, watching as we tasted, smiling at our nods of approval. 'I'm happy you find it good. We make the peppers every year at this time. It's very simple. You make ribbons of the peppers, and cook them very slowly with raisins and a little vinegar. And you must also try our syrup of wild plums – I think you call them sloes? Sometimes we make a jam, when we cannot get the sugar. We must boil it and boil it so it will keep without going bad. In the winter we like to take it hot with cloves for a cold.'

She poured a little into two glasses and diluted each with water from a jug. 'Here. Taste.' The blue eyes watched us once more. 'Good. You have children, I think? Then they will gather for you and you will make your own.'

I laughed. 'I'm afraid all mine are grown and gone. When they come home it is only to eat and sleep.'

'Then you will have to buy from the gypsies, but carefully because they are not always to be trusted – they sometimes include little stones to make up the weight. To make the syrup, you must first take the fruit and make little cuts – like so. You must put them with fresh water – very clean water from the well. You shall leave them in the water for three days. After this you can throw the fruit away. To each litre of the water you must put the same amount of sugar. Mix it together in a – what do I mean? I shall fetch it for you to see.'

She rose, returning with a large enamel pail. 'See? This is what I mean. It has a handle for hanging it on the hook over the stove. Sometimes we take it into the orchard to make jam. For making the syrup, the water must boil, but not too quickly. And you must stir it so the sugar disappears and the water is quite clear, like glass. When it is boiled, you may take it off. When it is quite cool, you must put it into very clean bottles. If this is done just as I say, the syrup will keep until the spring. And in the spring, you will no longer need to drink the syrup because you have fresh foods to eat and there will be no need of store-cupboards.'

She rose and went over to the linen-chest from which the papers had been removed to make space for a sideboard, returning with a rectangular porcelain plate on which were slices of golden cake studded with raisins, crystallized fruit and walnuts. 'Now that you have listened to my stories, I think you are ready for our Bishop's Bread. My grandmother baked it every Sunday, when we lit the oven to roast the meat. Now we have no meat, but because of the sugar in the market yesterday we can at least make cake. When I was a child, I was never sure if it was called Bishop's Bread because it was richer than poor people's bread, or because it was good and the people liked it. Now I am old, I still don't know. Perhaps a little of both.'

Frau Klein supervised the appreciation of the cake. Then she put out her hand to her younger granddaughter. '*Schatzi*, now you may fetch what you have prepared.'

Silvya jumped up eagerly, returning from the sideboard with a white china bowl in which gleamed a handful of tiny blue-black damsons.

'Silvya picked them specially when she knew you would be here. The tree is very old and we are proud it gives such good fruit.'

The damsons, dewed with little specks of golden juice that had hardened into amber tear-drops, was as sweet as honey, with translucent green flesh and tiny almond-shaped stones. The girls began to crack the stones between their teeth to get at the bitter little kernels. Bits of shell flew all over the room in a sudden burst of anarchy, which their grandmother brought firmly to a halt.

Noticing Nicholas stifling a yawn, Frau Klein rose to her feet.

'I'm afraid, Frau Lisbet, we have tired your husband with all this talk of domestic matters. Tomorrow he shall be allowed to sleep late. But if you will come to the church at nine, we will go to market together.'

The following morning, after a brief inspection of the hotel breakfast table and finding nothing but poppy-seed rolls and pink sausage, I made my way to the church just as the clock struck the hour.

Frau Klein bustled out into the sunshine, her basket over her arm.

'*Guten Morgen*, Frau Lisbet. You slept well?'

Sibiu Bischofsbrot
BISHOP'S BREAD

A light fruit cake which is all the better when kept for a few days, well wrapped or in an airtight tin. Since it's fatless, you can spread the slices with butter.

─────────── SERVES 6 ───────────

3 eggs
3 oz/75 g caster sugar
6 oz/150 g plain flour
1 tablespoon candied peel, chopped

1 tablespoon glacé cherries, sliced
2 oz/50 g walnuts, chopped
butter and flour for the loaf-tin

─────────── TO FINISH ───────────

icing sugar – vanilla-flavoured, if possible

1. Preheat the oven to 350°F/180°C/mark 4.
2. Beat the egg yolks with all but 1 tablespoon of the sugar until white and light – this takes longer than you think, so keep going. Whisk the whites until stiff (don't overbeat or they go grainy), then beat in the remaining tablespoon of sugar. Sieve the flour into a bowl and mix in the fruit and nuts. Fold in the whisked yolks alternately with the whisked whites until all is well blended.
3. Butter and flour a small loaf tin – 9 in x 5 in/23 cm x 13 cm equivalent. Tip in the cake mixture, spreading it into the corners. Bake for 45–50 minutes until well-risen, shrunk from the sides and firm to the finger. Transfer to a baking rack to cool.
4. Dust with icing sugar, and try not to cut it until tomorrow, when it will be even better.

Indeed I had. Although the reception rooms were undergoing noisy refurbishment and the dining room was open only for the serving of the dismal breakfast, the hotel was modern and perfectly comfortable.

'And your husband? He slept well too? I had been worried about the soup. One should always eat lightly in the evening – so much better for the sleeping. But the men need to eat.'

She stood for a moment, looking round the square. 'Over there you may see the old walls that went round the town. And over there, the one with all the carving, that is one of our guildhalls. All the trades had them – the stonemasons, the carpenters, the iron-workers – each with its own fortifications and garrisons. There were very many of them in the old days, forty is the number written in the record books. The trades have all gone, but many of the houses still remain. You may still see them in the different districts when you walk through the town.'

As she talked, she walked, halting at the top of a flight of stone steps to allow me a preliminary glimpse down a narrow street of tall houses with tiled roofs into which had been set dormer windows, like little eyes.

'The market is on Tuesdays and Saturdays. Until last year, it was up here in the square and we could walk straight out of the church. At that time the people could come in and out of the church after the market and pay their respects and perhaps leave a little money in the box.'

Today being market day, stalls had been set up on both sides of the street. Piled on the wooden counters were vegetables and fruit, open sacks of beans and rice, strings of chillies, bunches of garlic and herbs. Queues had already formed. 'You can see how busy it is. The market is good this morning – everyone knows about the lifting of the restrictions.'

Frau Klein trotted down the steps, chatting over her shoulder. 'They said the market must be moved because of the public works – the restoration of the buildings and other things which would benefit the town. The people said it was because there might be demonstrations against the shortages. My own opinion is that they did not like the Church being so much part of the life of the town. My husband is sometimes a little outspoken. Perhaps the reasons were a little of both.'

Frau Klein's quick eyes took in the scene. 'You can see how poor it has become. A little meat sometimes, but the prices are terrible. It has been three years now since we have lost the Turkish market.'

'The Turkish market?'

'Some people call it the foreigners' market.'

I nodded. Indeed I had noticed the carpets, just as I had noticed them in the Black Church in Brazov. Frau Klein frowned. 'The congregation in Brazov is German Reformed. I'm told they have prayer rugs of the best quality silk. We would not tolerate such extravagance.'

As the Romanian national economy began to disintegrate, supplies of imported goods had dwindled steadily until finally they dried up and the Turkish market closed for good. 'This year, for the first time, we know we cannot buy any of the spices we need for our Christmas *Wurst*. And not only the *Wurst*. We have many special recipes for cakes and biscuits, some with cardamom, some with cloves, some with cinnamon. People mind that most of all, not being able to celebrate Christmas as we have always done – more than the shortages or the rationing.'

For as long as records had been kept, my guide continued, merchants and gypsies had set up their stalls under the colonnade in the great central square. They sold silks to the ladies and dyes for wool to the villagers. They sold tea and coffee, spices to meet the requirements of the dark-eyed native Latins as well as those of the pale-haired Saxons. The congregation of the Lutheran church had, besides, long been an excellent customer for Turkish carpets, hanging them from the high gallery to commemorate their prominent citizens. Had I not noticed them when I had visited the church on the day of my arrival?

Frau Klein settled her basket more firmly on her arm, and plunged into the throng. She was clearly a popular figure, stopping every few yards to exchange words with the stallholders or join a group of women with heavily laden baskets. Her progress was slow, the welfare of the flock taking precedence over the shopping.

Since there was little I could contribute in the way of social intercourse, I wandered off to explore on my own. The vegetables and fruit on sale were no different from those in Bucharest so I made my way towards the fringes of the stallholders' territory where those who deal in wild foods are usually found. Sure enough, the gypsy-women, small, dark, with weather-worn faces and bright wandering eyes, presided over wild-gathered fruits heaped in mounds on sackcloth. Wild fruits are tiny, bitter and strong-flavoured – sloes, cranberries, blueberries make the finest jellies and jams, rosehips the best syrup for babies. Displayed alongside the fruit were earthenware dishes of wild honeycomb, baskets of fresh walnuts still soft from the husk, bunches of herbs – marjoram, fennel, dill, parsley and parsley-root, green bayleaves tied up in bundles, earth-crusted roots of horseradish.

The older women were joined at intervals by young girls who sold their wares door-to-door and needed to replenish their baskets. The younger women – some no older than fourteen or fifteen – were slender beauties with gold hoops in their ears and bright embroidered shawls; some carried small babies swaddled in the shawls, others had older children balanced on one hip.

At the far end, continuing the stalls, was a line of wooden carts, their tailgates dropped to display potatoes, pumpkins, marrows, salad vegetables, some unfamiliar and needing to be recorded in my sketchbook. Beyond, in the shade of a wall, yoked pairs of water-buffalo patiently chewed the cud alongside a half-dozen rusting tractors. Lack of fuel, Frau Klein explained, had brought the great black beasts out of retirement.

Beside the gypsy-women, a group had gathered by a trestle table behind which stood a wild-looking figure in a heavy sheepskin cloak, unusually tall and lean among the crowd of stockily built Saxons. On the table in front of him was a bucket and a large enamel washing-up basin; on the ground beside him, a wooden barrel. The bucket seemed to be attracting the most attention and was full of something white and soft, which he was ladling into an assortment of containers held out by his customers. Every now and then, he refilled the bowl from the barrel, carefully removing the wooden lid and reaching deep into its depths.

Curious, I joined the queue as soon as I had finished my sketching. As we shuffled closer, I could see the bucket contained thick white cream and the bowl was filled with small round cheeses sprinkled with rough grains of yellow salt. Propped against one of the table-legs, quite casually, was what looked like a stuffed sheep. Closer inspection revealed this to be not far from the truth: actually, it was a sack made of a whole sheepskin, the top few inches of which had been rolled down like a crumpled sock to expose the stuffing, a cylinder of tightly packed curds.

The seller's face was half obscured by a black felt flower-pot hat pulled well down. From beneath it peered a pair of eyes that were neither blue like those of the Saxons, nor black like the Romanians, but of a pale honey colour and slanting upwards at the edges, like the eyes of a wolf.

By now I'd reached the head of the queue and decisions had to be made in a hurry. I pointed to the sheepskin bag. The shepherd reached into his belt, pulled out a curved steel blade and deftly carved off a sliver of the curd, proffering it on the tip of the knife for my approval. The texture of the cheese was firm, almost chewy, the flavour strong and salty.

'*Buna?*'

I nodded. It was good. I indicated how much I wanted between index finger and thumb. The strange-eyed shepherd carved off a slice, wrapped it carefully in a leaf before handing it over with a courteous '*Cu placere*' – you're welcome.

In payment, I offered him my open purse. He chose some coins, careful to make a public display of his selection so that others might witness his honesty. In a market such as this I would not have expected to be cheated by a trader. Hard bargains can be struck and every market has pickpockets, but open dishonesty would be unthinkable. Encouraged, I applied the same negotiating technique to the purchase of picnic food: a pound of apples, some fresh walnuts to eat with my cheese, and added, for convenience, a basket of woven rushes of similar design to Frau Klein's. The basket, though sturdy, was surprisingly expensive.

With all my purchases completed, I returned to the spot where I had left Frau Klein, making a mental list of the produce for Margaret Maclean. There were hutch-reared rabbits for sale, chickens, even meat – veal, lamb, mutton – and hanks of very dark minced meat which, the butcher indicated with gestures at the beasts of burden still waiting by the wall, was buffalo.

Frau Klein bustled up. 'Forgive me for deserting you, my dear Frau Lisbet, but I can see you had no need of me.'

She examined my basket, tugging at the handles and running her finger down the seams. 'Good. It is a good one. I know the old woman who makes them. See, here – she does a special knot where the seams are joined. You will find it strong and the handles will not come loose.' She rummaged around inside. 'And I can see you have found some *branza* – a very good cheese for keeping, the country people like it on their *mamaliga*. But for you, *zum mitessen*, I have baked fresh bread. I know you must be on your way, but you must pass by the house before you leave.'

She smiled, her bright blue eyes twinkling. 'I have not had an idle morning. I have been busy on your behalf, making enquiries among my husband's parishioners. We spent many years in the villages when he was a young pastor, and the people know me well. In an hour, when you pass by the house, I shall have something I know will please you.'

With this she bustled back up the stairway, leaving me to make my way back to the hotel where I found Nicholas refreshed by his lie-in and packing the car ready for our departure.

An hour later, back at the Bishop's Palace, Frau Klein came to the door. In her hands was a freshly baked loaf of bread wrapped in a linen cloth, and a bundle of handwritten papers tied with embroidered ribbon.

'I give these to you, Frau Lisbet, because these are the old recipes of the Sibiu Saxons, the ones the people still make today. In the workplace, we are modern. But when we are at home, it is *Kirche und Kinder und Küche*, just as it has always been – and, God willing, as it will always be.'

But Frau Klein was wrong. Even then the bull-dozers were on their way. Today the Lutheran bishopric of Sibiu no longer draws its congregation from its seven Saxon villages. In what was to be a final thrash of the dragon's tail, under the personal supervision of the dictator's son, the villages were razed, the churches flattened, the great square is no more.

CHAPTER NINE

Land of the Midnight Sun

*Norway is a hard country: hard to know, hard to shoot over,
and hard – very hard – to fall down on: but hard to forsake
and harder to forget.*

J. A. LEES, *Peaks and Pines* (1899)

NO VOYAGE ROUND THE CULINARY HABITS OF EUROPE COULD BE
considered complete without Scandinavia. I knew nothing of
the Land of the Midnight Sun, and Nicholas, whose Hebridean
childhood had left him with an insatiable appetite for the
sparkling beauty of northern seas, needed no persuading.

Summer in Scandinavia is short but brilliant – all the more so
since for nine months of the year it's twilight even at midday.
But for three months, the light is so bright it could earn itself a
place on Elizabeth Taylor's engagement-ring finger.

We took the plane to Stavanger – preliminary staging-post
for the oil-riggers of the North Sea – and immediately

transferred to one of the internal flights that serve the Scandinavians almost like long-distance bus rides.

Our true starting point was Trondheim, one-time capital of the seafaring Viking kings, where we had arranged to rent a car – a Volvo, what else? – for the long swing north.

On that sunny summer day of 1985, the streets of Trondheim were full of shoppers and the sunshine had brought everyone out into their gardens. On every lawn were tables and chairs. The air sparkled.

'Sunningdale-on-Sea,' said Nicholas, inspecting the neat villas with the eye of a man who knows a suburb when he sees one.

Trondheim is a new town. Flattened by the retreating German Army in 1944, it had to rebuild itself from scratch. This is not a nation that takes kindly to interference from outsiders: while Norway was under German occupation during the war, it took one German soldier to every four inhabitants – man, woman and child – to keep the population in a state of subjugation. The result was a retreating army that bulldozed everything, including the telephone poles.

The rebuilding allowed for the inclusion of every modern convenience in the housing stock. Creature comforts mitigate, even if they don't actually cure, the gloom induced by latitude.

Leaving Nicholas to book into the hotel, I made my way to the fish market by the harbour, a vast utilitarian warehouse that towered over the town. Trondheim depends on the fishing industry, as it has since the days of the Vikings. The market opened early, customers were few and the fishmongers were already sluicing down the aisles. Even at the end of the day, the space was scrubbed and sanitized, whereas in any Mediterranean market there would be slops underfoot and fish guts waiting for the gulls. Light poured on to marble slabs on which, fresh as a mermaid's minder, piled in the profusion only possible where the inshore fleet can find a ready market, lay the harvest of the Atlantic. Creatures caught in cold northern waters are all the colours of ice. The scales act like prisms, splintering the light. To the amusement of those still conducting their business, I settled down in a corner to complete a couple of sketches.

In the afternoon, needing some kind of visual orientation that did not come from books, we made our way to what was billed as the Trondheim Folk Museum. This turned out to be a collection of wooden houses, dark and brooding, like land-locked galleons marooned on some green island. The weathered walls and silvery birchwood tiles contrasted sharply with the white bungalows of the modern town.

It had never been a real village, explained the pretty young tour guide – a university student employed for her grasp of English rather than her knowledge of Scandinavian architecture – it was simply an arbitrary selection of those buildings that had somehow escaped destruction by fire or flood or any of the hundred and one disasters to which such perishable materials are prone.

Our young guide, attempting to convey to her group of English-speakers the difficulties of maintaining such houses, struggled to find a word. 'What do you call a person who builds houses?'

'Builder? Architect? Engineer?'

Each suggestion was greeted with a puzzled shake of the head. 'Not any of these. I mean the person who *makes* the houses.'

She made a vigorous sawing motion.

'A carpenter?'

She smiled and nodded. 'Of course, a carpenter. This is *exactly* the word I mean.'

The interior of one house – that of a rich merchant – had been restored so that it now looked much as it had a century ago. The impression was of genteel poverty rather than affluence, perhaps because the shortage of material goods – geography limits trade-routes – had obliged the inhabitants, however wealthy, to make do with what they could get. The walls had been hand-scrolled to look like wallpaper, pine cupboards were painted to mimic carved oak. On the pale polished wooden floorboards lay rag rugs; on the shelves stood beautifully patched and mended copper pans and hammered basins. The kitchen implements – spoons, plates, bowls, boxes, storage chests – were of birchwood, pale and smooth as ivory. Although the windows were small, the light poured in through the panes. There were no curtains or blinds.

'We never sleep in the summertime – we don't want to miss

a moment of the light. And in the winter, it is always dark and houses such as this were quite isolated, so there were no nosy neighbours.'

In what way, I asked, did this century-old interior differ from that of a modern house?

'Less than you would think. Nowadays, naturally, we have modern conveniences, and our houses are lit by electricity instead of gas, but the furnishings are not so very different. We are used to making do with little, so we do not change so suddenly. Many of our modern houses are also built by carpenters. Wooden houses do not last for ever, so we are accustomed to replace them. Many times they are burned down. We have many fires – more fires than anyone else in the world. This is something we can certainly claim.' There was pride in her voice.

Did the frequent fires not encourage people to look for another material with which to build?

'Not at all. Our wooden houses are very practical. They are warm in winter, cool in summer and there is no need to import expensive materials for building them when you may so easily take an axe and go into the forest to fetch for yourself what you need.'

She smiled. 'I myself live in a wooden house, the house of my parents. In the old days, it was very convenient. When the children of the household grew up and married, the parents just cut a hole for the door and put another room on the end – although this does not happen so much any more because the young people must find work in the towns. And people sometimes move their houses from one side of the fjord to the other – wooden houses are very easy to take to pieces and build again. It is easy for us, but it makes it difficult for the historians. If you want to build a new one, you use some of the old one, so houses like this, in a good state of preservation, are rare.'

On a small eminence there was a dark little church, its walls thick as the tree-trunks. Closer inspection revealed it to have been constructed from this very material. Our guide opened the door, leaving it ajar.

'You may enter. This I find very moving. It is the oldest building in Norway. The construction tells us it was made in the twelfth century. You will see there are no windows in the walls. This was because people and their animals took shelter here in time of trouble. In those days there was always very much trouble, from outside and from within.'

The interior was dark as the womb, quiet as the grave.

When the tour was over, our guide expressed curiosity about the direction of my questioning. 'You are researching the food ways? This is good. I myself am studying for a degree in ethnology at the University of Oslo. We have done much work on the domestic habits of our people – but I think in Scandinavia perhaps sometimes we take ourselves too seriously.'

'What do you mean?'

She smiled. 'First, we take coffee and a cake. All Scandinavians take coffee and cake in the middle of the afternoon. It is the custom. And then I shall tell you a story which perhaps may help you understand something of who we are.'

We had made our way to the cafeteria and settled down in a corner with large slices of cream cake and cups of coffee before the young woman would begin her story.

'You have perhaps heard of the Porridge Feud? No? It happened maybe a hundred, a hundred and fifty years ago, before the Folk Museum was made. There was a quarrel between the scientists and the cookery experts over our traditional way of making porridge. We call it *grod*, and we eat very much of it. In those times perhaps three times a day. Because we in Norway have a difficult climate and much distance to travel, we must eat those things we can grow. Porridge, as you will know, is made with oats. Oats and barley grow easily in our land. The feud was to do with the way the porridge was made. The farmers' wives were accustomed to making the porridge just as everyone does – like you do in Scotland – but when it was cooked and ready to eat, they would stir in another handful of oatmeal. This oatmeal did not have time to cook, but the people liked it.'

I nodded. 'Some people in Scotland do that too – they even have special names for it.'

'This is what my grandmother says – she is from Aberdeen, but many, many years ago.'

'You have Scottish blood?'

'This is how I learn my English, from my grandmother.'

'You were well taught.'

She nodded. 'I do not think it is so good, but is good enough to speak of the Porridge Feud. So, at this time one hundred years ago, we in Norway have an important writer of fairy-tales, Asbjornsen. This man is very popular with the children. He publishes a book on how to cook scientifically. He tells all the mothers who read his stories to tell their children not to put the extra oatmeal in the porridge at the end. He tells them it is scientific fact that, without cooking, the oatmeal goes right through the body without being used, and that this is unpatriotic because it means much money and labour is lost not only to the individual family but also to the country.'

I smiled. 'Sounds a little extreme. And what did the mothers say?'

'They do not know what to say. Everyone is arguing. Even the children are arguing. At this time there is much discussion of social matters. There has been revolution in France, and many people are thinking about what is to come. The discussion of the porridge makes everyone talk about what should be in the future. There is science on the one hand, there is tradition on the other. People are speaking in the universities on the role of women, the problems of poverty, the new scientific discoveries, the importation of foreign ideas, whether people should be educated or left to do what they have always done – the fishing and the farming.'

'A storm in a porridge pot?'

'This is what my grandmother says – the storm in the teacup.' She nodded. 'But to us it is very serious. You must understand we Scandinavians are motivated by the common good. Foreign sociologists will explain there is no such thing as common good, that this is just an idea and that it is not possible to apply it in practice. This is, perhaps, true where there are too many people. But we in Norway do not have such a problem. We have very much land and very few people. We have a climate which makes our lives hard. Because of this, we must look after each other. This is why we were the first to set up state crèches, the first to make comfortable homes for our old people to live together. We can tax our populations to pay for such things and they do not mind. This is who we are. And all these things we understand because of the Porridge Feud.'

Trondheim in the dusk looked almost elegant, even a little raffish. Certainly it was very modern. We had booked ourselves – for patriotic reasons, if none other – into the steel-and-concrete Britannia Hotel. Trondheim is recreation territory for the North Sea oil-riggers, and most of the clientele seemed to have something or other to do with the oil business.

In the dining room – as huge and impersonal as an airport lounge – only a dozen tables were occupied, a few with Scandinavian couples but most with our countrymen, all male. Keeping them company was a sprinkling of young persons, all female and local. The cold table, the Norwegian equivalent of the Swedish *smörgåsbord*, featured twenty ways with salt herring. I like raw fish – but only up to a point. Nicholas, on the other hand, is besotted with the stuff. Show the man a herring, and he'll follow you anywhere. I think it must be the Viking in his soul.

At breakfast the following morning, the oil-riggers and their companions – if such they had been – were notable by their absence. The other guests were all wearing clothes of a dazzling cleanliness, as if auditioning for a detergent advertisement. Each said grace before settling down to another dose of herring salad.

Norway is a prosperous country. Prosperity brings height, breadth and amazingly large bottoms – particularly in the ladies. One of these instructed Nicholas on the proper way to tackle the morning *kaltbord*.

'No, no, no, you are not putting the soured milk in the coffee. The soured milk is for eating with the *flatbrod*.' She held up a very crisp, very thin round biscuit. 'You crumble the *flatbrod* into the soured milk and you eat it with the compôte of the red fruits. We say it is the first cornflakes. But first we take herring, then we take porridge. This is our diet. It is well known it is making us the healthiest nation in Europe.'

Nicholas inspected the milk jug. 'It looks just like yoghurt.'

'No. No. No.' A plump finger wagged. 'Is Scandinavian *naturally soured* milk. To say it is yoghurt would be very wrong, very ignorant.'

243

Foreigners' ignorance of all things Scandinavian is something of a sore point among the Norsemen. Another sore point is that, although the Scandinavians can tell the difference between themselves and other Scandinavians, no one else can.

The Swedes, says a Swedish friend of mine, believe the Norwegians to be dim-witted. The Norwegians reckon the Swedes are too clever by half. The Norwegians and Swedes believe that the Danes are unreliable and drunk. And everyone knows the Finns are not only drunk but deeply gloomy, which is perfectly natural considering their proximity to Russia. No one likes the Russians.

Each group has different allegiances. The Swedes get on perfectly well with the Germans, the Norwegians are friendly with the British. But the Finns are probably Hungarian, so no one really understands them anyway. The Danes are the ones everyone else cordially dislikes – mainly because at one stage or another they appear to have owned most of Scandinavia. Jokes made by other Scandinavians about the Danes are the same as those the English make about the Irish, or the French make about the Belgians.

There are subtle differences in the dinners. For instance, take the *smörgåsbord*, at which you are likely to find hot food as well as cold. In Norway the inclusion of hot food would make the meal a little bit foreign. In Denmark it is called the bread-and-butter – *smørebord* – and basically consists of open sandwiches. In Finland – well, nobody understands the Finns.

And then there's the fast food. The Norwegians have fish hamburgers, little patties called *fiskekakker* sold only in a *fiskematbutik* – a minced-fish shop – which appear to be unknown elsewhere in Scandinavia, or in the world, for that matter. The closest equivalent is the Chinese fish-ball, although the French, those magpie gatherers of good things, might claim them as *quenelles*.

At midday, before we took the road to the north, a queue of schoolchildren and office-workers led us to Trondheim's only *fiskematbutik*. Nicholas's friend from the breakfast table told him there used to be many in the town but now there was only one. The minced-fish shop sold nothing but minced and pounded fish, cooked and ready to eat on the premises, or raw for

Norwegian Fiskekakker
CREAM FISHCAKES

Note the absence of eggs or anything to complicate the simplicity. Fish and cream are the only essential ingredients – the starch is not necessary if the fish is very fresh and therefore naturally glutinous. Frozen fish won't do – it's too watery.

───────────── SERVES 4 AS A MAIN DISH ─────────────

1½ lb/750 g filleted fish (haddock is   *1 teaspoon ground mace or nutmeg*
  best, cod will do), skinned   *salt and white pepper*
½ pint/300 ml ice-cold cream
1 tablespoon potato starch
  or cornflour

───────────── TO FRY ─────────────

about 2 oz/50 g butter

1. Chop the fish roughly and put it in the food processor (a large pestle and mortar is the only other option – and for that you'll need patience as well as brawn). Process thoroughly, adding the cream as for a mayonnaise. If it seems too thick, you may need to add a little milk. Beat hard, either in the processor or with a wooden spoon, adding the potato starch or cornflour and season with the mace or nutmeg, salt and white pepper. The more air you include, the lighter the mixture. Beat it some more.

2. Heat a heavy frying-pan or griddle. When it's good and hot, drop in a little knob of butter. When it stops sizzling, drop on tablespoonfuls of the fish mixture, patting each dollop flat with the back of a spoon, and fry, turning once. No need to flour the patties – they won't stick. Serve with melted butter in which you have fried a few cubes of bacon, and potatoes boiled with dill-heads.

preparation later at home. The fish was not ground-up bits and pieces of the leftovers from the day's catch but the best fresh haddock or pike or young cod the market could offer.

The *fiskekakker* turned out to be patties made with pounded haddock moistened with cream, spiced with nutmeg, fried in butter and sold by weight. The same mixture was also poached as little dumplings – *fiskeboller* – to be eaten with melted butter. Or baked in a loaf-tin as a *fiskepudding*, a delicacy available ready-made, whole or by the slice. My Norwegian friend Astri, a professor of domestic history at Oslo University, once told me her mother used to buy *fiskekakker* for her to nibble on her way home from school, rather as modern children are given chocolate bars. 'We liked it because it was good, because it tasted of what we knew was good.'

The recommendation was irresistible. We bought a bagful and ate them there and then with our elbows propped on the steel counter and butter running down our chins.

Norway is long and narrow, with precious little hinterland. There are only two ways to travel: due north or due south. A mountainous spine divides Norway from Sweden, a vast, empty region where only the reindeer herdsmen and a few hardy farmsteads survive. In the interior, mining and forestry are the only industries. For the rest, the entire population is concentrated on the coast.

The map indicated a few roads meandering through the valleys, following the course of the old transhumancing routes, or giving access to the old mining towns of the interior. Nevertheless, these were of limited interest to a seafaring people, who treat the ocean as their principal highway.

These days, the coastal trunk road is the main artery of Norwegian life. There are, say the guidebooks, a thousand miles of fjord between Oslo and the North Cape. We soon discovered that the road-builders had been obliged to acknowledge every one.

Our night's destination was the prosperous port of Bergen, the trade-centre for the north. During the Middle Ages, the town became the local headquarters of the Hanseatic League, a powerful trading cartel based in Lübeck in northern Germany, as we had been reminded by the tractor salesman in Bulgaria. The Hansas controlled the dried-cod trade, exchanging Norwegian stockfish and cod-liver oil for southern wine, wheat-flour and woven wool. They moved into Bergen in the thirteenth century, filling the vacuum left by the Great Plague, when more than a third of the nation succumbed to the scourge and only the outlying populations survived.

The Hansas were more merchant pirate than merchant prince. As rumbustious in their personal habits as they were careful in their accounting houses, they brought neither wives nor women, recruiting local ladies for recreational purposes, taking no responsibility for any consequences. They kept their purses well buttoned for their return to Lübeck, when they could expect to find themselves a good German wife to bear more sons for the League.

Their handsome wooden warehouses can still be seen on the Bergen water-front, a monument to thrift and industry. Comfort was not a priority: one of the warehouses has been turned into a museum, demonstrating that the living quarters were as cramped as the warehouses were cavernous. The boy apprentices were packed into the attic bunks head-to-tail, like sardines in a tin – that is, if they survived the initiation ceremonies. These included being hurled down the cobbled streets in a barrel, then dunked in a vat of boiling cod-liver oil, immediately followed by an involuntary ducking in the Arctic waters of the harbour. As might be expected, the casualty rates were high: many a mother lost her son and never knew why. But, if you survived, there was no doubt the rewards were considerable.

The business has remained profitable: to this day, the burghers of Bergen serve as bankers to the Arctic fishing fleets. Fishing is a notoriously uncertain occupation, offering plenty of opportunity for bankers. The modern descendants of the Hansa merchants dine in the elegant restaurant that has replaced the dormitories in the warehouse on the Bryggen wharf. We booked in for dinner. Local specialities advertised on the menu were – naturally – fishy.

We were just discussing the possibilities of Bergen fish soup – creamy and including bacon, just like that of New England,

Norwegian Skreimolje
BERGEN FISH SOUP

A fisherman's one-pot stew, much like the New England chowders in that it includes both bacon and cream. For the rest, ingredients are as variable as the day's catch – the more the merrier.

─────────── SERVES 4 AS A MAIN COURSE ───────────

4 cod steaks, weighing about
  4 oz/100 g each
1 fresh cod's roe, both 'wings'
1 lb/500 g fresh mussels in
  the shell, scrubbed and bearded
1½ pints/900 ml fish stock
1½ lb/750 g potatoes, peeled
  and diced

1 medium onion, finely sliced
1 thick slice gammon, diced small
1 oz/25 g butter
2 egg yolks
2 tablespoons double cream
salt and pepper

─────────── TO FINISH ───────────

few sprigs fresh dill, chopped
1 tablespoon pickled 'pearl' onions or spring onions, chopped

1. Wipe over the cod steaks and salt them lightly. Rinse the roes and wrap them in a double envelope of greaseproof paper. Bring a pan of salted water to the boil and slip in the packet of roe. Bring back to the boil, then turn down the heat immediately. Simmer

until the roe is firm – a medium-sized roe takes about 25 minutes. Leave it in the water to cool. Unwrap and slice thickly (you may not need it all – save the leftovers for fishcakes).

2. Bring the fish stock to the boil with the potatoes. Turn down the heat and lid loosely. Simmer for 10–15 minutes, until the potatoes are nearly tender.

3. Meanwhile, fry the onion and bacon gently in the butter in a small frying-pan until the onions are soft and golden. Tip the contents of the frying-pan into the soup and lay the mussels on top. Bring back to the boil, lid and cook for about 5 minutes – just long enough to open the mussels. Carefully, with a draining spoon, transfer the solids to a deep soup tureen. Slip the cod steaks into the broth and let them poach for 3–4 minutes, until firm, then transfer to the tureen. Reheat the sliced cod's roe in the broth for a few minutes, lift out gently and lay on top of the cod steak in the tureen.

4. Whisk up the egg yolks with the cream. Whisk in a ladleful of warm, not boiling, broth. Stir this back into the soup and reheat gently – don't let it boil. Taste and season with salt and pepper. Pour over the fish and vegetables in the tureen, and sprinkle with chopped dill and pickled onion.

possibly followed by grilled shark steaks with Hollandaise, or even lobster thermidor, when the waiter pointed out that since the weather had been stormy for the last couple of days, the fishermen had not been able to leave harbour. Everything was off except the whale. What kind of whale – I mean, the really endangered kind or just the B-list? The waiter shrugged. Whale steak it was. With brown onion sauce. Nicholas prodded his portion uncertainly, tucked it under a blanket of potato and ate up all the sauce. I, on the other hand, was not only hungry but professionally curious. Once a creature is dead, it's dead, and it seems discourteous not to eat it. I'd feel the same about myself. Whale meat turned out to have a quite unfishy flavour somewhere between beefsteak and calf's liver.

The following day we set off early, just as the sun was lifting over the fjords. We had an appointment to keep. Astri, my friend from Oslo university, had a daughter who had married a farmer and gone to live on the family farm high above the Arctic Circle.

'My daughter Andrea is from the south, like me, but her husband Bjorn is a true Norseman. She has learned all the things an Arctic housewife needs to know. Their lives are not primitive, but they live in the way which is suitable to the land. She can show you something of the old ways.'

The map that Astri had drawn led us to a remote cluster of pretty wooden houses and their attendant barns, much like those we had seen at the Folk Museum at Trondheim, settled into a fold of flower-strewn hillside perched above the sparkling waters of a fjord.

It was Saturday afternoon. The homestead appeared deserted. By the gate was a copper cow-bell with a rope hanging invitingly from the clapper. We rang it, but could get no answer. At that moment, an engine cranked laboriously into action, and an eldery Jeep backed out of a driveway opposite.

'Hey!' The commonest form of greeting among Scandinavians sounds like an admonition, but is actually perfectly polite.

'Hey!' we replied experimentally.

The driver's grey hair and wrinkles indicated that she could not possibly be the young mother of two small children.

'You are looking for Andrea. You must come with me.' The words were spoken slowly, as if learned from a phrase book. 'We are expecting you. You leave your car, you come in with me. My English is not so good.'

Her vocabulary exhausted, she waited for us to obey what was not so much a suggestion as a command. As soon as we complied, she set off at breakneck speed up a bumpy track through a spruce-forest so dense and dark it must surely have harboured trolls – the wicked little dwarfs of Norwegian legend who cause havoc among unwary travellers.

The track wound upwards for several miles, until suddenly it emerged on the open hilltop. We were at the edge of a little lake, its surface a perfect mirror for the cloudless sky. The edges were treeless, fringed with cotton-grass and tussocks of myrtle and reed.

Our guide pointed encouragingly to the far side of the water, where a scarlet-and-white Norwegian flag hung limp on its flagpole over a cluster of wooden buildings. Then, with a casual wave of the hand, she reversed firmly and vanished back down the track.

We trod cautiously at first. The terrain was marshy, with deep pools of water between the hummocks.

As we walked I noticed among the cotton-grass the sticky little rosettes of butterwort, an insect-eating plant with glaucous leaves which Paul du Chaillu, author of *Land of the Midnight Sun*, my chosen literary companion on the road to Scandinavia, had described as used in cheese-making. (The curds it formed, he took care to explain, were curiously long and stringy, like hanks of newly twisted wool.) At the centre of the leaves was a stalk, curved and covered with fine red hairs dewed with tiny drops of a sticky substance. At the end of this was a delicate flower of the same shape and colour as a violet.

Vegetable rennets were used by the country people to replace animal rennets, a natural digestive substance found in the stomach of any ruminant. The most primitive of these preparations is a nugget of curd from the stomach of the first-born lamb or kid which has taken its first milk, usually a weakling whose loss will not be too keenly felt by the shepherd. But among herdsmen, those whose milk-animals are cows, a young calf would be considered too great a sacrifice. Most renneting plants are members of the thistle family: artichoke, cardoon, or the various wild thistles that grow tall by Mediterranean roadsides and provide shelter for aestivating snails. In Greece I was told that the best vegetable rennet was fig-tree sap, although I did not get the chance to put the information to the test. But in Scandinavia, said Monsieur du Chaillu, *Pinguicula vulgaris* was the dairyman's choice. Taking care that there were plenty of replacements all around, I uprooted one of the plants; I would paint its portrait later so that I could make enquiries as we travelled.

We walked on. Above us, the sun hung high in a sky of brilliant blue, its brightness exactly mirrored in the water beneath. Small butterflies of the same blue as the sky danced over the white spheres of grass-of-Parnassus, sipping nectar from the star-shaped centres. Bumble-bees, striped like miniature football mufflers, hummed among the heather. The air was so still you might imagine you could hear the rustle of birds moving around in the willow trees, the small sounds made by lizards and snakes, the crackle of tiny insects that burrow into the bark of the birch trees. The air sparkled, making each leaf and blade of grass distinct, as if a crystal globe had been dropped over the earth, shedding a radiance to reflect and refract the light.

So absorbed were we by the beauty all around, tempered somewhat by the necessity to avoid quicksands, that for some time we did not notice the figure in sun-bleached denim overalls striding purposefully round the lake towards us. 'Hey!'

This time there could be no mistaking our hostess. 'Welcome to our mountain-top! We are so happy you are here! My mother telephoned to say you would be coming, but we didn't know exactly when, or we would have waited down below.' She chatted over her shoulder as we followed, struggling to keep pace with her long countrywoman's stride. 'But then we thought you should see our summer farm, so we left the message with our neighbour. We come here every weekend until the first snows, unless we have too much work with the harvest. These are the summer pastures – the *setor* – where the dairymaids came for the summer with the cows. The pasture up here is very good because it's under snow all winter. All the farmers round here had summer farms. All summer they milked the cows and made the cheese and butter to send to market. But now we no longer have a dairy herd – except for what we need for ourselves – we do not have to do the transhumance. But we do it just the same for the pleasure.'

By now we had reached the front porch of the wooden dwelling. Our hostess pushed open the door, and turned back to us with a smile.

'Welcome to our summer home. The *setor*-house is very simple, but this is how we like it. My husband and the children will be back shortly – they have only gone to catch trout for supper. But first, like all good Norwegians, we shall take coffee together. I have already put it on the stove to welcome you. You will need reviving after your long walk.'

This was undeniable. The coffee was mild and fragrant, cooled with a thick layer of buttercup-yellow cream. With it came crisp little biscuits flavoured with aniseed. While we drank our coffee, Andrea told us a little of her life.

Although born to the lakes and sunshine of southern Norway she was drawn by the romance of the north. She had chosen to complete her teacher-training course at Mo-i-Rana, a fishing port some two hundred miles above the Arctic Circle. Here she had met a young farmer. 'He was a Viking, he captured my heart, so what could I do?' As soon as she qualified she married him.

With marriage came responsibility for the family farm. The young man brought his bride to Karvol, the little enclave on the lower slopes of the fjord where we had found our guide. Andrea's initiation into her new life was immediate. The summer pastures were at their richest and the cows were giving good milk. Her mother-in-law had twisted her ankle returfing the roof of the milking-shed and the young bride's first task was to take her place on the milkmaid's stool.

'What could you expect? I knew nothing. My mother-in-law could do the job in thirty minutes. That day it took me three hours.'

Three generations ago the farm had belonged to a single family. In the years since, war and the attractions of city life had taken or lured away many of the young people, and the original family was not able to provide enough labour. 'Fortunately we do not have a housing problem – we can always build more wooden rooms. This is why you will find many Norwegian houses are long and thin – we just add another room on the end.'

The farmstead, she continued, now provided a living for three separate and smaller families, none related by blood. 'This is good because we can all help each other, just as it was my neighbour, Margaret, who brought you here. We are very fortunate we are all friends, because in the winter, we are very isolated, sometimes for months at a time. But because Bjorn was of the original family, we have the use of the *setor*. When you are finished, I shall take you on a tour of the property. It is not very large, so it will not take long.'

The cabin's living space was about the size of a large potting-shed, but well insulated and cosy. It had been partitioned to provide two small rooms for sleeping, each equipped with bunks. The rest, a single larger space, was used for living, cooking and eating, with toilet facilities in a lean-to tacked on the back. Everything, both inside and out – Andrea demonstrated with pride – was made of wood. Little wooden pegs even did duty for nails.

Although few concessions were made to luxury, the furnishings had been chosen with care and many were handcrafted; the finishing touches spoke of pride in good workmanship. The tablecloth and cushion covers were made of bleached linen, thickly edged with crocheted lace; the bedcovers were patchwork quilts, simple patterns in white and blue sewn by hand with tiny stitches. These had been folded back over blankets of hand-woven scarlet wool. At the windows were curtains of the same scarlet fabric.

'I thought the Norwegians never had curtains?'

Andrea laughed. 'I can see you've been doing your home-work. You are right. These are for insulation in the winter, when the *setor*-house is buried under snowdrifts. If the house is warm, the snowmelt runs off very quickly and does not do so much damage. But, however careful we are, in the spring there is always much to do. We must mend holes in the roof, repair the walls or occasionally replace the window-frames. Wooden houses are easy to mend – we only have to go into the forest to fetch everything we need.'

Andrea led us outside to admire the patched shingles, the new wood smoothly grooved into old. 'My husband is very good with his hands. He does all the carpentry. The children and I help him, but we can only do the easy things.' She glanced at her watch. 'They should be here very soon. It takes an hour to walk back down to the house, and I do not want us to be late because they must do their homework. I am a teacher at the school, so they must set a good example. Their father is a typical countryman and he never remembers the time.'

The tour continued round the back of the house, where Andrea showed us what looked like a neat little grass-covered mound in the middle of which had been set a flight of steps, leading to a dwarf-sized door. Closer inspection revealed the structure to be a wooden hut half dug into the earth, which had been roofed with turf.

'This is my wood store. It is very special because we put grass on the roof. You see how it is done? It's made in two layers: underneath is the birch bark, and on top of it we put the grass with all its roots so it will continue to grow. It's very practical as it keeps out the water when the snow melts after the winter – but I like it because it is so pretty. I make sure there are strawberries for the children to pick. Look – they will soon be ripe.'

Sure enough, there among the smooth greenery were the leaves and little starry flowers of strawberry plants, the blooms just dropping their petals to form fruits.

Andrea glanced at her watch again. 'I hope they have caught some trout. If so, we will have fish for supper. If not, my store-cupboard is well stocked.' The strong teeth flashed in the tanned face. 'I think we will not go hungry.'

A few minutes later, the sound of voices heralded the return of the fishing party. Both children were blue-eyed, blond-haired, with deep-set blue eyes and tanned limbs, both identically dressed in ragged shorts and white T-shirts. Close behind came Bjorn, tall, broad-shouldered, with the high cheekbones and muscular good looks of his Viking ancestors. Swinging from his fist, threaded on a loop of reed, were six little brown trout, beautifully patterned, freckled, no longer than a man's hand.

'Very good, very clever.' Andrea examined the catch. 'I have been promising our visitors one each for our supper – but now we must be on our way.' She glanced at us. 'I hope you don't mind the walk? I thought you would like it because you can ask all the questions you want on the way.'

With the children racing on ahead, we followed the narrow path through the birchwoods which led directly down to the farmstead. The forest trees, so threatening on the other side of the mountain, had not colonized the steep slopes of the fjord, and the only hazards were the occasional ravine and a few broad swathes of marshland. In the middle of one of these, Andrea stopped suddenly and bent down, cupping her hand under a cluster of leaves.

'See? Look here. The cloudberries are ripe already – it's early for them. They must have ripened specially for you.'

The cloudberry, unlike most berry-bearing plants, is not a shrub but a flowering plant. My identification manual showed an exquisite five-petalled blossom like a miniature wild rose, and a fruit that looked not unlike a golden raspberry. Sure enough, glowing like tiny lanterns among the patch of dark green strawberry-shaped leaves were the starry little flowers and raspberry-shaped fruits, some green, some scarlet, some golden.

'The yellow ones are ripe, the red ones are still sour.' Andrea cupped her hand tenderly under one of the berries. 'Aren't they beautiful? This is our treasure – we think of it as mountain gold, and only we have a right to pick it. Our properties run from the sea to the mountain-top so that we have rights to the fish below, the hay between, and the cloudberries above.'

The gathering, she continued, was never predictable because only the female plants bore the fruit. 'Some years there are more males and then there is very little to pick and people are very angry if they catch anyone stealing their cloudberries. I think this will be a good year, but last year we had very few and many people had them stolen. Once we had to chase away some backpackers, but luckily they dropped their basket. The thieves can sell them, so they're worth stealing. Finns pay much money for our cloudberries – they use them to make a liqueur. I have tasted it. It is good, but it is not the same.'

She began to pick, her fingers swift and sure as she selected the ripe berries from their nests of greenery. Finally she straightened up, and handed me a single golden fruit. 'This is the first time? Good. You must taste it now, while the sun is on your skin, in the place where it grows. Then you will never forget, and every time you taste it, you will remember us, and the sunshine, and this day.'

I tasted. She was right. As with the first sip of fine wine, such moments, so small, so seemingly unimportant, are so rare that we are allowed no more than a few in a lifetime. These, indeed, are the stuff of memory.

The cluster of little yellow globes yielded a thick, almost buttery juice, each globe centred by a hollow seed that yielded easily to the teeth. But it was the flavour that haunted the mind. Neither sharp nor sweet, but with a fragrance, intense but delicate, of pine trees and birch, of heather, juniper and thyme – subtle, addictive.

Andrea watched me, smiling at my pleasure.

'I knew you would understand,' she said happily. 'They are very special, are they not?'

Andrea continued the lesson as we picked. 'Be careful to take only the yellow ones, the red we will leave for tomorrow. We have many other kinds of berry, but those are free for the picking. We have some you do not know, such as the Arctic bramble and many little berries used for flavouring. But we also have raspberries, strawberries and what you call cranberries but we call lingonberries – and the bilberries you might think of as blueberries. All of these you have, but not in such quantity. When the berries are ripe I'm kept busy for a whole week making syrups and jams. The small fruits are very important to us. They are the only fruit we can rely on to ripen in our short summers. The smaller the fruit, the quicker it ripens. All the family picks them. It is a duty as well as a pleasure. We need them for our winter stores because they make a balance in the diet. The cloudberries are unusual because you don't need to preserve them with sugar. I'm told they contain a natural antibiotic, and certainly my husband's family used them to dress wounds. I pack them straight into a jar – firmly, so they make a little juice – and they keep in the cellar all winter. Some people put them in the deep freeze, but it's not really necessary. We have apple and pear trees, but many years the fruits do not have enough time to ripen. Of course, we can buy fruit in the supermarket but it is not the same.'

She handed me the basket with its precious harvest. 'Here. You shall have the privilege of carrying our little treasure. We must hurry, or we will never get to the table at all.'

By the time we reached the farmstead and had made our way into the bright, modern kitchen, the trout had been cleaned, gutted and laid out ready for the pan. The children had also gathered a few handfuls of yellow-gilled chanterelles, and these, too, had been carefully brushed and trimmed.

Andrea examined the harvest speculatively. 'It is good. But it will not satisfy our hunger. Come with me and I will show you my store-cupboard. We still use the old *stabbur*. You will not find many of those in the south.'

The *stabbur* turned out to be a hut on stilts, one of the many outhouses that ringed the farmhouse. The floor-beams had been left protruding and to each was lashed a large boulder. 'This we must do so my store-cupboard is not blown away in the winter. The wind is so strong it can carry away even something as heavy as this.' It took a moment for our eyes to grow accustomed to the darkness, and then Andrea began to list her stores. In one corner, several barrels of herrings. 'These I buy from the fishermen but I salt them myself.' Hanging from the roof-beams were ranks of what looked like hams. 'This is not pork, as we have in the south, but mutton-ham – *spekemat*. Our domestic meat animal is the sheep – they are hardier than pigs.'

One corner was given over to dairy equipment. All was made of wood – buckets, troughs, spoons. Beside them, strung up on hooks, was the family's winter essentials: snowshoes, like small leather-thonged tennis racquets, reindeer-skin boots slung from a reindeer antler, skates, skis, hats and gloves made of some kind of thick fur – fox, perhaps, or even wolf. 'Yes, we have wolves,' said Andrea, with a smile. 'But they do not frighten us. They hunt in the forest. We are happy when we hear them.'

Andrea was a true Arctic farmer's wife, out harvesting long into the sunlit nights alongside her husband. Arctic crops, like the berries, have a short growing season. Often the ground is too hard to be broken for sowing until late May. Then the cereals and potatoes have to be planted immediately. Their growth, she added, in a good year was miraculous. In a bad year, when the sun was weak, the crops did not ripen before the autumn freeze set in, the potatoes shrivelled in the ground, the oats stayed green and rotted on the stalk.

The only dependable crop was hay for the cattle, a wild crop that needed no tending. The meadow grass had to be cut as soon as it reached maturity. The hay was dried on poles: some of these could be seen in the clearings in the birchwood, like bulky giants. Below, round the farmstead, the first cutting had been flipped over rope washing-lines and left to dry in the wind.

'If it rains after the hay has dried, we throw in salt when we move it into the barns. The cattle like the salted hay best.'

The barns, explained Andrea, were as essential to the life of the farm as the land itself. 'We keep everything in here in the winter. Sometimes the barns catch fire, and then there is no shelter for the animals and they die. This is the problem which faces us. The land is our friend, but also our enemy. You would not think it today, but it's true.'

There were ventilation slats between the planks to channel the wind which kept hay and cattle dry. Today, with not even a light breeze to disturb the air, the light poured through the gaps and made stained-glass-window patterns in the darkness.

'This is where my father-in-law used to make the aquavit – of course, we cannot make it any more because it is illegal,' she said, her eyes bright with laughter. 'I cannot vouch for my father-in-law though, except to say that he has very good aquavit. He *used* to make it with the potatoes which are caught by the frost, with berries for the flavouring. He buried the crock underneath where the cows stand. This was good because the warmth from the manure encouraged the fermentation, and the smell discouraged the excise inspectors. Now, of course, we have central heating, so everywhere is warm,' she added. 'I cannot say what happens now.'

The hay was stored on a platform over the cow-stalls – empty now since the beasts were out to grass – so that the fodder could be tossed straight down into the feeding baskets. 'We have only three cows, although in my father-in-law's day there were many more. In winter we keep them in milk as long as we can. In spring and summer, when there is plenty of milk, we make our own butter and cheese.'

This reminded me of my rennet plant. I had had just enough time up at the *setor* to make a small botanical painting before returning the plant to its habitat.

Andrea listened thoughtfully. 'I have never heard of it myself, but we'll ask my father-in-law.'

The old man was taking the sunshine with his feet up on the verandah of one of the neighbouring houses. He examined the drawing, and then nodded vigorously. '*Ja*. I know just what this is. When I was a boy, we use this plant to make cheese. We use all – all the plant, all the roots and the leaves. We put it all into the milk and it makes strings, long strings like knitting wool . . .' The knotted old fists made pulling gestures.

This reply pleased both of us greatly, Andrea because she resolved to try the method next time she made cheese, and me because Monsieur du Chaillu had proved the reliability of his powers of observation. Travellers, particularly nineteenth-century travellers, tell tall tales: you can never be sure of the truth until you test it.

'Come, now, I will show you my larder.'

Beneath the main farmhouse was a cellar dug deep into the earth. Andrea led the way down some steps and into what looked like a vast, cavernous dungeon. Immediately inside the door were wooden boxes full of sacking, beneath which were the last of the previous year's potatoes. 'The new ones are not yet ready – they are a pleasure for July.'

All round the walls were shelves laden with jars and bottles glowing like dark jewels, jams and syrups, pickles and wines.

Andrea ran her hand over the bottles. 'I think perhaps the rhubarb – we are proud of our rhubarb wine. It will be good with our harvest meal. See? It is the colour of the cloudberries.' She held it up to the light from the open door, turning it in her hand. The wine was clear and amber-coloured. 'Good. Perhaps we shall have two. We make all our own wine, but the best is the rhubarb. It comes from Tibet, so it does very well in the Arctic. A little wine keeps us cheerful in the winter – sometimes a little too cheerful. But in the summer we don't need it so much, so we keep it for special occasions, like today, to celebrate your visit.'

We carried the bottles back to the kitchen, along with the various stores Andrea had collected during the course of the inspection. During our gatherings she had decided to prepare a traditional harvest supper.

'It's the meal I take out to the family when we are cutting the hay. We sit among the wild flowers and we make a picnic. The hay smells good, the sky is blue and we are glad. Sometimes it is midnight before we eat, but you would not know it because the sun shines all night long. The summers make us happy.'

One wall of the living room was made entirely of glass, framing the jagged cliffs of the fjord and the soft haze of mountains beyond. The moon hung like some pale fruit caught between the branches of the pines, sharing the sky with the sun.

The table looked very festive. There were soft-boiled eggs, which had been collected that morning, pats of home-made butter, potato salad, pickled herrings with dill and soured cream, a plate of fine-cut slices of the mutton-ham from the *stabbur*. The little trout had been fried in butter with the chanterelles, sauced with cream. 'We use much cream in our special cooking – we put it in our little fried biscuits for Christmas. The children like them very much. I have saved some, and you shall taste them later with the coffee. We call them Reindeer Antlers because of the shape.'

There was also a brick-shaped lump of *geitost* – a whey cheese made with buttermilk, the knowledgeable Monsieur du Chaillu had already informed me – in a wide earthenware pan, which is left on a low heat to cook down until sugary and brown as toffee.

Pride of place on the table had been given to a pile of *lefse*, flatbreads much like the Mexican tortilla or the Indian chapatti, all warmed through and carefully wrapped in a damp cloth to keep them soft.

'The *lefse* are special – not from the shop but home-made,'

Norwegian Hjortetakk

REINDEER ANTLERS

Fried biscuits – in the old days the frying medium would have been pure butter – are the special treat where baking ovens are not traditional, as in northern Norway.

———————————— MAKES 25–30 ————————————

3 eggs	1 tablespoon cardamom pods,
6 oz/175 g sugar	husked and seeds crushed
2 oz/50 g butter, melted	1 tablespoon lemon rind, grated
6 tablespoons double cream, whipped	1 lb/500 g plain flour
2 tablespoons brandy	

———————————— TO FINISH ————————————

vegetable oil with a large knob of	sugar and powdered cinnamon,
butter, for frying	for dusting

1. Whisk the eggs thoroughly with the sugar until light and white. Stir in the butter, cream and brandy, the cardamom seeds and lemon rind. With a wooden spoon, beat in the flour – you may need less or more, depending on the size of the eggs and the absorbency of the flour – to give a soft, workable dough. Allow it to rest in a cool place, overnight in the fridge if possible.

2. Roll the dough into a sausage shape and chop into short lengths the size of a quail's egg. Roll each into a pencil-thin rope, then bend it to form a ring, pinching the ends together with a wet finger. Cut a few notches in the outside of each ring.

3. Heat a pan of deep oil with a knob of butter until a faint blue haze rises. Slip in the rings a few at a time and fry until puffed and golden. Drain on absorbent paper.

4. Serve sprinkled with sugar and cinnamon, prettily piled on your best white dish. They will keep well in an airtight tin.

explained Andrea. 'Do not misunderstand, please. I do not have to make them myself. There's an old lady on the other side of the fjord who still makes them in the traditional way. You must first make the dough with oatmeal and rye-flour – some people put in a little potato. Then you roll them out with a special rolling-pin to make the pattern, and then you cook them on the special baking-stone – we call it a stone, but it is really made of iron. It is very important that the fire must be hot when you begin so the outside blackens a little and the dough is light.'

The children gave a demonstration of how the *lefse* is eaten, first filled with sliced egg or mutton-ham or *geitost* or a combination of whatever you like, then rolled up with one end tucked in to enclose the filling.

The children ate quickly, and formally requested permission to leave the table. Andrea listened and turned to us. 'They ask your forgiveness if they join their friends on the shore. The salmon are running and there's a chance of a fish.'

We, the adults, lingered, talked quietly of those things that strangers share: our hosts of the hardships and pleasures of this harsh land; Nicholas of his childhood home in the Hebrides, the magic of waterfalls, the bounty of autumn woods, of the shepherding communities of the Western Isles.

We shared with our hosts a reluctance to abandon so bright a world to sleep, preferring to savour the wine, waiting for the moment when the globe of day dropped towards the curve of the earth, bathing the hill-tops in golden light, and then immediately began its slow ascent into the heavens again.

'Is it not beautiful? To me it is always a miracle. The midnight sun brings joy to the soul.'

Last of all, before we took ourselves to our beds, we were offered the promised taste of Reindeer Antlers – deep-fried, rich with butter, dusted with sugar and cinnamon – to dip into a bowl of cream into which had been stirred the cloudberries.

Berries from the clouds, fish from the streams, cream that tastes of wildflower meadows and new-mown hay – if that sounds like paradise, there could be no doubt that this was a garden of Eden won against the odds. All activities were dictated by season and weather. To live in comfort, even a family as self-sufficient as our hosts' needed access to two incomes. Money was needed, not so much for ordinary living, since many things could be gathered or bartered, a basket of chanterelles exchanged for a dozen eggs, a haul of herrings for a cheese, but to make life less harsh, to mitigate the lack of social life.

The necessary income came largely from the maintenance of public services: Andrea had her salary as a teacher, and Bjorn drove the snowplough that kept the roads passable throughout the winter. Because of their relative affluence, the household was well equipped with twentieth-century electronic gadgetry. Everyone used computers, and sophisticated satellite equipment meant they could watch TV programmes from all over the world. At the time of our visit, the memory of the Falklands War was still fresh, and the entire community had undergone many anxious evenings watching the news from the southern hemisphere.

A sense of isolation, the endless leisure of the winter months, combined with the ability to witness almost at first hand the major events taking place in the rest of the world, made them far better informed on world politics than we. Perhaps because of this, the Scandinavian nations are among the most reliable contributors to the UN's peacekeeping forces.

This is a highly moral nation, which allows itself little latitude. The Calvinist ethic has a firm grip on the law-makers of Scandinavia and drink is not only prohibitively highly taxed but obtainable only at state liquor stores, their façades as discreet as that of a Victorian brothel. Since the stores are several hundred miles apart, it's a little hard to understand how the Scandinavians acquired their reputation as the dedicated drinkers of Europe. Until, that is, you take a look at the shelves of the grocery stores: even in the most insignificant corner shop, you will find a cluster of tiny bottles proclaiming the contents as London gin, Scotch whisky, Cointreau, Campari – it's all available, packaged as non-alcoholic essences.

'What do you use them for?' I enquired naïvely, the first time I spotted them on arrival in Trondheim.

'Who knows?' replied the young woman, with a giggle. 'Perhaps they mix it with Finnish aquavit.'

'After a drive of five hundred miles, at thirty dollars a bottle?'

'Is possible.' She gave me an old-fashioned look. 'All things are possible.'

Including burying the aquavit under the cowshed, I thought, as I drifted off to sleep under the midnight sun.

The following morning we took our leave of the kindly inhabitants of Karvol, and headed for the Lofotens, a string of wild, beautiful islands that form part of the Arctic archipelago.

For anyone interested in domestic history, the islands have one irresistible draw: the Lofoten fishing industry provides most of southern Europe's supplies of salt cod.

For centuries it was the Portuguese who had a monopoly on this profitable trade. They not only had access to the cod shoals of the North Atlantic, but their salt-pans had been in use since Roman times. The trade became doubly valuable during the Middle Ages, when the Church of Rome decreed that more than half the year was to be spent fasting, not only on Fridays and throughout Lent but also on Wednesdays, on the eves of all saints' days and for a lengthy period before Christmas. Salt fish had long been the fasting food of Mediterranean Europe. With increased demand, it became both scarce and costly, so valuable a trade item that it attracted the attention of the merchants of Lübeck. The bullion dealers, who controlled the fur trade, moved smartly into fish futures. They persuaded the Norwegian cod fishermen to use salt mined in Salzburg to prepare their catch for export to Mediterranean markets. Until the Hansas intervened, the cod was simply wind-dried in the salty air. There were no salt-pans on the rocky Norwegian coast, and no particular need for additional salting since the climate was neither humid nor warm. If any extra conservation was necessary, the fish was treated with lye – a by-product of wood-ash. It was this that victualled the Viking longships, and the Norsemen traded what they did not consume. Wind-dried rather than salt fish is still popular in Italy and all along the east coast of Africa – and thence to the West Indies through the slave trade.

Our visit to Bergen had whetted my appetite. I meant to learn more, and if learning more involved a three-hour ferry-ride, that was the way it had to be.

We arrived at the jetty just as the ferry was preparing to embark its cargo. As soon as we had stowed the vehicle in the hold, Nicholas went up to the prow of the ship, while I found a sheltered corner on the upper deck where I settled down with my sketchbook.

'Excuse me – I think you are English?'

This was undeniable. Not that I would have wished to deny it. The speaker was remarkably handsome, remarkably tall and his teeth were remarkably white. He was wearing oilskins and on his head was a fisherman's cap.

'Please. I hope it does not disturb you, but I would like to practise my English.'

'It doesn't disturb me at all. I like company while I paint.'

'How do you do? My name is Olaf. I am pleased to meet you.'

A strong brown hand was extended to mine. It was dry and hard, and smelt a little of fish. He had been chewing absent-mindedly on something that looked like a chicken leg. Before taking my hand he had replaced this in his top pocket, rather as someone might store a stick of chewing-gum.

'My name is Elisabeth. What are you eating?'

He removed the object of my interest from his top pocket and gazed at it for a moment, holding it out for my inspection. It appeared to be a hunk of dried fish. 'This is *klipfisk*. Cod, but it is without salt. It is dried on the cliffs. You do not have it in England?'

'No. We chew other things. Gum, mostly.'

'Fish is better. Gum is not good. It will not give you strength.'

'No indeed.'

Silence fell but for the rhythmic working of Olaf's jaws.

'You know why we are calling our waterproofs oilskins?' he enquired suddenly.

'Tell me.'

'We are calling them oilskins because, in times gone by, the fishermen are putting the oil from the liver of the codfish on the sealskin coats to make them so the water cannot come in. They say when the wind is coming from the north, the people in Bergen are smelling the fishing-boats when they are many miles away. They say it is terrible – the women of Bergen all scream and run for their houses to get away from the smell.'

'How did the fishermen's wives feel about it when they got home?'

'I suppose they also are smelling of fish so they are not noticing.' The white teeth flashed. 'Today, of course, is different. Today, the women of the fishermen smell of lilies and roses. I myself am from Svolvaer, and I can tell you this is so.'

He tore off another hunk of fish, chewing thoughtfully and watching my reaction. 'Today I am visiting my girlfriend in Svolvaer. I can tell you she is very beautiful and she is not smelling of fish. Her name is Inge. She is smelling of Miss Dior. We are being very happy together. We are making love many many times. She is the most – how you say it?' He placed two fingers in close proximity. 'Like this all the time. She is the most loving of all my girlfriends.'

'Sounds wonderful. Do you have very many girlfriends?'

'Very many. We are very liberated.' He masticated some more. 'I think perhaps I marry her. We will have children together. Perhaps you have children?'

'I do. But rather a long time ago.'

More thoughtful mastication. 'Tell me, does your husband make love with other women?'

'If he does, I'd be very angry if I found out.'

'This is strange. Inge also does not like me to make love with other women. The other girls, they do not mind. So with Inge I do not tell her.'

'If you're going to marry her, keep it that way.'

'This is very interesting. You think this is marriage – that you do not tell the woman who has your children that you make love to other women?'

'Something of the kind.'

'This means you do not tell the truth?'

'Perish the thought.'

'Please?'

'I mean yes. It means you do not tell the truth.'

My interrogator tucked away his fish in his pocket and made

a formal little bow. 'I thank you very much for this conversation. I will think over what you have said. Please present my regards to your husband.'

'Indeed I will. Give my regards to Inge. I hope for your sake she accepts. She sounds like a good woman.'

The white teeth flashed. 'I hope we will meet again some day and you will meet my children.'

Quite apart from the unexpected pleasure of Olaf's company, our arrival in Svolvaer, the island's capital, proved the wisdom of travelling on the ferry. We had contemplated the alternative, one of the small aircraft which service the island from Mo-i-Rana, and are considered a more reliable form of transport since the ferry does not always run. Norway had applied the profits from North Sea gas to the building of bridges and air-strips to make the islands more accessible. Even so, Andrea had warned us, it was possible to be marooned on the islands for days, even weeks.

Today, an unseasonal fall of snow had been enough to flip the little plane over on its back. It lay on the shoreside runway, propellers skywards, helpless as an upturned tortoise.

We disembarked, grateful for our choice. The houses round the harbour-front were dwarfed by wooden racks on which, at the right time of year, the catch was hung out to dry. Now they were empty, but in spring the forests of pearl-grey wooden poles would be laden with stockfish, tied together by the tails in pairs.

The fishing industry depended on individuals. A single boat, manned by a fisherman and his son, could catch enough fish to fill the hold and still return on the tide. The cod was gutted and salted, and hung to dry in a single day, or sold to the merchants to be salted down for *bacalão* in the town's wooden warehouses. Afterwards, the nets that fished the cod were flung over the whole edifice to frustrate marauding seabirds.

Enquiries revealed that the only hotel on the island was on the harbour-front, a few yards from the ferry-port, handy for visiting salesmen and those involved in the salt-cod trade. The Lofoten tourist industry consists mostly of playing host to passing cruise ships so beds were not a priority. The only alternative accommodation was in the wooden fishermen's huts – *rorbu* – which are much in demand among the summer visitors, and the bed-and-breakfast available in the little harbour villages that shelter on the east coast of the island.

The travelling salesmen, who were our only companions in the hotel, are early. By seven o'clock the dining room was almost empty.

Nicholas, intrigued by my report on Olaf's fishy chewing-gum, ordered the *klipfisk*. The fish had been soaked and stewed and came with a sauce of melted butter in which tiny scraps of bacon had been fried. It was still pungent and chewy. Nicholas likes pungent and chewy.

'Old sock,' he said happily.

I chose fresh fish, which turned out to be salmon rather than the cod I had anticipated. The spring fish, *skrei*, as the mature fish heavy with roe is called, are the islands' great delicacy. I had hoped for a famous dish of cod with cream, one of those one-pot soup-stews traditionally prepared on board ship by the fishermen themselves.

'This year was not good for the cod, not even in the spring, when the fish came inshore to spawn,' explained the manager, a Dane from Copenhagen who had learned his English at the London Business School. 'It is very worrying.' He brightened. 'But perhaps, as you say in England, every cloud has a silver lining. We have begun to exploit the possibilities of the cod in a new way. This year we held a cod festival in the hotel to celebrate the arrival of the shoals. It was on television. People came from Sweden, Denmark and even from Finland. It was very good for tourism – we are thinking of promoting it through the tourist authority in Stockholm as well as Oslo. Perhaps even London and maybe Montreal. We had many Canadian visitors. A hundred years ago, when the fishing was bad, many Norwegians went to Canada. We think there should be international interest in the cod festival. It is interesting for the fishermen to diversify. They show us how they cook cod in the old way, and we do it here in the hotel.'

'And how do the fishermen like to cook it?'

'They cook it in salt water with the roe and the tongue, sometimes with cream and potatoes, and they make a sauce with the liver. Fresh cod's liver is very good, it does not taste of fish, but more like butter, or the marrow in beef bones. Even though I am a Dane, I know how good it is. With it we drink not beer and aquavit, as you might expect, but red wine. It has to be French and it must be claret.'

He paused expectantly. I expressed astonishment. He nodded happily. 'You will certainly be astonished to find such a thing traditional among the fishermen of the Lofoten Islands. You know very well there are no grapes to make wine up here in the Arctic Circle. I'll tell you why we drink red wine with cod. You have heard people speak of the Hanseatic League, the merchants in Bergen?'

'Indeed – we were there a few days ago.'

'Then you'll perhaps know it was these people, who were not Norwegian at all, who developed the business of the salt-cod trade?'

'I was told a little about that.'

'Then you'll also know that the Hansa merchants brought back wine in their ships on their return voyages to make up the weight. For special occasions, such as when there is fresh cod to eat, the fishermen liked to drink claret better than beer. Ever since that time all over Scandinavia – you will find it in Sweden too – claret has accompanied fresh cod.'

His bright blue Danish eyes were round with enthusiasm. 'You must try it. You will like it very much. Everyone does the *skol* and we are all very happy. You know how to do the *skol*? You must look in the eyes and nod and raise your glass before you drink. When you have finished drinking, you must look in the eyes and nod one more time. This is polite.'

'What happens if you don't want to wait?'

'Surely you must wait. You would not drink without a *skol*. This would be rude. But you can be sure you will not wait too long. That too would be rude.'

'Like passing the salt?'

'I do not know what this means.'

'I mean you have to look after your neighbour. We would say it's good table manners.'

'Of course. And we have also the singing of the cod songs. We have many speeches about the cod. Many stories. You know of Lief Erikson who discovered America? There is a very fine song about him. We call it a saga. The saga of Lief Erikson is very famous. We had a famous saga-singer who performed it which was very popular.'

That night, we slept fitfully, dreaming of the saga of the cod fishermen and listening to the gulls that screamed over the harbour all night long. Up here, the midnight sun was even brighter, slanting its beams through the thin curtaining – surely a concession to tourists – turning night to day.

The following morning we rose late, breakfasted on pickled herrings and soured milk, the *fjoelmilk* – a taste that grows on you, said Nicholas – and made our way down to the quayside. The wooden fishing-boats of Svolvaer's inshore fleet had already raised their triangular sails and were heading for the fishing-grounds. The larger boats were not allowed into the allotted fishing sector until ten o'clock, when the smaller boats with their hand-nets and hook-and-line tackle must haul in and clear out.

In summer, the rocky inlets and pastel-painted wood-built fishermen's houses are bathed in the clear twenty-four-hour sunlight. The meadows are ablaze with buttercups. Each house has its potato patch fenced with raspberry canes heavy with fruit.

The scene would have been idyllic – an Arctic paradise – had it not been for an angry-looking crowd engaged in the removal of a large billboard on which was displayed an advertisement for a season of Brigitte Bardot's movies. Unaware of local sensibilities, the newly appointed forward-thinking young manager of the islands' only cinema, attempting to drum up custom in high summer, had announced a gala season of Mademoiselle Bardot's more celebrated roles. The twenty-foot-high billboard had attracted some highly imaginative graffiti, very little requiring translation. In other words, what the fishermen of the Lofotens would really like to do is land Brigitte Bardot one in the eye with a wet haddock.

We went in search of the hotel manager for an explanation.

The reason for their displeasure, he said, was that, as we might already have observed, the inhabitants of the rocky islands depended for their livelihood on a rather different romantic entanglement. As long as records had been kept, the shores of the islands, bathed in the warm currents of the Gulf Stream, have played midwife each spring to the cod's plentiful spawn, between 500,000 and five million tiny eggs per female fish. In theory, more than enough to replenish the stocks.

This year the cod had not come to spawn. The fish were there all right, but they would not leave the safety of the deep water, which was where the factory ships operated. The fishermen had been doubly deprived of their livelihood.

'The fish are scared.'

'Scared of the factory ships?'

'Of the seals.'

Why more so now than last year or the year before that?

Easy. The lack of cod could be laid squarely at the door of the star of *And God Created Woman*. The one-time sex-kitten had taken up cudgels in defence of baby seals, a popular cause, since the little creatures have huge trusting brown eyes and expressions that make them look not unlike Bardot herself. This somewhat sentimental view of nature did not square with that of the fishermen, who were only too well aware that the delightful little pups take only a few months to turn into large, hungry predators.

Those who knew nothing, snorted the owner of the fish-salting factory, brought in to reinforce the argument, thought that little lambs would be left to frolic in the fields if all the world turned vegetarian.

'Now, because of that film, in Canada they are no longer permitted to kill the baby seals. On the other side of the ocean, there is a population explosion. A seal needs five kilos of fish every day. The seals must follow the food, so they travel to the Lofotens. It is like wolves and a flock of sheep. The cod understand very well the danger in the shallow water.'

He shook his head. 'We are fishermen. We have been here for a thousand years. Our ancestors came here because of the cod. If the cod doesn't come, we cannot live on these islands. Every year the cod has come, every year since time began. This year and last year were different. We know where the fish are, but we cannot reach them. Fish are like people – they hide in the mountains. But in the ocean it's not the high mountains but the deep valleys, which is where their enemies cannot find

272

them. The cod are in the ocean just beyond the fishing-grounds. They came in November to wait for the ice to break up in the spring. In February every year they come into the shores of the islands to lay their eggs where the water is shallow and the Gulf Stream makes it productive – full of food for the baby fish. Baby fish cannot survive in deep water. Just like human babies, they need a nursery where they can grow in safety. The seals do not usually come in because they do not like warm water, but this year they were too hungry to care.'

It takes a lot of seal to deflect a breeding cod from its purpose. If it were herring, say the locals, that would be another matter. The herring, the alternative catch, is a frivolous fish. The shoals come and go like wilful chorus girls – here for a decade, there for the next. But the cod is a reliable fellow, regular as clockwork: it takes something very unusual to scare him away.

The opinion of the crowd was that Mademoiselle Bardot had done what a thousand years of harvesting could not: upset the delicate balance between predator and prey. This year the fixed nets of the inshore fishermen, set at night and drawn in the morning, were full not of fine fat cod, their bellies swollen with roe, but with the drowned bodies of the film star's furry protégés.

'The seals see the fish in the nets. They are warm-blooded like us. They drown, like us, when they cannot get free. They have no choice. They are starving. No meat on them at all, and what there is has already rotted. They are good for nothing, even if there were a market for the pelts. In my father's day, we caught seals through the ice. We were hunters then – not murderers. We needed the skins to keep us warm. We were not wasteful. We used everything. The blubber went for lamp-oil and for waterproofing the skins. The choicest of the fat was chopped up with the meat and kept as winter stores. These days the government pays a bounty. What use to us is that?'

From our informant we begged a day out on one of the bigger boats to see for ourselves. Fishermen are a secretive lot, like all hunters, but the suggestion was greeted with courtesy. 'We are happy to take you with us. People should understand the problems we are facing.'

At seventy foot from stem to stern, with the breadth and

strength necessary to withstand the Arctic gales, the MK *Skarheim* represented a considerable investment: fifty thousand pounds' worth of engine, radar and depth-sounders, all of it funded by the bankers of Bergen, and certainly not for much longer.

The ship nudged slowly out of the harbour mouth, creating its own small waves to sparkle in the sunshine. The great Lofoten Wall, a precipice of pale rock entirely covered with ice in winter, glittered with ice-cream colours: apricot, strawberry, raspberry, pistachio. The ocean was a deep indigo on which floated brilliant rafts of sea-birds – king-eider with their noble Roman noses, diving ducks, mergansers. Troupes of dainty little terns, graceful as ballerinas, cropped the billows.

The ship was shadowed by rival predators on the waves: it seemed that all the world was waiting for the shoals to come in to spawn. Black-back gulls, killer whales, a pair of white-tailed fish eagles, together we proceeded to the fishing-grounds.

Torbjorn Skarheim, the owner-skipper, scanned the horizon, counting smoke-stacks. This year there were twenty boats where, in a good year, there would have been two hundred. Considering this, whatever the effect of the burgeoning seal population on the cod, Torbjorn did not discount over-fishing as the cause of the shortages all through the food chain, which is fragile.

'The seals really prefer ling, but the factory ships take ling for pet food. The cod feeds on three fish – capelin, herring and shrimp – but humans like to eat that too. The factory ships take everything. Everything is processed. You have only to look at the products on the supermarket shelves. Who cares any more where it comes from?'

All the same, the ocean remains a mystery. No one really knows what goes on in the depths. 'We can only guess at what has happened – and anyone who tells you otherwise knows nothing. It is not the first time there have been black seas. There are records in Bergen which tell us of fifty years and more when the cod did not come in to spawn. The bankers lent us the money, and we did what we could to pay the interest. But we do know that the lifespan of the cod is shorter. There were huge fish in the old days – in the Hansa's warehouses you will see the king-cod displayed. He is so old he has grown a formation of bone which looks like a crown on top of his head. Even in my father's day they caught such creatures, but never in mine. These days, with our modern equipment, we are capable of fishing out a whole generation in a single season. But what can we do? If we do not fish them, others will.'

The chains rattled, the nets fed out in our wake. We made three passes with the nets: they take an hour to set and gather each time, dragging deep down to the ocean floor. Slowly the net was hauled in. Long before the final loop appeared, no one on the boat was in any doubt that almost nothing was there – maybe a few kilos of herring, a scattering of red-fish from the lower depths, pop-eyed and suffering from the piscine equivalent of the bends. The fish-eagles swooped on the rejects – at least someone had a square meal. At the end of the day, the catch, said the skipper, would hardly cover the day's fuel, let alone the wages of four employees.

'Why should they do it?' Torbjorn shrugged. 'They can earn a fortune on the big trawlers out of Tromsø, even if they work shifts, eight hours' duty to four hours' sleep.' He rubbed his beard. 'Tomorrow we will go out into the ocean, over on the western side. We know the fish are there. The trouble is, they are even deeper than the shoals here, and out there we are competing with the factory ships which can freeze the catch as soon as it's caught. But we must do it, or stay at home and lose our livelihood.'

One of the employees turned out to be the school psychologist in the little fishing port of Hennigsvaer, where the fishing-boat berthed. I enquired after the effect of the black seas on the fishermen's families whose children are in his care.

He shook his head. 'It is a disaster. The town's population has dropped by a third in the last two years. The young people leave to find work on the mainland. Already the weaknesses are showing. We have many more cases of child-neglect among the wives who have been left behind. Last autumn a little girl climbed over the wall of the playground and drowned in the harbour. It was a terrible thing. Afterwards, there was no money to make the wall higher and safer, so we had to close the kindergarten. I fear very much we cannot survive.'

That these are familiar problems, which afflict communities in decline, was no consolation.

'In twenty years, none of us will be here.'

CHAPTER TEN

Ice Queens and Dairy Maids

*I watched the reindeer milking with great interest. The women
knew every animal around the tent. Those which were to be
milked were approached carefully, and a lasso was thrown
gently over the horns, and knotted over the muzzle, to prevent
the deer from running away; but they made no effort to
escape . . . The process was peculiar: the women held in one
hand a wooden scoop, frequently pressing hard with the other,
for the thick fluid seemed to come with difficulty; it was poured
from the scoop into a keg-like vessel closed by a sliding cover,
and so contrived that it could be carried on the back of an
animal . . . Skin bladders were filled, to be used by the Lapps
who were to remain the whole day with the herds. I was
surprised at the small yield – some not giving enough to fill a
small coffee-cup; but it was very thick and rich – so much so
that water had to be added before drinking, not unlike goat's
milk. The milk of the reindeer forms a very important item in*

the food of the Lapps. Butter made from it is like tallow, so they make very little.

PAUL DU CHAILLU, *Land of the Midnight Sun* (1881)

THE DUN–COLOURED BEASTS WANDERING ALONG THE SHORES OF the North Cape, splay-footed, their heavy hoofs clicking on the pebbles, were munching their way through a black ridge of glistening seaweed.

In Finnmark, Norway's most northerly province, reindeer are as common as cows. Nature has equipped them to be the only herd animal that can survive in the permafrost. They looked surprisingly small, no bigger than Shetland ponies, with angular rumps carried higher than their heads, velvet-clad horns and heavy aquiline faces. For the Lapps, the native people of the north, they serve the same domestic function as cattle. My attempts to sketch them when we had found a campsite for the night were curtailed by a huge cloud of mosquitoes that settled on every exposed area of skin.

Where there are reindeer there are Lapps. We had passed small encampments of reindeer-skin tepees on the trunk road to the North Cape. Although the traditional way of life of these nomadic herdsmen is inseparable from their identity – there are sea-Lapps, mountain-Lapps, river-Lapps, each with their own skills – they have adapted their migratory route to take in the tourist trade. In these modern times, man cannot live on reindeer alone, and the herdsmen had long since learned that in the short Arctic summer a useful cash crop could be earned by selling surplus reindeer products. 'Do not patronize the Lapps,' said a notice on the wall in the tourist office. 'They have provided many teachers and scientists and university graduates. They wear their traditional clothes, their pointed hats and medieval jerkins and red ribbons, because the garments are practical and distinctive, and adapted to the traditional way of life, not to entertain the tourists. They are a very ancient race – probably the oldest inhabitants of Scandinavia.'

The part-time tradesmen in their blue, yellow and red ribbon-bound jerkins presided casually over their wares. We stopped several times to make small purchases, but there appeared to be no particular anxiety to sell. Nevertheless, reindeer-skin rugs, boots, hats and mittens were popular with these customers, who had managed to persuade the salesmen to discuss their prices. For the traveller prepared to pay for workmanship, there were little birchwood boxes perfectly stitched and seamed with sapling twigs, wooden bowls fashioned from the elbows of ancient twisted tree-trunks, birch-root cups inlaid with bone. And for those who could afford the real thing – or didn't know the difference – there were toy trolls, round and coy, with rolling plastic eyes and a Far Eastern stamp somewhere on their reindeer-skin bottoms.

The main Lappish encampments are at Kiruna and Karasjok. Each group has its own traditional dress, worn even today as a declaration of identity. The Lapps of Karasjok wear tall three-pointed hats made of brilliant blue felt ornamented with scarlet wool. In the old days, explained my modern guidebook, their wives used to sport a peaked Punch's hat stiffened with a wooden block, until the elders of the Church, saving souls for Christ, forbade the wearing of the headgear because the blocks might harbour devils.

The pretty young woman who greeted English-speaking visitors to the Karasjok Lapp Museum had sensibly eschewed what might, in such a place, seem like fancy-dress, for a pink towelling tracksuit and American trainers. The slanted dark eyes and the high cheekbones characteristic of her race were uncharacteristically framed by a mop of curly blonde hair, cut as short as a boy's. She introduced herself with formal courtesy in excellent American-accented English: 'My name is Sara. I am happy to welcome you to Karasjok. Please allow me to conduct you round our museum. I have been for one year on student exchange at the University of Ottawa in Canada, but I'm afraid my English is a little out of practice.'

'You learned your English in Canada?'

The blonde curls bobbed. 'Of course. Many of our people emigrated to Canada because of the climate, which is so like our own, so we all have relations in the New World. The exchange is very common among young people of my generation.'

Nevertheless, in the three months she had been working as a student-helper at the museum, she had not had much call to use her newly acquired fluency. 'It is a pity we see so few English visitors. We are important in your folklore – you have taken our Santa Claus and our reindeer, even though you may sometimes think us just a fairytale for Christmas. We are proud of our Saame heritage, as you are of yours.'

'Saame?' This was not a word I had heard before.

'This is what we call ourselves. Lapp is not a word we would use. To our ears it sounds like nigger.'

Our guide smiled to soften her words. 'You will find we do not wear our traditional dress so much now. But our culture is strong. Everything in the museum is authentic. All the artefacts have been used for the purpose for which they were made. Many families have contributed precious possessions so our visitors may understand our way of life. We believe this is important. Our museum houses the largest library of Saame writings in the world and the best collection of Saame artefacts.'

The cabinets on the walls contained simple utensils, exquisitely crafted. The long winter nights breed careful time-profligate workmen – Why hurry, when an evening lasts for half a year?

The largest of the galleries was entirely occupied by a magnificent Viking longship.

Sara stood beside it with pride. 'We built boats such as this for the Vikings – they knew our worth and paid us well. Although we did not ourselves choose to be pirates and raiders, we were perfectly happy to accept their gold. We ourselves use boats made of skins because they are light and portable. But we are also very fine craftsmen in wood.'

The next gallery was devoted to the fisherman's trade. There were glass cases full of hand-knotted nets, birchbark-wrapped weights, fish-traps, hooks. For each display, a printed notice supplied two paragraphs of explanation, one in the Saame language and one in Norwegian, which Sara translated meticulously for our benefit.

At the last case, she studied the explanation for some time, and finally shook her head. 'There is no translation. In the Saame language, it means a particular kind of fish-hook designed for a particular kind of fish. There are many words which have no direct translation, but I can usually find a way.

We have words to describe different kinds of snow, of ice, of clouds, of the noise the wind makes through particular trees.'

In the final gallery, in solitary magnificence, was a tepee-shaped structure just like the ones beside the North Cape road, a construction of skins and birch branches.

'Here, as you can see, is one of our homes.'

Sara stood back and motioned that we should enter. Birch-brush sleeping pallets flanked a central aisle. On each pallet were piles of reindeer-skin rugs and hand-woven blankets dyed in soft colours. At the back were three wooden storage-chests, beautifully carved and polished but very simple. Hanging from hooks on the central tent-pole were garments made of hand-woven wool dyed a rich navy blue, trimmed and lined with fur. On smaller hooks hung hats, gloves and reindeer-skin boots, all decorated with handwoven scarlet ribbons. The tent was womblike, strangely comforting.

'The space is limited, so each person has their allotted place. On the right as you enter the tent would be the husband, with the older children nearer the door and space for guests by the entrance. The mother was the most important person in the tent – you can see that she has plenty of space. The women had much power before the Church taught otherwise. Over there, beside the mother, is the wood and leather cradle for the smallest child. We Saame had many children. Many would be expected to die, so you would need to replace them. The fire for cooking and warmth is on the central aisle, as you can see. The dog lies over the threshold. He is a special breed for herding reindeer. People say he is not a separate breed, but I can tell you that he is different from other breeds. He has a curled tail and he can be any colour – mine is brown with black patches and I have had him since I was small. My brother's was black with white patches.'

She glanced at me and smiled. 'We had women's liberation long before you did. We all performed the same tasks. We went hunting and fishing with our brothers. The old people took care of the younger children, so the mother did everything that the father did, unless she was nursing a baby at the breast. The only thing the woman did not do was hunt bear. That was not because she was a woman and therefore weak, it was because it was feared the spirit of the bear would do her harm. The people thought there were spirits in everything, not just in living things but in rocks, in water, in wind, in trees.'

'Did you have shamans?'

She considered this carefully. 'Not really. We were not patriarchal – we did not have witch-doctors. We were all equal, the women and the men. The girls had the same rights of inheritance as the boys. Perhaps there was even a prejudice in favour of the women. The three most important spirits were all female, the *noides*, the guardian angels. They were the spirits of the tent, one to guard the entrance, another who protected the outside, and the third, the spirit of the fire, kept watch over us all while we slept. Her name is Sara and she is my name-spirit. My father wanted to protect me from harm, so he named me for the most powerful spirit of all.'

She shook her head, laughing. 'But I say this is not true. I say he gave me my name because he loves to cook, so the fire-spirit is always in his heart. Among my people, the men very often cook – it is not considered to be women's business. My father makes wonderful stews flavoured with special berries, myrtle and juniper and the hard little fruits the birds like to eat. In the winter he used to take us to fish through a hole in the ice. We would catch salmon and char, I think you call it, and some kinds of fish which are only found beneath the ice. In the summer he used to hunt ptarmigan and my brother and I would set traps for the snow-hares and collect berries in the woods. Our berries have a wonderful flavour – even in Canada there was nothing like them.'

Knowing of my particular interest, Sara looked at me. 'Of course, you will want to know about our traditional cooking. I can tell you it's very simple – we don't need to follow recipes when we have good things all around us. We didn't have an oven because we didn't need one and, anyway, it would have been hard to gather enough fuel. You see the cooking pot hanging over the birch-brush fire? Everything can be made in that one pot. It can be raised or lowered, just as you want, so the heat can be great or small. You can cook meat, make porridge, even bake rye-bread in it – all you need do to make it into an oven is turn the lid over and fill it with hot charcoal. We use the

Lappish Kokt Rensdyrkjott

REINDEER STEW

In the likely absence of reindeer meat – or even the alternative, moose – this recipe is just as delicious made with venison or beef.

──────────── SERVES 4 HUNGRY HERDSMEN ────────────

*4 lb/2 kg braising joint reindeer
 or venison, boned and rolled*
*2 marrow bones or 6 oz/150 g
 pork belly, cut into chunks*
2 oz/50 g dried porcini mushrooms
*1 teaspoon juniper berries
 or allspice*
1 teaspoon myrtle berries

*4 tablespoons dried rowanberries or
 cranberries or sultanas*
2 tablespoons chopped mint
2 tablespoons chopped dill
1 tablespoon salt
1–2 tablespoons vinegar

──────────── OPTIONAL, TO FINISH ────────────

4 oz/100 g black pudding, skinned and crumbled

1. Put the braising joint and the bones or pork belly into a heavy casserole that will just accommodate it all. Pour in enough water to submerge everything completely. Bring to the boil and skim off the froth that rises. Add the mushrooms, the various berries, aromatics and the salt, lid tightly and turn down the heat to simmer very gently for 3–4 hours, until the meat is so tender it can be eaten with a spoon.

2. Take out the bones and scoop any marrow that hasn't already melted back into the gravy. Slice the meat and sharpen the gravy with vinegar. Taste and adjust the seasoning. Slip in the slices of black pudding, if using. Best eaten out of wooden bowls with wooden spoons. Black bread and pickled cucumbers to accompany.

same pot to heat the milk to make cheese. You can make coffee in it too – we drop in a little bit of salmon-skin to send the grounds to the bottom. One of the nicest things we make are little blood cakes mixed with rye flour – you would call them black pudding – which you eat with melted butter. My mother still makes them every Sunday.'

It seemed impossible that this modern young woman in her bright pink tracksuit could ever have lived the kind of life she was describing.

'And you, Sara? Did you follow the reindeer herds?'

'Always, when I was a child. The care of the reindeer was the most important responsibility we had. All our butter and cheese came from the reindeer, just like you get yours from cows or goats. The reindeer milk is very rich and thick – much better than cow's milk. But the milking is hard work – you have to be quick and careful that the reindeer don't kick over the bucket. But that was how we lived, travelling with the herds. My parents still do, even today, although not all the year round. The reindeer travel great distances to find the mosses and lichens they like. In the summer, they crop the seaweed by the shore – I expect you will have seen them. These days, some of the herdsmen even have helicopters so they can follow their herds more easily. But the old people of my grandparents' generation still think everyone in the world lives like they do. My grandfather was quite surprised when I told him that in Canada they don't herd reindeer but cows, and that they eat wheat bread instead of oatcakes. He was very worried that I might not be getting enough of the right kinds of things to eat. He wanted to know what kind of fungi we could gather.'

'And could you tell him?'

'Of course. All my Canadian cousins gathered them – not as many kinds as here, but many that I could recognize. Here we gather them in the summer, when the snows melt. But we have to be careful which ones we pick. In the old days, my father told me, they used the red ones with white spots to make themselves drunk.'

'The ones we call toadstools?'

'Of course. Just like the ones in your *Alice in Wonderland* – I used to love that story when I was a child. My father told me that after the people had eaten the toadstools, they became excited and they danced and made love and quarrelled. Then they would fall asleep. Naturally, their dreams would be full of things that looked just like toadstools – fat red men with white blobs on their jackets, and little scarlet gnomes with white pompoms on their hats, and flying reindeer and sledges in the sky. That is the origin of Santa Claus.' Her bright eyes shone. 'What do you think of that? You have taken our magic mushrooms and made them into Father Christmas. We share the same stories, but we do not know what they really mean.' She smiled and added thoughtfully, 'Perhaps when you have finished your travels, you will have learned the truth.'

I smiled back. 'I doubt it.'

The last thing you expect to see in Lapland is a tribe of Romanies.

After we had taken our leave of our guide at Karasjok we found a campsite, which offered lodgings in *hutte*. These wooden cabins, well insulated but furnished only with the bare necessities, serve Scandinavia's travellers as motels, the more luxurious providing holiday accommodation as well as temporary shelter. Here we intended to settle down for a few days, recover our breath and take our bearings.

A quick inspection confirmed that the rooms included access to communal washing facilities, a communal kitchen and, most important of all after so many days on the road, a coin-operated washing-machine. Nicholas promptly disappeared in the direction of the campsite's little grocery store in search of a new fishing permit and advice on how best to fish the river.

He returned with news that the salmon were running.

To the game fisherman, the three mighty rivers of Lapland provide the best sport in the world, and plenty of it. In the 1880s, the Duke of Roxburghe's game book recorded a catch of a dozen fish weighing thirty pounds and more in a single day.

That evening, Nicholas managed to hook a fish – a respectable three-pounder which, curled round on itself, would just fit into my saucepan for poaching. We ate it with Hollandaise made with the yolk of a gull's egg – large, delicately fishy and of an astonishing orange – and washed it down merrily with a bottle of rhubarb wine Andrea had pressed on us as we left the enclave at Karvol.

The next day, not wishing to put too much reliance on the continuing goodwill of the spirit of the river, I thought it wise to lay in alternative supplies. The experiences of Eastern Europe had made me a little wary of relying on external catering. A Saame stall at the entrance to the campsite offered smoked reindeer meat and reindeer-milk cheese. To these purchases I added a pair of sturdily made birchwood cups, a couple of wooden forks, two spoons made of roots, a pair of wooden plates and a birchwood biscuit-box, which the hatted salesman assured me would be perfect for storing flatbreads.

I arranged the booty in our temporary home and set about those domestic tasks that cannot, of necessity, be completed while on the road. An hour or so later, I had bathed, washed my hair, hung out the washing and was looking forward to an evening recording the local flora and fauna when a deafening roar of machinery shattered the tranquillity.

A caravan of forty or fifty elderly diesel trucks pulled into the campsite, juddering to a halt to form a rough circle. At first I thought these strange people must be a tribe of nomadic Saame whose identity our young guide of the morning had somehow failed to mention. Then I decided they must be a circus troupe, a company of acrobats. The wagons spilled out a great crowd of people – men and women, children, babies. The women were big-breasted, broad of hip, dressed in brightly patterned skirts plumped out with many petticoats, topped by tight-fitting bodices and billowing white blouses. The men – young and old, even the children – were uniformly dressed in tight black trousers and full-sleeved white shirts with black waistcoats.

Even stranger than their appearance was their behaviour. The men immediately hauled battered chairs and tables out of their vehicles and arranged bottles of liquor and packs of cards, while the younger women settled down on the steps of the communal washing facilities, popped their breasts out of their blouses and set about feeding their infants. The babies did not seem to belong to any one woman in particular, but were casually passed on to resume their feeding with an alternative wet-nurse whenever one of the women decided some other chore deserved her attention. They were like a flock of brightly coloured locusts, covering and consuming everything in their path.

By the time Nicholas returned from the river, cooking fires were blazing all over the encampment, pots bubbling on them, every tree had a washing line hung with white shirts and scarlet petticoats, and there was no possibility whatsoever of making use of the communal facilities since the buildings had been commandeered as a makeshift nursery for the toddlers.

Nicholas went off in search of the campsite's manager, returning with the news that these strange people were indeed what they seemed: a tribe of Romanies.

'Apart from that, he says he doesn't know who they are or where they come from. Maybe Latvia or even Hungary. All he knows is that they arrive at about this time every year, stay for a few days and then move on. No one knows what language they speak. They travel without passports and no one knows how they get through the frontiers. The first year the police were called, but as there's no law of trespass, and as long as they do no damage to property or people, there's nothing anyone can do.'

All night long and all through the next day the Romanies went about their business, a tribe that had somehow managed to insulate itself from all exterior interference, whose sheer physical presence was enough to deter the curiosity of outsiders. Their sheer oddity gave them a faint air of menace. Apart from the strangeness of their appearance and their evident indifference to those who did not belong to their group, they would have been perfectly at home in a medieval fairground. Another peculiarity set them apart: while the men were slender, small-boned, wiry and gypsy-like in appearance, the women were big-boned and muscular, and it was they who appeared to do all the physical labour.

The following evening they packed up and were gone. Had it not been for the circular scars of the cooking fires, it would have been easy to believe they had never been there at all. Later, researching a new novel, I read of a tribe of travellers who kept to the old ways, spoke the old language, who were seen by modern Romanies much as anthropologists might see a tribe of South American Indians: the last relics of what we ourselves must once have been, disturbing to the rest of us in that they show only too clearly what we have become. Perhaps our ancestors once travelled in such a way, restless, nomadic, cropping the land and moving on to new pastures, indifferent to their surroundings, careless of all life but their own.

Finland is flat, rolling country. Memory delivers black clouds of mosquitoes, swarms of angry bees; forests of birch or pine; shimmering lakes vast as inland seas.

The mightiest of these waters is Lake Inari. Around its shores the scattered trading-posts had white fox furs for sale, the most beautiful skins imaginable – small wonder the Hanseatic merchants made their fortunes from Russian furs. The long drive across the roof of the world, which had carried us across the border into Finland, was blessed with the bright sunshine and clear blue skies we had come to expect. The broad mouths of the northern fjords shelter small fishing settlements, with miles and miles of empty tundra between. To the south of us, mountains veined with snow; in the distance the islands, long and low and hazed with blue, reached out into the icy waters of the Arctic sea.

Occasionally we would pass a herd of reindeer ambling clumsily alongside the road, lugubrious faces turned calmly to watch us, giving us advance warning of a Saame trading-post a few miles down the road. These posts provided us with our lunchtime stores – pine-forest honey, Arctic raspberries, a wedge of smoked cheese, once even a handful of little ghost-mushrooms, lacy and fragrant, familiar to me from my own gatherings in Hebridean woods.

Driving through one of the dense patches of forest between the lakes, we slowed to offer a lift to a hitch-hiker. He scarcely gave us time to draw to a halt, leaping into the back seat as fast as a ferret out of a sack – a creature with whom he shared several other characteristics.

'Wow,' said Nicholas appreciatively. 'Smells like a sergeant major's crotch after a week on the Luneberg Heath.'

'And how would you know?'

'Trust me.'

We had spent the previous night in one of the few good

hotels listed in the guidebook. There had been a sauna for Nicholas and a gloriously hot bath for me, so we were rested, clean and ready for anything – even a guide who smelt like a ferret.

Our hitch-hiker stayed with us for two days, before vanishing as mysteriously and silently as he had appeared. During that time, he was our silent guide to the landscape, providing Nicholas with opportunities for bird-watching with frantic wavings and chatterings, and – indirectly – allowing me the leisure to paint. Verbal communication was out of the question. To say that Finnish is not an easy language would be a serious underestimation of a problem shared by no other nation except perhaps the Hungarians and the Basques, whose language it may or may not resemble. 'May or may not' is about as far as the etymologists will go. Nobody actually knows anything for sure about the Finns, any more than they know anything about the Finnish language.

Spotting the fishing gear in the boot, our guide directed us down a bumpy track to the lake shore, where a sign indicated that a boat might be rented. The sky was cloudless, there was sufficient breeze to discourage the mosquitoes, and I had bought a picnic of dark rye bread, reindeer blood pudding and Lapp curd cheese, together with a bottle of fine Finnish vodka to keep out the chill. We were assured of a fine day on the water.

When it came to the moment of embarkation, I decided the men would be better off without me – or, rather, that I would be better off without them. Explaining that I needed to search the woods for the elusive Arctic bramble, I vanished into the undergrowth.

The reality is, I'm perfectly happy to cook what the fishermen catch, but can see no reason in sport for sport's sake. I'm a poacher at heart, prefer the worm-baited hook to the fly, am far more interested in filling the pot than playing the game. My idea of hell is sitting in a boat, twitching a length of cat-gut, with absolutely no guarantee that there'll be dinner at the end of it.

When I re-emerged from the woods with a basket of fungi and another of berries – gathering is more reliable than hunting – the clouds had rolled in from the north, the light breeze had become a cold wind, and what had been earlier a mirror-smooth surface was now gun-metal grey flecked with white. Of the boat there was no sign.

I waited another hour. Still no sign. By now the gun-metal grey had turned to churning billows and the wind was howling through the pines. Telling myself that the fishermen had surely taken shelter in one of the wooded bays, I donned boots and waterproof jacket and set off round the lake. The shore was marshy and the track soon vanished into the reed-beds. By this time the rain had begun to fall in earnest and a thick mist had cut visibility to no more than yards. The sky was black and the wind was building to a gale. There was no alternative but to return to the boathouse, wait out the storm and pray.

As I approached the wooden hut, soaked to the skin, shivering with cold and imagining all kinds of disaster, movement within and a dim light under the door told me the boathouse was already occupied.

Of the boat there was still no sign.

I opened the door cautiously.

In the flickering light of an oil-lamp hanging from a hook, perched on the gunwales of the rowboat which had clearly never left its berth, were four men engrossed in a game of poker. Two were unmistakably Finnish fishermen, the third was our ferret-scented guide. The fourth – dry, warm and holding a fistful of Finnish banknotes – was my husband.

'Had a good day, sweetheart?' asked Nicholas brightly.

My language was quite unsuitable for family reading. In retrospect, at least, it was very fortunate that all but Nicholas spoke only Finnish – but I think they got the message.

A broad fast-flowing river marks the border between Finland and Sweden.

From a wooden platform high about the churning waters, four muscular young fishermen were casting oversized shrimping nets into the rapids. The water was thick with small silvery bodies – whitefish, said Nicholas, examining the catch with a fisherman's eye. The nets were lowered and raised, lowered and raised, each time filled to overflowing. In the old ferryman's house beside the rapids an enterprising restaurateur was advertising freshly grilled whitefish straight from the nets and good Danish beer at reasonable prices. The place was famous. When the whitefish were running, our host explained, word spread, the tourists piled in and the fishermen were kept busy day and night.

Nowhere in this vast land is more than an hour or two's drive from the coast, and at weekends in the summer the entire population takes to the water. Everyone has a boat – to a seafaring nation, the lure of the sea is irresistible.

Looking for somewhere to spend the night, we were directed to a Church-run holiday encampment. Fortunately, a room was still available, but strictly for one night only. After the spartan accommodation that had mostly been our lot to date, a soft double bed with white cotton sheets and private bathroom seemed impossibly luxurious.

The bell tolled to signal the evening meal. Following the crowd, we joined a group of young families at long wooden tables set out by the lakeside. The meal was a self-service *smörgåsbord* – the usual array of pickled herrings dressed with soured cream, potato salad, whole tomatoes in bowls, sliced meats and *geitost* cheese, *knackebrod* and crispbreads. Plates were piled high, but no one touched their food until heads had bowed for grace. I remembered Frau Klein in Sibiu – this, too, was a godly community. Her granddaughter would surely have found this place to her taste.

The road we chose the following day was one of the few that traverses the spine of Scandinavia. Notices by the roadside warned drivers of the presence of elk. A small guidebook acquired at the Church encampment provided enlightenment: 'The elk follow their usual paths through the forest. When they come to a road, they do not bother to stop for the traffic. More people are injured by elk than anything else on the road. It is a serious problem – both for the drivers and for the elk.'

Unfortunately the elk seemed to get the worst of the deal. Elk meat, salted, smoked and fresh, was on sale in the supermarket where we purchased our supplies for the road.

The road to Norway was well signposted. Although not billed as a motorway on the map, it proved to be a sturdily built

Swedish Smörgåsbord Sillsalad
SWEDISH PICKLED HERRING SALAD

Herring enthusiasts will know the difference between a sweet *matjes* cure, Dutch in origin, and the plain salt-brine of the traditional Scandinavian cure. Either will do. After handling raw fish, which this is, wash your hands in *cold* water and they won't smell fishy.

SERVES 12, AS THE STARTER FOR A SMÖRGÅSBORD (SERVES 3 PER RECIPE)

POTATO AND HERRING SALAD

2 pickled herring fillets, cut into 1 in/2.5 cm squares

1 cold boiled potato, diced

2–3 spring onions, or *handful* chives, finely chopped

1 tablespoon brine from the herrings

4 tablespoons soured cream

1 teaspoon whole-grain mustard

1 small pickled cucumber, diced

BEETROOT AND HERRING SALAD

2 pickled herring fillets, cut into 1 in/2.5 cm squares

1 pickled beetroot, diced

1 tablespoon pickling liquor from the beetroot

2 tablespoons oil

4 tablespoons soured cream

1 tablespoon chopped dill

$^1/_2$ mild red onion, finely sliced

TOMATO AND HERRING SALAD

4 pickled herring fillets, cut into 1 in/2.5 cm squares

$^1/_2$ mild red onion, finely sliced

1 tablespoon brine from the herring

2 tablespoons tomato purée

1 tomato, skinned and diced small

1 tablespoon malt vinegar

1 tablespoon sugar

CURRIED HERRING SALAD

4 pickled herring fillets, cut into 1 in/2.5 cm squares

1 sourish apple, diced small

1 tablespoon mild onion, finely chopped

1 tablespoon walnut pieces

1 tablespoon brine from the herring

2 tablespoons mayonnaise or oil

2 tablespoons soured cream

1 teaspoon curry powder

In each case, combine the herrings with the other ingredients. Leave in a cool place for an hour for the flavours to meld.

These are the classic *sillsalads*, but that's no reason not to make up your own combinations. As a rough rule of thumb, in salads that include vegetables the volume should equal that of the herring.

Swedish Kottbullar

MEATBALLS

Delicious plain as part of the smörgåsbord table or for a summer picnic, or bathed in a cream sauce and served with a buttery potato purée with celeriac.

─────────── SERVES 4 ───────────

1 lb/500 g minced pork and veal
4 oz/100 g fresh breadcrumbs
1/4 pint/150 ml milk
1 medium onion, finely chopped
  or grated

1 egg
1 tablespoon raisins, optional
1 teaspoon ground allspice
salt and pepper

─────────── TO FINISH ───────────

butter for frying

─────────── OPTIONAL SAUCE ───────────

1/4 pint/150 ml stock
1/2 pint/300 ml soured cream
  or crème fraîche

1 teaspoon flour
salt and pepper

1. Using your hands, work all the meatball ingredients together thoroughly in a bowl – have a bowl of cold water beside you for rinsing the sticky mixture from your fingers while you work. Season with allspice, salt and pepper. Shape the mixture into bite-sized balls.

2. Fry the balls in hot butter in a roomy pan, turning to brown all sides. Remove when perfectly firm and deliciously browned, and serve hot or cold, as part of the smörgåsbord table.

3. To make the cream gravy, sprinkle the flour into the leftover juices in the pan, add the stock and bubble up, scraping in all the little brown bits. Whisk in the soured cream, return the meatballs to the pan, and bubble up once more.

four-lane highway which rose swiftly into the mountains, winding its way through the dense pine forests that cover most of Swedish Lapland. At intervals the forest opened out into broad swathes of meadow, at the centre of which was a homestead much like the one in Karvol.

We halted at one to watch a family harvesting a hayfield. Two women, waist-deep in daisies and Canterbury bells, their faded shirtsleeves rolled up sinewy arms, were tossing the hay on birchwood forks. An old man with a weathered face and deep-set eyes was driving a small wooden cart pulled by a brown pony slowly through the billowing grass. The scythes fixed to the wheels left double tracks in his wake.

The elder of the two women halted, leaned on her fork and studied us with an interest equal to our own. After a few moments, she moved through the lanes of grass towards us, gathering up an armful of the bell-shaped flowers that had fallen to the scythes.

'Please take them. I hear your voices, I think you are English. You are welcome. I have visited England. I like it very much.'

She tipped the flowers into my arms, waving away my thanks. 'I do not like to see the flowers die when they are cut. I have already taken some to my mother, who is not able to come to the fields. There are more than enough in the house.'

She held out her hand. 'My name is Margaret.'

The handshake was bone-crushing. Nicholas introduced us in return, explaining a little of the reason for my curiosity about the work they were doing.

She nodded gravely. 'This is good. We can so easily forget. I come over because I think you are admiring our Norwegian fjord pony. He is a special breed, a winter animal – there are not many of his kind left. He loves the snow, like a reindeer. Today he is a little unhappy because he must work in the sunshine.' She laughed, the blue eyes crinkling. 'Not like his master, my father. He is eighty-two. We think he is wonderful. If you are interested, perhaps you would like to meet him?'

As it was time for the midday break, the old man insisted we join them for their picnic by the edge of the meadow.

Margaret smiled. 'You must do as my father says. It is our tradition to be hospitable to strangers. If you come in the winter, there will always be room to sleep in the hay-barn, a bowl of soup from the stove. We share what we have. Today it is our famous Swedish meatballs, and we have my mother's sourdough ryebread. My mother is famous for her bread.'

We too had a contribution – gulls' eggs from Finnmark. These I arranged and presented to our host in a basket.

Margaret nodded her approval. 'You have understood our traditions. Each person brings enough of one dish for everyone else. This way we may all enjoy what we like of what other people bring, and nobody's store-cupboard is left empty.'

While we ate, Margaret explained a little of her family life. She herself lived in the city most of the year. A modern woman with a modern job, she was an administrator in Stockholm general hospital. It was clear, though, that she had not forgotten she was a farmer's daughter.

'The city is just the place where we go to work. We all know where we come from. No Swedish people are more than two generations away from the land. My family have been farmers in this place for as long as anyone can remember. We have always owned our own land. Perhaps it might be only a few fields, but when there was less need for money, it was enough to keep bread on the table if we lived carefully and helped each other. We had wood all around for making our houses and for fuel, and we hunted in the forest for meat.'

Today, she explained sadly, it was no longer possible to live without an additional income. It seemed that, unlike Bjorn and Andrea over the mountains in Norway, there was little local employment, and the state did not see fit to provide any. The village was mostly inhabited by retired folk and summer visitors. The cash crop that supports a modern lifestyle had to be earned in the city. Nevertheless, there was no trace of the city in the strong bodies and weathered brown faces.

'We come here whenever we can. Every year we help to gather the harvest. My husband is an engineer, and we have three children – two sons and a daughter. Sometimes they can come, but sometimes they must work in the city.' This year it was the turn of her daughter – still at university and reading life sciences – and the daughter's boyfriend.

'All Swedish girls have boyfriends,' said Margaret, with a

laugh. 'But I tell my daughter to be careful to pick one who is willing to help with the harvest. As you can see, she is a dutiful daughter and does what I tell her.'

Although Margaret expected her children to marry and have families, she did not expect the farm to continue in the old way – self-sufficiency was not possible these days. There was no longer a living, even for one family, to be made out of the four or five acres her father could bequeath to her.

Perhaps, she said quietly, after the old man was gone, she and her husband would move here when they retired. But they would be the last generation to crop the hay and feed the four cows her father overwintered in the barn.

'It has changed very much in my lifetime. My father rears for meat, not for dairy any more. The calves are fattened and sent to market. For the last two years, my mother is bedridden and there is no one to milk. And we do not have the time to drive the milk-cows up into the mountains to the *setor* pastures, still less to stay there all through the summer. Soon the *setor* will no longer be pasture but forest. The juniper is very tall this year, and my father does not like to see it so neglected.'

She reflected for a moment, then added, 'If the farm was for me to run, I think I would buy a small tractor. A pony is too much hard work. My father's is the last working pony in the valley. But if I could not move here myself, I would not sell it. One of the children might find a way to make it work.'

Meanwhile, she took pleasure in her father's happiness as he returned to the field, driving his pony, the scythe flashing through the grass and meadow flowers. In his wake fell violets, cranesbill, daisies, corncockle. His granddaughter gathered another armful of deep blue Canterbury bells for her grandmother to remind her of the meadow.

Meanwhile Margaret continued her story quietly. In the old days in the winter when the farm lay dormant, the chores were light. Only the cows had to be fed with the summer's crop of hay, and the men were free to supplement the family's income from the surrounding forest. Pine and spruce would be felled and floated down the river to the depot. The branches were taken home for firewood. Today the men only fell an occasional tree for their own use. The trunk is stripped, cut and trimmed

Swedish Rugbrod
SOURDOUGH RYEBREAD

Sourdough bread is naturally leavened without brewer's yeast – useful in a cold climate where fermented liquor is not traditional. Start four days ahead: it takes two days to get the starter going and another two for the dough to rise. It doesn't need hard work, just a little forethought.

──────── MAKES 3 LOAVES – FIRST DAY (STARTER) ────────

4 oz/100 g rye flour   ¼ pint/125 ml warm water

──────────── SECOND DAY (STARTER) ────────────

4 oz/100 g rye flour   ¼ pint/125 ml warm water

──────────── THIRD DAY (BREAD DOUGH) ────────────

1½ lb/750 g rye flour   1 pint/600 ml warm water
8 oz/200 g starter-dough (give
  the extra to a friend)

──────────── FOURTH DAY (BREAD DOUGH) ────────────

1½ lb/750 g rye flour   1 tablespoon caraway seeds
12 fl oz/360 ml warm water   2 teaspoons salt
1 tablespoon molasses, optional

1. On the first day, work the two ingredients together in a bowl to make a thick cream, cover and set aside in a warm place for 24 hours. On the second day, work in the extra flour and water. Cover and set aside in a warm place for another 24 hours. This is your starter-dough – the stuff that makes all the little bubbles in the bread.
2. On the third day, take out 8 oz/200 g of the dough to keep for

the next time you make bread. (Store in a tightly covered screwtop jar in the fridge – it'll keep easily for a week, but if you make it drier, it'll keep for longer and can even be frozen. You'll need a little warm water to revive it.) Work the flour, the measured amount of starter and the water together in a bowl to make a sloppy dough – keep a bowl of water handy to rinse your hands so the dough doesn't stick to them. Rye dough is worked much wetter than wheat dough.

3. On the fourth day, work the dough with your fists and palms for 10–20 minutes (you may need a little more water – it should stay very soft), cover and set aside for an hour. Knead again, divide into 3 equal pieces and settle into greased tins. These should be two-thirds full; use a wet spoon to flatten the dough into the corners, and sprinkle with water.

4. Prick the tops, cover with a clean tea-cloth – best to use a couple of boards propped against the sides of the tins to make sure the dough doesn't stick to the cloth. Leave for 1–1½ hours in a warm place to rise and fill the tins – look for the little holes that tell you the natural yeasts have worked.

5. Meanwhile, preheat the oven to maximum – 475°F/240°C/ mark 9.

6. Bake the loaves for 15 minutes, then turn down the oven to 350°F/180°C/mark 4. Bake for another 45 minutes, until the loaves are nicely browned and sound hollow when you tip the loaf out of the tin and tap the base. Bake for 10–20 minutes extra, if necessary – no need to pop them back in the tin. A good keeper. Next time you'll have enough starter-dough to get going without the preliminaries. The method also works with wheat-flour or a combination of flours.

into planks and left at the edge of the forest, ready to be collected when needed for repairs. We had already noticed the pearl-grey heaps by the roadside, end slotted into end to allow the wind to weather the wood and dry the sap. The rest of the forest was leased by the government and harvested commercially. The felling fed the massive wood industries that had grown up since the turn of the century. The world has a voracious appetite for wood pulp.

Margaret picked up her fork again. The two men had finished the scything and were wedging the forked drying stakes into the ground. The same holes remain from year to year, explained Margaret, and all the harvesters know just where to find them. The old man, meanwhile, had hitched the pony to a wooden rake made of birchwood, flexible and tough. He climbed on to a tractor saddle perched above it, and took up the reins. Obediently the pony pulled away.

Watching him, Margaret sighed. 'Such memories. You should have seen us on Christmas Eve when I was a child. My mother would dress us up in our warmest clothes and my father would come round to the front of the house with the pony harnessed into our beautiful wooden sleigh, all lined with reindeer skins to keep us warm. We would creep under the furs and wait for my father to climb into the front. Then the sled would slide out into the darkness and the snow and head for the church in the valley – you can see the spire from here. The neighbours came from the hills around – they all had sleighs with ponies then. Everyone had lanterns hanging to light the way. You could hear the harness bells, and see the lights coming into the valley from all around, the people all drawn to the church. It was the most exciting thing in the world.'

She waved across the field towards the wooden farmhouse, dwarfed by its two barns. 'There, in the barn with the open doors, you will find the sleigh. It is at the top of the ramp. Go and see for yourself.'

We wandered over to the barn, the scent of ripe grass and herbs in our nostrils. A ramp led up into a cavernous storehouse. Margaret's voice followed us: 'Grandfather says to forgive the disorder. Things cannot be kept as he would like. It worries him that it is not as it was.'

The loft smelt of the cattle's sweet breath. The sleigh was huge and beautiful. Carved out of pale smooth birchwood, it was large enough to accommodate a whole family with ease. Slung over the beam beside it were the reindeer-skin coverings. On a hook nearby hung the lantern, ready to light the way for a new generation of bright faces through the Christmas snow.

High in the mountains that form the dividing spine between Sweden and Norway, the copper-mining town of Rorøs is preserved as a living museum. I have an inbuilt distrust of such artificial constructions, but a fully inhabited working town is another matter.

Enough copper is still mined in Rorøs for its craftsmen to continue to make the beautiful hand-seamed pans for which the town has always been famous. Although the trade is no longer sufficient to earn the town a living, the tourists who come to admire the men at work ensure its continuing prosperity.

An efficient young woman in the tourist bureau by the car-park – no vehicles were permitted in the old town – directed us to a bed-and-breakfast in the main street. Our room, exquisitely if plainly furnished in the Swedish style, overlooked what might easily have been the Last Chance Saloon. At any moment John Wayne might swing through the half-doors into the street, thrusting his Colt .45 back into its holster. Even the hitching-posts for the horses were authentically Wild West.

That night a storm broke. Thunder rolled and lightning flashed. It was one of those thunderstorms that – certainly in John Wayne territory – herald some kind of celluloid disaster. I lay awake in the darkness between the wooden walls, imagining the room rocking like a ship on the ocean, listening to the soft thud as the first drops splashed on to dry earth, the rattle of the rain on the tin roof. At last I fell into a troubled sleep, to dream of trolls and wolves and scarlet mushrooms that produced hallucinogenic dreams.

The following morning, the sky had cleared and the storm clouds had vanished. The little town was scrubbed and shining, leaving only a few pools on the earth road to dry out rapidly in the breeze. We breakfasted on the usual array of pickled herring and soured milk, and spent a leisurely morning inspecting the tourist attractions.

These turned out to be a curious mixture of the practical and the theatrical. Seduced by the glamour of a working copper-smith's forge, I acquired two hand-beaten saucepans whose handles, the salesman assured me, were made of wood from a beaver's dam. I scrutinized it for toothmarks. Finding none, I concluded that Swedish beavers must have done their appren-ticeship among the Lapps.

This unplanned rush of blood to the wallet delayed the real reason for our detour, which was to pay a visit to one of the last of the working *setors* near Rorøs. As we had learned in Kanvol only a few of these were still used for their original purpose. Some, like Bjørn's, were used by the families for recreation. Most had been converted for holiday lets, but the more remote had simply been abandoned. There were no longer any milkmaids to tend the herds and make the cheese. Young unmarried girls could earn better money in the hotels and shops of the coastal towns than they ever could for their lonely summers tending cows in the upland grass. The prospect of a working *setor* was well worth a night's delay – even if we had to miss one aeroplane and catch another.

A return visit to the helpful young lady in the tourist agency produced the response, 'Of course.'

Of course seemed to be the standard form of agreement in Sweden – I could only presume it was a direct translation of some less unequivocal reply.

'I shall send you to Birgitta Olsen, she is a very interesting lady,' she continued. Rummaging in a drawer she produced a map, tracing the route with her finger. 'You must take this turning from the main road. You must follow the track up the valley for fifteen kilometres until you reach the end of the lake. Then you must continue until you reach the bridge over the stream. From here you will see the wooden houses of the *setor* on the hill. Birgitta provides beds for hill-walkers. She will be happy if you wish to spend the night. She can give you food – it will be simple but I am told it's good. She lives there on her own because she is a widow. The services she offers provides her with a small income and, besides, she enjoys the company.

But you will have to leave your vehicle there' – she pointed to a spot – 'and take your overnight bag. The last mile is on foot.'

She inspected our walking shoes with a critical eye.

'You are fortunate it is only a mile – until ten years ago there was no road and no bridge.'

There was no mistaking Birgitta Olsen's *setor*. Sheltered by a clump of well-grown birch, clearly visible from the lakeside, the *setor*-house and its barns looked at first sight like a small village. All the buildings were raised on stilts.

Nicholas shouldered the overnight bag. We crossed the bridge, thankful we could pass dry-shod, since the water beneath was swollen by the storm.

The owner herself came to meet us, a small, cheerful woman in work-stained overalls, with a round wrinkled face, white hair cropped short, and the cornflower blue eyes that seem to be the birthright of all Scandinavians. I would have guessed her to be in her early sixties, but the energy with which she strode back up the hill was that of a far younger woman.

'You are very welcome. You must make yourself at home – go anywhere you please, ask anything you wish,' she said, waving her hand round her domain. As the *lingua franca* was German, I anticipated that Nicholas would have to do some translating. Through him, I explained the purpose of my visit.

She nodded gravely. 'This, I think, is interesting. But you must always remember we are not monkeys to be watched in a zoo. This is a working *setor*. I could not do it without modern machinery. Even so, I must work hard. You may come with me, and I shall explain what is needed, but do not expect to find fairyland.'

Wise words. For ten years, with the assistance of modern milking equipment, she had succeeded in running her family *setor* virtually single-handed.

'I am not here all year, you understand. This is the summer pasture. The winter farm is by the lake.'

Birgitta explained that she drives her cows to the *setor* in mid-June, as soon as the hay, dormant under snow all winter, is ready for cropping. The journey is leisurely. The cows are nervous because they have young calves, and there is no reason for any hurry. At one mile an hour, it takes twenty hours to move the herd from winter to summer pastures. These days, she leaves again in September when the long Arctic night sets in, but in the old days, when there were more of them to shoulder the workload and the herd was much larger, the family stayed put until Christmas.

Inside, the house was as clean and neat as a new pin. Rag rugs were scattered over the scrubbed wooden floor. By the open hearth Birgitta's simple kitchen utensils were laid out: a heavy iron griddle for baking *flatbrod*; a large iron pot for oat porridge and soups; three plates, three cups, three spoons; a kettle for coffee; a frying-pan. The pans were all of hand-seamed copper, mined and forged by the craftsmen of the old mining town below.

'In these domestic matters I am traditional. But I have a washing-machine and a microwave oven, although the generator will not allow me to use both at the same time.'

Beneath the buildings ran a stream of clear water, which powered the small generator. A constant supply of fresh water is essential in a dairy: the cheese must be washed and the equipment kept spotlessly clean.

Across the stream, set well back from the watercourse, was the cowshed, a long, low building painted ox-blood red, its window-frames picked out in white. Inside, at first, it was too dark to see. When my eyes grew accustomed to the gloom, I noticed six sturdy wooden stalls, each with its cow patiently anticipating the milkmaid.

In the dairy, housed in a separate wooden building, the huge butter-churn stood scrubbed and ready for use. In one corner, a wooden barrel awaited the day's quota of cream. I settled down with my paper and paints. I did not have to wait long for Birgitta to appear with two pails of milk, the contents of which she tipped into a shallow wooden pan the size of a car wheel. 'The secret is in a good pan – this one is good because the wood is old. It has all the necessary microbes. We scrub it and scald it, of course, but there is still something in the wood. In the morning the cream will be ready.'

Birgitta's accommodation for hill-walkers was in one of the smaller barns. Bunk beds, duvets and the evening meal were provided. For the rest, it was every man for himself.

As evening drew in, two hill-walkers appeared, young Swedes on their way to Rorøs. They would share the bunkhouse and the evening meal, our hostess announced.

The meal she set on the table she claimed was typically Swedish. As it was Saturday, there was *risengrod*, the traditional Saturday supper: milk pudding made with rice and the *setor*'s own cream. On the table at the same time, *smörgåsbord*-fashion, was a pile of *knackebrod* – hard discs of rye bread, unleavened and with a hole in the middle so they could be stored on a broom handle set between the rafters. There was also a pat of newly made butter, a block of Birgitta's sugary-sweet *geitost* and a wheel of her own curd cheese.

For liquid refreshment, there was home-made blackcurrant cordial or a cool jug of fresh milk, left to sour a little and thicken in the Scandinavian way.

After supper, I brought out my little painting of the butterwort, and asked about the renneting. The answer, exactly mirroring the previous response, delighted me. 'But of course we used it. And it makes long strings – like this.'

For a *digestif*, there was a bottle of aquavit flavoured with cloudberries. Birgitta set out the little glasses and poured it with justifiable pride. 'This, too, is of my own making. I think it will please.'

The circle was complete. We might now take pleasure in the familiar.

When we had embarked on our journey through the Land of the Midnight Sun, I had no understanding of the strangeness of a land so much the prisoner of its own geography, peopled by nations that know far more about the traditions of others than others will ever know of theirs.

Those virtues that were once essential to survival in isolated communities – frugality, neighbourliness, generosity to strangers – have little place in our busy modern world; a way of life such as this, self-sufficient, dependent on good husbandry and sustainable methods of agriculture, is only viable when the young are valued and the old respected. As soon as these human

– and therefore imperfect – values are no longer of practical use, they vanish, to be replaced by the intervention of the state.

Since we all live in centrally heated houses, we are all creatures of warm climates. We all take our holidays in the Mediterranean sun. We tuck our old people away in old folk's homes, we leave our infants in the care of strangers. We pay our taxes so the state can take care of our problems. Small wonder we can see no reason to learn lessons from those who live such outmoded lives in the frozen lands of the North. And yet we could be wrong. The danger is that we will burn the books before they have been read – that we will lose the library that tells us who we are, where we come from and, through that knowledge, what we may become.

I know now that in all my travels, in all the years in Spain and France while my children were growing to adulthood, I had only learned a fraction of what there was to be learned. Books can be read then put back on the shelf. Lives are not so easily assimilable. No doubt my understanding was imperfect, certainly it remains incomplete. It can never be otherwise. We must learn what we can, and take care we do not misunderstand what we are told.

Aware of all these things, I set out to write my book.

PART TWO

So You Wanna Be A Star?

CHAPTER ELEVEN

Travels in the New World

America is rather like life. You can usually find in it what you look for . . . It will probably be interesting, and it is sure to be large.

E. M. FORSTER, *Two Cheers for Democracy* (1951)

'SO HOW DO YOU FEEL ABOUT *THE OLD WORLD KITCHEN*?' ASKED the editor of the American edition of *European Peasant Cookery*.

'As you please, but any Es on the end of that lot and you've lost an author,' I replied, somewhat tersely. I didn't want to sound ungrateful – a deal's a deal, and a good deal is even better – but the whiff of compromise had reached my nostrils.

And, then again, American editors know what appeals to American readers, so who was I to argue? For any British author, the transatlantic crossing is by no means automatic. The book had done well in Britain – very well. In America, the previews showed promise: tipped as a nominee for the James

Beard Award, jacket quotes had come in from some of the biggest names on the American culinary scene.

By the autumn of 1987, the omens were favourable and the publicity machine rolled into action. We're not talking Jackie Collins mega-stardom, mind you, but a six-city author tour is worth the publisher's airfare.

It was Yom Kippur when I was collected by publisher's limo from New York airport. Everyone was on holiday, and I had twenty-four hours to recover from jet-lag before the machinery cracked in. Publicity had checked me into one of the glass-and-chrome high-rise hotels into which the publishing company post their touring authors. Middle-of-the-range authors, like aircraft seats, are billeted according to profitability.

The most important feast day in the Jewish calendar had emptied the streets and closed the shops. Yom Kippur means the Orthodox go home to mother, the Wasps go home to their wives. As for the rest of us, the drifters loose in the city, the devil finds work for idle hands. Left to my own devices, I decided to look for lunchtime company. I made the telephone calls. Everyone was out of town except Anthony Haden-Guest. A man whose every *cri* is the *dernier*, a city-dweller with his finger on every fashionable pulse, a man of – how shall I put it? – a certain fame, notorious even, rumoured to be the model for Tom Wolfe's English anti-hero in *Bonfire of the Vanities*. Never a man for rural parts, Anthony.

'Morton's,' said Anthony briskly. 'I'll book.'

This was the big time. I had heard tell of the city's most fashionable watering-hole. It would be hard not to when its table-hopping celebrities provided the raw material for every gossip-column in every country under the sun.

If Anthony wanted to meet me at Morton's, it boded well for the status of my authorship.

I should have known my old friend better. Germaine Greer was in town. The leader of the sisterhood was also embarking on an author tour of considerably greater grandeur than mine. It might have been my misfortune, or Anthony's design, that the lady was holding court at the bar. Anthony's living is earned because he has a nose for the main story like a mutt for a truffle. Ms Greer is a hold-the-front-page story, while authors of

308

cookery books, however well received, most emphatically are not.

'Germaine Greer,' observed Anthony unnecessarily, since no one – with the possible exception of a member of an undiscovered tribe of Amazonian forest Indians – could have failed to identify the six-foot frizzy-haired Antipodean.

Anthony watched her much as Gawain, that medieval Goody-Two-Shoes, must have contemplated the Holy Grail. I knew all about the book, naturally – I had read the reviews, some of them hostile. To put it delicately, it was a chronicle of Ms Greer's adventurings in Tuscany. To put it indelicately, *coitus interruptus*, five times a night.

'I think you should meet her.' A hand on my elbow, and I was face to face with the legend. Anthony explained my presence, leaning heavily on my early (totally uncreative) connections with *Private Eye*, skipping lightly over the breeding and the cookery.

Ms Greer peered at me over her specs. 'You write cookery books?'

'Well, this is my first. *The Old World Kitchen*, no Es on the end,' I burbled. 'Six-city author tour. Boston, Toronto, Detroit . . .' My voice trailed away. Geography was no excuse.

'A *cookery* writer?' The voice carried unmistakable undertones of Lady Bracknell discussing handbags.

'I've always admired your work,' I offered limply. This is not entirely true. *The Female Eunuch* was terrific. After that, I reckon, she rather went off the rails. I had, in fact, attempted to acquire a copy of her most recent tome at the airport, thinking it would make illuminating reading on the flight. The attempt had failed at the first fence when I tried to explain the book's contents to the elderly female assistant.

'What section, dear?'

I repeated the title, louder.

'Sex in Tuscany?' boomed the hard-of-hearing one across the crowded racks. 'Never heard of it, dear. Try the top shelf. Adults only.' There indeed it was, *Playboy* and *Penthouse* providing gloriously inappropriate company. By this time every customer in the bookshop had turned to watch me. Scarlet with embarrassment, I slunk away.

The great author examined me over her half-moon specs. 'And where did you learn to cook?'

I explain in as few words as possible how my career came about. '*Really?*'

A single word, but enough. Bang goes motherhood, domesticity, those complicated compromises made by women to ensure that their mate stays around for long enough to bring up the children.

Ah, well.

Same sex. Different destiny.

The tour started in New York.

I was to be a guest on the weekly food spot of what I had been assured was a highly influential radio show.

The venue turned out to be somewhat unglamorous. A downtown hotel of the sort airlines block book for their passengers when the jumbo breaks down on the runway. The radio station – even less glamorously – rented a suite by the hour.

Our host, the presenter, was a veteran of the air-waves, red-haired, red-necked, laconic, like the bad policeman in a fifties movie. My fellow guests were Barbara Kafka, mistress of the microwave, and a tall, rawboned grey-haired woman in a creasefree blouse, sensible skirt and flat shoes whose name escapes me to this day. Suffice it to say that her contribution to the world of the food-fix was *The Brittle Bone Cookbook*, an evangelical work on the importance of milk in the diet of the elderly.

'It was my mother who inspired me to write the cookbook. When she was eighty she had this big lump on her back. Her spine just crumbled, it was terrible. Do you know how many elderly women suffer from brittle-bone disease? Forty per cent. Imagine.'

Brittle-bone disease?

'In England you call it osteoporosis.'

Dowager's hump?

'I guess that describes it. Except in the States hump means something else.'

A whole cookbook?

310

'Sure. I give milk recipes, cheese recipes – all low fat, naturally. This is a very health-conscious subject. We're aiming for the silver bullets.'

Silver bullets?

'Third-agers – retired folk. They drive around in convoys in big shiny motorhomes shaped like bullets. Maybe you don't have them in England?'

I considered this. Actually, I admitted, the only time I'd ever seen the strange moon-vehicles she described was in southern Spain. A pack of them had been moving at a fast gallop round the coastal road between Cadiz and Malaga. At first sight I had thought it must be the Spanish soldiers out on one of the practice manoeuvres designed to repel a new Moorish invasion, the main preoccupation of the elderly generals of Franco's time.

I explained this at some length, and with embellishments, while we were waiting for the sound engineers to set up the machinery. I had not yet learned not to waste my energy on the warm-up.

The sound system cracked in and we were away.

The interview was my first experience of American talk-radio. The presenter was of the laconic, seen-it-all school of broadcasting. We three were there to promote our books, the presenter expected us to promote them. Barbara Kafka was the only one of us who knew how to work the system. Brittle Bones was too polite to interrupt, and I had not yet lost my English habit of not speaking before I'm spoken to.

A round-table discussion is a bit like a rugby scrum: when the hooker goes in, there's no way out but to grab the ball and run for touch. As might only be expected, Barbara knocked Brittle Bones and me way out of the ball-park. Brittle Bones had her calcium-rich cheesecake smacked straight into the microwave; my *cassoulet de confit d'oie* was the fatted goose that never got cooked.

Never mind. The following day my publishers sent a reassuring limo to take me to the airport. Next stop, Boston, home of the bean and the cod, where – as the saying goes – the Lowells talk to the Cabots and the Cabots talk only to God.

I was unaccompanied, but not for long. A lady called Lucky plucked me anxiously out of the arrivals lounge. Every author has to have a minder. Heaven knows, authors are not a reliable breed, liable as they are to go off the rails, bounce off the walls, tumble the bellboys.

Boston has a population of half a million. Most of them read books, said Lucky. Boston, continued my informant, calls itself the Free City. You could follow the Freedom Trail from the Common to Bunker Hill. This was what we did.

I think I stayed in the Back Bay Hilton, but I cannot be sure. I am perfectly sure that Lucky and I dined together in the hotel restaurant on Boston baked beans and apple upside-down cake – neither of which is easy of digestion. During the course of the meal I learned that Lucky acquired her nickname in the same spirit as very small men are called Lofty – fate had not been kind.

The next day the schedule was light. Lucky decided to take me up the observatory for a look at the ship responsible for the Boston tea-party. I tried not to take it personally.

We shared each other's most intimate thoughts. I learned more about Lucky's life in a few hours than close friends ever learn about each other in a lifetime. I even acquired Lucky's mum's recipe for granola. The first night we dined together on Boston chowder and tales from the crypt. We ran through the first husband, the second husband, the third. Lucky announced herself hopeful of a fourth. I listened gratefully. Lucky's misfortunes were not only a slice of life, they had absolutely nothing to do with me or the responsibilities that had landed on my shoulders.

The last evening I climbed into my red suit, seamed stockings and high heels for my moment of truth. When the going gets tough, the tough wear tights. The Boston Culinary Historians had invited me to address their distinguished members. Their members were distinguished enough to scare me out of my wits. The scarlet suit served the same purpose as the threat display by a small lizard confronted by a large predator.

Before my speech, the *Boston Globe* had requested an interview. The *Boston Globe* is almost as grand as the Boston Culinary Historians. The *Boston Globe* was represented by a perfectly painted and impeccably coiffed female person in Halston basic black.

Boston Baked Beans

Two storehouse staples – beans and barrelled pork – combine to make the forerunner of the baked bean. In Boston the dish is made with the small white haricots known as the 'navy' or pea bean, which – like all the haricots – is native to the Americas. The indigenous peoples of northern America used sugar rather than salt to season their meats – a taste that appealed to the settlers.

SERVES 4

1 lb/500 g small white
  haricot beans
1 teaspoon English mustard
1 tablespoon salt
2 tablespoons molasses (black
  treacle)

3 tablespoons brown sugar
8 oz/250 g unsmoked streaky
  bacon, rind on

1. Pick over the beans and soak them overnight in cold water. Next day, drain and cover them to a depth of two fingers with fresh water. Heat slowly to just under boiling point, lid loosely and leave to simmer – the water should tremble, no more – for about an hour and a half until they're soft. To test, take up a few on a spoon and blow on them: if ready, the skins will burst. Add boiling water if the beans need it.

2. Drain the beans and transfer them to a casserole. Mix the mustard, salt, molasses and sugar with a cupful of boiling water and stir in the liquid. Bury the bacon in the middle, leaving the rind exposed. Add enough boiling water to submerge the beans completely. Lid or cover with foil, shiny side down, and bake very slowly (250° F/130° C/mark 1) for at least 5 hours – longer, if possible. Uncover the pot for the last hour so the top browns and crisps.

Home-made Granola

On the road, I lived on this, the American version of muesli, the best breakfast in the world. Once you've got the hang of it, vary the proportions of nuts to suit yourself. Dried cranberries are a nice addition.

——————————— MAKES ABOUT 5LB/2.5KG ———————————

4 oz/100 g butter
1 lb/500 g runny honey
8 oz/250 g unrefined dark
  brown sugar
1 lb/500 g rolled oats
12 oz/350 g slivered almonds
8 oz/250 g shelled unsalted
  sunflower seeds

8 oz/250 g shelled unsalted
  pumpkin seeds
8 oz/250 g shredded (not grated)
  coconut
6 oz/175 g shelled unsalted
  pistachios
2 oz/50 g pine kernels

1. Preheat the oven to 180°F/350°C/mark 4.
2. Melt the butter, honey and sugar together in a small pan. Combine all the remaining ingredients in a bowl and pour in the warm honey mix. Toss to blend thoroughly.
3. Transfer to a roasting tin and bake for 25–30 minutes, stirring occasionally to prevent sticking, until nicely toasted into fragrant little lumps – the time taken depends on the moisture in the raw ingredients. It'll crisp more as it cools.
4. Store in an airtight tin when perfectly cool. Wonderful with yoghurt or milk and fresh fruit. Sensational with sliced peaches and thick strained yoghurt or sour cream.

Boston Chowder

This celebrated dish takes its name from the *chaudière*, a heavy iron cooking pot used by the early French settlers. The soup was thickened with ship's biscuit or hard-tack, which needed a good soaking to be edible at all. In Boston, the dish is made with the native quahog (little neck) or steamer (long neck) clams.

──────────────── SERVES 4 ────────────────

2 pints / 1 l shellfish in the shell –
  clams, scallops, queens, cockles,
  mussels
1 thick slice unsmoked streaky
  bacon, diced small
1 medium onion, skinned and
  finely sliced
1½ pints / 750 g milk

1 lb / 500 g potatoes, peeled and
  cubed
2 bayleaves
1 lb / 500 g filleted fresh cod or
  other white fish, skinned and cubed
¼ pint / 150 ml thick soured cream
salt and pepper

──────────────── TO FINISH ────────────────

4 crackers (water biscuits, cream
  crackers or matzos), broken

knob of butter

1. Rinse the shellfish thoroughly – if necessary, leave them in a bucket of water overnight to spit out their sand – and spread in a single layer in a roasting tin. Cover with foil and pop them into a hot oven until they steam open – this can take 20 minutes or more. Shell them (save the juices for the soup), dice the meat and reserve.
2. Set a roomy soup pan on the heat. Add the diced bacon and fry gently until nicely browned, when it will have yielded all its fat. Push the bacon bits to one side and add the sliced onion. Fry until soft and golden. Add the milk and reserved shellfish juices, bring to the boil and drop in the cubed potato and bayleaves. Season and simmer for 10–15 minutes until the potatoes are quite soft. Add the cubed white fish and bring the milk just back to the boil. Stir in the chopped shellfish meat and reheat to just beneath boiling point. Remove from the heat and stir in the cream.
3. To serve, drop a broken biscuit and a little knob of butter in the bottom of each soup plate before you ladle in the hot chowder.

315

'I'm going to take you to dinner, Elisabeth. I'm going to take you to dinner at Legal Seafood. You won't have heard of it, but it's the best fish restaurant on the east coast.'

At five o'clock? Are you sure?

'What time d'you eat in England?'

Ah, well. My interviewer led me to the best table in the house. She leaned towards me, eyes wide, glossed lips a-quiver. I sat up straight and glanced nervously round for Lucky. Lucky had another engagement at another table. Absurdly, I felt a pang of jealousy. The Americans have a gift for instant intimacy which can be misunderstood by those accustomed to Old World reserve.

Meanwhile, the *Globe* was giving me the full tour of her orthodontistry. Americans have perfect teeth – I am told they can identify Old World persons as soon as they smile.

'Elisabeth, I can't tell you what a privilege it is to meet you in person, Elisabeth.' She leaned forward eagerly. 'Share your experiences, Elisabeth.'

Captivated by the triple repetition of my name, I obliged. In spades. No one had ever invited me to share my experiences before.

Meanwhile, we ate prodigiously: blackened bluefish, grilled lobster, little neck clams with melted butter. This was my second mistake. The first mistake, once again, was wasting the good lines on the warm-up. By the time we got to the Culinary Historians, I was full of food and all talked out.

The room was packed. In one corner, a laden buffet table. To my dismay, the Culinary Historians had paid me the graceful compliment of cooking several of the more robust dishes from my book – and these, no doubt, I would be required to sample.

As if this wasn't enough, just as the secretary was preparing to introduce me, a large party led by a very tall woman whose face and figure I recognized swept through the throng and claimed the chairs reserved in the middle of the front row.

My mouth opened and shut like a Lofoten codfish. Julia Child is truly famous. The author of *The Art of French Cooking*, she taught the post-war generation of American cooks what their ancestors had not: how to appreciate the pleasures of *haute cuisine*. But it was her lack of inhibition as a television chef – she

316

was the first real star of that strange medium – that endeared her to the viewing public.

Her reputation was made when, after dropping a whole cooked salmon on the floor, she bent down, picked it up and replaced it on the dish, adding in a swift aside to the camera: 'Anything which has been on the floor for less than ten seconds doesn't count.'

Mrs Child folded her hands in her lap and nodded – the sign that the audience might relax and the entertainment begin. I stumbled into action.

'Ladies and gentlemen . . .' and so on and so forth. It took me, as you might well imagine, a little time to get into my stride. Actually, I was terrified. If I hadn't been wearing my red suit, I might have run for cover and pretended I was part of the audience.

Mrs Child nodded and smiled all through. Possibly taking her lead, the audience was gratifyingly attentive. The speech passed, as all such speeches must. Applause, lights, questions, answers.

'And now, ladies and gentlemen, we are to sample some of Elisabeth's dishes.'

Peasant cookery is not by nature dainty. The display included a cassoulet, lentil stew, Balkan *djuvedj*, a German onion-bread, all of which might have been purpose-designed to mitigate the effect of the other remarkable feature of the city: the force-nine gale that howls, winter and summer alike, through its patrician streets.

Manfully trying to persuade my already overstretched digestive tract to overlook the grilled lobster, the blackened bluefish, the little neck clams, I struggled, smacking my lips appreciatively from one dish to another.

'Elisabeth, I have a little something planned.'

A hand on my elbow, Mrs Child's voice in my ear.

'We'll slip away just as soon as we can. I mean to take you to supper.'

My cheeks flushed, sweat broke out on my forehead. 'Absolutely,' I agreed.

Minutes later, we were on our way. My hostess's introductory remarks were strangely familiar. 'I'm going to take you somewhere you'll never have heard of, Elisabeth. It's the best fish restaurant on the east coast.'

'Let me guess – not Legal Seafood?'

'You've been there?'

'Absolutely not,' I lied frantically, cursing the too-recognizable scarlet suit, the peculiar timing of the *Boston Globe*. How could I explain to a legend that she'd been double-dated? Twice in one evening would be impossible to excuse. The truth would spoil all the fun. Maybe the *maître d'* would be tactful enough not to blow my cover. Maybe they'll have run out of little-necks. Maybe the chef who had been summoned to receive my congratulations had gone home.

The restaurant was already half empty. Mrs Child swept straight to her usual table. Did I detect a sympathetic gleam in the eye of the meeter-and-greeter? I breathed again. Maybe I just might get away with a small salad.

Not a bit of it. Mrs Child ordered double rations of everything, from little-necks through to blueberry pie.

Dear reader, I ate them all.

Detroit is Hood City. Its reputation is dangerous. The freeway swirls round the suburbs, which encase the city like the thick green skin round a walnut. On the surface all looks orderly and open. Small squat dwellings aproned by unfenced lawns line the road. Featureless gardens are overlooked by equally faceless picture windows. This is suburban America at its most benign, yet there are more gangsters here per square inch than anywhere else in all the other states put together.

There was no minder to meet me. Instead, a smartly uniformed chauffeur held up a card scrawled with my name. Or nearly my name. Liz Ward is a little wide of the mark, but there was no one else to claim the Cadillac, and perhaps, in this city, anonymity was advisable.

The hotel was vast, impersonal, upholstered from floor to ceiling in beige suede, presumably to absorb the conspiratorial whisperings. Reception had my name correctly. 'Welcome to Detroit, Ms Luard.'

'Mrs,' I said, unnecessarily.

With a tolerant smile, Reception handed over a key which,

she explained, gave access to the two top floors. These were reserved for VIPs.

VIPs are supposed to have a great deal of luggage and a lawyer. I had neither.

I inspected the restaurant. I had a dinner allowance, a lunch allowance and a breakfast allowance included in the price of the room. If I had a minder, she was not on baby-sitting night-duty.

I missed Lucky. The idea that one can be on one's own in a strange city was entirely new to me. I made my way to the hotel's restaurant to spend my allowance. I ordered a Hawaiian salad, low-calorie. Salads are supposed to be safe. They inhabit a kind of culinary no man's land, not really food at all. This salad involved tinned pineapple, low-fat cream cheese, and had been liberally dosed with cashew nuts.

The next morning my minder collected me at cock-crow. She was of indeterminate age, brisk, efficient, and her lipstick would have stopped the traffic. We were on the TV breakfast show. There was no dressing-room, no makeup, no facilities for preparing food apart from a collapsible table on which I just recognized the ingredients stipulated in the recipes.

These were mostly potatoes. As it was the eve of All Saints', among the dishes I had proposed an Irish Hallowe'en champ.

I suggested to the producer's assistant I would slip in the traditional good-luck charms – a hazel twig for a wife-beater, a button for a bachelor, a coin for luck. I had brought the items with me.

'Good-luck charms? They edible?' The producer's assistant sounded alarmed.

Of course not, I replied. They're not supposed to be eaten.

'Like the little bit of paper in a fortune cookie?'

Something like that.

'We'll get back to you right away. I'll have the legal department check it out.'

Legal department?

'Sure. People can sue. Some kid swallows a lump of wood, they sue. You got insurance?'

I got the message. Scrap the good-luck charms.

I concentrated on non-controversial potato peeling. There was no saucepan and no water. Unfortunately I had omitted to

Irish Hallowe'en Champ

All Hallows' Eve is the time for young girls to think of future husbands. Favours buried in the bowl of champ, much as with the Christmas pudding, reveal what fortune might be expected for the coming year. The favour might be a gold wedding ring, or it might be a twig for a wife-beater, a button for bachelorhood, a penny for a man of substance, a miniature horseshoe for luck.

─────────────── SERVES 6 AS A MAIN DISH ───────────────

5 lb / 2.5 kg potatoes, scrubbed
  but unskinned
1 green cabbage, rinsed and
  shredded

1–2 large leeks or spring onions,
  finely sliced
1/2 pint / 300 ml creamy milk
salt and pepper

─────────────── TO FINISH ───────────────

6 oz / 175 g butter

1. Set the potatoes to cook in enough salted boiling water to cover. At the same time, cook the cabbage, in a very little water and salt, in a tightly lidded pan until tender but still bright green, then drain well. Set the sliced leeks or spring onions to simmer and infuse in the milk.

2. Drain the potatoes when perfectly tender, skin them just as soon as they're cool enough to handle, and mash thoroughly with the hot milk and leek. Season well and fold in the cabbage. Reheat and and pile in a hot bowl, burying the favours so they're invisible.

3. To serve, either make a dip in the middle and drop in the whole lump of butter, to melt in a glistening creamy pool, or ladle each portion into a bowl with its own nugget of butter. Buttermilk is the traditional accompaniment.

mention that a person intending to boil potatoes needs both. A saucepan was produced, but my area remained a water-free zone. I intercepted a passing studio technician. We had a little trouble over the pronunciation of 'water', one of those small things that divide nations. Finally I managed to convey what I required.

'Sparkling or still?'

Water for cooking.

'Cooking?'

Yes. You know. Plain water for cooking.

'Use the microwave, honey.'

Who? Me? The author of *European Peasant Cookery* use the *microwave*?

'Sure.'

Where's the instruction book? I enquired wearily.

'And you a cookbook writer?' The technician looked at me pityingly.

Barbara Kafka, where are you now? I had volunteered to make six potato recipes, all involving mashed tatties. We were going out live.

By the time I was wheeled on to the set, I was still peeling. Meanwhile, the presenter, a lady with eyelashes like a baby tarantula and lip-gloss as thick as yacht varnish, had begun to panic.

Mashed potatoes, champ, clapshot, potato scones, potato pancakes. Nothing to it, really, I explained soothingly. Actually, I was rather hoping the presenter might get involved. You know, all girls together. One glance at the fingernails convinced me that this was not to be. As they say in Detroit, 'In your dreams, honey.'

Lights, action.

I grabbed the minder's lipstick and headed for the counter. I burbled on merrily about Irish Hallowe'en and the favours buried in the champ. This slowed the action further. I was still frantically flipping pancakes as the credits rolled.

Chauffeur-driven cars collected and delivered me to various appointments – radio, press interviews, another local TV station, this time cooking-free. Publicity had done its stuff. I spoke to no one about anything but myself.

There's a curious unreality to the visiting author's presentation. No one knows *who* you are, but everyone knows *what* you are. Cookery-writers are neither intellectual nor newsworthy. My subject is both friendly and threatening to the immigrant populations to whom my book was expected to appeal. Very often it was a lack of anything to cook that made everyone emigrate in the first place.

The final interview was on a shopping channel. Naturally enough, the station was in a shopping precinct. The interview was sandwiched between the car ads and the consumer-product advice. The host's wife had just had a baby. We talked about babies and *The Old World Kitchen*. What baby-food could I recommend? Whatever the rest of the family eats, was my advice – just bang it in the liquidizer and spoon it in.

My host went into shock. Baby-food comes in jars and you buy it from the cook-chill cabinet. That's how the system works. There's no room for banging things in liquidizers – what would the consumer think? In America, consumers are born, not made. Nappies, sleeping suits, bedclothes, bottles, you name it – it's disposable. When on the move, an American baby comes with more hand-luggage than Imelda Marcos has shoes.

We moved to safer ground. The phones were plugged in. An anxious female voice came on the line. What about the calorie content of the recipes in *The Old World Kitchen*? I told her I knew nothing about calorie-counting, but that I'd been in enough Third World countries to know that if you want thin, go to bed hungry. Looking for a fat-farm? Two weeks in northern Ethiopia should do the trick. A dose of dysentery or an unhappy love affair works wonders for the waistline. Anyway, that might not have been what the ladies of Detroit wanted to hear, because I was out of there faster than a jack-rabbit with a coyote on its tail.

This was a shame because I enjoy a good phone-in. The following day I had another opportunity on an early-morning radio programme. Real people asked real questions, even if some of them got what they might have considered to be unreal answers.

A group of Poles collecting fungi in the Appalachians

monopolized the air-waves. I was fascinated by what they were telling me, which is that they picked exactly the same varieties they once picked at home, give or take a minor variation in the species. The Poles are opportunist feeders. They had fitted into the new landscape like hands in a glove.

'Did you choose where you live because it reminded you of home?'

'Sure we did. We came here to be who we are, not who someone wanted us to be.'

Toronto was in the process of refurbishment. It looked like New York would look like if someone had reduced the whole place to rubble and started rebuilding with the debris.

My new minder was wearing a great many woolly jumpers and a harassed expression. As she ferried me in from the airport, she assured me anxiously that my hotel was the best in town. We drove up the main drag towards what looked like a gigantic doorstop.

I didn't know much about Canada, except that there were Lapps – Saame people – in Ottawa, a lot of expatriate Scots in Newfoundland, and all the French lived in Québec.

Furthermore I was feeling a little underequipped. The customs officers had inspected my hand luggage with unusual thoroughness and removed my chef's knives, just in case. Canada does not welcome offensive weapons. Well, no surprise there. They would be returned to me, they assured me, on my departure, which was no good to anyone about to embark on a cookery demonstration.

My minder booked me in, and promptly dumped me. She'd love to have been able to join me for dinner, but she was job-sharing with her husband. She was also worn out. A certain very famous actress-turned-author had been through last week. The pace had been terrible.

And was Miss Collins, how shall I put it? a little on the demanding side? Her reply was unprintable.

Tomorrow she would be all mine. We would have a terrific day, an exciting programme of events had been planned.

Such as?

Well, to tell the truth, Miss Collins had left everyone

somewhat exhausted. The media did not seem susceptible to blandishments. She had done the best she could. She had arranged lunch in the hotel with a hand-picked group of local journalists, although journalists, hand-picked or otherwise, are notoriously unreliable and never answer their invitations until the last minute, and then only if hard-pressed by publicity persons.

Quite.

In the afternoon, she told me, there was to be another radio phone-in – the highspot of my day – and a newspaper profile. But tonight, tonight I was on my own.

Tonight was Cinderella-time.

The hotel lobby was crowded. Towing my hostess-suitcase in my wake – who needs Gucci leather when you can have a set of wheels? – I pushed my way through the throng and joined a queue of smartly dressed business-persons awaiting the concierge's attention.

From the chatter all around I discovered there was a political conference in town. Pierre Trudeau was making his first appearance after sensational revelations about his wife's liberated lifestyle. Mick Jagger had been mentioned. Canadians being sensitive about their reputation for dullness, the prospect of Maggie and Mick had brought the newspapers out in a rash of coloured photographs.

My turn. I filled in the forms that would admit me to the VIP suite – but of course, where else? The concierge presented me discreetly with a second key.

Why the second key? I enquired, somewhat naïvely, in the light of Madame Trudeau's requirements.

In case Madame desires company, replied the concierge severely. Now, there's one for the feminists. Who would have guessed, when I had been in the market for such things, that such a courtesy could possibly be extended to the female of the species?

I made my way thoughtfully to the lift. Author tours are oddly isolating, a bit like being a minor rock star but without the groupies. A week into the tour, and I'm positively screaming for company.

Maybe room service could provide rent-a-friend. It wouldn't

even have to be human. A cat, a lapdog, even a goldfish would do. We could share the tub and order up fishfood.

The lift doors parted to reveal a Cona coffee machine, a cocktail cabinet and a young woman wearing a short black frock and an expression that would have sat well on a *Playboy* bunny.

'Welcome to the VIP suite. My name is Tanya and I am your hostess for the evening.' With a flick of the lip-gloss, she showed me a set of perfectly capped teeth. I was beginning not to like her very much.

'Champagne?'

I inspected the proffered glass. It was fizzy, but that was about all.

'Compliments of the house,' said Tanya, flashing the false eyelashes.

'Really?'

'Oooh, how darling! You're from England! I can always tell.'

'Scotland, actually,' I replied nastily.

'Just darling.' Tanya showed me her teeth again, rather like a terrier caught nipping the postman.

I inspected the ice-bucket, wondering briefly if I could take the bottle to my room, or if I was expected to behave like a cocktail-party guest and not pinch the liquor.

Behind us, the lift doors creaked. Tanya's eye-contact shifted. Pierre Trudeau walked out.

To put it frankly, he was a bit of a disappointment. We expect our powerful men to be taller than ordinary men, like heroes on Greek vases, but Trudeau was tiny, like one of our royals, with the same popping blue eyes and slightly gormless expression. I've never been much of a royalist myself. In my view, they're a much overrated bunch. In the old days, no one expected the king to be clever or well behaved – the very reverse, the stupider the better. All he had to be was handsome. They picked one every year, told him he could have all the girls he wanted and behave as badly as he liked. At the end of the year, they gave him a good trepanning and chucked him in the bog. Apparently there was no shortage of volunteers. Every few years, the archaeologists dig one out of the peat and put him in a museum. The Danes have dozens, all authentically displayed and beautifully lit, and very salutary it is, too.

My rooms were vast. We're talking serious space. I could have handed my guest key to the entire troupe of the Chippendales and still not have met them all. I even had a kitchenette, super-sanitized for my safety. I considered inviting Tanya and Pierre. On second thoughts, come back, Lucky, all is forgiven.

I turned on a TV the size of a garden shed and flicked the channels. Someone was saucing skinless chicken breasts with low-fat yoghurt. The pornography channel offered a brief glimpse of heaving buttocks, then vanished in a snowstorm. A notice on the screen informed me I could see more buttocks by dialling the concierge. Actually, I have never been one for spectator sports, I prefer the personal touch. On the house-movie channel, *Casablanca* was getting a rerun. The Ottoman princess would have loved it.

For the seventh evening running, CNN and room service had my custom.

Cleveland is known to out-of-towners as the Mistake by the Lake. Iron and steel were her reason for existence. Apparently people spend a lot of time trying to get out of Cleveland – as yet I had no idea why they wanted me in it.

Fortunately I had a new minder to explain such things. Her name was Colleen. She was, naturally, Irish. There were, she told me, a lot of Irish in Cleveland, and my book had quite a bit of Irish cooking, mostly – as you will know by now – potatoes. I found her interest a little unconvincing. If I was Irish and living in Cleveland, I'd never want to see another potato again.

Ohio grows potatoes, explained my minder patiently. Immigrants went where the landscape looked like home, and Ohio was fine for potatoes.

She abandoned me to my evening. I ate in the hotel's coffee bar. My experience brought me to the conclusion that the baseline of American cooking is German. All those frankfurters and hamburgers can't be wrong.

My schedule was not exactly arduous: a bookshop signing, a radio interview and a ladies' literary lunch-club. The signing included coffee and a chat with the punters. Thirty people took coffee, three bought books. The lunchtime ladies talked enthusiastically of pasta and polenta while picking at a lettuce leaf. I pointed out that soon we wouldn't need to eat at all: we'd just watch it on TV and pop a pill.

The radio interview was the late-late show. The presenter greeted me warmly. It seemed that he, too, was glad of the company.

We rambled on amiably over the air-waves, inviting people to telephone with their cookery queries. Silence reigned. If there were any cooks out there, they were all safely tucked up in their beds. The telephone rang at last. A group of Polish truckers in a pull-in on the freeway wanted me to identify fungi. I explained about habitat and the need to hold the specimen in the hand. This caused a good deal of ribaldry and several indecent proposals, which had to be beeped out by the presenter. He was very quick on the button.

Ten minutes later, we took a call from the Ukrainian proprietor of an all-night diner. He wanted a reliable recipe for pickled cabbage. Now, reliable recipes for pickled cabbage are my area of special expertise. Warming to my theme, I embellished the practical information with the story of my night in the whorehouse outside Lutomer. Something told me that this wasn't going to sell a lot of copies of a cookbook, but what the hell, it was late and the host had opened a bottle of Californian claret.

The next day, the *Cleveland Plain Dealer* was on the line before breakfast. Their night editor had heard the broadcast, liked the cut of my jib, could they do an interview?

Of course they could.

I telephoned the good news to my minder, a mother of three whose husband had run away with a tantric yoga teacher from California. She positively percolated with joy. I only hoped it would serve her well when the Christmas bonuses came up.

The *Plain Dealer* sent a photographer and a reporter. I slapped on the lipstick and posed obligingly by the lake with a cabbage. The interview went well. All I had to do was share my experiences: the *Boston Globe* may have had my authorial virginity, but, like any old boiler in a brothel, I could still strut my stuff.

Chicago is the spiritual home of Prohibition, jazz, begetter of the speakeasy. It has a population of three million, which is a lot of customers to groove on down.

I expected good things of Chicago. It was – still is – the home of Second City, a satirical theatre company, which once played the Establishment Club, owned by Nicholas and his friend Peter Cook in the days when satire was young and *Private Eye* scarcely weaned from its mother's milk. Several of the cast had dossed down on the floor of our London flat, and I remembered shared laughter over strange substances and oddly perfumed smoke. But those were the sixties, when such things were run-of-the-mill. As someone once said, and quite rightly the provenance escapes me, 'If you can remember it, baby, you weren't there.'

Chicago has newspapers published in Italian, Polish and Lithuanian. My minder turned out not to belong to any of these rolling stones from whom I might have been able to gather a little moss, but was another Irishwoman. I feared more potato conversations. Happily she was more interested in culture than cooking. Downtown in the Loop is the Art Institute and the Symphony Orchestra. She could probably get me a ticket.

Actually, I'd prefer Second City. On second thoughts, maybe not. We were due for an early start, the early-morning spot on a popular breakfast TV show. They were expecting a paella. The producer's researcher was on the line as soon as I walked into my room. What exotic ingredients did I need? A chicken, some rice, olive oil, garlic, I replied soothingly. And don't worry, I'd bring my own saffron.

The TV station had taken over a disused warehouse. They had not bothered to alter the backstage décor so there were no changing rooms or any facilities for cooking. On a luggage trolley in the middle of a pile of empty crates was a chicken the size of a baby camel. Spanish chickens are even smaller than Pierre Trudeau, so this was not exactly what I needed.

I rolled up my sleeves and got to work on what was no more or less than a full post-mortem. I still had no knives so I borrowed a hacksaw from a passing chippie. No one paid the slightest attention to me, which was just as well: the Americans are a little squeamish about raw meat, and the baby camel looked distressingly like a murder victim. I disposed of most of the body behind the crates, wheeled my trolley on to the set and almost immediately set off the fire alarms with the over-zealous application of heat to olive oil in raw iron.

I was rather pleased to be escorted off the premises before they discovered the remains of the camel. I had no desire to get into any little misunderstandings.

My Irish minder was oblivious to the drama. Her mind was on higher things: she had scheduled an interview with the venerable *Chicago Tribune* which, she assured me, was quite a *coup*. The *Trib* was class: usually they interviewed only intellectual authors. Like Joan Collins? Well, yes, actually. But that was different.

The *Trib*'s offices were at the top of an art-deco skyscraper, a romantic edifice crowned with what looks from below like the spire of a Gothic cathedral. Close your eyes and you might be able to see the gargoyles.

We were shown into a leather-panelled, tobacco-basted office decorated in Harrods-Egyptian, *circa* 1950. The reporter, actually the deputy editor, was of the same vintage. His tweed jacket and polished brogues spoke more of the club-room than the kitchen. We chatted vaguely about Jermyn Street and the terrible price of bespoke shirtings. Shirtings is a tailor's word: only those who have their shirts made to measure use it. When I was courting, as a birthday present I had Nicholas measured up for a dozen silk shirts from Turnbull and Asser. I did not, in my innocence, consider this gesture extravagant since this was the shop where my gambling grandfather bought his supplies, and he wouldn't have dreamed of buying them off the peg. When I got the bill it was the equivalent of six months' salary pushing a pen at *Private Eye*, my gainful employ at the time.

'Went pretty good, don't you think?' my minder enquired anxiously when I collected her from the anteroom. A good minder never leaves her author unattended at interviews.

'Pretty good,' I agreed warily.

I never saw the result on the printed page, which might have been just as well. Talk of silk shirts has no obvious link with peasant cookery, although I could probably make the connection if I tried. Actually, until the invention of nylon, the silkworm industry provided many a peasant housewife with a cash crop. I have fine stories of how the little worms spin the cocoons, and how they must be popped on the beam so the cocoons are perfectly clean for the silkworm man to take to the spinners. And that certain spices and other necessities were exchanged for the cocoons . . . See what I mean?

CHAPTER TWELVE

California Dreaming

> *Talleyrand said that two things are essential in life: to give good dinners and to keep on fair terms with women. As the years pass and fires cool, it can become unimportant to stay on fair terms either with women or one's fellows, but a wide and sensitive appreciation of fine flavours can still abide with us, to warm our hearts.*
>
> M. F. K. FISHER, *Serve It Forth* (New York, 1937)

LAST WEEK'S HOT TOMATO IS NEXT WEEK'S COLD POTATO. AT THE end of my tour I flew back to New York. Authors on author tours are like the bride on her wedding day: queen for a day, Cinderella for a lifetime.

I didn't sit by the telephone and wait for it to ring. I had a date in Hollywood, a red-suit date.

I had a date in Hollywood because I had been in discussion, as they say in the business, with an independent producer. For 'independent producer' read 'old warhorse'. The old warhorse had persuaded me to write a proposal for a thirteen-part documentary based on my book.

With a view to marketing, Producer had offered to meet me in LA, providing I bought my own ticket. There was no budget for air-tickets for presenters. Producers, yes, presenters, no. Nevertheless, the opportunity was too good to miss. Still being wet behind the ears, I had agreed. Anyway, I rather liked the notion of swanning down Sunset Boulevard, relying on the kindness of strangers.

Producer had set up a meeting with a Movie Mogul. The Mogul, he assured me, was a legend. He had made his money from the sequels to *Hallowe'en*. As far as I remember, the sequels to *Hallowe'en* were not much to write home about. The name was vaguely familiar but, then, I don't know much about movie moguls.

Mogul, said Producer, was a big cheese in Home Box Office. HBO is cable. Cable needed product. Cookery was product. Sorry about the syntax, but the indefinite article has no place in movie-talk.

What made Producer think Mogul might be interested in a cookery series? I queried cautiously. It might seem to the uninitiated such as I that *Hallowe'en* and cookery programmes have little in common. Pumpkins, possibly, but you can't build a career on a pumpkin.

Producer was soothing. Mogul owed him a favour. That's how things work in Hollywood. I wondered briefly if this was shorthand for some other more sinister activity. Bribes? Money-laundering? Hookers? Who cares? This might be the only time in my life I'm gonna be a star.

Producer flew in from London. Together we caught the plane for LA. Producer immediately downed four glasses of champagne and fell into deep dreams of deals. I skipped the champagne and watched the movie – *Gypsy Rose Lee*, I think it was – and dozed fitfully, dreaming of stardom.

We touched down at dawn. I knew it must be LA because, as we came into land, the city was screened by a thick blanket of yellow fog streaked with scarlet.

Producer decided we needed a vehicle. No one walks

anywhere in LA. We negotiated the rental of a car. Actually, I negotiated the rental. Producer couldn't drive. Tactfully, I did not ask why. Neither did he have a functioning credit card. On this I was a little less tactful. However, there being no alternative, we used mine to secure the car. Producer promised to make it good later; I devoutly hoped not too much later.

Producer had booked us into a luxury hotel in the suburbs. This was not to say we were not in the centre of town, more that LA doesn't have a centre. It is one huge suburb. Negotiating the streets, I told myself soothingly, was merely a matter of keeping your nerve and not worrying about the hooting.

The hotel was marble-halled, fully equipped with fountains, and had only suites. These had two bedrooms, two bathrooms and a sitting room – quite enough for our requirements, Producer declared. How would Sir like to pay? Sir produced cash. There's no such thing as cash in LA. Only hoods use cash. There's plastic and there's charge account. Credit cards are security blankets: you can trace people through credit cards if they steal the spoons. There being no other dignified option, I produced mine.

I decided to go for a walk. LA has a pedestrian problem: it has no pedestrians. This is not because of the cars – the speed limit is 30 m.p.h. and no one ever disobeys it – but because anyone caught walking more than the few yards from the limo to, say, Tiffany's on Rodeo Drive, is likely to be arrested for loitering without papers. A dearth of papers leads to being spreadeagled over the bonnet of the cop car and ungently frisked by a police person with a grudge against all Limeys. Flick an eyelid and you're dead. Anthony Haden-Guest – a man who's been spreadeagled over many a bonnet in his time – had warned me about this. A few yards down the road, sure enough, a cruising cop car drew alongside.

'You OK, lady?'

'Fine. Absolutely fine, Officer. Just taking a walk.'

'Lady, you got ID?'

I pulled my passport out of my pocket and held it up.

LA's finest climbed out of his vehicle. He was wearing a lot of heavy iron. He accepted the passport, pondered my photo, read out my date and place of birth.

'London, England. Limey, eh?'

He frowned. He clearly didn't find my accent darling.

'OK, lady. Just don't make a habit of it.'

The vehicle drew away, but the encounter had cracked my nerve. I decided to flag down a passing cab. Cabbies have the same view as cops of passing pedestrians. If you want a cab you have to telephone and order one up. I walked.

I came to the conclusion that LA is a weird town. It would be weird anyway, even if the lunatics hadn't been let out of the asylum – and all of us who watch the news on TV know that there are plenty of those in dark downtown alleyways, the no-go areas where white cops beat up black brothers and are only brought to court when they're caught on video. Yet LA is not as other weirdos. On the surface it looks like a normal home-town boy, a Neil Simon or a Leo Sayer of a city. To the casual visitor, it might seem a person of modest aspirations, nothing more ambitious than a ticket to the Superbowl and a nice girl who'll make a good wife. But beneath it all, it's the urban embodiment of a pop-eyed madman – and there are plenty to stop you on the street and tell you they're the Second Coming. And who knows? Jesus was a star: maybe when He comes again, it'll be to Hollywood.

LA is all about makeover. Nothing and no one is as they seem. Just as it's impossible to tell if the sunset into which John Wayne walked was painted or real, there's no way of knowing if the woman flipping through the clothes racks in Armani on Rodeo Drive is seventeen or seventy, no way of knowing if the blond hunk on the exercise bike in the hotel's health spa is male or female. It is, as I say, weird.

I looked for a bookshop, hoping for normality. No one had heard of a bookshop. No one reads books in Storyland unless someone pays them to do so. Writers rate somewhere between the focus-puller and the tea-boy. The cold-water walk-ups are full of aspiring young writers who read other people's manu-scripts for money. William Faulkner, never heard of him. Scott Fitzgerald, who he?

Defeated, I retreated to my billet. Producer decreed an

evening on the town. We must do the right things, be seen in the right places at the right time. The Polo Lounge for cocktails. Spago's for dinner – but we'd need to book.

I knew about Spago's, Spago's is big. Big stars, big food, big money, big hair – big bills. Producer attempted to book at Spago's. No joy. I rang Publicity because I remembered that Wolfgang Puck, Spago's owner-chef, had given the publishers a glowing quote for the jacket of *The Old World Kitchen*. Ten minutes later, Publicity came through: we had a table, nine o'clock, the fashionable time.

Producer cheered up prodigiously and started making telephone calls about his non-functioning credit card.

Remembering Legal Seafood, I got myself up in basic black, with lip-gloss. Never make the same mistake twice.

The Polo Lounge was oddly empty. Of stars there was no sign. Maybe, I told myself as I ordered a White Lady, we've got the timing wrong. Producer ordered a whisky and branch-water, no ice.

'How's it going, Star?'

Producer always called me 'Star'. I was beginning to have my doubts. Producer cased the room. His attention settled on an elderly gentleman carrying a cowboy hat.

'Know who that is?' enquired Producer from behind his hand.

'Tell me.'

'That's the famous Marvin Twitchbuttock.'

Well, admittedly the acoustics were not too good.

I inspected Marvin cautiously. There could be no doubt that Marv's days of glory were long past. From the open-necked shirt, the silver-tipped shoe-string tie, jeans well polished at the crotch, wishbone legs thrust into ornate Texan boots, he was every inch Clint Eastwood in the days of the spaghetti western.

'Terrific,' I said.

'Helluva guy, Marv. Worked with John Ford – you've heard of John Ford?' says Producer, a note of irritability creeping into his normally amiable tone.

'Absolutely.'

'Helluva guy. Knew him well.' Producer's eyes narrowed

with nostalgia. 'Good old Marv. Been in the business longer than any of us. Knows all the gossip. See if I can rope him in.'

Marv needed little roping. Producer signed the chit for yet another round of cocktails. Anticipating the creaking of my credit card, I switched to branch-water. The bill came. The star paid – *noblesse oblige*.

It being a lonesome time for cowboys, Marv was still on the end of the rope when it was time for dinner. At least the Beverly Hills didn't have a cab-calling problem.

Spago's is real star territory. You could tell because of the crowd of photographers round the door. Marv, Producer and I didn't rate a single pop between us. The paparazzi don't waste their flashbulbs on anyone they can't flog to *People* magazine. *People* magazine is *Hello!* meets *Newsweek*.

Producer was happy. Tables at Spago's, Marv confirmed, were harder to come by than picking prawns out of the teeth of a great white shark. We had been given a good table, close to the serving counter with a fine view of the open kitchen right alongside the pizza ovens. This, said Marv, was a sign of success. Not quite Tom Cruise's regular spot, but on the scale of one to ten, at least a seven.

Producer ordered champagne. I examined the menu. Linguine al limone – cheap, easy and very California. Producer dithered between ossobuco with truffles, and pizza with oysters. Marv decided on spaghetti Bolognese – my credit card and I could have kissed him.

The room hushed. The kitchen door swung open. A small figure in immaculate chef's whites emerged. Wolfgang Puck is famous. Really, really *famous*. Wolfgang is probably just as famous as any of his famous clients – and he has very famous clients indeed. He had just made a TV show which had been beamed into fifty million homes, prime-time. Last week, he had been on the cover of *Newsweek*. Right then, with his face beaming down from every hoarding in LA, Wolfgang was superstar. In the excitement stakes, somewhere between Steven Spielberg and Harrison Ford.

But the real joy was that the great man was heading straight for our table. He settled momentarily, like a swan among ducklings. 'So pleased you're here. Enjoy your meal.'

With a politician's skill, Wolfgang moved on, this time to greet a bronzed, blond-haired man who looked like Robert Redford. Marv said it really was Robert Redford.

A caviare pizza arrived, compliments of the chef. Caviare pizza, Marv explained joyfully, was what Wolfgang always sent out to celebrities. Flushed with success, Producer ordered vodka to go with the caviare. Marv loosened the shoe-string tie, undid three shirt buttons and gave me what I feared might be a smouldering glance.

I buried myself in the pizza. Marv and Producer lost interest and settled down to chew over old cud. The meal proceeded to its conclusion. Star or not, Wolfgang is a seriously good cook. A vast plate of Austrian chocolate desserts arrived, compliments of the chef. By now all I wanted to be was Wolfgang Puck. I planned the opening of a restaurant in LA. Everyone became somewhat tired and emotional – particularly Producer. I am relieved to say that the remainder of the evening escapes my memory completely.

Next day, my hangover matched Producer's. I knew this because when we met over the orange-juice he failed to call me Star. This was unlike Producer because today, at eleven o'clock, we had our all-important meeting with the Mogul. The occasion demanded the red suit, the heels, the lipstick – and no shirking.

Mogul's suite of offices – this is a suite culture – turned out to be just what one might expect of a Big Cheese. His office occupied much of the top floor of a glass-clad block, from which could be seen the famous Chinese Theater. On a clear day, should such a thing ever happen in LA, you could probably have made out the handprints on the forecourt.

Producer vanished into the inner sanctum to deliver a briefing while I read a copy of *Variety* in the reception area and chewed my fingernails.

Time passed. Pamela Anderson – or some other *Baywatch* Babe – appeared.

If I'd like to follow her, Mogul would see me now.

A door opened. Cigar smoke and whisky fumes curled out to greet me.

Linguine al Limone
PASTA WITH LEMON

Roll your own pasta dough – it's as easy as apple pie. Make double quantities so that you dry the rest for later. Just hang it on the clothes-airer until it's perfectly brittle. If you can't get Italian durum wheat flour, bread flour with a handful of semolina (the hard kernel of the wheat grain) makes a good substitute.

──────────── SERVES 4 AS A MAIN DISH – THE PASTA ────────────

1 lb/500 g durum wheat flour
  or *strong bread flour with a*
  handful fine-ground semolina
1 teaspoon salt

4 eggs
1–2 eggshellfuls water
1 tablespoon olive oil
extra flour and semolina for dusting

──────────────── THE DRESSING ────────────────

¼ pint/150 ml double cream
1 lemon, juice and finely grated zest

salt and pepper

1. Sieve the flour (with the semolina, if using bread flour) with the salt into a roomy bowl, or tip straight on to a bread board. Make a dip in the middle and crack in the eggs. With a circular movement of your hand, work the eggs into the flour, plus enough water to make a soft, pliable dough. Knead thoroughly for 10 minutes to develop and stretch the flour (easily done in the mixer with the

dough-hook). When you have a smooth elastic dough ball, pour the oil into the palm of your hand and slick it over the surface. Drop it back into the bowl, cover with a cloth and set it aside to rest for 20 minutes.

2. Dust a board and rolling-pin with flour. Divide the dough into 4 pieces and knead each into a ball. Roll out each piece as thin as parchment, dust with more semolina, cover loosely and leave to rest for another 20 minutes. Roll up each piece loosely, as you would a carpet for storage. Slice across into strips as thin as a baby's ribbon. Lightly loosen the strips as soon as you cut them and drop them in hanks on to the flour-dusted board. The pasta is now ready for cooking.

3. When you're ready to eat, set a large pan of salted water to boil – pasta needs lots of room. Put the cream to warm on the side of the stove and have ready a warm bowl for serving. When the water reaches a rolling boil, drop in the pasta ribbons one hank at a time – don't let the water go off the boil. Give the pasta a quick stir to separate the strands. Drain as soon as it's tender, 2–4 minutes, depending on thickness. Tip it into a sieve and pass it quickly under the cold tap – don't soak it, just a splash to halt the cooking process. Tip the pasta into the bowl and dress with the warm cream mixed with the lemon juice and zest. Season with salt and pepper. Very California-style.

Caviare Pizza

Pretty star-struck stuff. A classy pizza from Spago's, the classiest joint in LA.

1 lb/500 g strong white flour	½ pint/300 ml warm water
½ teaspoon salt	2 tablespoons olive oil
½ oz/10 g active dry yeast	

SIMPLE TOMATO SAUCE

1 tablespoon olive oil	2 tablespoons tomato paste
1 can plum tomatoes	some Parmesan rind, grated
few basil leaves	(optional)
2 garlic cloves, finely chopped	salt, a pinch of sugar and pepper

TOPPING

2 tablespoons freshly grated	4 oz/100 g cream cheese
Parmesan or dry Cheddar	1 tablespoon pine nuts
4 oz/100 g mozzarella, grated	4 oz/100 g Parma ham

TO FINISH

soured cream and caviare

1. Make the dough first. Sieve the flour and the salt into a warm mixing bowl. Dissolve the yeast in a cupful of the warm water and pour it into a well in the flour. Work it into the flour along with

the rest of the warm water and the oil until you have a soft, slightly sticky dough. Knead on a lightly floured board for 10 minutes until you have a smooth, soft ball. The wetter you can handle the dough, the lighter the bread – keep some flour on the side to dust your hands. Put the dough in an oiled bowl, brush with a little more oil and cover tightly with cling-film. Leave in a warm place to double its bulk – about an hour.

2. Meanwhile, turn the oven to maximum: an ordinary domestic oven will need an hour to heat up properly. While the dough is rising, tip all the tomato-sauce ingredients into a pan, bring to the boil, squish the tomatoes down a bit, turn the heat down to simmer and leave to bubble gently, uncovered, for 40 minutes, until nice and thick.

3. To assemble the pizzas: divide the dough into 4 pieces, knead each into a ball, and pat out by hand until thin as cardboard – you need 5 oz/140 g dough for an 8 in/20 cm pizza base; or 6 oz/175 g for an 8 in/20 cm pizza base; or 6 oz/175 g for a 10 in/28 cm base. Transfer each round to a baking-sheet dusted lightly with flour. Spread with a thin layer of tomato sauce, a layer of grated mozzarella, scraps of Parma ham, grated Parmesan and pine nuts. Drizzle with olive oil and bake at maximum temperature for 10–15 minutes, until the dough is nicely blistered. To finish, top each pizza with 3 little dabs of soured cream topped with a teaspoon of caviare.

Mogul was at his desk, which was vast, almost empty. Producer was perched on the edge of it. Both men had glasses in their hands and were smoking cigars.

As might be expected, Mogul was a small man with a big belly, very little hair, extremely small eyes and a smile designed to avoid dislodging the Havana.

'Here she comes,' said Producer, somewhat unnecessarily.

Mogul examined me rather as one might a rabbit that had just been pulled out of a hat, then removed the cigar, replacing it as soon as he had finished speaking. 'So this is the little girl who wants to be a star?'

I bit my tongue. A blind water-rat could have seen that I hadn't been a little girl for thirty years.

'Drink? No? Coffee? Pammie's got this great little machine, makes it just like Italy. Great girl, Pammie. Get it, girl.'

With a swish of blonde hair, the great girl vanished.

'Got to be on my way – got a plane to catch,' said Producer, unhitching his broad pinstriped bottom from the desk. 'Sure you can handle it, Elisabeth?'

Handle what? Not, I hoped, what I thought he meant.

'Siddown, girlie, siddown,' said Mogul.

I was already beginning to regret the red suit. I glanced around quickly for the casting couch. Sure enough, a low sofa stretched along one wall.

I sat down firmly in an upright chair and folded my hands in my lap. The red suit had definitely been a mistake.

'Not there, girlie. Over there, on the couch. Gonna fix us a little whisky. Buddy of mine sends it over from someplace. Scotland, I guess. Here you are.'

'Thank you very much, but no. Coffee will be fine.' My voice sounded alarmingly like the Queen's. I perched on the edge of the cushions, pulling my skirt well down over my knees.

Not a man to take no for an answer, Mogul poured us both a large one. Pam knocked discreetly before reappearing with the coffee.

'Great kid, Pammie. Makes terrific coffee.'

Pammie flashed a set of perfectly capped teeth and closed the door a little too firmly behind her.

Alone at last, Mogul settled himself beside me on the sofa, removed the stogie and replaced it with a mouthful of whisky.

'OK, girlie?'

When he smiled I noticed the gold fillings. There were plenty.

Mogul smiled some more. 'I like you, girlie, I really like you. I've been hearing all about your great little project. Sounds great.'

'Oh, but it is,' I answer idiotically, inching down the sofa. 'I mean, it's really great you think it's great. My producer thinks so too.'

Movie Mogul sighed and rolled his eyes. 'Always happy to hear from my old buddy. We go way back.'

'So he tells me.'

Mogul's hand hovered over my knee, landing an exploratory pat that might just have been fatherly.

'So. This is the girl who wansa be a star?'

I hesitated. 'Up to a point.'

'Up to a point?' The hand hovered playfully.

I panicked. 'Mr Mogul, I would hate it if there was any misunderstanding.'

The gold fillings came back into play. 'Miss and Understanding! You got it! We gotta get an understanding, girlie!' Mogul hooted appreciatively. The hand landed back on my knee. 'If we gonna do business – and note the preposition – we gotta get acquainted. Gotta be *trust*.'

To celebrate this suggestion, Mogul removed his hand, leaned forward to stub out the cigar, at the same time replacing his other fist around the whisky glass.

I rose swiftly. Unfortunately the sofa, which was well sprung, bounced back. Some of Mogul's whisky landed in his lap.

I swallowed a giggle. 'I'm terribly sorry.'

While Mogul swatted his groin with a none-too-clean pocket hankie, I wandered over to the desk, picked up the proposal – still in its envelope – and waited discreetly until repairs had been effected.

'Perhaps you might like to look this over, Mr Mogul, before we take our discussions any further?'

Mogul's small eyes glittered. 'Later, girlie.'

'Later? I don't understand, Mr Mogul.'

'We take a little lunch. We get a little acquainted. And later we do business.'

I digested this unpromising line of thought. 'I'm afraid I've a lunch date, Mr Mogul.'

'So break it.'

He ground out the cigar, splaying the end and scattering ash over the table, selected another, clipped the end with a gold cigar-cutter, lit it slowly, examined it carefully, and clamped it back between his teeth. A small brown flake of tobacco remained attached to his lower lip.

'I booked Spago's. You know Spago's? Smart girl like you. My usual table.'

'I can't. Really. I'd love to. But I can't.'

'Girl wants to be a star. So make the girl a star.'

'I'm all for that, Mr Mogul. But I still can't make lunch.'

A long silence. Negotiations reopened abruptly. 'How 'bout tomorrow?'

'Tomorrow I'll be in San Francisco.'

'What you wanna go to 'Frisco for?' Mogul sounded aggrieved. 'Nothing there but conchies. Bunch o' faggots.'

'I have interviews. People to see. Books to sign.'

'Chicken-shit, pardon my French. Smart girl like you gotta be in movies. Gotta be on TV. Stick around, I make you a star.'

'I know, Mr Mogul. And please believe I'm grateful for your enthusiasm. But there's the problem of getting acquainted.'

Mogul stopped smiling. 'You got it, girl.'

I picked up my possessions, replaced the proposal on the desk and smiled brightly. 'Well, I think that about wraps it up, Mr Mogul.'

I held out my hand as politely as the Queen Mother greeting a lord lieutenant, just in time to sidestep the final lunge. By now, Mogul was somewhat the worse for the whisky and landed unceremoniously back on the couch.

'Goodbye, Mr Mogul. Don't bother to see me out.'

It's surprising how fast a person in high heels and a tight skirt can move when circumstances demand.

It might have been my imagination, but the familiar mantra seemed to follow me plaintively down the corridor.

'Girl wants to be a star. So make the girl a star.'

I, too, had a plane to catch. I was indeed on my way to San Francisco. Publicity had not entirely cut me adrift. A couple of newspapers had expressed interest in interviews. And since I was in the area, my American editor, Fran McCulloch, had arranged for us both to attend a conference of the American Institute of Wine and Food up the Napa valley.

It'd be good for the book, she said, I'd meet all the movers and shakers. Fran is a *bon viveur* and a good companion, so I had been easy to persuade. When she met me at the airport, I almost burst into tears when I saw her cheerful face and welcoming smile.

'How did it go?'

I told her.

She laughed. 'It's a learning process. Don't even think about it.'

I didn't. There was too much else to do. The conference was already getting under way. We set off immediately. Our hosts were the winemakers themselves, the food was to be prepared by visiting chefs. California invented the hot-shot chef – long before Marco Pierre White popped his head round the green baize door, the egalitarian Californians were cutting the mustard with the customers.

It would be impossible to overestimate the influence of the west-coast cooks on the gastronomic habits of America. The style was, remains, inventive, ingredient-led, sophisticated Mediterranean market-food. Alice Waters, doyenne of the style, acknowledges her debt to our own Elizabeth David, the mighty Julia Child, but above all to M.F.K. (Mary Frances Kennedy) Fisher. Mrs Fisher's strength lay not so much in recipe-writing but in the powerful storytelling which transported her readers to places they might never have imagined existed. She is often credited with a major role in bringing the United States into the Second World War. Her evocative prose – highly personal and beautifully crafted – reminded her countrymen of what they stood to lose.

On her books, she used initials only – feminist instincts made her anxious to avoid typecasting by gender – but to friends she was always known as Mary Frances. Although her books sold respectably and her reputation made her one of the most admired writers in her profession, she never made much money. Fortunately, in her old age, she found a benefactor, a rich Englishman who owned a large estate in the Sonoma, the parallel valley to the Napa, who was prepared to provide her with the security she needed.

It so happened that Mrs Fisher had written to me after first publication of my book and invited me to visit her if I ever came to California. Fran was keen for me to take up the invitation.

On the second day of the conference – the Institute took its responsibilities seriously and we scarcely had a moment to ourselves – I made the telephone call.

The housekeeper consulted the great lady. 'Mrs Fisher has just returned from hospital. She needed a new hip.'

After a few moments, Mrs Fisher herself was on the line.

'But of course you must come to tea. You must forgive me if I'm bed-ridden, but we shall do the best we can. If you speak to my housekeeper, she'll tell you how to find us. Shall we say tomorrow?'

Tomorrow it was to be. We were to watch out for a gravel driveway with white gates that led through an English garden to a low bungalow. The housekeeper's directions led us to what looked like any well-maintained parkland in the Home Counties. Horses cropped the pastures, a bell-tower chanted the hours.

No one appeared to be at home, but the door was ajar.

'Come in, my dears. Don't mind the mess.'

The voice emerged through the open door of an adjacent bedroom. Whereas the living room was polished, tidy and had the air of being little used – the upper level was equipped with a professional-looking range and large kitchen table, the lower by sofas and armchairs arranged around a plate-glass window with a view across the rolling, deceptively English landscape – there was no doubt that the bedroom was the heart of the household. Furnished in the Mediterranean style, with dark polished wood, pale fabrics, pottery bowls filled with lavender, it had an English feel for comfort. The room was lined from floor to ceiling with books, with yet more piled in corners and on every spare surface, except for one wall which was entirely occupied by a floor-to-ceiling computer, a vast winking console that emitted a low hum.

Sunshine slanted through small windows set on either side of the double bed. Lying within, like a bony young bird in a nest, was Mrs Fisher. She waved her hand towards the machinery. 'An experiment, my dears, the very latest thing. Costs a fortune – ten thousand dollars, I think. I couldn't possibly afford it but the university thinks I should have it. A good-looking young man comes in and shows me how to use it. I can lie in my bed and dictate whatever comes into my head and, hey presto, it prints it all out. Though heaven knows . . .' The covers were littered with books and papers.

'So. You've come to visit the old lady? You must forgive me for not coming out to greet you.'

The voice was strong, but the blue eyes were milky and faded.

'Come closer, my dears.'

Then, to me: 'Not there but over here, where I can see you. Later, my housekeeper will bring us our tea, but now I want to hear the news.'

I obeyed. We talked of France, of the recent elections – she was pleased with the arrival of a Socialist government – she had long been a fan of François Mitterand.

Proximity gave me a chance to study my hostess at leisure. Mary Frances Kennedy Fisher wore her ninety years with grace. She was still a beauty, with high cheekbones, arched eyebrows and the clear complexion that in youth must have been rosy, but which time had stretched to a fine blue-veined transparency. She had the physical confidence, sometimes mistaken for arrogance, that only physical beauty can bestow. That she had always been a beauty was evident in the set of the head, the care with which the hair had been coiffed, the hands which, though bony and freckled with age, were beringed and manicured.

She sensed my scrutiny, and sighed. 'Old age is such a bore. I cannot recommend it. Did you know I'm nearly blind? Each morning one must be grateful to find oneself still alive.'

The voice trailed away and the bony hand emerged from the covers to stroke a calico cat, its white fur marked with ginger and black patches.

'Ungrateful animal. She's sulking. We changed her food, and I'm afraid she doesn't like it. I can't think why. I tried it myself and it's perfectly good. One should always taste – a teaspoon – just to make sure it's palatable.'

The cat arched its back and slipped off the bed to take up a new position on the window-sill among the pots of scarlet geraniums. 'Cats are such independent creatures. Not like humans at all. It makes me realize how little I can do for myself these days, how much I must depend on others.

She sighed 'Tell me about your own life in France, my dear. Have you been back since you wrote your book?'

Indeed I had, and only a few months earlier, when we had spent the Christmas holiday in the places she knew so well. In fact, I had taken one of her books with me to reread while I was there. There was a passage that described a violet-seller in Aix-en-Provence who scented his flowers surreptitiously from a little vial of essence he kept in his pocket. She laughed to hear that the self-same violet-seller – or perhaps his heir – was still working the same trick on unsuspecting customers.

'And the Saturday market, that's still there in the square?'

I told her it was. I could also confirm that the fungi-woman still offered her wares for sale under a striped umbrella by the newspaper stand. And that the sea-urchin man still took his place on his stool with his prickly harvest in a bucket between his knees.

'Sea urchins – such a delicious flavour. I used to make him open them right away so I could eat them straight from the shell. He kept a special spoon for greedy people like me. You know it's only the females who produce the little orange roes? I'm told it's the ovaries. A curious thing to enjoy.' She paused. 'You must forgive me if I ramble. Old age, you see.'

'We ate them with scrambled eggs.'

'Did you, indeed?'

The faded blue eyes looked into the distance. 'The chocolate shop on the corner by the cathedral? I loved their bitter chocolate – such chocolate, the best in the world.'

'Still there. Still good. Last year, we bought our Easter eggs.'

'Very expensive, but the French were always willing to pay for what they like.'

The cat shifted its position among the geraniums, then returned to settle down by its mistress. Mary Frances ran her fingers through the soft fur.

'Such sensual creatures, cats.'

The voice trailed away. She settled herself back on the pillows. I took advantage of the temporary lull to slip my sketchbook out of my pocket. All I could find to work with was a little box of eyeshadow. My hand moved quietly across the paper.

Time passed. Her eyelids drooped. I rose silently, slipping my sketchbook back into my satchel. The rustle disturbed her. Her hand fluttered, delicate and fine-boned, signalling that the audience was not yet at an end.

'Don't go. You mustn't leave without your tea. I shall ring for my housekeeper.'

She searched for a button by her hand. A bell tinkled in the next room. Tea arrived. The tea set was exquisite: Sèvres, perhaps, bone-china decorated with small blue flowers. The housekeeper, a motherly woman with pink cheeks and bright eyes, fussed around her mistress to make sure the tea was just as she liked it.

Mary Frances sipped and pronounced it good. 'One of my pleasures. A friend of mine brought it from England. Earl Grey, I think – anyway, the one with the bergamot. The sense of taste has not yet deserted me. Everything else, but not that. We must be thankful for small mercies.'

'Perhaps not so small.'

With the tea came buttery little ginger biscuits, home-made, and small triangles of bread and butter and a cut-glass dish with an amber-coloured jelly.

'Peach. You must tell me what you think.'

I tasted. 'Delicious.'

She nodded gravely. 'You must tell my housekeeper you approve. We make it ourselves. It's in my latest book. The publishers did not pay me for the work, but I asked for a hundred copies to give away to visitors and friends. So many

Fanny Plagemann's Peach Marmalade

'There is probably no better smell,' reads Mrs Fisher's annotation to this recipe, 'than the forthright cloud that fills a room, a memory, as the bubbles in the jam pot rise darker from the bottom. Stir! Stir fast!'

――――――――――――― MAKES 3 JARS ―――――――――――――

2 lb / 1 kg peaches – about 8   juice of 2 lemons
1 lb / 500 g granulated sugar

1. Scald and peel the peaches, cut them in half and remove the stones. Crack 5, extract the kernels and stew them in a little water in a small pan for 5 minutes, until tender; then skin and chop.

2. Put the peaches and the kernels in a large saucepan and bring slowly to boiling point, mashing the peaches with a potato masher as they heat. By the time the mixture boils, the peaches should be really mushy. Stir in the sugar and the lemon juice and cook rapidly for 10 minutes, stirring all the time – it may look juicy enough, but it can easily stick and burn. Turn down the heat and cook slowly for about another 5 minutes. It should be ready by now, but maybe you'd better put a test spoonful on a cold saucer in the refrigerator just to be sure of the set.

3. Pour the jam into clean, scalded jars and seal it down. Ready immediately. This is not a good keeper – but there'll probably be no need to put longevity to the test.

things still left to do. So little time to do them. I still work every day, you know. I shall give you a copy – it's on preserving. Quite appropriate, don't you think?'

The housekeeper rummaged in a box. The book was a reprint of an old household manual, *Mrs Plagemann's Fine Preserving*, with annotations by Mrs Fisher all down the margins. She signed it, careful to ask me how to spell my name. The activity tired her. I finished my tea and rose once more. Again the hand came up to stop me.

'You're a painter?'

I hesitated. 'I was – at the beginning. That is, painting was the way I earned my living.'

'Then you must have been very good. Or very lucky.'

I shook my head. 'Not enough of either. I had several exhibitions, sold quite a bit of work, then I became an illustrator. To the illustrating I added the writing. And finally the writing took over.'

Mary Frances nodded. 'I was married to a painter once. It's a hard way to earn a living. These days, if one is an artist, one should make films. If one is a writer, one should be on television.'

I laughed. 'So I'm told. I'm doing my best.'

'Good. Everyone tells me it's the thing to do. One must always be doing new things.'

The voice faded again, once more the eyelids drooped.

'Goodbye, my dear. Close the door when you leave. I don't expect we shall meet again, but it was good of you to come.'

The calico cat returned to the window-sill to sun itself among the geraniums. The computer hummed quietly in its corner.

But the audience was not quite over.

'One more thing, my dear, before you go.'

I waited. The voice was faint now, but gathered strength.

'You and I understand the value of the past, my dear, but we must not let it blind us to the future. I may be old, but I live in the present. I hope you will remember that too when you grow old.'

PART THREE

On The Road Again

CHAPTER THIRTEEN

Andalucia Revisited

*In a culture like ours, long accustomed to splitting and dividing
all things as a means of control, it is sometimes a bit of a shock
to be reminded that, in operational and practical fact, the
medium is the message.*

MARSHALL McLUHAN, *Understanding Media* (1964)

HIS NAME WAS CHARLIE. ACTUALLY, SINCE HE WAS ITALIAN BY
birth, it was Carmelo, but his mates in Perth preferred the
Australian vernacular version. The Oz accent, the fuzzy carrot-
coloured hair, the laid-back New World manners, these things
offered no hint that the man had been born on an earth floor in
Sicily.

The Australian director-cameraman of what was to become
'my' TV series had finally arrived on my doorstep in the
Hebrides in the spring of 1991.

To Charlie the making of the series was more than another

job, it was a crusade. His grandmother still lived in the house where he had been born. At his home on the outskirts of Perth he had planted a fig tree and kept a goat. Even more persuasively, he had the money. Just. With the kind of open-minded enthusiasm, or blind optimism, that jumps in where angels fear to tread, he had persuaded the Australian Film Finance Corporation to put the initial funding in place. The problem was, the money had to be taken up before the end of the fiscal year.

I did not hesitate. I'd had enough of expense-account lunches with movie moguls, and something told me Spago's was not high on Charlie's list of priorities. If he rummaged around in the back of a cupboard, he would probably have been able to find a suit and tie, but business class was not in his nature.

A director-cameraman needs physical strength and a hide like a rhinoceros. Charlie had both. Furthermore, this was a man who was prepared to put his house on the line for something he believed in. If the series was going to be made, it seemed to me that this was the way to do it. What was needed was not a Hollywood juggernaut, but a small mobile outfit that could work fast and economically, like a documentary crew in a war-zone.

With the entire organizational capacity based in the Antipodes, I delivered outline treatments of the thirteen episodes, the most that could be reasonably done in advance. As many location recces were done as the budget could afford, and by September it seemed we were as ready as we would ever be.

Nevertheless, when I flew into Seville to join the film crew I was already a little apprehensive. I already knew I was an outsider – the Oz view of the Poms, to put it delicately, is ambivalent. There had already been a few warning shots fired across my bows.

The original idea had been to be as light and as mobile as possible. Unfortunately there's a law of the movie business which says that the more you have the more you need. Even in Charlie's world there were egos to be massaged, empires to be built. The crew list now included three extra bodies: Charlie's best friend Jon (a.k.a. location producer, or our man with his finger on the cashbox), first cameraman (Charlie had decided he must be free to direct); first cameraman's wife (alternative function, continuity).

There had also been a somewhat sinister series of faxes explaining that the location producer didn't think it was necessary for the presenter to appear in all the episodes.

'Daft,' said Nicholas crisply, and returned to correcting the proofs of his new novel.

The arrivals lounge at Seville airport looked as if it had fallen to an invasion from Mars. In the middle of the marble promenade was what appeared to be a self-assembly kit for the construction of an intergalactic mobile home. Round this mountain of steel debris, a jumbo-jetful of holidaymakers surged like floodwater round a broken bridge.

In one corner, sprawled over a mountain of dollies, gollies, trolleys and brollies – the peripheral paraphernalia of a film crew on the move – was Charlie.

'And what,' I enquired nervously, 'are we going to do with all of this stuff?'

'Essential equipment,' said Charlie tersely, his Sicilian eyes narrowed to slits.

I retired to my corner. The people we were hoping to film would not have the kind of dwellings that could absorb such a mob. As I knew well enough from twelve years' living with my young family in the hills of Andalucia, there was a good chance we'd find ourselves in places where there was neither running water nor electricity. All of these things I explained.

Charlie stared at me bleakly. 'Let's go.'

We had a large van and a small runaround. Soundman Piercy was to double as van driver, with Producer at the wheel of the runaround. We divided into separate groups and consulted maps. None of the Australians had ever been to this part of the world before.

The budget was tight. Tomorrow the camera must roll. For the first section, I had picked *feria*-week in Cabra, a small town in the hills between Seville and Granada. As well as the week-long festivities in town, which would give us flamenco frocks and plenty of atmosphere, we would be able to film the *romeria*, the religious procession which precedes the festivities.

The Cabra *romería* is famous for the fervour of the worshippers and the beauty of the descent from the shrine where the Virgin guards the town's water-source. Water-sources are all that matter in the dustbowl Andalucia becomes in summer. The midsummer pilgrimage is the equivalent of our own Guy Fawkes.

The Virgin herself is something of a newcomer, replacing the goddess Diana as the guardian of the well. The rituals that have slipped over into the Christianized festival owe rather more to Roman saturnalias than the decorous processions of the Church.

For our opening sequence we should have music, singing, dancing, feasting, all the elements that characterize a celebration among a peasant community.

Throughout the following day's filming, confusion reigned. None of the Australians had a word of Spanish. There were explanations to be made, palms to be greased, priests to be pacified with invitations to be interviewed.

I was on a sharp learning curve. There was piece-to-camera to be mastered: this is when the presenter looks straight into the lens and speaks directly to the viewer. In a studio, this is easily done: you can read it all from the tele-prompt. In the field, it's more a matter of trying desperately to remember exactly what's in the script. Considering that I had written the words, one might have thought this would be easy. Not so. Ask any presenter: the mind goes blank, the brain turns to jelly. Every time I had a word out of line, Piercy unclamped his ear-muffs and we'd have to begin all over again. The soundman's outtakes must have provided much amusement for many a winter evening back in Perth.

Meanwhile, Charlie had discovered that I spent my waiting hours – and in filming there is always an inordinate amount of waiting – sitting in a corner sketching. He began to film the wet paint going on to the paper with the intention of using the images as a link between takes.

We spent the morning at the top of the mountain filming the doll-like image of the Virgin swaying down the slopes among her retinue of worshippers.

'*Muy auténtico*,' said the young priest, with satisfaction, watching his flock careening down the ravines in their flamenco flounces.

'Perhaps a little pagan?' I prompted gently.

He glanced at me sharply. 'But of course. Why do you think I am dressed like this?'

For the first time I noticed that he was wearing neither soutane nor dog-collar. 'You're off-duty?'

He shook his head. 'Not entirely. Let's say I make an intelligent compromise. I perform the blessing, but I do not wear my robes.'

'Very subtle.'

'*Naturalmente*. What else?'

Meanwhile, the crew had decided it was time for a lunch-break. I consulted my priest. He suggested a restaurant we had passed on our way up to the sanctuary.

'It's not elegant but it too is *auténtico*.' He kissed his fingers enthusiastically. Authenticity that rates finger-kissing is high praise in Andalucia.

What might we expect of the menu? Pig, actually. Just pig? Of course, the restaurant was entirely devoted to pork. The family slaughtered their own. Delicious.

I conveyed this information to the crew, but failed to mention the limitations of the menu.

We set off in procession. The runaround arrived ahead of the van. The crew had already ordered what they imagined to be steak and chips with ketchup, but turned out to be a heap of assorted innards, Pilgrimage Tripe, bathed in a richly garlic-scented scarlet sauce, which bore absolutely no relation to anything that might appear on a respectable table in Perth. With *patatas fritas*, chips. The crew ate the chips, I ate the innards.

Rumbles of discontent accompanied the coffee. How on earth had I managed to pick a dump like this? I made a mental note that the catering would have to be a little less *auténtico* if the crew was to get anything to its taste.

More trouble was in store as soon as we got down to the *plaza* to await the arrival of the procession. Continuity was a voluptuous young woman whose wardrobe appeared to consist of an all-in-one garment of skin-tight Lycra in lipstick pink, with a very small matching skirt encircling her waist rather like a

Spanish Callos de Romeria

PILGRIMAGE TRIPE WITH CHILLI AND CHICKPEAS

The soft, gluey texture of tripe – you love it or hate it – combines particularly well with the floury texture of chickpeas.

─────────── SERVES 6 ───────────

1 lb/500 g chickpeas, soaked for 8 hours or overnight
1 lb/500 g prepared tripe, cubed
2 bayleaves
1/2 teaspoon black peppercorns, crushed
4 oz/125 g Serrano ham (a slice of gammon will do), cubed
6 tablespoons olive oil
2 cloves garlic, peeled and crushed

2 onions, skinned and chopped
1 red pepper, hulled, seeded and chopped
4 oz/125 g chorizo, 2 links
1 lb/500 g tomatoes, scalded, skinned and chopped (or tinned)
2 chillis, fresh or dried, seeded and finely chopped
1 glass dry sherry or white wine
salt

1. Drain the chickpeas and put them in a roomy pot with the tripe, bayleaves, the peppercorns, the ham and enough water to cover. Bring to the boil, skim off any grey foam that rises and let it bubble gently for 1½–2 hours until the chickpeas are soft. Some take much longer than others. If you need to add water, let it be boiling.

2. Meanwhile, warm the olive oil in a frying-pan, and put in the garlic, the onions and the red pepper. Fry gently until the vegetables soften. Chop up the chorizo and add it, followed by the chopped tomatoes, the chillis (don't rub your eyes with chilli fingers) and the wine. Cook uncovered for 20–25 minutes, until you have a spicy sauce. Stir this mixture into the stew, season and cook gently for 15 minutes to marry the flavours. Serve with chips fried in olive oil.

Spanish Patatas Fritas

THRICE-FRIED CHIPS IN OLIVE OIL

Chips fried in olive oil have a delicious flavour – the Spaniards use only about a finger's depth of oil in a small pan. The oil can be reused, so it's not wasteful. The triple cooking ensures crispness.

───────────────── SERVES 6 ─────────────────

4 lb/2 kg old potatoes, peeled
and sliced

olive oil for shallow frying
salt

1. Cut the potato slices into chips about the length and width of your finger. Sprinkle with salt and leave them to drain for 10 minutes in a colander.

2. Heat a frying-pan and pour in about 1 in/2.5 cm depth of oil. When lightly hazed with blue, slip in the chips – they should immediately acquire a jacket of bubbles. Fry over a high heat until the oil has returned to its original temperature, then turn down the heat and cook the chips gently until they are tender but have not coloured. Transfer them to a colander over a bowl to drain off any excess oil. Continue with the rest of the chips, pouring the extra oil back into the pan and reheating each time until the blue haze rises again.

3. Fry the chips a second time until they are pale gold and beginning to crisp. Remove as before, drain and save the oil.

4. Reheat the oil – this time it should be very hot. Slip in the chips: they'll gild and crisp immediately. Drain on kitchen paper and serve piping hot.

pie-frill round a lamb cutlet. Unfortunately, a close encounter with a thorn bush had caused the Lycra to split in a strategic position on her left buttock, sending a ladder right down her inner thigh, rather like a streak of lightning seeking earth.

The ladder unravelled slowly during the chip-enriched lunch. By the time we reached the main square, it had developed into a large hole which the pie-frill was quite unable to disguise.

This opened a culture gap just when I was negotiating with the Mother Superior for the positioning of the cameraman, Continuity's husband, on the wall of the convent to film the arrival of the Virgin at the church. '*Ni hablar, señorita.*'

The Mother Superior took one look at the Lycra-clad one and threw us out on to the street.

Somewhat warily, fearing our lack of sartorial tact might already have queered our pitch, I reopened negotiations with the priest over a small cup of coffee and a large brandy in the Bar Central. Would a donation to the fund for widows and orphans permit us to film a candlelit sequence in the church, once the opening ceremony had been completed? It would.

That evening Location Producer called a meeting. He wished to make a speech.

We took our seats expectantly. I recalled that his visiting card had declared him a qualified doctor, practising psychiatrist and nightclub owner. Excellent qualifications, no doubt, for keeping an unruly crew in check. It was not, however, the behaviour of the crew that was to be called into question. The thrust of the speech – after a passing allusion to the fiasco over lunch and the need for adequate sustenance of which all may partake – was that, artistically, the outfit was a co-operative undertaking.

'I want there to be no misunderstandings. Everyone must feel free to suggest anything they wish. No one's opinion matters more than anyone else's.'

Everyone glanced at me. I'm not particularly sensitive, but the subtext was unmistakable. In the land of Oz, it seems, women are either wives or sheilas. Sheilas are not supposed to use their brains. Sheilas, to put it delicately, are supposed to use their mammaries. Sheilas are the ones who parade around in wet T-shirts while the judges decide who has the biggest and wobbliest tits. It's nobody's fault, that's just the way the cookie crumbles.

The result of this prejudice was a credibility gap, a great deal of time – and budget-consuming faxing Sydney to check not so much facts as the acceptability of ideas.

If I stood with my back to a hillside full of chanting Andaluzes and explained that the songs they were singing were called *dianas*, the information had to be approved by Sydney.

'And where does the buck stop?' I enquired, with all the calmness I could muster.

He-who-must-be-obeyed hesitated, but only for an instant. 'The buck stops here.'

Well, at least we knew where we were. And as far as I was concerned, it was more than possible that it was the next plane home.

I fell asleep as soon as my head hit the pillow. It was two in the morning when I woke, bolt upright and shaking. Many years of bellowing babies have left me a light sleeper. Bellowing adults usually leave me cold, but this was unusual in that the bellowing was accompanied by the sound of furniture breaking. A late-night quarrel was in full swing. At first it seemed that the cacophony was coming from the street. A moment later, doors began to crash open.

Soundman Piercy had confided to me on the drive from the airport that the cameraman and his wife were newly-weds. The noise was coming unmistakably from the honeymoon suite.

'What the hell's going on?'

Female screechings interwove with remonstrating Australian voices, shortly followed by the heavy tread of outdoor boots and a torrent of Spanish abuse.

Footsteps approached my door. Without a moment's hesitation I nipped out of bed and shot the bolt. The handle turned. A fist banged on the door.

'Spanish speaker!'

I tucked my head under the bedclothes. The fist banged again, but this time the voice was less peremptory.

'Please, Elisabeth, will you give us a hand with the Spaniards?'

I burrowed further under the bedclothes, like an ostrich burying its head in the sand. It worked. The footsteps retreated.

Meanwhile, the cacophony had subsided. Doors clicked. Silence descended once more, but not for long. The noises off were replaced by the rhythmic moaning that indicates the kind of enthusiasm only honeymoon couples can muster.

I drifted back into oblivion. Two hours later, as dawn was breaking, the cacophony began again, this time punctuated by the crash of metal. The Australian vocabulary was nothing short of colourful.

'Shit a brick!'

'Couldn't have put it better myself.' The voice was that of Soundman Piercy, who had joined us from his billet on the other side of the hotel.

Together we contemplated the fray from a safe distance.

Just visible through the open door of the honeymoon suite was the blushing bride, still in Lycra, slippery as a hippo in a mudbath, whirling a tripod round her head. Charlie was trying to sneak out with the cameras, while our in-house psychiatrist attempted to fend off the blows of her bridegroom.

'Jesus wept,' said Piercy.

We were a depleted and somewhat shell-shocked group in the breakfast room. He-with-whom-the-buck-stopped called the meeting to order.

'The good news,' he announced carefully, 'is that Continuity's on the next plane out.'

'And the bad?'

'The cameraman can't live without his woman.'

Until this moment, I had assumed that the cameraman had been the unwilling victim of his wife's unreasonableness. I had underestimated the power of love.

'So what do we do now?'

'I'll drive the pair of them back to the airport and drop them on the first available flight. Continuity's on tranquillizers, so it shouldn't be a problem. Piercy'll take the cameras to Madrid for an overhaul. Meanwhile Charlie can read up on the manuals. Seems like he'll be doing the camera-work himself.'

I hesitated. 'How's Charlie behind the camera?'

The reply was swift – too swift. 'Best in the business.'

'So why wasn't he doing it from the start?'

The producer's reply verged on the unprintable, and characterized the difference between those who knew about such things and those who most emphatically did not.

I retired from the fray. Clearly this was not the moment to bring up the budget. Instead, with what I considered to be astonishing self-sacrifice, I volunteered to accompany the party back to Seville to make sure that all was well. In reality, it was to make sure the Lycra-clad baby hippo was actually cranked on to the plane. There had been ominous rumblings from the hotel manager about charges being brought, and I had no desire to spend the rest of the week at the police station, arguing the toss with a magistrate resentful of the interruption to his annual *fiesta*.

Things began to improve. With Continuity and First Cameraman out of the picture, the cameras mended and the crew reduced to manageable proportions, the Spanish episode was back on track.

We left Cabra to its *feria* and moved to Tarifa, a little windswept port overlooking the Pillars of Hercules where I used to do the weekly shop. For me it was home territory.

What I had not realized was that in the fifteen years since I had last lived there Tarifa had changed its character, turning from a sleepy little harbour with fishing-boats and a few rusting naval patrol boats, to a mecca for windsurfers.

Fortunately, several of the young Spaniards who found a calling catering for the tourists had been at school with my own children, and were willing to set up what I had in mind: a paella party on the beach.

Come the day, the gang turned up on time – most unusual in Andalucia on a Sunday. Most of the guests, however, sported the multi-coloured hair and nose-rings fashionable in the new Tarifa.

Producer shook his head. 'Completion guarantors won't like it.'

'Tell them it's just as it should be,' I offered cheerfully. 'Shows it's a living tradition.'

The next problem was the crayfish for the paella. These had been acquired fresh from the crayfish farm that same morning –

Spanish Paella con Langostas

PAELLA WITH CRAYFISH (LANGOUSTINE, SPINY LOBSTER)

A paella must be cooked in the open air in a purpose-made utensil – the same ingredients prepared to the same method in the kitchen is merely *un arroz*, a rice. A paella pan is a shallow, double-handled raw-iron frying-pan, which requires a wide bed of heat so that the rice can cook evenly. Paella pans come in people sizes. The governing principle is that the diameter of the pan should be broad enough to accommodate in a single layer the correct amount of rice per person, roughly 4 oz/100 g per head. The ideal cooking fire is a bed of charcoal although, if more convenient, you can pop it on the barbecue. The key ingredients are round, absorbent 'pudding' rice, good olive oil and saffron. The rest is as variable as location and seasonality dictate – always remembering that all ingredients should be uncooked when they go into the pan so they can transmit their goodness to the grains. A paella pan with a top diameter of 17 in/ 43 cm is right for the quantity of rice. Otherwise, use a large iron frying-pan or flat-bottomed wok (you may have to turn the rice as it cooks).

———— SERVES 6 ————

4 large ripe 'beef' tomatoes

12 threads saffron, lightly toasted in a dry pan

3–6 crayfish or small lobsters, live

6–8 tablespoons olive oil

1 rabbit, or 1 small chicken, jointed into 16–20 bite-sized pieces

4 garlic cloves, crushed

1 large onion, chopped small

1 red pepper, seeded and cut into strips

1 lb/500 g round rice (risotto or 'pudding')

about 1¾ pints/1 l water

salt and pepper

1. Halve the tomatoes, scoop out the seeds and, gripping them firmly on the skin-side, grate the flesh to give you a skin-free mush. Put the saffron to soak in a splash of boiling water for 15

minutes – whizz it up in the blender to extract maximum flavour and colour.

2. Use a sharp knife to dispatch the crayfish humanely: hold the creature firmly in one hand, then pierce the back of the head to sever the spinal cord, and press down firmly to divide it neatly in two; remove the dark vein that runs along the back.

3. Have the crayfish and all the other ingredients ready to hand by the fire – make sure the coals are good and hot and evenly spread. Heat the pan before you add the oil (this avoids sticking later). When the oil is lightly smoke-hazed, put in the jointed rabbit or chicken. Cook gently until the flesh is no longer pink, turning to fry on all sides. Add the garlic, onion and pepper and fry for a few minutes until the vegetables soften. Add the rice and turn it in the oil until all the grains are coated and transparent. Toss in the tomato flesh and bubble up. Pour in the saffron liquid and as much water as will cover the layer of rice to a depth of one finger. If using a paella pan, the liquid should come up to the screws that fix the handles to the pan.

4. Let everything come to the boil, season with salt and pepper, and pop the crayfish on top, cut side down: they'll cook in the steam and all the delicious juices will run into the rice. Leave to bubble gently for 18 minutes, adding more boiling water as and when necessary to avoid drying out. Don't stir it if you're using a paella pan over a bed of charcoal. If you have chosen some other method, you'll have to stir it. When the rice is ready, little craters will appear in the surface and the grains will be almost soft but still retain a nutty little heart. It should still be a little soupy when you take it off the fire.

5. Cover with newspaper or a cloth and allow to rest for 10 minutes: this gives the grains time to finish swelling. A paella should never be dry, but remain succulent. Best eaten straight from the pan, with cos lettuce leaves to scoop up the rice and bread for wiping fingers. Quartered lemons may accompany.

another modern convenience, and one of which our young persons were justifiably proud.

Producer opened the sack and inspected the contents. 'They're still alive.'

'Much better that way. They go off if you kill them.'

The crayfish climbed out of their sack. They were very large and had very long whiskers. Their liveliness could not be overlooked.

I attempted a reconciliation. 'It'll be fine. They go to sleep in the pot, like a boiled missionary.'

'You mean they put them in *like that*?'

'Well, yes. Sort of.'

'You mean, you don't kill them first?'

'Not usually. Not unless they get out of hand.'

'They're already out of hand.'

The Australians went into a huddle. The paella party and I busied ourselves with the preparations. At least the chicken was dead – even if it was still in possession of its feet and head. I armed myself with a sharp knife and rolled up my sleeves.

I had no wish to upset the home team, which was already busy making brush-fires and chopping up garlic. I had no wish to upset the camera crew, which was already turning green.

I waited anxiously. Charlie was delegated to negotiate.

'Be reasonable, Elisabeth. We'll never get that one through the animal-rights people.'

This was probably true. I put it to the paella party, but tactfully. We'll have to slaughter the crayfish, preferably not on camera.

The paella party agreed that the ways of Australia were unfathomable. The crew returned to its post. We rolled. The first episode was in the can – thankfully, but not by much.

We moved lock, stock and barrel to the Hebrides, to our cottage on the Isle of Mull, where Charlie had found me for that first auspicious meeting.

I hoped he was not beginning to regret it. Location Producer had hightailed it back to Oz, leaving the rest of us to battle it out, like ferrets in a sack. I had had brief glimpses of the kind of pressures the film-makers were under, the usual ones that haunt such enterprises: lack of back-up resources, lack of money, the completion guarantors who demanded daily reports on exactly what had been filmed.

Attempting to defuse what the people from Perth seemed to consider my somewhat cavalier attitude to the storyline, I had taken to producing single sheets of cartoon drawings, primitive storyboards that offered guidelines to the logical sequence of the events we were filming. This seemed to soothe Charlie's frayed nerves – at least he had more idea of what we were doing, sheila or no.

I, too, was more confident in the Hebrides. To me, at that time, Mull was my home. Nicholas and I spent most of our working year there. We didn't return to the city until the depths of winter, when the stream was frozen over each night and we had no water even at midday.

That particular autumn, Nicholas was away in Africa, so we had the place to ourselves. The need to present my own patch to an audience made me consider my experience of life on the island. I am not from the isles myself, although I have been a regular visitor for more than thirty years. Nicholas, on the other hand, has fair claim to be a native. His paternal grandmother was a McVean and island-bred, and there are plenty of his kith and kin buried in the island's churchyards.

The theme of the programme on Mull was to be the daily tasks of the crofting communities. A croft is a piece of land that supports a man and his family, and might not even have a dwelling on it. A crofthouse without a croft is a cot; the land is essential to the crofter. At this time of year the work was constant – hay needed to be harvested, the tattie patch had to be dug over, winter preserves put up. For me, too, there were wild fungi to be gathered in the woods, blue-black mussels as big as a baby's fist to be dredged up from beneath the waterfall. And Jessie, the island's most famous shepherd and Nicholas's childhood companion, had volunteered a gathering of the sheep for the autumn tally.

Our little house was not a croft but a cot. A two-room dwelling with a scramble of tin-shackery added in the 1930s to provide two extra rooms and a lean-to bathroom, it had once housed the gardener who grew the fruit and vegetables on the Quinish estate.

The estate had little in the way of stalking or fishing, the attributes that make possession attractive to a southern fortune. Its charm lay in the woods and the water. Charm alone won't pay the bills, and Quinish had never been able to earn its own living. Successive owners, finding themselves unable to change the pattern, moved on. Some five years before we bought our cottage, the estate had passed into the ownership of an amiable East Anglian pea-farmer, who had sold up, taken early retirement and gone in search of the good life.

As always with the good life, bad things happen. The twin problems of rising damp and collapsing stairwells, and the failure of various business ventures designed to pay for the necessary repairs, had obliged the pea-farmer to asset-strip. Reluctantly he set about selling the various cottages dotted around the estate – but only to those people he found acceptable to his vision of what a laird's neighbours should be. Fortunately, we fitted his bill.

Garden Cottage was perched on the lip of a two-acre stone-walled kitchen garden, whose site, while lacking a view of the sea, was remarkably sheltered and sunny. Although we worked hard on the garden, a few lines of lettuces, a hank or two of herbs, radishes and a small neep-and-tattie patch were all we had ever managed to wrest from the weeds of twenty years' neglect. Nevertheless the place was beautiful. In the middle of the four-acre spread, a magnificent cedar tree soared skywards, flanked by a grove of moss-draped apple trees and a rhubarb patch. There was, too, the remains of a shrubbery, in which were several rare species brought by some previous plant-hunting owner from New Zealand or Tibet, or some other climate which approximated our own.

The cottage, however, had been built to the same pattern as a croft dwelling. The black-house which preceded it and whose stones were incorporated into the new building, had had curved walls, partly to accommodate the winds from the Atlantic and partly because roundness suits the Celtic vision of how life ought to be. The old single-room dwellings were square with rounded corners. The heat came from a central cooking-fire, and the milk-cow provided a primitive form of central heating in her stall by the entrance. The old black-house lacked windows: soot from the fire was far too valuable a fertilizer to be permitted to escape unharvested. We had been modernized. The electrical supply had been connected not long before we moved in. Until then the house was gas-lit, and the old copper pipes still ran behind the wainscot.

I knocked down all unnecessary partitions and installed my kitchen against one wall of the old dwelling room. This meant that all living was communal. Most of my larder stores – barley, beans, oats and flour – were stacked in an old meat-safe, or balanced on narrow open shelves made from a Victorian butler's table.

We lacked all but the minimum conveniences – an electric cooker, a huge elderly fridge which acted as a cold larder, and a plug-in kettle. I had no electric toaster, preferring (as I still do) to use a little iron toasting-grid that fits over any heat source and gives the bread a lovely singed flavour. Pots and pans were tossed into a huge Spanish bread-basket under a big wooden table made for me by an Andalucian shipwright. The table was far too big for the room, but ever since it first arrived in my Spanish kitchen twenty years ago, it has been my favourite kitchen tool, a source of culinary inspiration, the place to lay out and admire good raw ingredients. The table adapted to its new habitat, providing the perfect background for a bucketful of crabs, or a few of the small speckled brown trout someone had managed to coax out of the burn, and in high summer there were blue-blushed sloes and scarlet raspberries from the hedgerows to make into jams and jellies.

The living room – *aig an tein* or at-the-fire room – was equipped with an open hearth, behind which was the copper boiler that heated the bath-water. There was, indeed, a bathroom although this, sandwiched between the tin-shackery and the exterior stone wall, was as wet inside as it was out. On the fire we burned fuel gathered from the beechwoods, augmented with a bit of peat or coal to hold the warmth overnight. The fireplace had been converted in the last century to accommodate a black-iron open range, removed before my time, so the overmantel was high and equipped with a triple flue.

We had made the necessary concessions to modern living. There was no need to cook on the fire since we had an electric stove; we built a little porch so that we might take shelter from the rain; we added on a sunroom at the front where we could watch the rabbits bouncing about in the lettuce patch and catch the warmth of the midsummer sun. We also placed a mesh-and-brass fireguard round the fire for drying kitchen cloths, towels and the wet socks that are the inevitable daily hazard on the lush rainwashed island – but beyond these additional comforts, the cottage was more or less as it had been for a hundred years.

I had much of my information about the island from Chrissie, our crofting neighbour, who supplied us with eggs from her own small tuft-topped hens, and – given advance warning – gingerbreads and apple pies from her oven. A fluent Gaelic speaker, Chrissie would sometimes tell me stories of life on the island in her grandmother's day. 'The kitchen was always the heart of the crofthouse. Everything of importance happened there. There was a sitting room on the other side of the staircase, with a carpet on the floor, but that was kept for best – visiting posh folk, a wedding, or for the lying-in before a funeral for practical reasons: you could never have got a coffin up and down the narrow stairs. 'There are a few kitchens around which still have the old open range. Ours was a black iron grate all gleaming with brass, very handsome, but a lot of trouble, what with all the blacking and polishing, but my grandmother said it was considered very modern in its time. There was a black kettle, which sat right in the fire and got all sooty, and a shiny kettle, which went on the hob ready to fill the teapot. My grandmother could remember a time when all the cooking was done in the fireplace.

'My grandmother put in an open range around 1912, which was replaced with a closed range in 1954. My mother never lost the habit of putting her hand in the oven to test the heat – she never trusted a thermometer. But, then, she could put her hand straight into boiling water and lift out a cloutie dumpling without so much as a blister.

'In those days what is now the larder was the dairy.

Grandmother sold butter and milk to make a bit of money. The dairy was painted white, a distemper wash, I think – it seemed cold to me. I remember when I was a child I sat on the kirst – the oatmeal chest – to turn the butter-churn handle. We would sing as we churned, and there was a songbook kept in there. We liked the Irish songs – "Kathleen Mavourneen" and the like. My mother used to come in and tell us off for kicking the kirst as we kept time.

'In the larder there were flat basins for setting the milk for the cream to rise, a skimmer to lift it off ready for the butter-making. All the dairy implements had to be scalded and set to dry, never washed with soap. We had a flat rectangular dish, like an ashet – a meat dish – but without an edge, with holes in it for draining the cream. There were tall earthenware crocks for the milk. For everyday, the butter was always patted with a criss-cross pattern before it was put on the table. But there was a mould for the butter with a thistle on it, for best. After the calving there was beestie cheese – so rich and thick mother had to cut it off in slices to lay it on the scones.

'The kitchen table had two drawers, one at either end, where people would put aside cake for visitors, and store special food. There was no need to keep cake in our house, as there was always baking. We had the iron girdle for scones and oatcakes, with a hinged handle over the top for hanging over the fire, and we had a pair of irons for drying the oatcakes. The boiling pan was the three-toed pot that stood by the fire or could be suspended above it. There was a pail of water behind the door for cooking. Water for washing and washing-up was put in the middle of the table after the meal. Fetching the water from the well just outside was the children's job, and we really hated it. It was cold and damp and the bucket was heavy. Now we have the same water piped in, but Father still likes his straight from the well.'

Chrissie's neighbour, Betsy, was another of the islanders in whose kitchen I was welcome. Betsy had married an islander, although she herself was born on the Firth of Clyde. She had learned her cooking from her grandmother, who used to bake on an open range. Although she was always willing to experiment – she explained she read recipe books like other people read novels – Betsy's cooking remained firmly rooted in her own heritage.

The traditional cooking of the Hebrides relies on fine raw materials and a light hand with the baking. Betsy uses her own good ingredients – above all, the beautiful eggs from her own chickens. The hooded crows also appreciated the hens' creative efforts. Seven hoodies, two parents and five fledglings, had taken up permanent residence in a nearby tree, a vantage-point from which to survey the flock's favourite scratching ground under the kitchen window.

Betsy shooed them away, but they always came back. 'They always seem to find the eggs – they'll get right into the coop and take them from under the hen's own feathers. And when the hens lay in the nettles, they find them there too. And they're not averse to helping themselves to a bit of chicken instead when the hens are not laying in the winter. They'll lift the dummy china eggs too, which are in the nest to encourage the laying. Down they go in one gulp, and not even a morsel of cracked china to show for it. Everything's been tried – even a blown egg filled with mustard – they loved it, didn't even leave a scrap of shell.'

Scones are the daily bread of the islanders, sometimes, but not always, taken with butter, honey, strawberry jam or bramble jelly.

Betsy's speciality is girdle rather than oven-baked scones. Hers have no rival on the island. She gave me the recipe, but added a warning against taking it as truly authentic.

'Older ladies would be horrified by the sugar, but I tend to make recipes that the family like. In the old days, the scones never had sugar, and all the baking was done without chemical raisings. But sugar is always a matter for argument. The other day, I was talking to a friend from Salen who dips her knife in the syrup and trails it into the mix when she makes pancakes. She says it gives the same result as the egg in the girdle scones – a smooth golden brown crust – but keeps them soft.'

Even today, there are few among the rural housewives who cannot rustle up a batch of scones in a shake of a lamb's tail.

'It needs to be quick. The shepherding is not regular hours. I never know when the lads'll come in off the hill of an evening,

Oven Scones

In the old days, ordinary folk in the Highlands and Islands ate scones or oatcakes with home-churned butter or cream crowdie, a fresh curd cheese. Shop bread and jam were kept for visitors.

───────────── MAKES ABOUT 2 DOZEN SCONES ─────────────

1½ lb/750 g flour
1 level teaspoon salt
2 oz/150 g butter or lard

1 teaspoon sugar (optional)
1 pint/600 ml milk (unpasteurized
  soured is best)

1. Preheat the oven to 450°F/230°C/mark 8.
2. Sieve the flour and the salt and rub in the fat with your fingertips. Add the sugar if you are using it. Fork in the liquid. The mixture should be wet – the wetter the mix, the lighter the scone. You should hardly touch the dough: pat it out, don't knead it, to a thickness of 1 in/2.5 cm. Cut rounds with a pastry-cutter, or use a knife to cut into squares.
3. Transfer the scones to a well-floured ungreased baking tray. Bake them for 7–12 minutes, until golden.

but when they do they'll surely be hungry. From the time I take the flour from the cupboard to the moment I put the plate on the table would be about twenty minutes. But often as not the scones are plucked straight off the girdle.

'High tea is what we have in the evening. We might have sardines, tomatoes, maybe cheese. The main meal is the midday dinner – a knife-and-fork is what it's called. I make a nice thick soup with good home-made chicken stock, vegetables and maybe rice. Or it might be lamb with barley. If you soak the barley overnight, it takes no longer to cook than the carrots. The meat doesn't have to be expensive – flank is a good cut and economical, or I might use just the little shank bone from the leg or shoulder. Or I might cook yellow lentils with a bacon stock, carrots and leeks. Then we'd have the gammon with potatoes as the meat course. In winter we always have hot puddings. Crumbles are much liked: apple and brambles, rhubarb, damsons, whatever. Lemon meringue pie is popular, but the standby is gingerbread, sliced, warmed through in the oven and served with custard made with my own eggs and fresh milk.'

Each household has a potato patch. Gardeners' skills are competitive, and news of who has lifted the earliest of the crop travels fast. The Hebrides are famous for their beautiful tatties. A piece-for-the-pocket to be taken out on the hill would often be a baked potato, set to cook overnight in the range.

High tea is not the last meal of the day. 'We take a bite of supper before bed – tea and cake, bread and butter, scones and pancakes, fancy cake from the shop. If visitors come, we buy white bread from the shop. I don't really know why – it's the custom.'

In my days on the island, I had learned many things from Chrissie and Betsy, not least that limitations imposed on daily life intensify the experience of living. When I returned to the island with news of my travels, both ladies accorded my tales the interest good manners dictated, but were neither astonished nor particularly curious. How many twin lambs had been born, how many salmon there had been in the Aros pool, these things were of far more immediate interest. The subtle compliment was in the expectation that I, too, would share these preoccupations.

The islanders have their priorities in the right order. Spring is not simply a matter of sunshine and blossom: new beech leaves and hawthorn buds are the first edible leaves, and every child who walked to school knew the pleasure of wild-gathering. The appearance of the young shoots of wild garlic among the bluebells is greeted with delight by those who like the flavour, but with dismay by those who had to chase the cow from the garlic patch lest the milk be tainted with its rank flavour. I learned to add nettle-tops to the last of the winter barley-broth for very good reasons: they added much-needed vitamins and welcome variety.

The spring in the Hebrides is always late, but when it arrives it is with astonishing swiftness. By mid-July the first chanterelles appear in the woods, free for the foraging and infinitely more delicious than any cultivated mushrooms. I did all my own baking: the truth of it was, it took less time to make a batch of scones, or put a loaf of bread to rise, than it did to drive the forty minutes round the island to the shops of Tobermory.

The crofting communities were once as numerous as the oyster-catchers on the shore, but Chrissie's was one of the last working crofts on the island. As is the way with the Celts, a market-going people, she likes living by the road: the croft is well placed in that the single tarmacked track, which encircles the island, passes within a few yards of her door. From her window she can see the silvery shapes of the Inner Isles, the soft violet of the Outer Isles beyond, and closest to hand, the sister islands, Coll and Tiree.

Coll is rocky and wild, a stronghold of warrior kings, but Tiree sits low to the water, a sandy slip of an island, all macchair and dunes, its shimmering meadows bright with buttercups in summer, bleak in winter when the sea wind bends the birches and rips at the roots of the rowan. At its highest point, it's scarcely more than a yard or two above the ocean's lip.

Coll is the last of the islands where the kelp is gathered, a living reminder of a resource that was once the livelihood of thousands. In the 1860s, before the Clearances, *The Times* carried a report on the problems of overcrowding on the islands. Today, in this deserted landscape, it's impossible to imagine what it must have been like in the old days – the settlements and the people and the lines of stone-built dwellings rimming the shore. Each day there was the back-breaking labour of the gathering of kelp, a seaweed thick as a man's arm, tufted with hanks of weed like an elephant's tail.

The dwellings remain. Their construction is particular to the island, the peculiarity being that they're double-walled, with sand poured between the two walls, which holds the water for warmth in winter and keeps the stones cool in summer. The roof, made of packed heather painted with jet-black tar, a by-product of the kelp industry, covers the inner wall but leaves the outer rampart exposed.

The life was hard, say those who remember, but hardship was bearable when a living might be scraped from the shore. The worst came when the politicians in London passed laws that deprived the gatherers of their livelihood. Then the absentee landlords instructed their factors to clear the land, torch the roof-beams, break open the byres, scatter the kye and the people starved.

To this day there's a prejudice against eating those foodstuffs that can be gathered from the wild, starvation foods: the memory of deprivation stays in the heart long after it has vanished from the head. But even when there was money to be made to fatten the landlord's purses, even when there was a market for the salt-rich chemicals extracted by the boiling cauldrons, there was never enough work for all.

Chrissie married a man from Tiree, one of seven brothers, five of whom were sailors. 'The men of Tiree are all for the sea. The land cannot support any but the first-born – so what could you do but that?'

The sea is a dangerous mistress. Many go before their time, Chrissie's man among them. The gravestones in the churchyard on Tiree record the same names over and over again. Because the island's stone is so soft and the wind so fierce, the names are not carved but made of little lead letters tapped into the soft surface. In time, whether twenty years or fifty or a hundred, the letters fall to the ground in little heaps, to be gathered and used again.

When she was widowed, Chrissie brought her daughters home to her own island, to the crofthouse where she was born.

'My father had just lost my mother, so he was grateful for the company. Or perhaps I was homesick. Tiree is a very different place. On Tiree, there are fewer choices. On Mull, even when times were hard, we always had a choice. We could fish, there was the croft to be worked, we could grow potatoes and kale, keep hens, pasture a cow. We will always turn our hand to whatever needs doing.'

That's the way it works on the island. The paid work is done by the incomers, working for other incomers. The crofters will help the incomers, but only when it is judged necessary, or if money is particularly needed. If the grandparents are visiting and you lack fuel for the fire, your neighbours will move heaven and earth to fix the heating, and take nothing for their pains but a dram of whisky, a slice of gingerbread and a moment of conviviality by the fire. But if you want to install frivolity – a barbecue, a bidet – you must look to the incomers.

The film crew moved slowly round the island, gathering what was there. We filmed Chrissie making her cloutie dumpling in her little crofthouse kitchen, the schoolmistress in Tobermory rolling her oatcakes, Betsy baking her scones.

On the final day, at Chrissie's suggestion, since it was one of those magical days in the Hebrides when the morning mists lift to reveal the islands scattered like pearls in a silvery sea, we drove down to the Ross, the southern tip of the island, to pay a visit to Duncan and Morag of Bunessan.

'I would say they were the last of the true crofters, as I would call the island-born who speak the Gaelic from the cradle. There's none of us now in the north, but you may find a few more left in the south,' said Chrissie.

Although the Ross, being on the way to Iona, birthplace of Scotland's Christianity, is firmly on the tourist trail, having no town like Tobermory it lacks the modernizing influence. It is here that the old ways have survived and the island's remaining Gaelic-speaking families are mainly to be found.

Chrissie, who takes lessons in Gaelic in the infant school at Ulva Ferry, is well aware of how few are left who speak the native tongue of the islands. She teaches it to the children of the incomers and those of the island-born who have not the language from birth – and there are many. The incomers are now far more numerous than the islanders, and it is they who rebuild the more viable of the crofthouses and are anxious to learn what they can of the old ways.

Few of the island-born still wish to live as their forefathers once did. Most have moved to modern bungalows built by the council, where there's central heating and piped water and mains electricity. The shoreline is littered with the crumbling stones of abandoned crofthouses grouped together in clachans, small settlements whose size was limited by the practical considerations that govern good husbandry.

'To understand the crofting system you must know that it worked to a different rhythm,' Chrissie explained to me when I first moved to the island. 'The work and the hardships were shared, as were the ceilidhs and the feast days. The folk who lived in the clachans cared for each other. The working households had an obligation to those too weak to work for themselves – the widows and orphans and those who had other misfortunes. There was no landlord, no man who might be called master. The landlord was an invention of the English so that the king could collect the taxes. The clans heard the call of the chieftain and he was obeyed as the leader in war, but that is not to say he was the overlord. There were wars and feuds and battles and betrayals, but these were between the clans, as is only to be expected. But the crofting life was a co-operation, never an imposition. Every man – and woman too – was born equal to every other, and remained so till the day they died. That was how it was, and how when times are hard, it still remains.

'Four families were needed to make a clachan, eight was the maximum. Each clachan had to have access to crops from land and sea. Although many of the tasks were shared, the men were the fishermen and the women worked the in-bye land – the arable land close to the clachan. Four households were necessary because four able-bodied men were needed to draw the boats sufficiently high above the tide to keep them safe from the winter storms. Four men were needed, too, to put their shoulder to the plough. While the men were at sea, the women and children saw to the animals and tended the crops, but other tasks were shared – cutting peat for the fire, harvesting hay, planting kale, sowing oats and barley. And in the autumn, everyone was needed to dig the tatties out of the lazy-beds before the frost.'

The lazy-beds belie their name. They were the potato trenches dug into the moorland between the high-tops, buried under snow during the winter. In summer the peaty soil and natural dampness provides ideal growing conditions. The crop lifted from the lazy-bed was the last of the year and might be expected to last until spring.

The crofthouse of Duncan and Morag is surrounded by twenty acres of arable and seven hundred acres of hill pasture.

Charlie set up his machinery. Duncan was a natural performer, surveying his hayfield from the whitewashed porch of the crofthouse.

'It's a good enough life for man and wife, good and healthy, a place where you can live in quiet and content. You're always in the open air, you're your own boss, you may grow the crops you choose. There's no one near to trouble you, unless it be your neighbours. Ours are good enough, since they are our own daughter and son-in-law. The grandchildren visit all the time. They like to help me with the haymaking, they gather the eggs from the hens for their grandmother and there's always the barn to play in when it's wet.'

He glanced up at the sky, where small white clouds were scudding across the sun. 'The only thing you don't like is when the rain comes down in torrents. It can be terrible wet for the haymaking.' He picked up his scythe, examined the curved blade and smoothed the polished wood of the haft. 'Otherwise, as I say, it's a good life. You're free to enjoy the sunshine and take shelter from the shower. And what more can a man and a woman ask but that?'

For our concluding sequence, Chrissie had organized a ceilidh on the little island of Ulva where David Livingstone was born – although some will dispute this – just across the bay from the crofthouse where my father-in-law lives in the summer months.

A ceilidh is any gathering that might provide an excuse for a party and is always a co-operative effort. Much as in Scandinavia, the centrepiece is a meal to which everyone contributes so that no one's store-cupboard is left empty, a convivial arrange-ment which gives everyone an excuse to show off their culinary expertise and provide according to their means.

The preparations gave us an opportunity to film the cooks at work in their own kitchens. Certain rules apply to the food suitable for Ceilidh. Celebrations must be marked by all those good things you don't expect to eat every day. Festive food must be frivolous – the less virtuous the better. Neither soup nor stews nor vegetables, but fruit cakes and iced biscuits, gingerbreads and cream-stuffed sponges. What is everyday must be made special. There must be crowdie to top the oatcakes, a whisky-flavoured custard to pour over the cloutie dumpling, the best butter from Tiree to spread on the girdle scones.

The laird of Ulva had offered us the use of what was once a boat-house and was now a tea-room converted for the summer tourists. Reflections from the lighted windows danced like fireflies on the dark waters of the bay as the boatman ferried the guests across the narrow stretch of water. These days, the crossing takes no more than a few minutes, but I remember a time when you had to wait by the jetty for the boatman to return from hauling up the lobster-pots, when it was the broad shoulders of a muscular oarsman that propelled the boat and not the noisy little outboard motor. Even then, the craft had to be broad enough to take a cargo of sheep, sturdy enough to tug in its wake a couple of reluctant cattle swimming against the tide. When the sea was running each passenger was handed a bailing bucket, and few escaped a soaking.

This evening, though, the sea was smooth as glass and the boat ran back and forth like clockwork. Once inside, in the cosiness and comfort of the refurbished boat-house, with its shimmering plate-glass window and glossy wooden tables, there were mugs of scalding tea to warm our hands and the prospect of a feast to cheer the heart.

The tea, as always on the islands, was well mashed, thoroughly milked and generously sugared. The whisky bottle circulated. Among the Celts, gatherings tend to the circular. To facilitate this, the chairs had been set against the walls. The Celts built their dwellings to an ancient pattern like that of the beehive dwellings of pre-history, and the cooking-fire was

Ceilidh Oatcakes

It's not hard to make your own oatcakes — anyone who can make pastry can do it in two shakes of a lamb's tail. Serve with cream cheese worked with a little softened butter, or crowdie, the soft white curd cheese the crofters made with soured milk. Top it off with the best of Scotland's smoked fish.

SERVES 4

8 oz/250 g medium oatmeal
generous pinch salt
1/4 teaspoon bicarbonate of soda
1 tablespoon dripping (bacon or beef)
  or softened butter

boiling water from the kettle (about
  4 tablespoons)

1. Make the oatcakes ahead of time. Preheat the oven to 350°F/ 180°C/mark 4. Grease a baking-sheet with butter paper. Mix the dry ingredients in a bowl. Work in the dripping or butter with the boiling water to give you a dampish dough.
2. Knead it lightly into a ball. Dust a pastry board with oatmeal and flatten the dough-ball, as if making pastry.
3. Roll it out as thinly as possible without cracking (thin means crisp) — use the pressure of the rolling-pin rather than a pushing action. With a sharp knife, cut into squares and then into bite-sized triangles (if you cut traditional rounds or farls, nobody will know you made them yourself). The trimmings will need an extra splash of water before they can be rolled. Using a palette knife, slip the oatcakes on the baking sheet. Bake for 20–25 minutes, until quite dry. Transfer to a baking rack.
4. When you're ready to serve, pop the oatcakes under the grill or in a very hot oven to warm — nice if they toast at the edges. Spread each with a little crowdie. Serve with smoked salmon finished with a trickle of a mustardy vinaigrette and a sprig of dill; smoked trout finished with a dab of whipped cream whisked with grated horseradish; rollmop herrings finished with finely chopped onion and dill; filleted Arbroath smokies finished with chopped parsley and capers; flaked boned kipper or smoked haddock finished with a dab of whipped cream and mustard.

always in the centre. Although flick-of-a-switch central heating has long since replaced the kindling on the hearth, a group of Celts will still gather in a circle, backs to the wall, women on one side, men on the other, their faces turned towards a ghostly flame, like roofless wanderers round the evening bonfire. No wonder the southerners found the northerners both primitive and subversive – and still do.

The presence of the camera crew was a cause for celebration. There was pride to be taken in public acknowledgement of survival against adversity. We had come to record the traditions of a people who had known oppression. For centuries, ever since defeat on Culloden's field transferred the nation's sovereignty to the southerners, the wearing of the plaid, the speaking of Gaelic and the playing of the pipes was outlawed by the overlords. Those same landlords who, though they might themselves be Scots, took their power from the English and swore allegiance to a foreign Crown. The landlords of the island – the Campbells, the dukes of Argyll – employed the factors who cleared away the dwellings of the kelpers to make way for the more profitable sheep. The laird of Mull was a Maclean. To this day the Macleans and the Campbells do not sit easily together at table. The ancient feuds are not forgotten.

The wail of the bagpipes called the meeting to order. The young laird might pride himself on the swing of his kilt and his skill with the pipes, but the island-born are more at home with the accordion and the fiddle. These days of new-found tolerance, the pipes speak a little too strongly of the southern landlords' tastes. The islanders, too, will never wear the tartan except when entertaining tourists.

But tonight old enmities were forgotten. There was singing, dancing and laughter. The men sipped their whisky and the women gossiped over tea and cake. And later, after the last crumbs had been swept from the board, when the dancers were weary and the toasts had all been drunk, the fiddle and pipes fell silent to make way for the teller of tales. Tale-telling is an island-born skill valued above all others.

An old man, dignified and solemn, rose without prompting, moved slowly to the hearthstone where once the hearth fire blazed. He halted, swayed a little to find his balance, and lifted his eyes to the far horizon. Not for him the frivolous courtship of an audience, he waited patiently for the attention that was his due.

The Gaelic is an ancient language. Soft and sibilant as the wind through the trees, it was never the language of cities: in concrete and steel, it withers and dies. When used as intended, for the formal cadences of the storyteller, it rises and falls like the hills and valleys, or the swell of billows on the sea.

The stories are neither sung nor spoken, neither prose nor poetry, but something in between. No music provides accompaniment, but as the tale is told, the teller's fingers count the rhythm on the thumb. These are legends, the raw material of poets, which have been told many times before, yet each is different every time it's told. These are not fairy-stories for children – although they draw their water from the same well – but the universal tales of love and loss, of ancient battles and never-forgotten rivalries, the making of heroes, the courting of queens, the burial of kings.

The tales of the ancestral fires are the words that infants hear in the mother's womb, that old men mutter when they die. The songs of the Western Isles speak not to the conscious mind, nor even to the heart. They speak directly to the soul.

CHAPTER FOURTEEN

Have Camcorder, Will Travel

*Learn how to cook! That's the way to save money. You don't
save it buying hamburger helpers, and prepared foods; you save
it by buying fresh foods in season or in large supply, when they
are at their cheapest and usually best, and you prepare them
from scratch at home. Why pay for someone else's work, when
if you know how to do it, you can save all that money for
yourself?*

JULIA CHILD, *Julia Child's Kitchen* (1975)

'TO MAKE THIS WINDMILL GO ROUND,' SAID THE DISTILLERY
owner in the Savile Row suit, 'it is necessary to pass a state
exam. One blow to the head, and – phut!' He banged his head
and rolled his eyes. 'No brain. We say it is mill-crazy.'

Charlie pushed a new video into the camcorder. 'Again,
Elisabeth. Tell him to do it again.'

'Just for me?' I wheedled.

'I think I am not doing it again,' said the distiller. 'I think we are now drinking some genever.'

'OK,' said Charlie.

There's no mistaking a film unit on the move. It was early March, far too early to be out on the road, but the powers-that-be, the mysterious men in Sydney, had spoken and, having spoken, must be obeyed.

The crew was down to half its original strength. We were due to be on the road for six weeks, longer if necessary. We had assembled the previous day at Charles de Gaulle airport. Perth to Paris is a direct route: the logistics of shifting half a ton of equipment dictate that overnighting in Djakarta is to be avoided.

The group was compact enough to pack into one van. We headed north in driving rain for Rotterdam, our first night's destination. The landscape was bleak and wintry. It would be at least a month before the patchwork of muddy fields showed the first green of spring, but the street markets were full of spring leaves and hothouse flowers and early-flowering bulbs. Northerners need their pot-plants and their greens.

He-with-whom-the-buck-stops had decided not to join us this time: Perth in summer was preferable to Europe in winter and, anyway, he had a nightclub to run. In his place, we had acquired a new team member, a lanky, bespectacled Dutchman, now a resident of Perth.

The Dutchman's name was Hans. Hans was the reason for Charlie's decision to film a gin distillery in Holland. Me? I'll go anywhere, do anything. At first Hans's role was not entirely clear. Charlie presented him as an award-winning photographer. I had no objections – we would certainly need photographs to illustrate all future publicity material – but Hans's principal virtue was entirely practical. He spoke fluent German – a language essential in Eastern Europe.

Charlie was apprehensive about the schedule. He wanted his storyboards, and he wanted them *now*. His fuzzy head bristled, a sign that he was not in the best of humours. To complete the series, he had been obliged to mortgage not only his house but his goat and his fig-tree. Storyboards would soothe him. Since we did not know what we were filming before we filmed it, until now my storyboards had been retrospective, designed to tell the cutting room back in Perth what we were trying to convey.

We reached a compromise: storyboards would be updated daily, and I would do my best to anticipate requirements.

The Dutch gin distillery in which we were filming resembled all other distilleries: a bottling plant with steel vats in the background and something reassuring in the way of furnaces and copper piping to dress the front-of-house.

The gin-makers were professional and very efficient. Charlie cheered up when he got some classy shots of the furnace's interior. I became very excited over the windmill, which I thought was being used to grind the grain in preparation for distilling. I collect windmills – they're like the pestle-and-mortar: simple, versatile and gastronomically stimulating. The windmill is a jack of all trades – anything can be grist to the mill. Without the windmill, gin would never have been invented. Mother would never have been ruined. The Dutchman would never have been able to afford his suit.

'We Dutch like genever very much,' continued the Hollander, pouring a viscous golden liquid into a small glass. 'Especially this genever – the recipe is very secret. Fourteen herbs, that's all I know. Only one person in every generation must know the secret. Australians like genever. Americans like genever. Ha! English like genever *very* much. Call it mother's ruin, no? We cross the English Channel with the ships. We put the broom on the mast and sweep down the Thames – You remember our William of Orange?'

'Bit before my time, I'm afraid.'

'Yah! Good. Now we drink genever.'

Fortunately the following day was spent in the bracing breezes on top of a dyke.

'Very famous dyke, the Ijsselmeer,' explained Hans kindly.

Soundman Piercy fitted me up with a directional microphone. Charlie wanted me to wander down the road saying something intelligent and free-thinking about dykes. Not *too* freethinking, he added hastily.

'Hello and welcome to Holland,' I screamed into the wind.

'We are on the edge of the Ijsselmeer, the largest dyke in Holland—'

'Not Holland,' shouted Hans.

'Why not?' I yelled back.

'*Nederland*. We are in *die Nederlands*. There's more than one. And Piercy says don't shout. You're giving him a headache.'

'Welcome to *die Nederlands* sounds a bit naff,' I muttered. I had just discovered I could talk into the thing and it'd pick up half a mile away.

'*Nay*-derlands.'

Well, you're the Dutchman.

'Hello, it's me again,' I improvised cheerily, just to liven up the action.

My directional mike crackled furiously.

I tried a compromise. 'It's me again. It's a windy day in Holland. Welcome to *die Nederlands*.'

I smiled convincingly in what I hoped was the direction of the camera. Making a mental note to invest in a pair of long-distance specs, I could see Piercy hopping up and down like a monkey on hot coals. He usually only did this when the mike picked up a jet overhead or car-horn at close quarters. He did the same thing, I was beginning to learn, when I didn't repeat myself on the retake.

Charlie unglued his eye from the camera. He had no need of a directional mike to make himself heard.

'Stick to the script!'

What script?

Unlike the gin, the dykes keep Holland dry. This is just as well, since the Netherlands, a union of eleven provinces with very firm opinions about their separate identities, would otherwise not exist at all.

Religion had a hand in dictating the differences: there are Catholics, Protestants, Huguenots, Jews and Lord alone knows how many factions in between. Hans's family turns out to be Dutch Reformed, followers of John Calvin, the dourest Frenchman of the lot. The Calvinists are hard-working, thrifty and say grace before meat. They are also very family-minded, which was just as well since Hans had managed to persuade his sister Lisbet to prepare *hutzpot*, the national dish, for Charlie's camera.

Lisbet lives with her family on a houseboat in Utrecht. Well, not actually in Utrecht but on a canal that passes right through the middle.

Lisbet's two young children had come home early from school to provide a family group round the table. The houseboat was warm, cosy and very full of large Australian film-makers. We clambered aboard and set up the machines. Every ten minutes or so an enormous tanker slid past the window like a mobile skyscraper.

The *hutzpot*, Lisbet explained, is a slow-simmered stew with a political message, since the recipe was the spoils of war. When Philip II of Spain and William of Orange met on the battlefield, the Spaniards were in such a hurry to flee that they left their stew simmering on the camp-fire. *Die Nederlanders* claimed their supper along with the victory – and they've been cooking the dish ever since.

'Lisbet is making a *hutzpot*,' I told the camera confidently.

'*Hutzpot*, we say *hertz*pot,' interrupted Hans. 'H-u-t-z—'

'Lisbet is making a *hertz*pot,' I repeated obediently. 'The basic ingredients are onions, carrots, potatoes and meat—'

'The meat is a luxury,' said Lisbet, dutiful daughter of Calvin. 'We do not like to be thought extravagant.'

Again. 'The meat is a luxury, but finely sliced onion—'

'Cut! Stick to the script!'

We had a date at the clog-makers. The Dutch wear clogs not as fancy dress but for entirely practical reasons, on barges and as protective clothing for factory-workers and farmers, all of whom for one reason or another get wet feet.

First we filmed an avenue of poplars, with me painting it, just to give the impression of a little action. The poplar, a tree that is perfectly happy with its roots in water, is the wood from which, for the obvious reason, the clog-maker makes clogs. The clog-maker's machinery was computer-operated. This meant that a block of wood could be inserted in the lathe, numbers dialled, and with a whirr of cogs and wheels, the clog appeared like magic. Size seven? No problem. And for those in too much of a

Dutch Hutzpot

CARROT AND ONION HOTPOT

A slow-simmered stew, which depends on plenty of onions and well-flavoured carrots. The meat is a luxury – some days you'd have to make do with just gravy, say the frugal Hollanders.

SERVES 4

2 lb / 1 kg stewing beef (flank is good), cut into small strips

2 lb / 1 kg onions, skinned and finely sliced vertically

2 lb / 1 kg well-grown carrots, scraped and matchsticked

salt and pepper

1. Put the meat with its fat in a heavy pan, add a little water – 3–4 tablespoons, no more, season with salt and pepper, cover tightly and leave to stew very, very gently for 4–5 hours, until quite soft – you may need a little more water, it all depends on the meat.
2. Drain off the juices and add them to another pan with the carrots and onions. Cook these very gently until tender – about an hour. Stir in the meat and reheat. Serve with plain-boiled or mashed potatoes.

hurry to wait, he had rows and rows of ready-made ones on his shelves. The designs for ladies were lower cut than the men's and had leather straps across the instep.

I played Cinderella for Charlie's camcorder. My glass slipper was somewhat less dainty than Cinders's – more the pantomime dame than the fairy princess. I clopped about for the camera as elegantly as anyone wearing a pair of miniature wooden boats can manage. Heaven knows how anyone manages to dance in the things, but they do.

Just as some villages are famed for their cheese-makers or their television-assembly plants, Aalten is famous for its clog-dancers. It is also famous for its handsome half-timbered houses and cobbled streets. Hans had arranged for the town's cloggies, De Klepperklumkes, to perform for us in full national dress in the market square. National dress in Holland, as you might imagine, involves a lot of starched linen and lace. Starched linen and lace is to a cameraman as catnip to a cat.

Hoping no one would drag me into the fray, I settled down quietly in a corner of the square with my paintbox, a crowd of the town's children and several dogs. I can handle a sketchbook under pressure – in fact, I pride myself on being the human Polaroid – but showing a clean pair of heels in a pair of clogs is a matter best left to the experts.

You may by now be wondering what clog-dancing has to do with cookery. Blame Hans. The song that accompanies the clog-dancing is the brown-bean song. It is, amazingly, a complete recipe for baked beans. To confirm the connection, the ladies of the clog-dancing troupe had volunteered to cook the dish for us in the museum house. I attempted to persuade them that we didn't need special treatment – why not cook the beans at home, in a modern kitchen, where we can show that this is a living tradition?

Round pink faces framed in starched linen stared at me in consternation. The mayor was consulted. The mayor consulted his wife. Certainly everyone still cooks the dish at home, in fact, tins of it are available in every supermarket, but the museum house was a far more appropriate setting. It's traditional, declared the mayor, and Aalten earns its living from tradition.

In the face of mayoral consternation, I borrowed a starched

Dutch Bruine Bonen

BROWN BEANS WITH SOURED CREAM SAUCE

A simple combination of flavours and colours, a sturdy dish for
the winter months.

─────────── SERVES 4 CLOG-DANCERS ───────────

8 oz / 250 g red kidney or *borlotti*
  beans, soaked overnight
2 lb / 1 kg floury old potatoes,
  peeled and chunked
6 thick slices bacon

2 onions, skinned and chopped
1 tablespoon plain flour
^{1}/2 pint / 300 ml soured cream
salt and pepper

1. Drain the beans, cover them generously with fresh water, bring
to the boil, skim, turn down the heat and cook, loosely covered,
until perfectly tender, between 2 and 4 hours. Add more boiling
water when necessary. Bubble up at the end to evaporate excess
water. Season.

2. Cook the potatoes in boiling salted water until perfectly tender,
about 20 minutes, drain and shake over the heat to dry thoroughly.
Meanwhile, fry the bacon until the fat runs. Remove 4 of the
slices and transfer to a warm dish. Dice the remaining 2 slices and
return them to the pan with the chopped onion. Fry until the
onion is soft and golden – you may need a little butter as well.

3. Mix the flour with the soured cream, stir it into the bacon and
onion in the pan and bubble up for 3–4 minutes to thicken and
cook the flour. Taste and adjust the seasoning. Serve the beans
with the bacon and potatoes and hand the sauce separately.

apron and kerchief, and meekly joined the group. Filming in the museum house was clearly a municipal obligation as inevitable as taxation.

The next stop was a herring-port. Since this was my idea in the first place, I had only myself to blame. Plump spring herring – *groene herring* – can be bought from the quayside at Dutch ports. The fish is filleted to order to be swallowed whole. Spring herring is particularly well endowed with winter fat and is considered so great a delicacy that the first catch of the new season is presented ceremoniously to the monarch.

The raw-herring purveyor demonstrated the correct procedure with great artistry. He ripped out the head and backbone in one smooth movement, flipped the fillets expertly into a bowl of chopped onion, threw back his head and – bingo, just like a penguin.

'Now you, Elisabeth.'

'How about piece-to-camera?' I offered wildly. This was a sign of desperation. Piece-to-camera, everyone already knew, was not anything I volunteered lightly.

Well aware that I had initiated the whole thing, Charlie decided to flex his directorial muscle. 'Don't try to wriggle out of it.'

Actually, it wasn't me that was wriggling. I did as I was told. The herring tail wouldn't go down. I choked and spat.

'Again.'

Lord preserve me.

This time the onion failed to stick to the fish.

'Again.'

We waited while a new lot of herring was filleted.

This time the fish went down as smoothly as, well, a sardine into a tin. I took a little bow and waved cheerily.

'Continuity. Again!'

'No. Absolutely not. I'm not a penguin.'

'Piece-to-camera, Elisabeth.'

We were in Germany. I posed obligingly on a wall by the four-lane highway that flanks the river Rhine. Behind me, huge barges moved slowly up and down the broad, brown ribbon of sluggish water. Between me and Charlie thundered an endless procession of juggernauts. We had to wait for a gap in the traffic.

'Rolling.'

'Hello again, and welcome to Germany. We're on the banks of the river Rhine,' I explained jovially. I was beginning to get the hang of this. Nothing to it, really, as easy as falling off a wall.

'The river was a source of prosperity and a commercial highway long before trade travelled by road.' With a screech of gears a juggernaut crashed by. We were using the directional mike. Although the bat-eared Piercy could hear what I was saying, Charlie couldn't, so Piercy had to give the signal for me to speak. Meanwhile, Hans hopped up and down in the road, trying to slow the traffic. They reminded me of the three monkeys – hear no evil, speak no evil, see no evil.

Piercy gave the thumbs up. 'Rolling!'

'The river offered a route into the heart of Germany both to friend and foe,' I continued rapidly. 'Raiders came from the sea. All along the Rhine, fortified citadels like the one behind me—'

'Cut!' It was the Minister for Absolute Accuracy. 'There's no citadel in shot.'

I swung round. Sure enough, on the far bank, was a socking great castle. 'Well, get it into shot,' I said, not unreasonably, adding, just to be a bit more convincing, 'I put it in the storyboard – remember? Citadels, fortifications, the Iron Knights – that's the whole point of being here.'

The monkeys went into a huddle.

Charlie came on the line. 'Cut the citadel bit.'

Ah, well. The Iron Knights rode off into the sunset. Bang goes two thousand years of history. The camera never lies.

Although Germany is a thoroughly modern nation with the best communications in Europe, geography still dictates culinary habit. Central European housewives have always seen their larders as a safeguard not only against the natural shortages of winter, but also to protect their families against the deprivations that followed war.

I suspect that one reason why English cooking is comparatively unsophisticated is because, as islanders, our main concern was to survive from one season to another; we did not normally expect our fields to become a battleground.

The dark swathe of the Black Forest climbs the steep slopes of the Alps. In spite of the ecologists' warnings, the trees look green and thick-needled and the forest seems as impenetrable as ever, even though over the years so much of it has been cut down and floated off to wherever wood was needed to provide ships' masts and telegraph poles. It's hard to tell with the naked eye if the few patches of defoliated tree-trunk are the natural cycle of birth and death in any forest or are, indeed, victims of industrial pollution.

The farming community has other things than acid rain to worry about. Life in these uplands has always been hard; they are snow-bound in winter, when the lakes freeze solid and the icy earth yields no fodder for man or beast. It's only a thousand years since this was unmapped territory, inhabited only by wolves and bears – and, of course, the hobgoblins, about whom the burghers of the Rhine basin told stories to frighten their children into good behaviour. When we lived in Andalucia, my own children listened, shivering, to the neighbours' tales of the wild men in the woods – the fear of the wild is universal.

Nowadays, four-lane highways carry tourists into what has become Germany's favourite hiking and skiing area. People here have preserved the old habits: they still keep and slaughter their own pigs for hams and sausages, distil their own schnapps, pickle their own sauerkraut, churn their own butter. As you would expect of those who husband their own raw materials, the cooks of the Black Forest have fair claim to being the best in Germany. Nothing here for slimmers – but, then, you need a square meal after a walk in the Black Forest.

The houses here are huge, their roofs reaching down to the ankles of the dwellings like Victorian skirts, sheltering domestic animals and at least three generations of humanity under the same dark beams. The overhanging eaves provide protection against the weather for the stacked walls of firewood. Self-sufficiency is not a lifestyle but a matter of life and death. As in Norway and Sweden, the homesteads are dwarfed by the huge barns needed for the storage of fodder and to provide shelter for the larger domestic animals which must be overwintered in the warmth.

Hans had booked us into a farming household, which offered rooms to walkers in the summer, and to those brave souls who enjoy the solitude and the snow in winter. In the spring there was little custom, and we were doubly welcome. The household was of the old school – central heating and bathing facilities took second place to looking after the inner man. In one corner of the kitchen was a huge tiled stove, as ornately decorated as a baroque church, which served to heat the water and to keep the kitchen warm and cosy. A tiled bench ran along the base where sick barnyard creatures or humans could huddle for warmth. A clutch of ducklings, which had lost their mother, were nestled in a basket at one end; at the other, a newborn baby slept in a wicker cradle.

There were pigs in the sty, chickens scratching in the yard, a line of hutches for rabbits, a flock of white geese parading round a pond. In the barns, cows and their calves stirred in the straw. The farmer's wife – the baby's granny, in charge of its welfare while her daughter-in-law went to work in the town hall – was a brawny matron with arms like tree-trunks and shoulders that would not have disgraced a champion weight-lifter.

The daughters of the Schwarzwald are built on a heroic scale. No slender young *Mädchen* – said our hostess, piling plates with *Bratwurst* fried with apples, and potatoes cooked in cream – would easily find herself a husband in these parts. Not only are there domestic animals to be tended, but the pig must be transformed into the *Wurst*, bacon and hams that will see the household through to the following autumn. There is not so much call for meat in the summer, when there are vegetables from the garden, but everyone enjoys veal when the calves are ready for weaning.

And who apart from herself, I enquired tactfully at the end of the gargantuan meal, would our hostess consider the best cook in the village, someone who might be prepared to make, say, a potful of *Spätzle*, the hand-scraped noodles that are the speciality of the area?

'*Ja*, is possible.' Our hostess frowned thoughtfully. There was

German Spätzle
EGG NOODLES WITH CHEESE

A very eggy pasta, which takes only half an hour from the moment you crack the first egg to when you set the finished dish on the table. An excellent recipe if you have unexpected guests. Classic proportions are 50 g flour to 1 egg – basically the same weight of flour to egg.

SERVES 1 TRUE SON OF THE SCHWARZWALD, 4 OF THE REST OF US – THE DOUGH

14 oz/400 g plain flour   *1 teaspoon nutmeg, grated*
8 medium eggs   *salt and pepper*

———————————— TO FINISH ————————————

14 oz/400 g cheese, lightly grated   *large knob of butter*
2–3 tablespoons fresh breadcrumbs

1. Mix all of the dough ingredients until you have a runny, glossy dough. You now need a little wooden board with a handle – the wrong side of a butter-bat will do, or one of those small cheeseboards – and a knife.
2. Bring a large pan of salted water to a rolling boil. Heat up a serving bowl, and set a draining spoon and the grated cheese ready to hand. Spread a couple of spoonfuls of the runny egg paste on to the end of the dough board. Using the full length of the knife blade, flick slivers of the egg paste into the boiling water, not much, only enough to cover the surface of the water. Or you could press the noodles in small batches through a colander with large holes (or you can use a special instrument like a large garlic press with irregular holes). The *Spätzle* will puff up and firm in a minute or two. Scoop them up with the draining spoon and drop them into the warm bowl. Sprinkle with grated cheese. Carry on layering until the dough and the cheese is all used up.
3. Meanwhile fry the breadcrumbs in butter. Top the last layer of *Spätzle* with this crisp hat, and serve immediately.

really only one candidate. No one made *Spätzle* like Frau Erica – and, if she agreed, we must be sure to take a look in her cellar. Not everyone had the time or skill to put up their own jams and pickles any more, but Erica was a diabetic, and this was one way to ensure that she knew exactly what went into her store-cupboard.

Frau Erica was at home.

Her house was not one of the ancient brooding farmhouses, but a modern bungalow, one of a dozen or so clustered together along the road, each also with its own cabbage patch and stock of fuel under the eaves. A slender young woman came to the door, wiping her hands on a snowy white apron.

'*Willkommen* – come in, you are welcome to my home.'

Erica had an intelligent face and thick glasses that made her look serious in repose, but which lit with a smile of wonderful sweetness. Our hostess had warned her of our requirements. She would be delighted to cook for the camera.

'It will be a pleasure. I cannot eat many of the things I make – the cakes and all sweet things are forbidden – but I like to cook them just the same. It is enough that my family can appreciate what I cannot.' With one of her beautiful smiles, Erica handed me an apron. 'We shall begin immediately. Perhaps you will be my kitchen-maid?'

Hans translated for us, since Erica's English was even less adequate than my kitchen German. She was patient with the process of filming, repeating her actions as often as necessary with gentle good humour. 'It does not worry me. I have always loved to cook.'

With tranquil skill, she piled flour on to a scrubbed board, cracked in half a dozen eggs one-handed, and swiftly formed the dough. 'You will be surprised by how easy it is to do, and quick. Just as well, since my husband is capable of eating all of this on his own.'

Every cook has their own rhythm for making dough: some are gentle, some rough, some seem to work it effortlessly until it does exactly what is required. Erica belonged to the latter category, and I watched her, enthralled.

When she was satisfied with the sheen and texture, she found a wooden butter-bat and a little knife and set a saucepan of water on the stove to boil. 'The noodles must be scraped from the board by hand straight into the water, so they make uneven little shapes – see?'

Her movements were quick and sure. 'I like to do it like this, but some people use a special instrument. You can find it in the market.'

Little worms plopped into the water, bouncing almost immediately to the surface. 'They rise quickly because of the egg. They are always very light and very good.' The slender fingers ceased scraping. 'At one time, you must cook no more than will cover the top of the water. You take them out as soon as they are done. So.'

The little yellow noodles were transferred into a buttered pudding bowl, which Erica had already set in the oven to warm.

'You must have plenty of cheese. You may grate it for me, Elisabeth. But make sure you grate it lightly, so there is air between the threads.'

I did as she bade. On top of each layer of noodles, she dropped a generous handful of the grated cheese, which melted immediately in the heat.

Meanwhile, the noodle-scraping had been resumed. 'And so on, until all are done.'

When the noodle-making was complete, she dropped a large pat of butter into a frying-pan and put it over the heat. 'This is good butter. We make our own butter and cream, but only in the summer-time, when the calves are weaned and the milk is good. I do not make butter in the winter when the cows are eating nothing but hay, even though we have milk.'

As soon as the butter foamed, she stirred in a handful of breadcrumbs. The exquisite scent of hot butter filled the kitchen.

Erica smiled as I took a deep breath. 'You, too? It smells good, does it not? I, too, love to breathe in the scent. I think perhaps this is why I love to cook so much – I can enjoy everything through all my other senses, even if I cannot taste.

She tipped the sizzling panful on to the bowl of noodles. 'This give a crisp little top. See?' She showed the glistening bowl to the camera. Charlie's head bobbed appreciatively. 'My husband will be happy when he comes home tonight. He is a good son of the Schwarzwald – he has a good appetite.'

She rinsed her hands carefully under the tap and turned back to the camera, smiling and wiping her hands on her apron.

'Now I shall show you how to make our famous *Zwiebelkuchen*. This is like the Italian pizza, but much more delicious because of the eggs and cream we use. I shall make enough dough for an *Apfelkuchen* as well – this, as you must know, Elisabeth, is made with apples instead of onions. I always make both because the dough is the same.'

Her dough was extraordinarily soft and highly yeasted, puffing up under her hands like a feather pillow even before she set it to rise.

After it had risen to her satisfaction, she cut the dough ball in two, rolled out each piece in turn and transferred it to a baking-sheet. The first piece she topped with fried onions and eggs beaten up with cream. The other she finished with a carefully arranged pattern of apple slices. 'With the apples I put cinnamon and sugar. With the onions I put plenty of pepper and marjoram. See? It is very good. It must rise a little. We will bake it when it is ready. Before, even for the *Apfelkuchen*, I would serve a good thick vegetable soup, or perhaps a big salad, with sauerkraut and grated carrots. We like to serve a good dumpling or an applecake as the most important dish in the meal. We do not serve cake at the end of the meal, as I believe you do. We serve it with coffee at other times – we call it *Kaffee und Kuchen*.'

Erica waved away our gratitude.

'Not at all. I hope your film will make people know how good these things are. It pleases me to watch other people enjoy what I do. I will be happy to think of their pleasure.'

On Erica's recommendation, the following day we took our vanful of machinery down to Freiburg, the area's market town.

Freiburg's cathedral is a mighty Gothic masterpiece, twin-towered and copper-roofed, visible for miles across the plain. Unlike so many of Europe's fine churches, it has not been crowded by houses and shops, but sits proudly in the middle of a well-proportioned market square.

That day it seemed to me that this was what it must have

German Zwiebelkuchen
ONION BREAD

Erica's favourite lunch dish. Quite marvellous, a kind of superior pizza – creamy, oniony, yeasty, all the flavours at their simple best. Non-meat eaters can leave out the bacon.

—— SERVES 2 BLACK FORESTERS, 4 OF THE REST OF US – THE DOUGH ——

2 oz/50 g fresh yeast	2 teaspoons salt
1 small teaspoon sugar	1 teaspoon dried marjoram
14 oz/400 g flour	4 oz/100 g soft lard or butter
about ½ pint/250 ml milk and water	

———————————— TOPPING ————————————

1½ lb/750 g onions	1 teaspoon nutmeg, grated
4 oz/100 g bacon, chopped small	salt and pepper
1 egg	
4 fl oz/100 ml soured cream	

1. All the dough ingredients should be warm: put them out in the kitchen well ahead of time. Mix the yeast with the sugar, and then stir in some of the milk and water. Sift the flour with the salt and

marjoram. Put all the ingredients in the food processor and use the dough-hook to knead everything into a very wet dough. Or make it by hand in the usual way: work the liquid into the flour gradually. Leave the dough in the bowl, cover it with a clean cloth and put it in a warm place for 20 minutes for the yeast to get working – there's plenty of yeast so it works quickly.

2. Meanwhile, slice the onions finely. Fry the bacon gently until the fat runs. Cook the onions in the bacon fat until they collapse. (Erica says the topping can go on raw – but it's not so good.)

3. Preheat the oven to 425°F/225°C/mark 7.

4. Grease a baking-sheet and tip the dough out on to it. Pat it out flat with a well-floured hand to the thickness of your little finger. Top with a juicy layer of onions and bacon. Fork up the egg with its own volume of soured cream, nutmeg, salt and pepper, and trickle the custard over the onions – don't worry about it trickling off, it just kind of soaks in. Bake for 20–25 minutes on the middle rack of the oven, until fragrant and exquisitely gilded. Cut in squares and serve with a salad – lamb's lettuce and mustardy rocket are popular in this neck of the pinewoods.

looked like in medieval times: a mass of stalls and busy shoppers, for all that their clothes and money were modern.

The Germans value quality. One corner of the square had been given over to organic produce. Perched on a barrel alongside the stall that sold free-range eggs, a handsome black cockerel crowed, advertising the products of his hens; trestle-tables had been loaded with trays of plump pink frankfurters, fresh *Bratwurst* spiced with nutmeg and rich with cream, firm slabs of fat bacon cut from the piece, whole hams dark with smoke. There was honey, too, and bottles of spiced plums and damsons, home-made cheeses studded with caraway seeds.

The vegetables were still winter varieties, sandy from store or dusted with damp black loam: carrots and cabbages, chard, chicory, salsify, celeriac, big bundles of woolly stalked cardoons. Less familiar to me were the black roots of horseradish for grating in long strips to eat with the sausages. Alongside were the pot-herbs used by German housewives: parsley-root, soft blue-green bouquets of dill, dark heads of celery, untrimmed and unblanched, to flavour soups and stews. On one small stall, providing a welcome sign that spring was on its way, the first wild-gathered leaves: dandelion rosettes and little bundles of hop-shoots to be steamed like asparagus and eaten with soft-boiled eggs mashed with butter.

The sun shone and the townspeople were taking advantage of the café tables set out on the pavement. Those who had finished their marketing formed orderly queues for street-food: dough-nuts hot from the frying vat, schnitzels and *Bratwurst* straight from the grill. Each stall offered the appropriate seasonings and sauces – a dusting of vanilla or cinnamon sugar for the fritters, thick slabs of bread, pickled cucumbers and mild mustard for the meats.

After my initial inspection of the market, the crew found themselves a vantage-point on a balcony. Following Erica's advice, I went in search of a *Spätzle*-maker. This turned out to be an instrument like a giant garlic-crusher with irregular holes through which the noodle mixture could be pressed. Since I was never likely to acquire Erica's skill with the knife and the board, at least it would give me a chance to try out what I had learned.

German Bratwurst

SPICED PORK SAUSAGES

The basic German sausage is all meat, made without bread or rusk, designed to be eaten fresh. It can be fried in lard or butter. Gorgeous with plain-boiled potatoes and slices of apple caramelized in the pan.

———————————— MAKES 4 LB/2 KG ————————————

3 lb/1.5 kg lean pork (leg
  or shoulder)
1 lb/500 g pork belly
2 tablespoons salt

3 tablespoons freshly ground
  black pepper
4 tablespoons herbs, rosemary,
  thyme, sage, chopped

———————————— ACCOMPANIMENTS ————————————

mild German mustard

horseradish, freshly grated

1. Mince the meat very finely – put it through the mincer twice (or have your butcher do this for you). Mix with the seasonings and herbs.

2. Using a funnel, stuff the mixture into well-washed intestines – a butcher who makes his own sausages will be able to sell you a hank of these, usually preserved in a great deal of salt, so they need to be soaked. When working with sausage mixtures, have a basin of cold water beside you so that you can rinse your hands frequently: this prevents the fat from sticking to your fingers and making you clumsy. The trick is to roll the casing up the stem of the funnel, like a kid glove up a dowager's arm. If you can't get the casing, no matter – with wet hands, form into fat fingers and dust with a little flour.

3. Fry or grill the sausages until perfectly firm – check that the juices no longer run pink. Accompany with mild mustard and horseradish grated into long thin strings.

The crew occupied itself with filming the bustle, only occasionally summoning me to walk through the market or buy something from one of the stallholders. This arrangement allowed me time between takes to settle down to sip coffee and sketch, which attracted the usual audience. Most drifted past, glanced down, then moved away – but some had time to stay for a chat.

'I think you are English. I speak English. You paint our beautiful cathedral?'

I glanced up. A pretty young woman was watching the paintbrush move over the paper.

'Indeed I do. It's very fine.'

'I see you earlier. You are with the filming.'

'Yes.'

'They are English?'

'Australian.'

'Australian? Very far, Australia. I am happy you find our cathedral fine. We are fortunate you did not bomb it.' A smile and a shake of the head. 'I do not blame you. We are not of the generation of the war. We are all Europeans now. I learned my English so I can be a good European.'

'I'm afraid my German is terrible, but you're right.'

She shrugged. 'German is good for poetry. Is good for Goethe and Schiller, but is not good for business. Perhaps I can take coffee with you? I like to practise my English. It does not disturb you?'

'Of course not. Please do.'

She settled herself down. When the coffee arrived, she stirred it thoughtfully. 'You see, I am in business. I am in import-export. I hope I can travel to England, or even to America. Maybe even Australia.'

'Australia is very beautiful. Very big. Huge farms.'

'This I already know. They speak English in Australia. I will be able to do business. We must look to the future.'

'True.'

'Is the same for us all. I am typical of the new Germany. I was born on a farm in the Schwarzwald. Now, because of the business, I am living in Freiburg, but I go home when I can. We have a good farm. We are fortunate. My grandfather receives the land after the equalizations.'

'Equalizations?'

'The equalizations which happen after the war. When the land is given to the people.'

'Tell me.'

'You do not know?' She looked at me in surprise. 'Is very famous.' She paused, composing herself. 'This is what my grandfather told me. When the soldiers came home after the war, they had no money. There is a very great danger they steal, they rob, they have nothing to eat and nowhere to live. Is very dangerous time for Germany. So this is what happens. After the war is finished, the government told the people who own much land that they must give some to those who have not. It is not easy for us at that time. My grandfather is coming from Frankfurt and my grandmother from München. These are big cities and my grandmother does not know milk is coming from cows. There are many things to learn. It is very hard, but they go to classes paid by the government. The government gives very much help, advice, money to buy machinery. This is why there are so many small farms in Germany. It is political.'

'Political?'

'Of course. Is because we are so many. In Germany, farmers have very much power.'

'Is that a good thing?'

She nodded vigorously. 'Of course. Is the future. In Germany we have very strong bio-movement, very highly political. Because we are so many farmers, we see every day what happens to our crops when we put chemicals. We see very well in the Schwarzwald what happens when the rain is black with smoke from the factories. We understand very well what we must do.'

'Would you like to say that for the camera?'

She studied me for a moment with great seriousness, then shook her head and smiled. 'I think perhaps that is for you. I give you this responsibility. It is important that people understand.'

CHAPTER FIFTEEN

Adventures in Hungary

> *In Hungary is the strongest, most pervasive nationalism in Europe. In the chauvinism sweepstakes the Hungarians beat even the Poles. A little story is relevant. The proud father of an eight-year-old schoolgirl entering a geography class bought her a globe. She surveyed it and burst into tears. 'Papa,' she wailed, 'I want a globe with only Hungary on it.'*
>
> JOHN GUNTER, *Inside Europe* (1938)

MIKHAIL WAS A UNIVERSITY PROFESSOR WITH A CHAIR IN ethnology and a prodigious appetite. He ate constantly, like a squirrel storing nuts.

We acquired Mikhail in Budapest as our translator in Eastern Europe.

Hungary's capital, newly liberated from Communism, was celebrating its freedom by cleaning itself up with the enthusiasm of a cat that had fallen into the cream bowl. Our plan had been to film in the magnificent covered central market, but since this was closed for renovation, the outdoor market would have to suffice.

The outdoor market was a warren of covered stores beneath a flyover, which was itself in the process of reconstruction. The noise and bustle was both deafening and dusty. At the market's entrance, a gaggle of countrywomen in bright kerchiefs and embroidered aprons had established a bridgehead. The market-eers and their customers bellowed at each other across the din.

While Mikhail disappeared in search of permission to film, the rest of us idled around the perimeters, eating salty dough fritters hot from the frying vat. These came with a bowl of garlicky sauce of indeterminate ingredients to be brushed on with a goose-feather quill.

Mikhail soon returned with an official in uniform and a fat wad of documents, all of which had to be signed in triplicate. Money changed hands. This was our first taste of Eastern European bureaucracy – and it was certainly not our last.

Meanwhile, I had negotiated the purchase of an enormous wooden spoon, which I thought might be useful for unblocking a drain in my garden on Mull. Mikhail inspected it enthusiastically. 'This I remember from when I was a little boy. This is the correct instrument for stirring the *bogracs* when we make the plum jam.

'The *bogracs*,' he continued 'means the bucket – we cook many things in the *bogracs*, paprika stew, jam, soup. We always cook outside in the *bogracs*. This is because we are Magyars and we are cooking like nomads. The cooking of the jam takes a very long time because we put in no sugar and the fire must be very hot. We make it in the orchard when the plums are ripe. Perhaps we find some in the market.' He wiped his eyes with a handkerchief. 'Is so very good, it makes me cry.'

Sure enough, at a nearby stall, an old lady in a dark flower-printed pleated skirt and embroidered waistcoat worn over a full-sleeved shirt, was stirring a copper cauldron with a wooden spoon identical to the one I had just acquired.

From the cauldron rose little puffs of steam and the rich scent of jam at just that moment when it begins to caramelize. Under it was a little flame, just enough to keep the soft black velvety mass bubbling gently, like a dormant volcano. Every now and then the stirrer paused to ladle dollops of the sticky jam into containers proffered by customers.

Seeing my interest, she offered me a taste – a little smudge of dark gloop. I tasted. It was almost chewy in texture, with a startlingly intense flavour.

Using my sketchbook, I asked if she had included sugar. A firm shake of the head and a handful of plums indicated the paste was pure fruit.

'Rolling!'

Charlie's voice rose above the din.

'Can you do that again, Elisabeth?'

Mikhail explained to the jam lady what was needed. He nodded. 'Is good, but she wants to know who pays for the jam.'

'We do,' I answered swiftly with a glance at Charlie, always a man with an eye on the budget.

By now the whole market-place had involved itself in the drama of the filming. The jam-lady gave me another dollop. She could recognize a big spender when she saw one.

Charlie filmed my appreciative lipsmacking. 'Again.'

The camcorder trundled closer. I handed a spare dollop of jam to Mikhail, who wolfed it down ravenously. Out came the hankie. The flavours of childhood had, indeed, brought tears to his eyes.

Charlie came in for the kill. 'Again. Ask her to do it again.'

I pointed to the spoon. The jam-lady ladled out another blob on to a square of paper. I picked it up on a none-too-clean finger and licked and chewed enthusiastically for the camera. Meanwhile, yet more jam had landed on the paper. We appeared to be about to acquire most of her stock.

Encouraged by my enthusiasm, the jam-lady demonstrated, with stirring movements of my wooden spoon and puffing at imaginary flames, that the jam had been cooked very slowly. This burst of activity acquired her an admiring audience. She immediately lost interest in the camcorder and turned her attention back to her customers.

Charlie's fuzzy head popped up. 'Continuity's all shot up! Get 'em out of here!'

'Shoo!' shouted Hans, flapping his arms. Long and thin, with pebble glasses and a beaky nose, he looked like an over-anxious heron in the mating season.

Mikhail explained something in rapid Hungarian to the ladies in the queue. Whatever he said, it had the desired effect. They melted away like snow in summer.

'Again! Get her to do it again!'

More rapid-fire Hungarian had the jam-lady looking bewildered. She dipped in the spoon. This time the taste was definitely on the mean side.

'Get her to fill it up!'

By the fourth take, the jam-lady was panicking. She could see the day's profits vanishing down my throat with no sure prospect of any reward. She wagged a finger at the camera. Then she spooned another lump of plum-jam on a square of paper and dropped it on the weighing-machine, pointed at my mouth, and leaned firmly on the scales. They registered treble. She explained, with surprising clarity considering the lack of a shared language, that I should pay the bill and let her get on with her customers.

I paid up. There were now four kilos of jam in my basket and no more *per diems* – the daily allowance of petty cash. Mikhail offered to relieve me of my sticky burden. The packets disappeared into a plastic airline bag that turned out to be the portable equivalent of the Bermuda Triangle.

As we walked back to the van after the shoot, I asked Mikhail the question that had hovered at the back of my mind all morning.

'What did you say to the ladies in the queue, Mikhail, to make them disappear?'

Mikhail grinned. 'I told them I was Stasi policeman, the old lady was a spy and the camera was really a gun.'

'And they believed you?'

'Of course. Why not?'

'Seems a little improbable.'

'Not at all. My country has been under Communism – how many years? Forty? Fifty? It will take many more for the people to forget.'

* * *

That evening we were to attend one of the municipal functions that are the inevitable price of negotiations with City Hall.

The new wine was being presented to the press. The presence of a foreign camera crew would add cachet.

An array of little stalls with striped awnings had been erected in the main square of Buda. Young men in national costume were handing round trays with small plastic glasses half full of slightly fizzy semi-sweet white wine. From the presence of the men in dark suits with well-polished shoes and gold teeth, it was obvious there would be speeches.

Charlie began to edge his machinery out of range, only to be intercepted by Mikhail.

'It is obligatory to film the speeches,' he said firmly.

Out of the corner of my eye, I noticed Charlie surreptitiously removing the film. Good manners required that we comply; good housekeeping dictated that there was no sense in wasting expensive stock.

A great many speeches were made. The camera whirred convincingly. Charlie stood there hand on hip, eyes slanted, simmering. Half-way through, his patience snapped. He smacked a video in the camera and looked at me.

'Piece-to-camera. Hello, and welcome to Hungary.'

We usually filmed the welcoming sequence somewhere in the middle of the shoot, after we'd got our bearings and I'd worked out what I wanted to say. But by the look on Charlie's freckled face, something told me I'd better deliver.

'We are privileged to be the guests of the wine-makers of Hungary,' I burbled.

'Just drink up the wine and smile.'

I sipped. The wine was truly awful – with a chemical flavour, like flat lemonade.

'Rolling.'

'Hello, and welcome to Hungary. It was here, on the bend of the Danube, that the Magyar horsemen first beat their sabres into ploughshares.'

I was rather pleased with that line. I thought it summed it all up rather nicely. I took another sip of the wine to celebrate: it still tasted horrible. I pulled a face. This meant there'd be some unflattering outtakes to watch on the rushes in the hotel that evening. I usually avoided watching the rushes. I found the sight of myself with my cheeks puffed out like a chipmunk with the fourth doughnut of the morning a little depressing.

'Rolling.'

'Behind me is the basilica of St Matthias,' I improvised, thankful I'd skipped through the guidebook. 'The building has had an ecumenically chequered career. Built during the twelfth century—'

'Excuse me!' Mikhail interrupted excitedly. 'Is started in twelve. Is continue in thirteen. Is finish in fourteen.'

'OK, Mikhail.' I took a deep breath and faced the camera again. 'Building commenced in the twelfth century, continued through the thirteenth and was completed in the fourteenth. Originally intended to house the relics of King Matthias Corvino, subsequently canonized . . .' I paused, pleased with myself. No one could possibly object to 'subsequently'.

'Rolling!'

'Under Turkish rule the basilica became a mosque—'

'Excuse me. *Domination*. Is not Turkish rule. Is Turkish domination.'

One Minister for Authenticity is tolerable, two is a little over the top. 'Under Turkish domination,' I continued, with some irritation, 'the cathedral became a mosque. When the Ottoman Empire retreated, the building fell into disuse under the rule of Communism . . .'

To one side, I could see Mikhail filling his lungs. 'And finally returned to the Church of Rome,' I finished in a rush.

Mikhail wagged his finger. 'Is not Church of Rome. Is schismatic.'

'Mikhail, this programme is not about the internal politics of the Church. It's about food.'

'If this is so, why are you in front of basilica?' enquired Mikhail, with impeccably professorial logic.

'Because – oh, never mind.'

At this moment, a curious sound reached my ears. It started quietly but rapidly built to a deafening crescendo. It was a very strange noise indeed, as if an army of mice was being ground up slowly between the wheels of imperfectly maintained industrial machinery.

'What the [unprintable Oz expletive] is that?'

Piercy's face was a study. His hands were clapped to his metal ear-muffs. Charlie swung round to point his camera at the source of the weird screechings. During the course of our acquaintance, I had noticed one thing about the red-headed Sicilian. He changed personality as soon as he stood behind an eyepiece. Instead of the laid-back beach-bum in the bomber-jacket, which was his usual presentation, he turned into a true professional, a man with a mission. Neither tides nor earth-quakes would unloose his grip.

Nothing so dramatic met Charlie's lens. Instead, beneath the porch of the basilica, an organ-grinder was cranking his barrel. On his shoulder was a stuffed parrot. The sound appeared to be emanating from the bird itself. Gradually the noise resolved itself into the tinkling rhythms of a children's skipping song.

Later, in the evening rushes, which for once I decided to watch, half a mile of celluloid was loaded with an organ-grinder's singing parrot.

'What did you do that for, Charlie?'

'Local colour,' said Charlie happily. 'Isn't it great?'

'How on earth do you think I'm going to work that into the script?'

Charlie waved his hand. 'You'll handle it.'

'Don't count on it.'

Next morning at the breakfast briefing, Mikhail, not a man normally given to outward expressions of pleasure, was grinning from ear to ear. We had a treat in store, a very special invitation – an evening of music and dance.

'Municipal? In national dress?' I enquired cautiously. I don't share Charlie's artistic enthusiasm for folk-dancing and frocks – but far be it from me to spoil the fun.

'You think I'd take you to something for *tourist*?' protested Mikhail, with all the outraged innocence of a man who would never dream of setting up a municipal evening. 'This is *subversive* dancing.' Mikhail paused dramatically. 'Is political. We go to folk-dance house. Is in modern apartment in Pest. You will like it very much.'

We finished our filming early to humour Mikhail, who

414

seemed extremely anxious we keep our appointment on time. We piled into the van and drove through the seemingly endless grey suburbs on the outskirts of Pest. Mikhail made us stop outside an apartment block, grey and blank-eyed, like all other apartment blocks.

The apartment was on the third floor. We dragged up the equipment. The room, open plan, low-ceilinged, empty of furniture, lit by striplights like a ballet-dancer's practice room, was packed. Every head turned to watch our arrival.

Most of the dancers were young, no more than teenagers. All were wearing the uniform of modern Hungary – American jeans, check logger-shirts, and not an embroidered waistcoat among them.

'You will see there is no wearing of the fancy dress,' Mikhail announced unnecessarily. 'You may set up the camera, Charlie. They are ready to begin.'

Charlie leaned on his camcorder, hitching his hip in a gesture I had come to learn meant *so what?*

'What are we filming, Mikhail?' I asked.

Mikhail drew himself up to his full height. 'You are filming the Hungarian people's declaration of freedom. For you this may be hard to understand, but for many years we were not able to express our national identity in this way. We were not permitted to sing the traditional songs or dance the traditional dances. This dancing we will be watching was considered to be an attack on the state. Anyone who is doing what we are seeing now would be thrown into prison and their families would never see them again. In the cities, in the years of Communism, the knowledge of the dancing and the music is lost. The young people who wish to be Hungarian had to go into the countryside and talk to the old people; they had to ask their grandparents in the villages. This is how they learn the music and the dancing, and this is what they are bringing back to the city so others may learn what it is to be Magyar – for that is what we are, the children of the steppes, the sons and daughters of the wind.'

Mikhail reached in his airline bag and produced a booklet. 'This you must read, Madame Lisbet. It will tell you about these people and what they have done.'

The Kalamajka folk-music band plays such typical Hungarian folk-instruments as koboz, gardon, jew's harp [I read]. *One of the most interesting features of the folk music, namely that of improvisational and spontaneous decoration, is strictly forbidden in written music in our country nowadays. Hungarian instrumental music has preserved some almost forgotten elements of European Renaissance and baroque instrumental techniques. The manner of performing differs from today's written music in many ways. The Renaissance modesty of modal harmonies, the suite-like traditional forms – all these are representative of the common European heritage, while a great number of asymmetric rhythms and the ancient melodies are those of the Eastern heritage.*

'You understand now?'

'Up to a point, Mikhail.'

While I was reading, Charlie was busy with the camera.

The dances were circular, intertwining, arms linked over arms. The body was held in firm control from the waist up, the feet and hips moved like lightning, first forward, then reverse. The steps were swift and repetitive.

'This is very difficult for Westerners to do,' said Mikhail, with satisfaction.

Charlie bobbed around among the dancers, trailing the rather less agile Piercy by his umbilical cable, while I joined the dancers. It looked easy enough – until you tried. I pride myself on an ability to follow where anyone leads, but Mikhail was right. Accustomed as I am to Western rhythms and patterns, I find the dances of the East astonishingly difficult to master. The music is assonant, like listening to a tune that slips in and out of key. You can float over the top, catch it momentarily, but then the intellect takes over and the feet revert to the pattern they know.

'Hah! You cannot do it!' said Mikhail triumphantly, as my feet worked themselves into a cat's cradle.

'I thought I did pretty well,' I answered indignantly, withdrawing from the floor with as much dignity as I could muster.

'Hah! As an ethnologist, I say the genetic inheritance is different. You may think that we are all the same people, with our white skins and thin lips and Caucasian faces, but you have only to see the way the bodies move, and all becomes clear. Our traditions are very old.'

'Older than ours?'

'Of course. We are shamanistic. You know what is this? Is what you would call the witch-doctor – men witches. This says our culture is very old.'

I waited for enlightenment. It came. 'You can see this in our embroideries where you will see the tulip motif. You know what this means? It is the vulva, the sex organ of the woman. This is common in all shamanist cultures. The woman is the receptacle. She is like the tulip waiting for the bee.' Mikhail's strength was clearly not horticultural. 'In the tulip,' his hand traced an imaginary flower in the air, 'this is the *labia majora*, inside is the *labia minora*. And here, where the flower and the stem are joining, this is the clitoris.' He sighed. 'Is beautiful, is it not?'

This was not a question to which Mikhail seemed to require an answer. I wondered how Mrs Mikhail took to the shamanistic culture.

'Do you have a wife, Mikhail?'

'Certainly. I have little children still in school. Is very expensive. We must pay for books and extra lessons. Today, all life in Hungary is very expensive. Since there is no more Communism, the prices are terrible.'

'Communism had its advantages?'

'Certainly. There was respect. Respect for learning, for teachers. We were not paid much money, but we were respected. Today we are still not paid much money, but there is no respect. We speak and no one listens. Everything is coming from television. If it is not on the television, no one will believe it.'

He looked at me.

'Ha! You, Madame Lisbet, even though you will never learn the folk-dancing, many people will believe you.'

* * *

417

We headed south for Szeged, hard by the Romanian border, a market town on the Tisza, a sluggish marsh-rimmed tributary of the Danube. As might be expected, Szeged's speciality is river-fish soup.

I delivered my piece-to-camera. 'The Tisza marshland was settled by nomadic Magyar herdsmen about a thousand years ago. Their descendants still use the Magyar iron pail, the *bogracs*, for much of their cooking. The shape of this pot – round-bellied and swing-handled – means it can really only work on an open fire. You can buy a *bogracs* in any Hungarian hardware store. Szeged Fish Soup – the famous *halaszle*—'

'Hal-aaa-slay.'

'Hal-aa-slay,' I repeated obediently. 'Hal-aa-slay is a fresh-water bouillabaisse traditionally prepared by the fishermen on the riverbank, although now it's a great draw in the restaurants. The soup is a broth made with the small river-fish which cannot be sold in the market —'

'Is not market. Is people come down and buy from the fishermen.'

'Cut,' said Charlie.

Next day, Mikhail produced a gang of river fishermen, who volunteered to empty their fish-traps and cook us the famous soup. Mysteriously, they were all wearing identical army-green boiler-suits. They looked vaguely sinister, like the prisoners in *Cell Block H* – I didn't mind, since it's my favourite Australian soap-opera, but the crew didn't seem to think it appropriate.

Somewhat sulkily, Charlie trundled his camcorder down to the water's edge. The riverbank had been reinforced by a wooden walkway to which had been tethered a line of elderly punts, their planks bleached white by the sun.

'What's the matter, Charlie?'

'I get seasick.'

I tried to reassure him. 'Don't worry. It's as calm as a millpond.'

I climbed into one of the punts with the fishermen while the crew piled into the other with an oarsman. We set off in stately procession. The punt-poles were used to propel the boat and keep the prow from bumping against the bank or ramming itself into the reedbeds. At first we rocked gently on the swell, but further out the current was surprisingly strong. The boats picked

Hungarian Szeged Bogracsgulyas
RIVER-FISH SOUP WITH PAPRIKA

A dish for fishermen, to be cooked in the open air, made with small river-fish – pike, tench, roach, bream, catfish, small sturgeon, whatever swims into the net. River-fish have a great many bones – nice and gluey for a soup. Larger fish (I have recommended farmed carp) should be sliced into thick cutlets and poached in the soup at the end.

——— SERVES 6 ———

4 lb/2 kg small river-fish
2 lb/1 kg onions, finely chopped
1 tablespoon paprika paste
2 heaped tablespoons ground paprika

1 large farmed carp, cleaned and
sliced into thick cutlets (optional)
salt

——— TO FINISH ———

1 chilli, finely chopped or 1 teaspoon chilli powder

1. Rinse the small fish, gut but don't scale them. Put them in a large stew-pan (the *bogracs*) with about 4 pints/2 l water and simmer uncovered for at least an hour until the fish is absolutely mushy.
2. Strain through a potato-ricer or mouli, pushing through all the little threads of flesh but leaving the bones behind. Return the broth to the pan and add the onions and paprika paste. Simmer gently for an hour until the onions are perfectly tender.
3. Sprinkle in the paprika, taste, and add salt – you'll need plenty because freshwater fish has no natural salt. If using a large carp, slip in the cutlets and poach – they'll take only 3–4 minutes. To finish, pour a ladleful of the hot broth into a bowl and mix in. Serve the chilli separately for people to add their own.

up speed, the reeds flashed by as the punter transferred his energy to the oars.

I glanced back at Charlie, waiting for the usual instructions. He didn't look too good. His eyes were closed, the camera was across his knees, his face was as green as the fishermen's boiler-suits. Even the red hair had subsided into a gloomy little mop, like a feather-duster left out in the rain.

Meanwhile, the oarsmen had manoeuvred us out of the current into the lee of an island where the fish-traps had been set. We nudged into the reed bed. I glanced back at Charlie. His hand was twitching on the camcorder's grip. Then, like a man sleepwalking, he raised the machine to his shoulder.

'Rolling.' Mind had triumphed over matter – but only just.

The traps yielded a modest haul of small river-fish and one large pike. The fish were transferred to a floating cage that bobbed along behind the punt like a toy lifeboat. Inside the cage, the water thrashed. By the time we reached the shore, most of the small fish had vanished into the pike. The fishermen consulted with each other and disappeared up the path.

'They got to go to fish-farm for carp,' explained Mikhail. 'They say no more carp in the river. Too many tourists eating soup. Is problem of *glasnost*.'

Mikhail had a Slav appetite for a good disaster. It was the tourist's appetite for Szeged fisherman's *halaszle* that had led to the necessity for farming carp, which in turn fed the tourist appetite for Szeged fisherman's *halaszle*, he explained happily. 'Is round and round, one thing leads to another. You see?'

I did indeed. In a few years' time, I suggested, the famous *halaszle* would not only be mispronounced by people like me on TV, but would be prepared by young persons with degrees in tourist-resource management. By this time the soup would contain pseudo-carp pieces fashioned by laser technology from reclaimed minced fish, and there'd be a microwave hidden in the fish-kettle.

'Is true,' said Mikhail gloomily.

'Look on the bright side, Mikhail. Everyone will come to you to tell them how it once was. You will have respect.'

'Is true,' said Mikhail, brightening.

★   ★   ★

The workers in the paprika factory at Koloksa, an enterprise which produced one of Hungary's most valuable exports, wore overalls cut to exactly the same pattern as the fishermen's, except that theirs were paprika-coloured rather than marsh-green.

The machinery was very modern, all gleaming steel and pre-formed plastic. 'Is very hygienic,' announced Mikhail proudly. 'You may tell this to the camera, Madame Lisbet. You can tell them Hungary is not all primitive and folkloric. We are very proud of our paprika industry. It is commercially very important.'

The management, continued Mikhail, was in some confusion since production had recently been transferred from state ownership into private hands. Actually, he added, the state and the private hands were the same. The existing management had simply been given shares in the enterprise and told to raise such finance as was required from the private sector. Unfortunately there wasn't a private sector. Confusion reigned. As long as everyone was stealing from the state, everyone knew exactly what to do. Now the right hand was in the left hand's pocket, and everyone was bewildered.

'The paprika of Koloksa is the most famous paprika pepper in the world. This you may say to camera, because it is true,' Mikhail offered by way of consolation. 'Now I must pay a visit to my friend the manager.'

I waited till Mikhail was safely out of earshot before tackling the business of the morning.

'OK, Charlie. Piece-to-camera.'

Charlie put his eye to machinery.

'Paprika has anti-malarial properties,' I announced confidently, 'bestowing a degree of immunity that preserved the lives of Hungarian workmen who went to work on the Suez Canal. The paprika-eaters shrugged off the fever where many others died.'

The camera stopped whirring. 'Are you sure?'

'Mikhail told me,' I lied, with a quick glance to check that our guru was still otherwise engaged. Actually, I had the information from George Lang, highly respected author of *The Cuisine of Hungary*, the classic work on the subject. Books didn't impress Charlie. He was a man for the horse's mouth.

The camera whirred once more.

At this moment, a lorryload of dried paprika peppers was tipped out on to the warehouse floor.

Charlie swung the camera round on its tripod to capture this new excitement.

One of the paprika-uniformed workers set to work sweeping up the peppers with a paprika-coloured broom into a holding-tank set into the floor, where a suction tube pulled the rattling cones directly into the mill. From here the ground-up spice was transferred directly into the machinery, which measured it into little glass jars that were then sealed down and labelled. The entire process could be viewed at any stage because the tubes were made of clear plastic.

Charlie's view-finder was in black and white, which made it impossible to tell the difference between minced mouse and ground paprika. 'Charlie,' I said conversationally, 'you've just filmed a dead mouse going into the paprika mill.'

'It's a wrap,' said Charlie.

Mikhail had obtained permission for us to film the Easter festival in Holoku, a conservation village in the hills to the north of Budapest. The authorities were pleased since the area had recently been declared a World Heritage Site, which qualified it for international funds to promote tourism.

'Very authentic, very ethnologically correct. You will like it, Madame Lisbet.'

'Are you sure, Mikhail?' I wasn't sure I could handle another museum house.

'I am sure. These are working people. They are not like your Disneyland.'

Mikhail was right. He usually was, despite his dogmatism. Actually, I was beginning to enjoy his certainties: you knew exactly where you were.

Although the centre of the village was postcard-pretty, Holoku had a modern residential quarter consisting of mostly prefabricated bungalows set in their own little farmyards with fields before and aft.

Our intention was to film the preparation of the Easter feast in one of these little working homesteads. 'No costumes, Mikhail?'

'But of course there are costumes, but these are for the processions. You will like this, too. The young women must wear crowns of wheat, which, as you know, Madame Lisbet, is a symbol of fertility. Only the young women who have made babies in the year before are allowed to wear the crowns. It is very symbolic. They are making processions on Good Friday and going to church on Easter Sunday. Is very authentic.'

We all agreed authenticity was much to be desired. Our timing was perfect. While Hungary is predominantly Roman Catholic, Slovakia, our next destination, follows the Orthodox calendar. Although Easter follows the lunar calendar in both Eastern and Western rites, the split between Constantinople and Rome left the former working to the old calendar, while the latter switched to the new. A two-week gap, which separates one from the other, allowed us two bites at the cherry.

The Easter festival conveniently coincides with the spring plantings. Even under the Communist system, all those with rural roots – few are more than a single generation from the land – were permitted to return home not only to celebrate but to give a hand with planting the 'unofficial' crops that filled country store-cupboards and became available to townsfolk through the black market.

'There is much barter,' said Mikhail. 'Not only in the country but even in the towns. I myself give extra classes to children whose father mends my electric typewriter. We may always find ways to pay. If we go to our villages in the spring and help plant the potatoes, or prepare the fields for growing vegetables, we have an entitlement to a share.'

The old part of the village was centred round an austere little black and white church, newly painted and spruce. Inside, two black-clad women were dusting and polishing the wooden pews, the altar rail, the sills. Everything that could possibly shine shimmered.

'Is the custom and is always done before Easter on Green Thursday. Is important to clean both inside and out. Even if you are not spiritual, is still the custom. Is the time of year when all

Hungarian Porkolt Csirke
CHICKEN GOULASH

A *porkolt* – the name means 'singed' because the stew is allowed to cook right down so it is almost frying in its concentrated juices – is what might be recognized as Austrian goulash. Serve with Hungarian pinch-finger dumplings – a pasta dough given its shape by pinching small pieces between the finger and thumb. If you don't want to make your own, any little pasta shapes will do as an accompaniment. The stew can be made with any kind of meat or game or even fish – but do as you please.

---------------------------------- SERVES 6 ----------------------------------

2 oz/50 g lard

1½ lb/750 g onions, finely
  sliced vertically

2 garlic cloves, skinned and crushed
  with a little salt

1 chicken, neatly jointed small
  (use the whole bird, back and all)

2 tablespoons mild paprika

1 teaspoon ground chilli

salt and pepper

---------------------------------- THE DUMPLINGS ----------------------------------

1 egg

½ teaspoon salt

about 3 oz/75 g plain flour

a little butter to finish

1. Melt the lard in a heavy casserole and add the onions and the garlic. Fry them gently until golden. Put in the pieces of chicken

and fry them gently too. The whole operation will take 10 minutes and is more like stewing than frying. Add 4 tablespoons water, and stir in the paprika and chilli, then season with salt and pepper. Reheat, then lid the pot tightly and stew very gently for 50–60 minutes if you have a young bird, and for 1½ hours if the bird is an old boiler. Check regularly that the pot has not boiled dry, but add the minimum water necessary.

2. Meanwhile, prepare the dumplings: fork up the egg with the salt and work in enough flour to make a soft dough. Knead until it's a smooth ball, cover with cling-film and set it aside. When you are ready to serve, using finger and thumb, pinch off little pea-sized pieces of the dough, and toss them, a batch at a time – no more than will cover the surface – into a pan of boiling lightly salted water. The dumplings will be cooked in 2–3 minutes – as soon as they bob to the surface. Remove with a draining spoon, drop into a colander and run under the cold tap for a second, no more. Transfer to a warm bowl and toss with butter.

3. To finish the stew, turn up the heat and take the lid off the pot. Watch carefully as the liquid boils nearly clean away; remove from the heat just before anything burns. Paprika is a vegetable and the flavour is fugitive. Serve in its own minimal but wonderfully aromatic juices, with the dumplings.

people paint the houses. This you may say in piece-to-camera,' said Mikhail.

'Welcome to Holokö,' I offered experimentally.

It was very rare that I could pronounce a Hungarian word to Mikhail's satisfaction. Holokö was one he seemed to take particularly personally. Whatever I did, I could never get it right.

'Hol-oo-*koo*.'

'Local colour,' said Charlie, rolling contentedly.

Right on cue, a man with a bucket of whitewash and a broom appeared from one of the little houses that lined the broad track of beaten earth leading to the church. He propped a ladder against the roof and began the laborious process of laying skins of powdered lime over wattle-and-daub.

I sketched, Charlie rolled, the morning passed pleasantly.

In the afternoon, Charlie and the crew began to assemble the equipment on our hostess's verandah. The kitchen was tiny and full of large Hungarian ladies in flowered overalls, making the Easter brawn.

At the back of the stove, a cauldron bubbled. Out of it protruded the head of a pig, ears pricked, snout wrinkled in a Hannibal Lector smirk.

'Is salted pig. Has been in the salt pot since Christmas,' said Mikhail, smacking his lips in anticipation. For an instant I had a vision of the pig's head vanishing into the Bermuda Triangle, along with a whole ham purchased to keep the wolf from the door on the road, and the jars of paprika ceremonially presented to us by the Koloksa co-operative, which I had somehow forgotten to tell him was flavoured with minced mouse.

The ladies of the household found me a flowered overall, extremely pungent and bearing the evidence of much previous culinary exertion, and tied a kerchief on my head.

Mikhail nodded approvingly. 'Is not appropriate, Madame Lisbet, for you to wear your hair uncovered. This for the young maidens, not for the matrons.'

Thank you, Mikhail. We set about dismantling the pig's head. The kitchen began to look like a scene from a medieval charnel house. The bones – skull, jaw, teeth and all – piled up grimly on the table. With a sudden attack of uncharacteristic squeamishness, Charlie decided it would be appropriate to film through the open door.

Meanwhile the ladies had arranged the meat tastefully in a large shallow dish and bathed it in its own glutinous broth. They set this outside the kitchen door to cool. By now the kitchen was becoming distinctly overpopulated. The open door drew in a flock of chickens to forage under the kitchen table, an elderly dog of no discernible breed to chew reflectively on a pig-bone, and a cat.

Charlie took his eye from the view-finder. 'Good. Let's have some noddies.'

Noddies are the reaction of the interviewer to the inter-viewee, stockpiled so the lads in the cutting room have something to break the monotony of talking heads. Since it's never clear what segment the back-room boys are going to consider suitable, nods and smiles are all that's appropriate. Noddies always look ridiculous to those not directly involved, consisting of changes of expression and small movements of the head which convey that the listener is taking an interest in an event that is not happening at the time.

I did as I was asked. From their expressions, the ladies clearly thought I was crazy. But, then, since all foreigners are crazy, particularly those with camcorders who want to make television about something so ordinary as boiling up the Easter pig's head, they went on quietly with the business in hand.

From my vantage-point inside the kitchen, I alone could see the cat. I could also see the plate of brawn. So could the cat. I went on nodding. The cat dipped an experimental paw in the sticky juices, licked it, liked what it found, and set about making a meal of it.

'Charlie,' I said quietly, into the directional mike clipped to my pinny, 'the cat's eating the brawn.'

Charlie waved a dismissive hand. He was concentrating on the noodle-rolling, which had replaced the brawn-making. One of the noodle-makers went to the door to fetch a large sack of poppy-seeds needed to dress the noodles.

All these things I knew because Mikhail was supplying a running commentary.

Spotting the cat, the poppy-seed lady unleashed a

Hungarian Husvetgulasch

EASTER SOUP

If you can lay your hands on a salted pig's head, it'll take about 3 hours to simmer until the meat is dropping off the bone. This should be stripped from the bones, cut into bite-sized pieces, and left to set in its own jelly to be eaten on the return from the Easter service. Otherwise, make a soup.

----- SERVES 6 -----

1 bacon hock (as a substitute for a pig's head)

3 onions, skinned and sliced

3 large old carrots, scraped and chunked

1 celeriac root, peeled and chunked parsley root or a small bunch leaf-parsley

1 bayleaf

1 teaspoon allspice berries

----- TO FINISH -----

1 small cabbage, sliced finely (optional)

dill and savory

1. Put the bacon hock in a roomy pot with all the other ingredients. Cover generously with cold water. Bring to the boil 3 times, skimming and adding a little cold water each time to send the cloudy bits to the bottom.

2. Simmer for about 1½ hours, until the bacon hock is tender.

3. Fifteen minutes before the end of the cooking time, add the sliced cabbage, if using. Finish with the chopped herbs. Serve the soup with bread and wine.

machine-gun burst of invective, and picked up a broom. Piercy, his instincts for trouble fine-honed, yanked the umbilical cord that joined him to the camera, catching the fetcher of poppy-seeds behind her knees and bringing her cannoning into Charlie.

At this moment, the cat took a flying leap, which landed it four-square among the chickens, which exploded in a flurry of feathers, only to find Charlie, hunched protectively over the camera, blocking the doorway.

In the ensuing panic, the sack of poppy-seeds split open, scattering the contents like tiny ball-bearings all over the floor. By now our hostess was moving faster than a fox after a barnyard goose. Her feet shot from beneath her, bringing her into contact with Mikhail and his bag, which detonated in a shower of mouse-flavoured spice.

Meanwhile, the ever-helpful Hans was in the process of reversing the van into the courtyard at precisely the moment the chickens managed to make their escape from the cat. With a mighty squawking, four of the feathered refugees got trapped beneath the van's wheels, adding paprika-feathered chicken to the possible options on the Easter menu.

In the ensuing panic, I retired with my phrase-book to add, 'I'm sorry we've squashed the chickens. How much do we owe you?' to the list of useful Hungarian phrases written on my arm in indelible ink.

Our billet for the weekend was, quite literally, palatial. A hunting lodge built for a grandee of the Habsburg empire, it had been converted into a hotel to accommodate the expected influx of tourists into the newly announced World Heritage Site.

Since Monday was a holiday, the place was packed not only with guests but locals enjoying an evening out in the cafeteria. In the sumptuously restored reception rooms – and no one restores more sumptuously than a Communist regime that has recently returned to capitalist ways – rows of chairs had been set ready for an audience. A troupe of musicans and dancers, extravagantly beribboned and booted, was limbering up for a performance.

'Very good, very lucky, very famous. You film,' announced Mikhail, with unusual brevity.

'Any excuse for a party,' said Charlie cheerfully. He was in a good mood this evening, his sense of well-being restored after the chicken episode by the luxuriously appointed bedrooms.

Charlie shouldered the camera and began to move around among the dancers. The hand-held camcorder was a sign that he was having fun. The presence of a foreign camera crew pleased everyone else, including the performers. There were rumours, not discouraged by Mikhail who was basking in reflected glory, of Hollywood presences.

'They are thinking there is a movie star,' he said cheerfully, as the audience craned its collective neck in an attempt to reconcile my appearance with their expectations.

'What did you tell them, Mikhail?'

Mikhail glanced at me sheepishly. 'Nothing bad. They think you are Sigourney Weaver.'

This cheered me greatly. You can mistake me for Sigourney any day.

'Now, Madame Lisbet, I shall explain everything.'

There's nothing like an ethnologist confronted with a bit of authentic ethnicity – particularly if it's remarkably pretty and flashing its legs in a pair of thigh-length Russian boots – for rolling out the symbolism.

'You see the lovely ladies, how they dance? You see how they make the circle and do the kicking with their legs – this thing you cannot do at the folk-house in Budapest?' A triumphant pause. 'You know what this means?'

'No, Mikhail, but no doubt you'll tell me.'

'It is for this that I am here.' Irony has no meaning in Mikhail's world. 'It is the dance of the clitoris.'

'Not the same clitoris, the one we met in the folk-dance house?'

'Ah!' This admiringly. 'You can say this word, clitoris. You are not afraid. Many women are afraid of this word. But you, you are not.'

The ladies did a quick flurry of high-kicking. I devoutly hoped that Mikhail was not going to tell me that the clitoris connection was that they were not wearing any knickers.

430

'You see the female in the middle, how there is always only one?'

'Indeed I do.'

'She is there in the middle. The others are doing the dancing all around. Is celebration of the clitoris.'

'Mikhail, it looks like a ring dance to me. Like our maypole.'

'Ah. I will tell you about maypole.'

'I know, Mikhail, a bunch of little virgins dancing round the oldest phallic symbol in the world.'

'This is true. All these dances, they are sexy. This is what they are for.'

At this moment the lovelies came on in a line, arms linked in a reasonably decorous imitation of the can-can. They were wearing knickers.

Mikhail sighed happily. 'You see.'

He cupped his ear. There was a lull. A group of young men leaped on to the stage and burst into song. The women waited until they finished, then sang a chorus of their own. The arrangement appeared to have taken the form of question and answer.

Each young man performed an energetic solo, involving much intricate boot-slapping, balletic back-flips and kicking of the heels from a crouching position. The audience applauded each performance enthusiastically. The young women on the stage appeared unmoved by the vigorous display of masculine prowess.

Every now and then, one of the girls yelped, a curiously unmusical noise.

'This is the making love of the young men to the young women.'

'The young women don't seem very interested.'

'The lovemaking is not yet beginning. Listen.' He cupped his ear urgently.

The young men sang some more and the young women repeated the yelping, this time with what seemed to be a degree of animosity.

'The young men are singing of the women's loveliness. They are saying it is a great pity the young women are down there in the valleys, and they are up here in the mountains. It is very beautiful, very natural.'

431

'Very clitoral.'

Mikhail looked at me severely. 'I think you are teasing me, Madame Lisbet. These are important matters, they are not for your English sense of humour.'

'Tell me, Mikhail, what are they saying?'

'They are saying – how may I translate? – the young men are saying—' He spread his hands dramatically. 'I wouldn't mind a bit of your big black bunny.'

'Are you sure?'

'Of course I am sure,' replied Mikhail indignantly. 'You do not have big black bunny in English?'

'Hard to tell,' I answered noncommittally.

'Yeah yeah, yeah yeah, yeah yeah, *yeah*!' yelped the girls.

'What are they saying, Mikhail?'

Mikhail gave me a scornful glance. 'They are saying what all young women are saying to all young men, Madame Lisbet.'

'And what would that be, Mikhail?'

'You'd be lucky, matey.'

CHAPTER SIXTEEN

Into the High Tatras

'My dear old man, we made some new nations after the peace that might well not have been created. A Czecho-Slovak is what came up and fermented after Austria putrified.'
RUDYARD KIPLING, in a letter to Rider Haggard (1925)

CONTRARY TO RECEIVED WISDOM, ROLLING STONES *DO* GATHER moss.

In Bratislava, capital of what was then eastern Czechoslovakia, we acquired Katya, a dark-haired beauty with very little English but fluent Hungarian. Fortunately we still had Mikhail and, although two translators was a little cumbersome, Katya came with the blessing of the Czech tourist board, which would certainly come in handy as we ventured into the unknown. The High Tatras was here-be-dragons territory.

'Many people in Slovakia speak Hungarian,' said Katya brightly. 'Is not difficult language.'

Our first night was spent in a municipal hotel whose walls, ceiling, bedcovers and soft-furnishings were of a uniform cow-pat brown. The matching carpet was relieved only by geometric blotches the colour of raw liver, as if someone had committed a particularly messy murder and no one had yet got round to clearing it up.

There was no food, but there was a bar. Since we had arrived too late for dinner anywhere else, the lads settled down to an in-depth investigation of the virtues of Czech beer, which they pronounced excellent, while the ladies retired prudently to an early bed.

It was not a promising beginning. Next day we drove north into the foothills of the mountains. 'I do not like this place. In this place there are bears and wolves,' said Mikhail, scanning the forest nervously.

Since we were in the area, Katya proposed a visit to the village of Krasna Luka, where her cousin had just had a baby. 'Is the ceremony of the birth-baskets – like in America when they do the baby-shower – but the people bring food instead of presents,' translated Mikhail. 'Katya says we are very fortunate there is this baby born. It will be very authentic.'

Charlie brightened. 'Costumes?'

'Of course. Is very beautiful. Is play-acting.'

'Play-acting with a real baby?' I asked.

'I think, perhaps, this is very primitive place,' said Mikhail. 'Is usual that the people make theatre when they do not have books. I think it will be very interesting for me too.'

A broad-shouldered matron in voluminous skirts and much embroidered waistcoating came to the door, greeting Katya with a motherly hug and the rest of us with a stream of impenetrable Slovakian.

'This is Monica, she is the mistress of the ceremonies,' Mikhail translated. 'She is the village midwife. She says you are welcome and you are just in time because they are ready to begin.'

Each visitor, fully costumed, brought a different offering tucked into a basket, delivering the gift with a formal little verse, which sometimes needed Monica's prompting.

As soon as each new visitor arrived, they were handed a small glass of something fiery, and invited to join the fun.

'The poppy-seeds are for fertility,' Mikhail announced predictably. 'Piece-to-camera, Madame Lisbet.' Mikhail took great delight in dictating the content of my pronouncements, but this was a suggestion I found not entirely convincing. In the present company, fertility seemed the least of anyone's problems, since the object of all the attention was contentedly rocking in its mother's arms, suckling a milky breast.

The little ceremony, a kind of Slovak 'Knock, knock,' took place in the museum house, one of the traditional village dwellings complete with all domestic furnishings, including a large wood-fired oven positively brimming with stuffed strudels, sugar buns and trays of snowy little dumplings keeping warm on the side.

The ladies turned their attention to washing a large bowlful of sauerkraut.

'The sauerkraut, Mikhail, is that also for fertility?' I enquired mischievously. A certain amount of mild professorial teasing kept my stress levels down, mostly since Mikhail took everything I said without a single grain of salt.

Mikhail consulted Katya.

Katya nodded and went off for a conversation with the midwife.

'The sauerkraut is for the every day,' Mikhail announced, on her return. 'Katya is saying you will notice the visitors have brought many other things and put them on the table. The chicken is for the feast, the soup of red beans gives strength, the bag of flour is so that the cupboard will never be empty, the eggs – I do not know what the eggs are for. And there will be sugar buns so the baby will always have sweetness. Katya says we must not forget the sweetness.'

By the time Charlie was ready to roll, the room was so full of excited Slovak ladies wielding rolling-pins that the presenter and translators were reduced to peering through the window, like the bad fairies who hadn't been invited to the feast.

Fortunately Katya kept up a running commentary on the events taking place inside.

The midwife's two gifts, Mikhail translated, were peace and a

Slovakian Beigli

CHRISTENING STRUDEL

Celebration cakes such as this horseshoe-shaped strudel have lots of little seeds to denote fertility and prosperity. In the West, the equivalent is raisins and crystallized fruits.

SERVES 6 — THE DOUGH

8 oz/250 g plain flour
½ teaspoon salt
1 oz/25 g fresh yeast

2 oz/50 g butter or lard
1 tablespoon sugar
½ pint/300 ml warm milk

THE FILLING

4 oz/100 g poppy-seeds
½ pint/300 ml milk
1 oz/25 g butter

2 tablespoons sugar
a little egg and milk, to glaze

1. Sieve the flour with the salt into a warm bowl. Rub in the yeast and butter or lard with the tips of your fingers. Mix in the sugar and, with the crook of your hand, work in enough warm milk to make a soft dough. Knead until it no longer feels sticky – the wetter the dough, the lighter the end result. Work it into a smooth ball and set it to rise in a bowl under a damp cloth (or seal under cling-film) in a warm place for an hour or so, until spongy and light. Knead to distribute the air, and roll out with a floured rolling-pin, using short, quick strokes, to an oblong about the length and width of a swiss roll.

2. Meanwhile, grind the poppy-seeds in an electric coffee-grinder, or crush them in a mortar. Bring the milk to the boil in a small saucepan and stir in the powdered poppy-seeds. Boil until the mixture thickens. Remove from the heat and beat in the butter and sugar. Let the mixture cool and spread it over the dough. Roll it up like a swiss roll, tucking in the ends as if making a bed, and curl it in a horseshoe shape on a buttered baking-sheet. Leave it to rise again for about 30 minutes.

3. Preheat the oven to 375°F/190°C/mark 5.

4. Brush the strudel with egg and milk and bake for 45–50 minutes until well risen and golden brown. Transfer to a rack to cool. Dust with powdered sugar. It's at its best after a day or two in a tin.

tranquil heart. A herb slipped under the baby's embroidered linen pillow was camomile to bring sleep; a little white bulb tucked under the tiny feet was garlic to keep witches at bay. Each of the cooking ladies made the motion of spitting in the cradle, a discreet little pursing of the lips and a quick expulsion of air, no more.

'You know of that, Madame Lisbet?' Mikhail's voice had the eagerness that could mean only one thing.

'Let me guess, Mikhail. Fertility?'

'Very good, Madame Lisbet, you are learning a little of our ways.' He paused thoughtfully. 'Some people will tell you that this spitting is to bring luck. Do not believe them. This is a little true, but it is not, as you say, the whole story. They say this because they do not want you think them *primitive*. This spitting, this watering of the cradle, this is for the growing of the seed. I know this because I have made a study of it. It is in my doctoral thesis. I will explain it all.'

Thankfully at this moment Hans's pebble glasses popped up at the window. Charlie wanted me to hold the baby. Holding a baby seemed a lot more like reality than listening to professors of ethnology, however knowledgeable, explaining the meaning of life.

I left Mikhail to expand on his thesis to the beautiful Katya, whose face wore an inscrutable Slavic expression that spoke of many years of being bored by middle-aged professors.

'I think this is very interesting,' said Katya. 'But it is also very primitive.'

Banská Bystrica is a grey industrial city surrounded by belching factory chimneys. Culturally, it has a single claim to fame.

'Now I am taking you,' said the beautiful Katya, 'to see Anton Anderle. Anton Anderle is the most famous puppet-master in the world.'

It was no accident that the Czechoslovakians elected a playwright as their first post-Communist leader. In Slovakia, play-acting is more than an entertainment: it is, as we had witnessed at the birth-basket ceremony, a primary method of communication.

The puppet-masters of Slovakia can trace their roots back to the mystery plays of the Middle Ages – the wooden dolls were a substitute for real actors when the Church discovered the script was getting a little out of hand. As with modern nativity plays, much was made of the peripheral figures. Among these, the ringleader was always the wise Caspar: it was he who was given all the good lines and told all the bawdy jokes. Although the inanimate was not capable of the same directness of self-expression as the animate, a little subversion began to creep back in. The misbehaving cleric might carry a large sausage under his robe, the corrupt mayor a money-bag behind his back – there were many ways in which the woodcarvers could deliver their subversive message. When they attached strings to the figures, the puppet theatre was born.

Following Katya's instructions, we turned off the road on the outskirts of the city and found ourselves in a vast housing estate, a collection of gigantic upturned Kleenex boxes distributed at random over bare earth. Only the lines of washing hanging on the tiny balconies indicated that these dwellings might house a human community. It seemed impossible that anything creative could come out of these bleak little cells in which all the inhabitants must be as indistinguishable from each other as bees in a hive.

Even Katya was beginning to look dubious, checking the scribbled address anxiously. Suddenly she dived into one of the faceless blocks, then reappeared immediately, beckoning and smiling.

'Here is the famous puppet-master,' announced Mikhail triumphantly.

He had slipped into the somewhat less stressful role as interpreter to the interpreter. Katya was in charge of day-to-day arrangements, and Mikhail was free to fill up his airline bag where and when he could. At the birth-basket ceremony it had swallowed two sauerkraut pies and a dozen sticky buns.

Beneath the upturned Kleenex box was a huge subterranean garage. In one corner was a bricked-off bunker with a pair of heavy steel doors, which yielded to the knock. Just like the White Rabbit bolting down the magic rabbit-hole, the door gave access to a wonderland. The bunker was crammed with children, their attention so concentrated on what was happening on stage they did not even turn their heads as we entered.

Charlie set his camera quietly in position and began to roll.

Anton Anderle's puppets were not so much characters in a play as actors who play different parts. The youthful audience knew exactly what to expect of each puppet.

The stars of the little stage were the handsome hero, the beautiful heroine with her supporting cast of handmaidens, a caddish Don Juan, a cloven-footed Devil and a scarily skeletal Death.

The master of ceremonies was Gasparko, the heir to the wise Caspar – like Punch, he was the joker in the pack, neither good nor bad. The villain was Hansi Paprika, a flamboyant scarlet fop who spoke his lines in what Mikhail assured me was a thick Hungarian accent. There was no doubt that Hansi represented the old enemy. Maybe in time his wooden effigy would be replaced by a vodka-swilling Boris or a burger-chewing Bill, but for now, Hansi claimed his place among that merry band of Frogs, Krauts and Bifsteks whose undesirableness can most easily be identified by their eating habits. The children hissed the villain, denounced the Devil, cheered the hero and applauded the heroine. They greeted Death with terrified shrieks. The tales retained their morality – good must ultimately triumph over evil – but what happened in between was dictated by the audience as much as by the puppet-master. Fairy-tales are never entirely innocent: the messages they deliver are not always what they seem.

Whatever the subtleties of the political content, the audience was entranced, even though they must have heard the same stories a thousand times before. The old ones are the best – the old man who told his Celtic tales on the island of Mull would have felt perfectly at home in this magic grotto, as we did too.

As Andy Warhol's birthplace, Svidnik in the High Tatras is probably the most famous little town in Slovakia. History does not relate whether the world's first superstar learned his subversive art in a puppet theatre in a garage underneath a concrete Kleenex box but I wouldn't be surprised.

Svidnik also had the Hotel Dukla, which provided an

excellent reason for leaving Svidnik immediately, never to return. It had concrete cancer, a visible disintegration of the exterior from the top downwards, like a slowly-peeling banana. The black Tarmac bib on which the crumbling edifice had been dumped was speckled with the little bits of concrete, like specks of dandruff on the shoulders of an undertaker's assistant.

Svidnik also had Andy Warhol groupies. As soon as we began to dismantle our luggage in the Hotel Dukla's car-park, we were approached by a gentleman in a tightly belted mackintosh. After a brief and excitable conversation, our twin interpreters vanished. Ten minutes later, they were back, beaming. We were very fortunate. They had negotiated an interview with the late superstar's parents, the price to include a photograph of the infant Andy in his birthday suit, and a bootleg copy of a Factory hand-held movie starring Divine.

'Much nakedness,' said Mikhail encouragingly. 'We see it on playback.'

'Nah,' said Charlie decisively.

Our two interpreters withdrew sulkily, leaving us to negotiate with Reception on our own.

Wearily we dragged our equipment into the grim foyer. If Reception was representative of the local talent, Mr Warhol need never have left home. His taste for corpulent, choleric transsexuals would have been well satisfied right on his doorstep.

Reception, barricaded behind a vast steel desk, was wearing a great deal of loose powder, which masked an impressive moustache, purple lipstick and a frilly blouse that delivered an expanse of elderly but surprisingly pneumatic bosom. She listened impassively while Hans explained our presence in fluent German.

'You American, *dah?*'

'We're from Oz,' said Piercy firmly. The lads from Perth didn't like being taken for Limeys, even by Reception at the Hotel Dukla.

'You speak English?' enquired Charlie, with one of those gestures that occasionally got us into hot water since they mean one thing in Sicily but something quite different elsewhere.

Reception studied us impassively. '*Amerikan, dah.*'

'We have booking. *Reservazion*,' cut in Hans hopefully.

Reception swung ponderously back on her chair and pulled a large plastic-covered ledger from a shelf between her knees. She set it carefully on the desk. One pudgy finger worked slowly down each page. The finger stopped. Reception reversed the ledger and pushed it across the desk.

'*Dah*. Passport.'

We obliged. Reception studied each one in turn, checking the photographs with slow deliberation.

Finally she leaned back. 'How many room you want?'

Charlie did a head-count and held up five fingers. Reception also did a head-count, looked at me and sucked her teeth.

'You are madame. You have husband.'

I hesitated. 'I have husband,' I agreed.

'Which one you husban'? This one? That one?'

'Husband not here.'

'Where husban'?' Clearly, Reception did not share her celluloid alter ego's moral tolerance.

I flap my hands. 'In England. London. Over there.'

'*London, Englan'*?'

Reception put down the pencil, examined me severely, then scribbled some more. 'OK, lady. You no want sleep with these mens?'

'No. Absolutely not.'

'OK, lady. I give one person *Zimmer mit Toiletten*. You pay separate.' She banged a stamp down on a bit of paper and pushed it towards me. 'You want toilet paper?'

I agreed that toilet paper was useful if one had *Toiletten*.

'Ten kopek. You pay now.'

I scrabbled in my pocket.

'*Nein*. You get paper *Toiletten* woman.'

Obediently I followed the pointing finger to the public facility at the other end of the reception area. *Toiletten* was locked. There was a bell. *Toiletten* woman appeared. She looked like Mrs Krushchev on a bad-hair day, carrying a roll of lavatory paper. It was brown and stiff. I proffered a handful of small paper money. Mrs Krushchev tore off two sheets and held them up triumphantly.

I indicated it would be nice to have the whole roll.

'*Neh.*'

I offered more kopeks. The paper came off the roll sheet by sheet, fluttering into my hand like a ticker-tape reception given to some particularly unpopular politician.

When I returned to the desk for my key, Hans was getting down to essentials.

'Restaurant? *Essen und Trinken?*'

'Restaurant. *Dah.*'

'*E aperto? Cuando e chiuso?*' When in dire straits Charlie reverted to the language of childhood. He made closing gestures while raising his eyebrows. In Eastern Europe, we had learned, you have to catch public catering facilities by surprise. In Slovakia, they take it one stage further: the restaurants time their closing by the precise moment at which a foreign customer appears.

'Restaurant she is close.' For the first time since our arrival, Reception was smiling.

Hans pointed to a prominently displayed notice.

'It says here,' he said, in a reasonable voice, 'all-day cafeteria.'

Reception examined the notice briefly and placed it face down on the desk, like a wronged wife censoring a picture of her philandering husband.

'Is Sunday. All is close Sunday. Cafeteria is close. Restaurant is close. All is close.'

The lift did not stop at any floor but the seventeeth, the start of the concrete cancer. The rooms matched Reception's scowl. The décor was rat-grey, the mini-bar was not connected to the electricity and had grown an interior covering of soft green fur. The central heating had long abandoned its purpose, the lavatory had failed to digest the last incumbent's toilet paper, the mattress was a two-inch slab of furrowed foam and the base had no springs.

Half an hour later, we all met again in the foyer. By now Katya and Mikhail had returned to the fold. Mikhail looked very happy.

'We find wine cellar. Wine cellar is very popular with the young people for the dancing. There is also drinking of wine and eating of fried cheese.'

Whatever the ethnological content, eating of fried cheese and drinking of wine sounded like the best news we'd heard since we crossed the border.

'Come.' Mikhail grabbed his airline bag and set off at a gallop towards an elevated railway line with bricked-in arches.

One of these had fairy-lights over the door and wine barrels on either side. Katya disappeared down a flight of steps into the darkness. She came back, chattering excitedly.

Mikhail translated. 'Katya say, you like M. C. Hammer?'

'To eat?' enquired Piercy, the hollowness of hunger in his voice.

Katya giggled. 'I like M. C. Hammer very much.' She did a quick burst of rap-artistry.

'Fried cheese?'

Katya placed the two first fingers of one hand on her thumb and kissed the air.

Mikhail led the stampede.

The interior of the cellar was smoke-sodden, the crush of bodies impenetrable, the music the sensory equivalent of the outbreak of the Third World War. We felt our way along the walls like three blind mice, and found, miraculously, an unoccupied table.

As my eyes accustomed themselves to the smog – everyone in Slovakia smoked like chimneys – it was possible to see that the cellar was a subterranean passage lined with wine barrels, which left just enough space on either side for half a dozen wooden tables. Benches were provided, but these were jammed beneath the tables to allow more room for the dancers. The dance-floor was packed with slowly moving bodies. Hands waved above the throng, the only possible physical manifestation of the beat. A jug of something pale, alcoholic and slightly fizzy was set on the table unasked for.

Katya and Mikhail took to the floor, the rest of us waited impatiently for our fried cheese. I was pleased to observe from his disjointed movements and agonized expression that Mikhail was having just as much trouble with M. C. Hammer as I had with the rhythms of 'Wouldn't Mind A Bit Of Your Big Black Bunny'.

Some time later – much later – the fried cheese arrived. It

Slovakian Sri Cvreti

FRIED CHEESE

This is the simplest of dishes. It makes an excellent light lunch or supper, served with a salad.

SERVES 2 AS A MAIN DISH, 4 AS A STARTER

1 teaspoon paprika
2 tablespoons flour
1 large egg
1 tablespoon milk
8 heaped tablespoons home-made
  breadcrumbs (fresh or dried)
  oil for frying

4 thick slices mature cheese
  (sheep's cheese, Cheddar or any
  other hard cheese)

1. Mix the paprika and the flour on a shallow plate. Fork up the egg with the milk on another plate. Spread the breadcrumbs on a third. Dust the cheese slices through the flour, dip in the egg, making sure all sides are well coated, and press firmly into the breadcrumbs. Carefully patch any bald bits with egg and bread-crumbs.

2. Heat the oil in a frying-pan – just enough to submerge the cheese. Test the heat with a cube of bread – it should bubble and brown immediately. The oil must be good and hot to seal the coating before the cheese melts and seeps out. Slip in the cheese slices and fry until golden, turning once. Drain on kitchen paper. Serve piping hot with tartare sauce.

came in a jacket of breadcrumbs and was hotter than Hades. There was a cream sauce to eat with it, rather good, since it seemed to be made with proper eggs and cream, like a savoury custard.

'Is tartare sauce,' reported Mikhail, through bulging cheeks. 'Is good.' He seemed to have asbestos instead of mouth tissue.

Dizzy with exhaustion and wine, we returned to the Hotel Dukla and made our way to our separate billets. The building simmered and crackled through the night, like a lizard shedding its skin. I curled up as best I could under every blanket I could find, reflecting on my good fortune that my room was on the second floor and that if I had to jump the worst I could expect was a pair of broken ankles.

Thus comforted, I slept like the dead.

'The Ruthenes of Ludomirova are a community of Ukrainians marooned in Slovakia in the aftermath of war,' I explained to camera, mercifully without interruption from Mikhail, who had a terrible hangover and a burned tongue.

During the morning, Katya had disappeared, but returned with the good news that she had managed to persuade a household to allow us to film their preparations for the Orthodox Easter. Luba, the daughter of the house, spoke Slovak. The chain of information had acquired another link.

It was Ludomirova's good fortune that a slip of the politician's pencil had somehow permitted the Ruthenes to maintain their traditional customs and way of life, whereas those on the other side of the border had lost theirs.

'These people are speaking Old Ukrainian. Is not the same as Russian,' said Mikhail, cheering up at the prospect of another link snapping in the chain of responsibility.

Trolleys, brollies and dollies were unloaded from the van. Charlie applied one bleary eye to the lens and began to set up a shot. Piercy clamped his headphones to his ears and settled his face into his normal anxious expression. He had much to make him anxious. There were many strange noises, mostly of the farmyard kind.

Spring had sprung with a vengeance. The household cow was giving birth to her calf in the byre across the yard. The hens

Slovakian Omaka Tartar
TARTARE SAUCE

The real thing – not unlike an old-fashioned English salad cream – delicious with breaded cheese. Optional extras include stirring in finely chopped gherkins and capers. Serve it in a jug.

MAKES ABOUT 3/4 PINT/450 ML SAUCE

3 egg yolks	2 tablespoons vegetable oil
1/4 pint/150 ml soured cream	1/4 pint/150 ml white wine
1 teaspoon sugar	2 tablespoons thick cream
1/2 teaspoon salt	1 tablespoon dill, chopped
1 teaspoon mild mustard	1 tablespoon chives, chopped
a squeeze of lemon juice	

1. Whisk up the yolks, soured cream, sugar, salt, mustard and lemon juice in a small pan, and stir over a gentle heat, or in a bowl over simmering water, until the mixture begins to thicken like a custard.
2. Add the oil as for a mayonnaise, then the wine, and lastly the cream. Whisk over the heat until smooth and no longer smelling of alcohol. Allow the sauce to cool.
3. Stir in the chopped herbs and pickles, if using.

were protesting vigorously against the removal of a clutch of eggs they had been nurturing throughout Lent. The sow was trying to teach her squealing piglets some manners. Turkeys gobbled, geese hissed, roosters crowed.

'Come inside,' said Mikhail.

The kitchen did triple duty as living and dining area. It was as warm as a furry Russian hat, heated with a huge tiled wood-fired stove, against whose welcoming flanks sat Mama Anna.

Mama Anna was the matriarch. We could do nothing, explained Mikhail, without Mama Anna's permission. The kitchen filled up rapidly. The younger members of the family arrived from the city. Everyone worked in the city. The important thing was to come home at Easter and plant the potatoes. No potatoes, nothing to eat for the pig. No pig, nothing to make the bacon. No bacon, no eggs, because the eggs would have to be sent to market. No eggs, no milk, because the milk would have to go to make cheese to be sent to market to pay for the petrol to take the eggs to market. No petrol – but I'm sure you get the picture.

Charlie set up his camera and rolled.

There were the breads to be made. A sack of flour was tipped into a huge wooden trough, mixed with yeast, copious quantities of melted butter and enough eggs to repopulate the whole barnyard. Equipped with the obligatory pinny and kerchief, I joined the women at the kneading trough. It was back-breaking work. After half an hour's hard labour, Charlie filmed me collapsed in a corner, my face drenched in sweat.

Mikhail examined me with interest. 'You do not mind this, Madame Lisbet?'

I looked at him wearily. 'Don't mind what, Mikhail?'

'That they are making film of you when you are perspiring like a pig and your hair is wet and you are very dirty from the flour. My wife would not like this. Not at all.'

'Piss off, Mikhail.'

'What does this mean, "piss off"?'

'It means – oh, never mind, Mikhail.'

Mama Anna invited us to inspect the cellar. This, confirmed Katya, was not only a privilege but a considerable demonstration of trust. Larders were always kept locked.

Larder-inspection was not lightly granted by those who had ample reason to protect what little they had.

We descended into the cavern beneath the house. In the flickering light of the oil-lamp, it looked as if we had stumbled into a rustic Fortnum and Mason. There were sacks of potatoes, beans, grain, a barrel of pickled eggs, another of salted green beans, shelves of jams and honeys, relishes and pickles – horseradish in cream, beetroot with honey, cucumbers in brine, jars of plum jam and apple purée, pickled peppers and an amber fruit that looked as if it might be medlars.

'I think you are most surprised, Madame Lisbet,' said Mikhail confidently.

I was indeed. Considering we were at the end of winter and as yet there were no crops to refill the larder, let alone anything of gastronomic interest in the market, the bounty seemed nothing short of miraculous.

Mikhail picked up a bottle of something dark and viscous and held it up to the light. 'You know this, Madame Lisbet? I can tell you is plum brandy. Very good. Very nice. Very strong. Thank you,' said Mikhail, accepting an offering for his hand luggage.

Mysteriously, perhaps because they were a minority who posed no real threat to the state, the Ruthenes were left to practise their faith throughout the years of Communism. The inhabitants of Ludomirova supported a Russian Orthodox monastery.

A store-cupboard well stocked by the end of winter was the sign of good husbandry and prudent housewifery, worthy of the blessing of the church. It was customary, translated Mikhail, for the Easter food to be taken to the monastery to be blessed.

'They are calling this the Easter baskets. You must listen carefully and not interrupt,' said Mikhail firmly. 'Is not permitted to make the blessing of the baskets inside the church. This is political. This is because in bygone days the people like to go into the churchyard and eat the meal with the ancestors, but this is not permitted in modern times. This is the meaning of the plaited breads, the *babkas*, which represent the cutting of the woman's hair on the wedding day. When the husband dies, his woman's hair is put in the coffin with the corpse.'

'Like committing suttee by proxy?'

'Please?'

'Thank you for the information, Mikhail.'

'You are welcome.'

Easter Saturday was the allotted day for the mass of the Resurrection and the blessing of the baskets – maybe a little early for the risen Christ, but no matter. Inside the church, bodies packed the aisles. There was a low buzz of meeting and greeting.

'Many people, Mikhail.'

Mikhail nodded. 'The people come here because is cheaper than Catholics. Is economic. After the revolution, there are fifty Russian monks who come to Ludomirova. Stalin is in the Kremlin and no one is permitted to worship in the churches in Russia. People send money to Ludomirova so that masses may be said for their souls. The Pratoslavs have plenty of money, so they can make everything cheaper. Is the power of economics.'

Inside the church, the air was thick with incense. The walls had been freshly whitewashed, contrasting sharply with the dark-faced icons framed in gold. Narrow frescoes, like brightly embroidered silk ribbons, traced the curve of the arches. The priest and the altar were dressed in the sombre splendour of the Easter mourning garments.

Taking up a vantage-point in the gallery, Charlie found himself competing with a film crew from Kiev.

'They are Ukrainians. Is the same as the Ruthenes. They are looking for their roots,' explained Mikhail.

As soon as mass was over, the church emptied quickly.

The men hovered behind the women and children, who lined up behind their baskets. The patriarch, heavily bearded and magnificently hatted, passed down the ranks sprinkling water from a silver bowl.

Each woman waited until the patriarch drew level with her basket before drawing back the embroidered linen covers. As soon as the covers were off, each made the most of the opportunity to take a good look at her neighbour's stores – the culinary equivalent of a peep behind the lace curtains. From this brief glimpse, a mother might draw her own conclusions on her neighbours' housekeeping – and thus, no doubt, the marriageability of their daughters or the likely profligacy of their sons.

'You know what is this sprinkling of water, Madame Lisbet?'

'Let me guess. A fertility rite.'

'Ha. Very clever, Madame Lisbet. The sprinkling of the water is for the fertilization of the womb. Many people think this is for the watering of the ground for growing of the crops. This is not so. The shamanistic peoples are for the hunting and herding, they are not for the farming. This watering is for the making of the babies. In my country in the villages, the boys are throwing water all over the girls for the Easter ceremonies. The young women are getting wet. Is very beautiful.'

'I'm sure it is, Mikhail. You should visit Australia. They throw water all over the girls there too. It's called a sheila-in-a-wet-T-shirt competition.'

'In Australia? This is true?'

'Honest. Ask Charlie.'

'But is for the same reason?'

'More or less.'

'This must be very beautiful.'

'It is, Mikhail, indeed it is.'

Darkness was already falling by the time we returned to Mama Anna's domestic citadel. A single candle had been set on the window-sill to light up our path.

On the way home, each family had paid a visit to the graveyard. Ancestors are important where life is hard, and these were people to whom death was a constant presence; the approval of those who had gone before was essential to the well-being of those left behind.

Since the feast of the spirit had been celebrated with the proper solemnity, it was time for the feast of the flesh. Luba's father went down to the cellar to fetch the slivovic while the ladies unpacked the basket. All that was required had already been prepared; this was not a moment for culinary exertions, but a time to enjoy the gathering.

On her grandmother's instruction, Luba, her pretty face wreathed in smiles, made a graceful little speech of welcome. The presence of strangers such as ourselves brought honour to the household. On behalf of the visitors, Charlie replied that the strangers must be forgiven for having appetites like a herd of starving 'roos, since this could be interpreted as a compliment to the food's excellence.

The preliminaries concluded to all parties' satisfaction, Charlie reapplied his eye to the lens, Piercy hooked up his umbilical, and I took my place at the table.

Corks were withdrawn from bottles and the scent of berries, must-laden and rich, filled the air. The table looked truly magnificent. There were generous slices of tender pink ham cut from the bone, thick wedges of smoked sausage and slabs of bacon, hard-boiled eggs peeled and quartered, a whole round cheese. There were also thin slices of egg-cheese – eggs that had been scrambled until thoroughly coagulated, dropped in a muslin bag and left to drip-dry on a corner of the cooker, until perfectly firm and spherical as an old-fashioned Christmas pudding. Because the cow had conveniently calved, there was new butter, pale and creamy, for spreading on the *babkas*.

Mama Anna set a basket of decorated eggs on the table. Mikhail moved forward eagerly to inspect them.

'You see pattern on eggs, Madame Lisbet?'

'Indeed I do, Mikhail.' They had been painted with little wax sunbursts, which I knew because I had helped to paint them, dipping a pin stuck in a cork into little dishes of melted coloured candle ends. It had taken us – Luba and me and three visiting grandchildren – much of the previous evening to complete.

'You know what this means?'

'I rely on you to tell me, Mikhail.'

'Is very ancient. The sunshine is painted on the shell, which signifies the earth, and within is the yolk, which signifies the seed. You see? The egg, the sunshine, the sprinkling of the water . . .'

'Rolling,' said Charlie.

'You know why there is a big bowl of salt, Madame Lisbet?'

'I expect you'll tell me, Mikhail.'

'There is always salt in the spring. My mother used to go to the market at Easter to buy salt. This is very important to these people.'

Slovakian Easter Egg-cheese

A very unusual dish to use up all the eggs that could not be eaten during Lent. The household gets through prodigious amounts of them at Easter — eggs are prohibited during the forty-day fast — but the hens who are not brooding a clutch of spring chicks keep right on laying, so there's quite an accumulation.

─────────────── SERVES A DOZEN ───────────────

4 pints/2 l rich milk   1 tablespoon salt
20 medium eggs

1. Bring the milk to the boil. Meanwhile whisk the eggs with the salt. When the milk boils, whisk in the egg. Keep whisking until the resulting custard is thoroughly scrambled.
2. Tip the mixture into a clean, scalded pudding cloth. Hang it to drain overnight with a bowl underneath to catch the whey, exactly as you would fresh cheese.
3. When it's quite firm, tip it out on to a clean dish, paint it with beaten egg and slip it into a medium oven (350°F/180°C/mark 4) for 10 minutes to glaze. The result should look like a large shiny yellow Easter egg.
4. Slice it thickly and serve with ham and sweet-pickled beetroot.

Wax-patterned Easter Eggs

1. You'll need multi-coloured candle-ends, a large-headed pin stuck into a cork, and the appropriate quantity of eggs for decorating. Either empty the eggs by making a pin-hole at both ends and blowing until all the contents have been evacuated (you can use these eggs to make an Easter egg-cheese, see opposite). Or hard-boil some white-shelled eggs – allow 8–10 minutes depending on their size.

2. Melt the candle-ends, keeping the colours separate – it's most convenient if you do it in metal jar-tops. Hold the egg firmly in one hand, big-end upwards. Dip the pin-pen in the melted wax and, starting half an inch below the apex of the egg, dab on a blob of wax and drag it up towards the apex of the egg to give a tadpole-shaped dash. With a steady hand, repeat the pattern all round the egg until you have a sunburst pattern.

3. It is prettiest if you use short and long strokes alternately and different coloured waxes. Repeat on the other end of the egg – obviously you don't hold the egg by the patterned bit or the wax will melt – then make more sunburst patterns round the sides.

4. Dip the eggs in diluted food colouring to throw the wax pattern into relief – a batik technique.

The gathering had taken on the character of a cocktail party. Everyone was talking and laughing, the children chased each other round the table.

Suddenly silence fell. Mama Anna rose from her seat by the tiled stove and came slowly to the head of the table. Even the children were quiet.

At a sign from Mama Anna, all the little glasses were filled and raised.

'*Nasdrovna* – good health,' she said, bowing towards Charlie's lens and raising the glass to her lips. Everyone else followed suit. It was a graceful gesture. We drank. The liquor was mind-numbingly strong.

The same gesture was then repeated round the table to each of the participants in turn. The tiny glasses were filled and refilled. My head began to spin.

'You must drink all, Madame Lisbet,' said Mikhail.

'Is not true,' said Katya. 'You may sip. The women do not drink so much as the men. Mikhail is teasing.'

At that moment, the rooster crowed in the yard. Everyone suddenly fell silent. All heads turned towards the head of the table.

There was one further ceremony.

Mama Anna alone remained on her feet. The wrinkled face, pale and slant-eyed, betrayed no emotion as she surveyed the laden table and the faces all around.

After a moment she beckoned to the youngest granddaughter, one of Luba's children, a little girl with bright dark eyes and long brown hair caught in two bunches at the sides of her neat head.

Mama Anna leaned down and whispered something in the child's ear. The little girl listened with quiet intensity. Her small face, so lively the previous evening, was as impassive as the matriarch's. She left the room, to return a few moments later. She walked solemnly round the table. Cradled in her hand, she held a single egg, white as snow.

Mama Anna accepted the offering, cupped it in her palm and raised it so that all the company might see. Then, with one single gesture, the egg was broached, the contents sipped. The shell, now transformed into a ceremonial drinking cup, was passed from hand to hand, each of those present taking only enough to glisten on the lips.

The silence was complete. Even the soft hum of Charlie's machinery had ceased. It was as if the world had stopped turning, as if this moment captured all the reality of the world – the cycle completed, birth, death and life.

The little ceremony was so simple, so ancient, the emotions it stirred so potent, so deep-rooted, that even now I cannot peel back the layers that hide its meaning. In that single gesture, so clean, so perfect, so ordinary, was the essence of all living things, shared by all living things, acknowledged by all living things.

The image haunts me still. Even now, revisiting those journeys in my heart and head, I do not know the true meaning of what happened that day. I think perhaps I never will.

Epilogue

Jonathan Swift's Resolutions When He Comes to Be Old.

Not to marry a young woman.

Not to keep company unless they really deserve it.

Not to be peevish or morose, or suspicious.

Not to scorn present ways, or wits, or fashions, or men, or war, etc.

Not to be fond of children, or let them come near me hardly.

Not to tell the same story over and over to the same people.

Not to be covetous.

Not to neglect decency, or cleanliness, for fear of falling into nastiness.

Not to be over severe with young people, but give allowances for their youthful follies and weaknesses.

Not to be influenced by, or give ear to, knavish tattling servants, or others.

Not to be too free of advice, nor trouble any but those that desire it.

To desire some good friends to inform me which of these Resolutions I break, or neglect, and wherein; and reform accordingly.

Not to talk much, nor of myself.

Not to boast of my former beauty, or strength, or favour with ladies, etc.

Not to hearken to flatteries, nor conceive I can be beloved by a young woman.

Not to be positive or opinionative.

Not to set up for observing all these Rules, for fear I should observe none.

JONATHAN SWIFT (1667–1745), at the age of thirty-two, in a
letter to a friend

SO WHAT DID I LEARN ON MY TRAVELS? AS MUCH AS ANYTHING, to hear but not to judge; to see but not to draw conclusions; to speak but only of those things I believe to be true in my heart – and always to remember that I may be wrong. And I am happy to be wrong. I am well aware there is no such thing as the right road, no such thing as absolute truth.

This is a light-hearted book with a serious intent. My learning tools were not the usual ones – the path of the intellect, the maps and guidebooks and leatherbound tales of long-dead travellers, although these were my constant companions. Instead, I chose that least threatening, most unpolitical of pathways, the study of domestic habit. The narrative, the account of my journeys, although seen through my eyes and retold in my own words, is a communal effort: the contributions of others are all that matters. It is only through the experience of others, those who share this particular moment, our contemporaries, whether friend or family or passing acquaintance, that we can learn the truth about ourselves. We need each other. Self-examination is a sterile business – like the sultan's mule, without hope for the future, a eunuch, the last of the line. Our children, whether our own or those we hope will succeed us, are our only certainty of immortality, and it is for their sakes that we must learn and pass on what we can. There are books in which we can read what has gone before, but there is also the unwritten record, the gatherings of those senses that are as much our birthright as speech or conscious thought, which are by their nature unrecordable but can nevertheless be captured in small things, in a word, a scent, an arrangement of limbs or a fleeting expression on a face. We learn these things only by observation and patience and good will – and these are the hardest things of all to communicate. Tellers of tales understand these things very well: what we may read as fiction may well be far more true than fact.

Oscar Wilde, that deflater of overblown egos, once said that nothing worth knowing can be taught. So how are we to acquire our understanding? The grace to see ourselves as others see us does not come naturally. If you hold up a mirror to a baby, it will not recognize its own reflection. It is not until the child sees a familiar face gazing back over its shoulder that it understands the truth of what is reflected in the glass. Innocence makes no judgements, cannot be held to account for its mistakes – but once we understand, we know the image in the mirror is our own.

Postscript

There was a long pause.
'Is that all?' Alice timidly asked.
'That's all,' said Humpty Dumpty. 'Goodbye.'
LEWIS CARROLL (1832–98), *Through the Looking Glass*

Index

(★ indicates recipe)

461